Praise for *Top Eight*

"For anyone raised in the era between the record store and the playlist, MySpace was everything. And yet we knew nothing about its rise or fall. Michael Tedder breaks through distant nostalgia with a masterfully written, compelling and emotional history of my generation's musical touchstone."

—**Conor Murphy**, Foxing

"A thorough and fascinating history, Michael Tedder's *Top Eight: How MySpace Changed Music* traces the unique collision of technology and youth culture that came to define an era. An essential examination that reveals the behind-the-scenes machinations of this music-biz boom-to-bust tale."

—**Bob Mehr**, author of the New York Times bestseller *Trouble Boys: The True Story of the Replacements*

"With all of the rush of being placed into the Top 8 of your crush, Michael Tedder's *Top Eight: How MySpace Changed Music* details the Internet's greatest (and sometimes horniest) social media/music/networking platform with the precision of a Scene Queen clipping raccoon tail extensions into her perfectly flat-ironed fringe. Rigorously reported, researched, and—in the case of your favorite twenty-first-century emo bands—remembered, this oral history celebrates '00s alternative culture, technology, and early online fandom with real expertise, proving once and for all that, *Mom, this isn't a phase.* (Okay, well, MySpace was. But the effects of it? Those are forever.) A real joy for nostalgic readers, and an eye-opening text for all others."

—**Maria Sherman**, author of *Larger than Life: A History of Boy Bands from NKOTB to BTS*

"This oral history takes you from basement shows to boardrooms to learn, in fascinating, hilarious, and yes, *emo* detail, why a low-tech website with eyesore graphics felt like home to so many music lovers. I loved it!"

—**DC Pierson**, author of *The Boy Who Couldn't Sleep and Never Had To*

TOP EIGHT

TOP EIGHT

How MySpace Changed Music

:::::Michael Tedder:::::::

CHICAGO
REVIEW
PRESS

Published by Chicago Review Press Incorporated
814 North Franklin Street
Chicago, Illinois 60610
ISBN 978-1-64160-658-5

Select interview quotes have previously appeared in the author's article
"The My Generation: An Oral History of Myspace Music," Stereogum,
March 30, 2020, https://www.stereogum.com/2056046/myspace-music-oral
-history/interviews/cover-story/.

Library of Congress Control Number: 2023935158

Typesetting: Nord Compo

Printed in the United States of America
5 4 3 2 1

For Charles Aaron.

Additionally, this book is dedicated to all those who love music enough to make it a part of their being. Even if we never meet, do know that you are my friend.

TABLE OF CONTENTS

PREFACE:
ENTER THE FOXHOLE

Everyone who was alive during the George W. Bush nightmare knows the picture. If you were young and wired, up too late, fretting over your Top Eight, on the verge of discovering your new favorite band, and practicing the duckface you'd make in your next several thousand selfies, it's burned into your memory like a CD-R.

There he is, Tom Anderson, sporting a white undershirt and a five o'clock shadow, his head tilted a few degrees toward the camera. His grin is as wide as the whiteboard hovering behind him like a scribble-filled thought bubble, and he's smiling with his eyes in a way that conveys authentic excitement. He's absolutely thrilled you've logged on to his site, and he's *so* happy to be your friend. Until the last millennial shuffles off this mortal coil, this image will linger in the collective unconscious like a hypersaturated, hyperlinked Proustian reverie.

No one who worked with Anderson seems to have a bad word to say about him. He was a bit of a hustler, maybe, but ultimately a benign one. He loved music with all of his being, the true love that only a teenager can feel but some lucky adults can still tap into. He wanted to share that love above all, and so he maneuvered his way into cocreating the best website music fans of all stripes and sounds would ever know.

MySpace did not start the social media age, but it unquestionably brought social media to the masses. There was a time when you could reasonably argue this was a good thing. But if social media has taught us anything, it's that people fuck up all the damn time. Every day, every minute. It's what we do, and we're damn good at it.

Sometimes it's a small faux pas, and sometimes the fuckup changes the world, dashing dreams and ruining lives in the process. Sometimes you don't know what you've done in the moment, and you won't realize your mistake until much later, if ever. But sometimes the universe lets you know quite clearly that you have fucked up. And if you're Tom Anderson, the universe's message takes the form of your best friend throwing a DVD at your head, wiping that signature grin off your face. It's hard to miss a message like that.

Anderson had a work ethic beyond his years—he was always the last to leave the office—and an irrepressible boyish spirit. A true believer in music's promise to bring people together, he wanted to connect the entire world through rabid fandom, hot jams, hotter babes, and a cool website with previously unimaginable bells and whistles. He just wanted us all to have a good time, together. But while he wanted to interlink the world, he didn't always pay the necessary attention to it. He didn't really know much about what Rupert Murdoch's whole deal was when his company News Corp bought MySpace for $580 million in July 2005. All that adult stuff fell to Chris DeWolfe, Anderson's partner and MySpace's cofounder.

Like any former punk, Anderson was worried about The Man, but Murdoch assured him and DeWolfe that they could do what they wanted with the site; he'd just handle the business end. DeWolfe had lived through the dot-com bust of early 2000 that brought down once-hyped websites like Pets.com, and he knew their parent company Inter-mix Media needed money to keep up the skyrocketing growth they'd experienced in the past two years, lest they crash and burn like Friend-ster. Anderson wasn't the type of cool guy who balked when his beloved indie act signed to a major. His favorite band in the world was Weezer, for goodness sakes. So what's the worst that could happen? And why was Bích Ngọc Cao mad enough to throw a DVD at Anderson's head?

Bích Ngọc Cao was a superwired, very online music fan in the '90s, well before terms like *streaming, MP3,* or *blog* had entered the public consciousness. She first joined MySpace in late 2003, well before you, I, or anyone we knew did. Some things impressed her, some things didn't, but the main thing that stayed with her about Anderson's MySpace page was that under favorites, he had listed alternative rock one-hit wonder Superdrag.*

There's an authenticity that comes with owning up to unfashionable tastes, and Ngọc Cao remembers thinking *Oh, he can't be too bad,* she says. *It's not the kind of band that you would brag about liking, because they weren't cool.*

She friended him and they chatted and started hitting the nightclubs together, scoping out fresh talent to feature on MySpace. Her plan for the summer of 2004 was to travel on the Lollapalooza tour as a volunteer for the political action committee MoveOn, helping to register voters for that fall's election. Those plans fell through after the show was canceled due to poor ticket sales.†

Instead she joined MySpace as the music editor, but you may as well have called her the Head Fan in Charge. She helped develop features that made the site a daily—or hourly—visit, which included a music player, a chart of the most popular unsigned artists that day, and an editorial page that highlighted both established and completely unknown artists, in the process creating careers and bestowing dreams.

The hours were long. The nights were late. The joy of knowing you'd helped someone find their favorite new artist or their new number-one fan was reward enough. She was aware that Intermix was being courted heavily by Viacom, owner of MTV, which Anderson had termed a dinosaur he was out to destroy. But while Ngọc Cao had DeWolfe's ear and trust, there are so many cool bands to discover and only so many hours in a day.

---

* Hailing from Knoxville, Tennessee, Superdrag had one big hit in 1996, "Sucked Out," a lament that MTV and the corporate music industry were sucking the true feeling out of music. With all due respect (and I mean that—both "Sucked Out" and follow-up single "Destination Ursa Major" are bangers), repping Superdrag is not akin to someone listing Pavement under their favorites so you know they're hip.

† Rumors have long circulated that the festival was canceled by the promotions company Clear Channel, now known as Live Nation, which had ties to George W. Bush and didn't want an uptick in younger voters.

"We were always talking about deals and things that might be rumbling through: the Facebooks and the Friendsters. I knew about a possible deal with Viacom. I didn't know about the deal with Fox. As the company grew, I became less connected to that aspect, all of the biz," she says. "I just didn't have the space and time to be part of it. So I really didn't know that that was happening. And so when the deal came down, I was really upset and sometimes really rude."

The idea that Fox News was a mendacious and unapologetic mouthpiece for reactionary right-wing talking points and was having a corrosive impact on the body politic was in the cultural air by 2005, but if you weren't mainlining *The Daily Show*, you might not have picked up on it. (A few years later, it would be much harder to avoid this truth, unless you really loved how sand felt against your face.)

By 2005, the reelection of George W. Bush still stung. Despite both of his wars increasingly turning into debacles, he won a decisive victory, partly due to a sickening anti–gay marriage stance and partly due to the relentless cheerleading of Fox News drowning out any criticism of his failed record. And now, the CEO of the Fox News Evil Empire was going to have his hands on Ngọc Cao's baby. "When they sold MySpace, I lost my mind, because I am a flaming liberal," she says. "I took a DVD of a film called *Outfoxed* about Fox News and I threw it at Tom's head the day they sold the company. He ducked."

He went home and watched it, she says. Directed by Robert Greenwald, the 2004 film lays out how the news company that touted itself as "fair and balanced" was anything but, exposing how it relentlessly pushed conservative talking points and helped cheerlead Bush's disastrous wars, all while spreading falsehoods and dog-whistling racism. On top of all that, the film also made it very clear that Fox's whole thing was angry grandpa fare and not something a cool, cutting-edge youth culture product would ever want to be associated with.

"He came back and he told me, 'I didn't know any of this stuff,'" she says. "Tom was obsessed with what he was obsessed with, so he wasn't necessarily connected to what was happening on a day-to-day basis in politics. I think he's a liberal person. But it just wasn't his thing."

As for DeWolfe, Ngọc Cao says, "I don't necessarily know that he is super political as well, although he is a smart and connected person. I don't know that either of them could have stopped the sale. They didn't own the company."

Maybe if Anderson had been more aware of what News Corp was, he could have spoken out and prevented the acquisition, or urged Intermix to pursue a better counteroffer from Viacom. Perhaps Anderson would still be at MySpace and would still be our number-one friend.

Or maybe nothing could have been done. Perhaps Facebook would have won out anyway. But it certainly wasn't predestined that Facebook's clean-cut professionalism would beat the anarchic fun of MySpace; a lot of shortsighted decisions made it that way. Adults may have preferred the former, but the youth always favor the latter, and there's never been a scenario in cultural history where the kids didn't set the agenda. But the feeling that the adults in the room have let you down again is the eternal burden of being young.

Shortly after the acquisition, DeWolfe "called an all-hands together to try to announce the deal in a positive way and told all of the employees that we would now be getting free lunch at work," she remembers. "I was a very defiant young person. There's still a lot of that in me, but it was a lot more freewheeling back then. I'm a lot more calculating in how I behave these days.

"I told everyone that we would now all be expected to work an extra hour every day because we wouldn't be leaving for lunch."

A year later, MySpace would be the biggest website the Internet had ever seen. Four years later, neither DeWolfe nor Anderson would work at MySpace. Ten years later, MySpace in any meaningful sense would be long gone, as would the era it embodied in all its messy glory.

INTRODUCTION:
WHY WE MISS MYSPACE

FRANK IERO DOESN'T EVEN LIKE SOCIAL MEDIA all that much. But without it, he might not be a rock star.

At the start of the 2000s, one of his bands played a party for Makeoutclub, a dating website and early social media precursor. This was his introduction to the future of music, dating, society, and everything else, a preview of how we were all about to get super-connected. He wasn't sold. Really, the whole thing just skeeved him out.

Oh, this whole thing is just for people who want to fuck each other, he remembers thinking. Plus, he admits, "I've always been kind of an idiot when it comes to computers or anything of that nature."

Then MySpace arrived. After launching in the summer of 2003, it slowly gained users as people began to figure out what exactly it was. It took some time to catch on, as things went viral much more slowly back then, though that would very soon change.

Social media was a new concept at the time. Friendster, generally considered the first true social media site, was barely a year old, and Facebook was a year away from launching. While more and more households and college campuses were beginning to adopt high-speed Internet, most people didn't live online the way we do now.

MySpace differed from Friendster in several ways, including a sharper design and the ability to curate the top eight people you wanted to present as your favorite bands and your closest besties, and for many people, the selection process was a source of great anxiety. (Whether those friendships were real or aspirational was immaterial.)

Beyond your profile, you had an entire customizable page to yourself, which you could trick out to your heart's content. These pages included places for status updates, an About Me section and, as copied from Friendster, a digital wall where people could leave complaints that you hadn't messaged them back yet.

But the crucial difference between MySpace and Friendster—and all other inferior social media platforms—was that MySpace let you embed songs onto your page, which allowed users to force new discoveries onto their friends, flaunt their cutting-edge taste, and document their shifting adolescent moods. Sometimes a small difference is all it takes to spark a paradigm shift, and the addition of a music player elevated MySpace from a fun digital distraction between classes to a gathering place for a community of music fans that never felt more alive than when they got to share their favorites.

It didn't take long for fledgling garage bands, hungry rappers, and aspiring pop stars to appreciate the possibilities at play here. It had been accepted since the late '90s that all musicians were required to have a website, even if almost no one had truly broken through to the larger world simply because they had a great web presence and a dedicated online fanbase going wild for them in the message boards. You still usually needed MTV and radio support for that. Some critical support and a grassroots fanbase were always nice, but never strictly required.

But MySpace was something different, something much easier to use, and easier to stumble upon. By allowing anyone to be a cool hunter just by futzing around online, MySpace fully changed the game, finally making the Internet *the* place where artists would be broken.

"The good thing about MySpace is it was a super user-friendly, point-and-click sort of thing," Iero says. "It seemed foolproof, and I was definitely a fool when it came to that kind of stuff." Before long, Iero remembers, all of his friends began flocking to the site and uploading their songs. "That was the thing," he remembers, "every time you start a new band, immediately, the first thing you do is you decide on a name, and the second thing you do is you start a MySpace page for it."

He never started a page just for himself. He never felt the need. But he had one for each of the bands he was in at the time. And he was in or had been in so many bands around that time that he can't remember them all. He grew up in Belleville, New Jersey, and like any Jersey punk with a tolerant parent, his basement served as a petri dish for all kinds of loud-fast-rules groups, from Pencey Prep to I Am a Graveyard to American Nightmare. But there was one group he was in that was getting a bit more attention than all the rest.

Iero had recently dropped out of Rutgers University to join My Chemical Romance. Their front man Gerard Way was a big thinker, a scholar of rock music, comic books, and juvenilia detritus in all its glory. He had ambitious plans for the band, including a concept for what eventually became their debut *I Brought You My Bullets, You Brought Me Your Love*. That album was released on the tiny New York label Eyeball Records in 2002, but Way was just getting started. A year after the album was released, the band still didn't have much in the way of resources or national attention, but at least they now had MySpace.

"We recorded one song because that's all we had the money for at that point. So we put it up on MySpace immediately and were like, 'Hey listen, we're gonna do a record soon, once we get the money, but this is a sneak preview kind of thing,'" he says. "And once we put that up, there were literally major label A&Rs calling the practice studio. How they got the number for the practice studio, I have no idea. And that's when we were all like, 'what's happening?' There's something way bigger than we could've imagined. Is it someone's job to troll MySpace and listen for new bands?"

Before long, record label representatives for all the big companies were showing up to My Chemical Romance's cramped basement shows. Eventually, they would later sign to the major label Reprise for their 2004 breakthrough *Three Cheers for Sweet Revenge*, which would eventually go on to sell three million albums and turn them into one of the most beloved bands of the decade. But before radio and MTV launched singles such as "I'm Not Okay (I Promise)" and "Helena" into the mainstream, MySpace was where My Chemical Romance's fans found the band, turning them from unknowns to cultishly adored to genuine, no-shit rock stars.

My Chemical Romance were one of the biggest acts to emerge from MySpace, but these outsiders weren't exactly lonely. The intellectually inclined Thursday and the boyish Taking Back Sunday, their friends in the New Jersey and Long Island emo-punk scene, were also around just before MySpace launched, but the fan communities fostered there gave them a career boost and would rocket younger emo groups such as compulsive oversharers Fall Out Boy, the fiery Paramore, and the theatrical Panic! at the Disco into arenas.

Angsty rock fans may have been among the first to flock to MySpace, as those sorts of fans had been trained since the days of punk and college radio to look anywhere but the mainstream for validation and community. But MySpace had room for everyone and every taste. Fans of stylish hip-hop, fizzy dance pop, strummy adult contempo bops, artsy indie rock, and everything else quickly got in on the search party, proving that underground types didn't have a monopoly on wanting to find tomorrow's icon today. Not to get too rose-colored glasses about it, but when MySpace was at its peak, everybody—or at least everybody of a certain inclination—was having fun. Or trying to, at least. MySpace helped high school students Colbie Caillat and Soulja Boy find fans across the world when they began dominating the site's unsigned artist charts. Record deals and MTV hits soon followed, but their stardom had already been coronated by a new generation of fans before the old gatekeepers caught up.

As MySpace grew in popularity, the stranglehold that corporate radio and MTV had long held on listening habits began to erode, allowing a new generation of artists to seize the spotlight. Music websites such as Stereogum and Pitchfork began anointing new voices of a generation, and MP3-based blogs such as Fluxblog, Nah Right, and BrooklynVegan became daily reads for fans searching for the latest and freshest. But MySpace was the glue that kept it all together, the place where fans of all stripes could get together to share, to gush, and to vent.

Ultimately, MySpace was the name that came to epitomize the Wild West of the new music industry. MySpace was right at the center of everything that made the time so exciting. And the same forces that killed MySpace also killed that free-floating feeling that everything was finally possible. At least for a time.

MySpace pioneered much of what is commonplace about the Internet today. Tila Tequila was a social media influencer before that was even a term, using her MySpace page and a shameless hustle to build followings. Comedians posted jokes to their pages to find fans and to launch DIY tours that were closer in spirit to get-in-the-van punk tours than traditional comedy shows. Movie studios and television networks began using the site to promote their latest endeavors, and cast members of *The Office* regularly blogged on the site (sometimes in character, while sitting in the background of a scene).

MySpace was far from perfect. As with literally any place on the Internet, it was overflowing with trolls, scammers, and abusers looking for their next mark. The music genre most closely associated with MySpace was the anthemic emo and pop-punk scene, which was rife with misogyny and sexual harassment and was overly, and distressingly, dominated by and marketed toward young white men. And then there's the Rupert Murdoch of it all.

To retrospectively romanticize the era would be to rewrite history. The same problems of greed, prejudice, and unthinking cruelty that have always been part of society were amplified by the new digital tools. But so were the eternal virtues of connection, curiosity, and community. Ultimately, MySpace was more than just a social media site. It embodied the feeling that the old rules were out, and the rule makers with them, and we now had the chance to make our own culture. It was an idea, a metaphor for the optimism of its time and a shorthand for the freedom the Internet once promised to a hungry generation and anyone else looking for more than just more of the same.

When MySpace was at its height, it felt like the hub of the Internet. Thanks to MySpace, desperately loving music online wasn't just a niche, online nerd thing anymore, because for a while, everyone was an online music nerd.

As you've noticed, the Internet devolved into a rather more frustrating, monopolized place, and the old rules seem more firmly calcified than ever before. Online leviathans Facebook and Google eat up the majority of advertising revenue, starving most of the vibrant and esoteric websites that make the Internet worthwhile out of business. This great money suck devastated the once thriving music blog community and put a serious hurt on the resources of the mainstream publications that once signal boosted the underground. All the while, the steadfast refusal of Facebook and Twitter to ban rampant disinformation and hate speech has turned social media into a cesspool as toxic as it is wearying.

Since the decline of MySpace, music discovery has regressed to the top-down phenomenon, with major labels spending millions to make their artists appear like viral sensations while true outsiders find it harder than ever to sustain a lasting career. Streaming services supposedly encourage discovery, but this usually amounts to fans passively accepting what algorithms have decided they will tolerate well enough to not skip, all while paying artists so little that giving them a singular crumb per stream would be more nourishing.

But when MySpace was at its strongest, fans were empowered to actively seek out new favorites for themselves. As any writer of fiction will tell you, an active choice is always more meaningful and exciting than a passive one. And there's no one who misses the old MySpace more than the bands that were there.

"Everyone was centralized in this one social platform. The audience was there, and the bands were there, and you could just click through and find out about bands that you liked," Iero says. "Now I just feel like there's so much shit everywhere. There's too many bands, there's too many sites, there's just too much. It's hard to get through."

A few defiant, unique, independently minded artists still manage to break through every year. But increasingly, there's only a few, as it's harder than ever to capture enough people's attention so that you can continue to make your art. The height of MySpace now feels several lifetimes away, and the idea that the right MP3 could change your life overnight now reads as a romantic idea too quaint to be true. But for a while, it was a regular occurrence.

The connection between artists and fans, and between fans and their fellow fans, is life-affirming. MySpace put that often messy connection right at the heart of its service, remaking countless lives in the process. This is how that connection was made, and lost, as told by the artists, journalists, bloggers, executives, insiders, and scene kids who were there.

1

BACK IN THE DAY

MYSPACE WASN'T THE FIRST SOCIAL NETWORKING SITE and wasn't the last social networking site, but it was the best social networking site. Which is an easy title for it to win, because it was also the only good social networking site. But that's hardly the point.

The reason MySpace is so fondly remembered, years after most people kicked their ex out of their Top Eight, is that the site still serves as a synecdoche for a feeling, a freedom, a time.

Before MySpace, being a voracious online music fan was a niche, nerdy activity. But MySpace changed all that. Because of MySpace, everyone spent the 2000s searching for their next favorite song. Or at least that's the way it felt at the time.

MySpace was a genuine pop explosion, like the British Invasion of the late '60s or hip-hop's conquest of the suburbs in the '80s. MySpace Nation exploded out of nowhere, and suddenly, obscure bands with no fans at all were stunned to find themselves with huge international followings of kids. Emo was the official sound of MySpace, but everything was blowing up on the site all the time. That's what made it great, bewildering, and aggravating.

MySpace created an entirely new way to be a lonely, confused teenager, and music was the site's beating heart. If you were a weird kid (and most kids, correctly, think they are weird, because being human is just a weird endeavor) with no friends, suddenly there was this thing called "a social network" that would help you find your people. So no one else at your school likes emo, indie rock, goth, hip-hop, punk, or whatever subculture you're obsessed with? So you don't feel like you fit in anywhere? So you're certain that everyone is off somewhere else having fun out there without you?

That's no longer a problem. With MySpace, you could finally find your people, your scene, and your home. You could also find your new favorite band. And if you were lucky enough and dedicated enough, you could even find a coveted spot in your new favorite band's Top Eight.

When MySpace launched on August 1, 2003, it changed the world overnight. But from the '80s underground bands that set the table for Nirvana to the Bronx DJs whose block parties would one day lead to hip-hop becoming the soundtrack of America, every earthshaking cultural explosion has a number of forerunners that never quite get the credit they deserve. MySpace was the moment that music fandom fully moved online, but several antecedents paved the road to the Top Eight.

Internet forums have existed since the 1970s, back when the Internet was mostly a tool for the military and academia. In the '80s and '90s, a relatively small group of early adopters, many of them from The WELL, an early virtual community that started in 1985, figured out what e-mail lists and Usenet bulletin boards were well before most of the general populace had even heard the term *dial-up*. Message boards and the very idea of "the Internet" became a lot more popular in the mid-'90s as Internet usage became more mainstream and American Online (AOL) mailed every household a CD-ROM to coax them to log on. But half the time, you needed to know someone or get lucky to discover a worthwhile forum, and not everyone is lucky enough to have a cool friend. But some people do.

Courtney Holt is a music industry veteran who built his career by noticing opportunities others let pass them by. While he was working at Interscope, he was one of the few people at a major label willing to meet with the creators of Napster to figure out how labels could get ahead of file sharing. When he joined MySpace as the president of the offshoot MySpace Music and later became the president of the company, he tried to save the flailing site by converting it to a music streaming subscription model, just before Spotify came in and made that idea workable (for some). But before any of that, he was an '80s New York punk kid who stumbled onto the earliest bulletin board systems.

"I was pretty lucky that I went to a high school in New York that had a computer lab. My friends and I would operate bulletin boards. We would hack into the phone system and get thirty people on a call together and then prank call people," he says. "There was Crazy Eddie, which was an electronics store that would match any advertised price. So we would get Atari 2600 cartridges for half off by creating these ads that looked real. Back then no one cared. I would say most of my interest was around general fuckery."

He continued to be a message board dweller as he grew out of his punk youth. Even in the early days of the Internet, free music was there for the downloading once the MP3 was created in the mid-'90s, but it was often too arduous a process to appeal to anyone but the diehards. "It just took a little bit more work because you had to look into it as opposed to it being a database that's searchable. There were communities that you had to go and basically search through what was effectively code. So it's really fucking hard, but it was still free music," he says. "But the digital listening experience was terrible, because you're limited to MP3 software like Winamp on a computer, which was still not a great way to organize music. And it wasn't portable. So a CD or a cassette was still a better listening experience."

MySpace harnessed and supercharged online music fandom, but it didn't create it. The popularity of message boards continued to grow throughout the '90s, and it offered something for every type of music fan.

By the end of the decade, small but thriving communities looking for something different were attracting enthusiastic and plugged-in denizens like Scott Heisel. Before he would become a music journalist for *Alternative Press*, a publication that found its final form as a MySpace-scene bible, he just wanted to talk about emo with someone.

Before she would befriend MySpace's founder and help guide the site's coverage as the music editor, Bích Ngọc Cao was an early online denizen as well. She seems to have a lifelong knack for being at the right place at the right time, as she was an early fan of the soft rock group Fisher, the first band to break online, and was active on the message board for the alternative rock singer Poe,* whose fans organized when they discovered rock radio wasn't playing her latest single, as female artists were rapidly disappearing from rock radio by 2000.

But the spread of the Internet was uneven and often quite regional in the late '90s, and it wasn't until MySpace hit that everyone more or less started getting online. Alain Macklovitch, aka A-Trak, was a Montreal-born DJ who began winning turntablist† competitions as a high schooler. In the late '90s, he didn't spend much time on the Internet, aside from the occasional scratch tournament forum, though that would eventually change. He later became an active blogger, cofounded the influential label and record store Fool's Gold, and served as an unofficial big brother to the '00s wave of alternative rappers.

A-Trak was one of the digital foot-draggers that didn't get themselves fully online until the MySpace Era arrived. But once it did, they got on board. We all did.

(All quotes have been edited for clarity and length.)

BÍCH NGỌC CAO (MYSPACE MUSIC EDITOR): Poe was the first person I ever heard sing a song where she mentioned a modem. I went online and I found a fan site by a guy named Jared, who's still my friend. We found a bunch of fans who joined an e-mail list in which we wrote

---

* Poe, aka Anne Decatur Danielewski, scored an alternative rock hit with "Angry Johnny," from her 1995 album *Hello.* Her online fan base felt that her 2000 album *Haunted* was underpromoted by Atlantic Records and took steps to correct that.

† Turntablism is the art of manipulating a record player to make noises previously unheard by the human ear. It became a very popular underground sound in the '90s and widely fell out of fashion a decade later. The most popular act in this scene was the group Invisibl Skratch Piklz.

to each other every day about the things that we liked about her music and sharing other music. These are all tools that we built for each other.

COURTNEY HOLT (MYSPACE MUSIC PRESIDENT): I was at A&M Records when the first MP3 player came out. I ended up purchasing one. I was working in digital, whatever they called it, new media, and I worked for a gentleman named Milt Olin, and I said, "Hey, give me five songs in order. Any five songs off the top of your head." It was a Byrds song, a Dictators song, a Soundgarden song, some other stuff, and a Bob Dylan song. Twenty minutes later, I walked back with the MP3 player filled with those songs in order, which I'd stolen off the Internet in a pre-Napster era on Usenet. And that was the wake-up call.

A-TRAK: In my scratch years, around '96, '97, '98 or so, the Invisibl Skratch Piklz had a message board. Sometimes I would go to other cities for shows and meet other scratch DJs who would bring up all types of inside jokes and things from that board.

NGQC CAO: The beauty of the early music Internet is that all of the fans banded together and became friends and made tools that kids today really take for granted. I've been trying to tell my boyfriend's kids about what the Internet was like back when we were young because they have everything just handed to them from corporations and they have no idea what it's like to build a listserv and figure out how to do a tape trade with a bunch of random people that you met and you have no idea what they look like, and yet they're your friends.

SCOTT HEISEL (*ALTERNATIVE PRESS* EDITOR): I was a huge Internet kid from the beginning. I had websites in the '90s, my brother ran a BBS [bulletin board system]. In terms of discovering music, I read Collective -Zine.co.uk a lot—they were a big emo and indie website for reviews.

A-TRAK: There were two or three online record stores that I remember going to regularly to order vinyl, basically—HipHopSite.com and Sandbox Automatic. I remember going to those and they would have a little RealPlayer snippet of a song and then you could buy records, vinyl, on mail order.

NGOC CAO: Poe's first album came out and had an alternative rock hit with "Angry Johnny." And then the second album came out, and by that time, radio was playing people like No Doubt, and radio program managers literally told her team, "We're already playing a woman. We don't need another one." And then there was a song called "Hey Pretty," and then she released it to a radio station in Portland, and we blew up their phone lines. We organized and we went nuts. They have no idea that we are calling from all over the world, and we created a rock hit. We're teenagers, for the most part.

While the polarities would one day drastically reverse, in the '90s, music was still mainly covered in print magazines, which either didn't even bother with a website, or had one that was neglected and run by junior staff members and interns, with maybe the occasional news update.

The idea of online music journalism was in its infancy back then, with the one major exception being the website Addicted to Noise. Started by former *Rolling Stone* journalist Michael Goldberg, it was the first online magazine and even featured the then-novel inclusion of audio snippets in its reviews. It later merged with a company called SonicNet.

"I actually used to work for SonicNet. And I guess this was '95, I wanna say. I gotta be frank with you, nobody really knew what to do with it, including the people who worked for it," remembers Norman Brannon, a writer, publicist, educator, and former guitarist for influential emo forebearers Texas Is the Reason. "It was very, very early music Internet. Viacom eventually bought SonicNet, and then they folded it."

But while the first major online music publication was the victim of corporate negligence, another one would have a more lasting impact. Pitchfork Media was founded in 1996 by Ryan Schreiber, a young Minneapolis high school graduate and record store clerk who would quickly move to Chicago. Influenced by college radio and '90s zine culture, he fostered a website for people who felt that the alternative music pushed by MTV and commercial radio wasn't alternative *enough* and who instead wanted something smarter and edgier and not diluted for mainstream consumption.

But in the '90s, few people noticed it, aside from Mark Richardson, who would eventually become the site's managing editor, editor in chief, and executive editor and is credited with helping to elevate the site's coverage into something less snarky and more thoughtful.

"Definitely my introduction to online music as a thing was really when I found Pitchfork, which was 1997. And then I started writing for it in 1998. I definitely read Addicted to Noise," he remembers. "I lived in San Francisco. I worked at this very large law office. I could waste time at work looking at the web. It was covering things I was familiar with, but also introducing me to stuff. So I became a daily reader, pretty regularly, then shortly after that, I was like, 'Oh, there's a call for writers.'"

Eventually, Pitchfork would become the dominant music publication of the '00s, often cherry-picking MySpace's artist profiles for fresh finds. But right alongside MySpace and Pitchfork was the explosion of music blogs. Often called MP3 blogs, they were ubiquitous at the time, offering downloads of brand-new and unheard-of artists; the best blogs had writing as fresh as the sounds. If message boards weren't your thing, here was something a bit more accessible. Soon, the blogs, Pitchfork, and the fans would work in synergy with MySpace to establish how music felt in the '00s.

———

MARK RICHARDSON (FORMER PITCHFORK EDITOR IN CHIEF): It's really hard to even describe what the Internet was like before Google, because there was no clear way to find anything that you were looking for. The existing search engines were very poor. I did discover Pitchfork before Google.* I remember that the first thing I read on it was an interview with Dean Wareham about Luna.†

———

* Google was launched in 1998 by Stanford University doctoral students Larry Page and Sergey Brin.

† A dream-pop band formed by Dean Wareham, formerly of '80s college radio favorites Galaxie 500.

HOLT: You really had to know where to look, and you had to be really deliberate about what you were looking for. Most of what you could find were things that weren't effectively mainstream but were in demand. I could find Bowie, Springsteen, and Dylan bootlegs and a bunch of the stuff that ended up becoming reissues. In the '80s and '90s there was always the bootleg section of the independent record store, and that stuff migrated to the Internet really quickly.

NORMAN BRANNON (TEXAS IS THE REASON): So after SonicNet, that's when the bulletin board systems started taking hold, and it was very sort of a decentralized platform. It was just a lot of kids talking shit, as the Internet is wont to do. And so very early on, everybody knew that that's what the Internet was going to be. I remember at the end of Texas Is the Reason, there was specifically, alt.music.hardcore was the place where everybody went to talk shit, and already, we were getting drawn into drama.

NGỌC CAO: I had a really weird existence as a child where my parents were very strict. But they didn't understand what I was doing because they were immigrants, so I got away with doing things that I think a lot of kids would not have. I basically spent my childhood in *Almost Famous*. I was on tour with bands. The only thing I wasn't doing was, I wasn't sleeping with them. I really wasn't writing about them.

BRANNON: We were in an analog world for the majority of our existence. It was a big deal when we were in *CMJ* or *Alternative Press* or *Spin*. I didn't think of Internet press as real press. Which is funny if you think about it now.

RICHARDSON: The consensus is the years of rapid growth are between 2000 and 2003. And that's when file sharing was also at a peak. I guess Napster stopped in there, but file sharing was still going on. So I always thought the early rise of Pitchfork is very connected with the early days of file sharing, in that it was an obsessive music magazine that covered a lot of albums and published a lot of content. You could tell that it was getting bigger and it was more of a thing.

One of the main reasons that online music journalism struggled for a foothold in the '90s was because it was still difficult to find music online unless you knew what you were doing.

While MySpace was the first website where you could stream music that the general populace noted, it had an important precursor in MP3.com, a website launched in 1997 and run by Michael Robertson that let independent musicians sell their song files.

The main success story of MP3.com and the pre-Napster music web was Fisher, a soft-rock duo composed of vocalist Kathy Fisher and Ron Wasserman, a former heavy metal musician who later wrote theme songs for *Mighty Morphin Power Rangers* and music for the '90s *X-Men* cartoon. They had a song on the *Great Expectations* soundtrack in 1998, and Atlantic Records had an option on the band but wouldn't actually sign them. "What you hear about every band always going through, where you're under contract," he says, "but they won't do a damn thing."

They began printing their own CDs and uploading their songs. On the strength of the lovely coffee shop jam "I Will Love You," they became the first group to jump from the web to the *Billboard* charts, with the song hitting number thirty-six on the Adult Top 40 countdown in 2000.

Fisher earned a short-lived deal with Interscope's subsidiary label Farmclub.com (also the name of a Interscope Records–produced show that aired on the USA Network in the late '90s, featuring performances from bands found on MP3.com and other online music industry feeders, an interesting but too-early attempt to find talent from the Internet). Fisher would later split with Interscope over business disputes, and no one else would quite follow Wasserman in breaking big off MP3.com, though not for a lack of trying.

No one tried harder to make the brave new world work for them than California's Sherwood. Led by the extremely determined Nate Henry, they were a pop-rock band with a Beach Boys–like wistfulness that pivoted, perhaps too hard, to a more straight-ahead pop-punk sound tailored with exacting precision for the Warped Tour crowd.

But before Sherwood would sign with MySpace Records, they were a bunch of college students lurking on MP3.com and, later, PureVolume, a similar streaming website that became popular with the punk and emo scene upon its launch in 2003.

––––––––––

NGỌC CAO: There's a band called Fisher. They had always been told, "these songs will never get played on the radio." And so they just released it as a free song on MP3.com. It became the number-one song for months. I found them off of the *Great Expectations* soundtrack. So I e-mailed them and I asked if I could intern with them, and they wrote me back. They thought I was a boy because I have a very straightforward manner. They said, "We don't really have interns. But here's our CD." They're family to me now. We do Thanksgivings together. I spent a ton of time moderating their message board and led their online marketing as a kid when they signed to the label. These are the kinds of experiences that I got off of the early Internet that have been life-changing and invaluable. And these are the kinds of things that I wanted to bring to MySpace.

RON WASSERMAN (FISHER): Back then, doing your own CD was like vanity publishing in a way. It was considered that you're not good enough. So because of the film soundtrack, we ended up pushing very hard and managed to book three Lilith Fair dates. And there were about five hundred people that showed up to see us. Complete shock. Didn't have a clue. We came back and I said, "We should do our own CD, and I'll start promoting it online."

NATE HENRY (SHERWOOD): We were all students at Cal Poly San Luis Obispo College [California Polytechnic State University], a tech school on the central coast of California. We were all around twenty to twenty-three years old, so second, third years in college. Our drummer graduated first and actually stuck around. And then a couple of us dropped out of school around 2004 to tour full-time. We were a local band going to college for about three years before we actually decided to hit the road and go for it.

HEISEL: MP3.com was huge. It was '98, '99. My band had stuff on there, and you'd find bands there all the time. It was just queueing up my parents' dial-up Internet for a million downloads overnight and then coming back in the morning, like, "Which ones made it through?"

WASSERMAN: It was right as the whole MP3 craze was starting. So I uploaded a couple songs to MP3.com. One of them was one I never thought would go anywhere, a piano vocal ballad called "I Will Love You." And it just took off at MP3.com. I remember the first day there was like eleven downloads, then it shot to thirty, fifty, two thousand, three thousand, and soon getting eight thousand a day. Now, it wasn't paying anything yet, but we were thrilled for the promotion. So we were sitting for almost a year at the top of the pop charts on MP3.com.

HENRY: Our guitar player was always on MP3.com, and he was always making me burned CDs, "Hey, check out *this* band, check out *this* band." I remember that was right when PureVolume started. Bands were kinda getting noticed there. But I wanna say the gist of when it all started was probably MP3.com. I remember going there a lot and checking up on that. But it hadn't blown up into the way you discovered bands quite yet.

WASSERMAN: I ended up knowing the owner of the site and tried to get into discussions with him about how to make it a more profitable business model, and how to also get some money to the artists. And he just had no interest in that whatsoever. In all things related to the music business, you're constantly running into a lot of "what the fuck" moments. It could have been the original iTunes.

The main precursor to MySpace that anyone remembers is Friendster. It has a reputation as the very first social network, even though that's not actually the case, and we're not printing the legend here.

CollegeClub, SocialNet, and SixDegrees were sort of proto versions of Facebook that were a bit too early and undercooked to really take off, arriving right before high-speed Internet was becoming widely available. There was also HotOrNot, a website where the brave could ask total strangers to rate their face, and in the process normalized the idea of posting selfies online.

AsianAve, BlackPlanet, and MiGente.com were all early social networking services that thrived on a small scale by targeting underserved communities, featuring active message boards and matchmaking services. A related forum online forum AsianRaps.com became the online destination for Asian hip-hop fans and artists, including members of the Los Angeles hip-hop group Far East Movement, a group that included Kevin Nishimura (Kev Nish), James Roh (Prohgress), and Jae Choung (J-Splif). That these sites are often left out of the narrative of social media is sadly typical, but Jonathan Smith remembers BlackPlanet fondly. Before he would go on to damage subwoofers and get all of America screaming "okay!" the man who would be Lil Jon was a bit of a computer geek, having gone to a technology magnet high school as a kid. "I've been on computers since the '80s, so I've been technologically inclined for a long time," he notes.

"BlackPlanet was like AOL. That's where people went to talk and share shit. BlackPlanet was huge in the Black community, and then it just slowly dwindled because MySpace just had all of these great features," he says. "But I think the chat rooms was what kind of blew BlackPlanet up. People would use it kind of like Tinder and shit, they would go meet and hook up."

But the social media site that truly set the path for the wild, lusty 24/7 music nerd party that was MySpace would have to be Makeoutclub. Started by punk fan Gibby Miller as a personal homepage named in honor of '90s college-radio favorite Unrest, Makeoutclub was a message board and dating service that catered to the emo subculture at the turn of the century. (What *emo* even meant was an eternal point of debate on the message boards.)

Like a passionate indie band with a jaundiced eye toward the mainstream, Makeoutclub was designed for subcultural appreciation. It was a place for an awkward emo superfan like Say Anything front man Max Bemis to find their kind, as well as future songwriting inspiration. People traded music recommendations as well as gossip there, a fair amount of which concerned Gabe Saporta, bassist and singer for Midtown. Anyone who attended one of the site's parties or who spent hours on the message board finding new artists and debating about old favorites was seeing an awkward glimpse into the future. But if they were anything like Thursday singer Geoff Rickly, they laughed it off at the time.

GEOFF RICKLY (THURSDAY): I knew Makeoutclub. I had been to some of their parties, but we had never played them or anything. At one of them, I was single, and I made out with a girl, but nothing really happened. It was a bit debaucherous, but it was also sort of like a joke. We said, "Oh, Makeoutclub parties. We gotta make out." It was sorta silly.

GIBBY MILLER (MAKEOUTCLUB): I was in Boston from 1993 to 2002. I was going to art school and I was part of the music scene. I started on the Internet in the mid-'90s and I had grown up sort of always interested in online activity, in ways of bringing people together. I ran a bulletin board system in like '91 to '92 called Minor Threat.

HEISEL: I certainly lurked on Makeoutclub, but I was never the person who was confident enough to have a profile on there. It felt very subversive, like I felt like I shouldn't be allowed to be on here, and that's what a lot of that early Internet stuff felt like. I felt like we were all a microgeneration looking around and saying, "How are we getting away with doing this?" because our parents weren't online.

MAX BEMIS (SAY ANYTHING/MAXIM MENTAL): I met the girl who one of our most popular songs "Woe" is about on Makeoutclub. I was living in L.A. at the time. I guess that'd be pre-MySpace era. There was a crossover for people my age with stuff like just the L.A. hipster scene in general, stuff like Buddyhead,* and then it went the way of Hot Topic.

---

* An oft-problematic hipster gossip site, affiliated with a confrontational and tuneless L.A. punk band called the Icarus Line.

But for a while there, it was not that weird to find an actually cool person on Makeoutclub. It was more like a basement show of social media.

MILLER: I was an FTP bulletin board guy. I was a member of the indie-pop lists, and all of these e-mail lists and Yahoo! groups. And I had all of the IP addresses for all of the FTP servers where people were trading music and shit. So, there was a Philadelphia-based record label called Track Star Records. And they had a personal section on their record label website. You would e-mail the owner your photo. And he would take your photo and rip you apart, in *Vice* magazine "hot-or-not" style. I was like, what would that look like if it was a purpose-built website where people could write their own profile and people could submit their own picture? And so I marinated on that for a little while.

KEV NISH (FAR EAST MOVEMENT): We would download beats from Napster and record freestyles over them, put them up on this website called AsianRaps.com, which was the early community for Asian rappers all around the US.

MILLER: With SixDegrees I was like, "Who the fuck is this going to connect me to, like, my grandparents or something?" It felt a little too dot-com-y for me. I do recall you entering in your information and then searching its database to find people that you might be connected to, remotely. "OK, that's cool, but where are the cuties at? Where is the music at?"

NISH: We were watching BET and saw Jin the MC* on the freestyle battles and freestyle Friday, and he shouted out AsianRaps.com. So we went on this forum and my heart stopped, like, "Damn, we're not the only ones!" We all started profiles. I would battle on there. They have these things called chatroom keyboard battles. You write verses freestyle and diss the other person.

---

* MC Jin, aka Jin Au-Yeung, was a Miami-born rapper who in 2002 competed in and won a competition called "Freestyle Friday" on the BET program *106 & Park*, one of the most important video shows, earning a deal with Ruff Ryders/Virgin Records. Though he never became much of a commercial or cultural force, his 2007 "Open Letter to Obama" got him in the future president's Top Eight.

MILLER: Makeoutclub was always a day late and a dollar short. The servers were always crashing. The hosting bills were always late. I struggled to monetize it because I really wanted to be cool. And I wanted *it* to be cool. And there was nothing to compare it to, so I didn't have anything to look at. Should I charge users a monthly fee to use this? Should it be ad-revenue based? But back then, it wasn't uncommon to meet someone who didn't have the Internet. Nobody had cell phones. Going online was an activity that you did, maybe for one part of the day. Maybe half an hour a day, or every other day. So, it was a different world.

MySpace's greatest cultural legacy was to help create a vibrant, online fan culture. But people who truly love music *need* it to soothe and reify feelings they otherwise can't quite touch. Ergo, MySpace was as much about young adult angst as it was about the soundtrack to said angst.

So considering the hormonal, teenage energy that fueled MySpace and led to uncountable numbers of Internet crushes and overthought About Me profile entries, MySpace should be considered to have three spiritual forebearers that stand apart from the rest of the Internet: Makeoutclub, AOL Instant Messenger (or AIM), and LiveJournal. All three started in the late '90s, priming the pump for a decade of oversharing.

AOL Instant Messenger introduced the bored teenagers of the world to the idea of chatting with your friends online all day instead of going outside. And it also introduced the idea of the away message, sort of the proto-tweet—your way of letting the world (or at least your friend list) in on your current emotional state. (Crushed Out and Mad at Your Dad were popular standbys.) AIM also, crucially, introduced the idea of using your favorite song lyric as your away message. How many people did I know who used lyrics from the band Dashboard Confessional as their away message? More than a few.

Launched in 1997, AIM was an offshoot of the company's popular chat rooms, which were miniature message boards devoted to everything from sports to ska. AIM was developed by a group of AOL employees as a stand-alone free product, much to the chagrin of the company's senior executives, who were worried it would "cannibalize" the main product, as Eric Bosco, VP community and communications engineering AOL told *InVision*. But AIM quickly caught on, with away messages establishing an easy way to check in on your friends and mark your presence online, even in a small way.

"Mostly people used it as an expression of themselves, a way to say not just 'I'm away' but 'this is who I am,'" said Jerry Harris, a system architect and technical manager at AOL, to *InVision*. Second only to the search for pornography, informing the world "This is who I am" became the fuel of the Internet. For a young Gareth David, future front man of the Welsh indie-rock group Los Campesinos!, AIM was an opportunity for budding music fans to flex their burgeoning cultural expertise.

"I would say probably until the age of like fifteen, maybe a little bit earlier than that, all I was interested in was soccer. I had zero interest in music. But there was a particular bar called the Wonder Bar, which sadly doesn't exist anymore, and I joined its message board when I was sixteen or something," he says, "and I very quickly got into a lot of music. I knew everything."

Minneapolis's Motion City Soundtrack were arguably the foremost band's band of their era—not the biggest, but the band that all the other ones in their scene looked up to, on account of their ease with hooks and neurotic wit. Led by front man Justin Pierre, a bespectacled man whose skyscraper-esque hair seemed to house his great many anxieties, and flanked by guitarist Joshua Cain, an archetypal Midwestern ballbuster, they used every outlet possible to get the word out and knew something was finally clicking when one day their AIM started blowing up.

AIM was discontinued in 2017, having been made largely redundant by Google's gchat feature, which succeeded in all but eroding the line between Work Internet and Fun Internet. AIM was also killed by Facebook, slayer of all things good. (Other notable victims: MySpace, print journalism, American social cohesion.)

Your AIM away message let you express yourself. But LiveJournal was where you went to really let the world know how you felt. Started by nineteen-year-old programmer Brad Fitzpatrick in 1999, LiveJournal, along with similar sites like Blogger and Xanga, was often messy, as

messy was the default mood of the Internet. But they also taught a generation of anxious, restless kids that they could find a sanctuary online
that they couldn't find elsewhere. Or if you were bored suburban New
Jersey teenager Cassie Grzymkowski, who one day would front indie
punks the Vivian Girls under the nom de punk Cassie Ramone, you
could just use your LiveJournal to vent about "angsty girl stuff," she
says, "like how I thought I was cooler than everybody because I liked
really good music, like a typical obnoxious teenager."

Graham Wright's band Tokyo Police Club would eventually make
the leap from a MySpace page to blog buzz, to Pitchfork raves, to Pitchfork shrugs, to late-night television performances and a respectable
middle-class indie-rock career, just before that stopped being much of
a thing. But before that, he was a sensitive young man with sensitive-
young-man tastes and a LiveJournal account. And he wanted the world
to know exactly what he was into and, therefore, who he was.

"It was just me and four people who I saw every day, blogging at
each other at night. It was performative, very much me constructing
the image of myself that I wanted to project outwards," he remembers,
"which, being fourteen to fifteen, meant that it was probably insanely
twee and verbose, like a Decemberists record on the turntable and a
Craig Thompson* graphic novel open on my lap kind of thing. No
shade to the Decemberists or to Craig Thompson. They filled a role in
my life that is no longer relevant."

LiveJournal had 2.5 million users by 2005, its peak year. It was an
essential part of being a teenager in the '00s until it wasn't. In 2007,
LiveJournal was purchased by the Russian company SUP Media. As
reported by *Slate*, Casey Fiesler, an information science professor at
the University of Colorado–Boulder, found that the company began a
crackdown on adult-oriented material, but the crackdown was poorly
enforced and entire online communities, including "support groups
for rape survivors," were deleted. Outraged users would flee to newer

---

* Thompson is best known for the award-winning, acclaimed 2003 coming-of-age graphic
novel *Blankets*, which became so popular it was name-checked on the Fox TV show/
cultural bellwether *The O.C.* It is earnest in the best sense, and Wright needn't apologize
for ever loving it.

platforms such as Tumblr and DeviantArt, though LiveJournal remains quite popular in Russia.

This all may sound quaint now, but if you were young and online back then, it felt like the future. And then MySpace showed up and we saw what the future was really going to look like, for better and for worse.

———————

CASSIE RAMONE (VIVIAN GIRLS): I was on Instant Messenger and I was on LiveJournal. I was not on Makeoutclub because I didn't think I was cool enough, which is kind of funny because looking back, Makeoutclub is not cool at all. But Katy* was on Makeoutclub, so we met some older kids who lived in Manhattan through that, and I was still a senior in high school. It was a good way for me to kind of dip my toes into the New York scene, whatever. But I never had a profile myself because I didn't think I was attractive enough.

GABE SAPORTA (MIDTOWN/HUMBLE BEGINNINGS/COBRA STAR-SHIP): When I was in Humble Beginnings, I was all over AOL chat, that was the big thing. There were a lot of chat rooms. I remember my username was *PunkPC*. I was very into being politically correct. I think the thing that people that grew up on the Internet don't understand is that at the beginning, the Internet was AOL chat rooms and all this stuff. Maybe my perspective is a little biased, but it just felt like it was all kids that were into music that wasn't popular. That's kind of the point.

GARETH DAVID (LOS CAMPESINOS!): From the age of sixteen, from the time that it was not likely that we would be receiving any phone calls that evening—it was still dial up back then—until I went to bed, it would be just talking to people. Early forms of shit posting and beefing with people, but also getting turned on to a lot of really, really great music, twee pop stuff, so my musical upbringing was fifty-fifty meeting people through Wonder Bar and then AOL chat rooms, and then onto MySpace. That was everything.

———————

* Future Vivian Girls bandmate Katy "Kickball Katy" Goodman.

BEMIS: My [AIM away message] would be a quote from a band that I didn't really like as much as I was acting like I did.

JUSTIN COURTNEY PIERRE (MOTION CITY SOUNDTRACK): I was on AOL Instant Messenger. I'm still technology adverse, but Josh [Cain] set up my name, which I think is basically the name I still use, just JCPMCS. At some point I remember signing on and then just suddenly being bombarded by 150 messages.

JOSHUA CAIN (MOTION CITY SOUNDTRACK): We're playing basement shows and then we started communicating with people, making these fan friends that let us sleep on their floors, and we just chatted and people would tell me about their lives. I would just sit at my computer; I think I drove my wife mad. And we were just girlfriend and boyfriend at the time. But I would just have Instant Messenger open and then I would just be talking to tons of random people in different countries. I think one of them was named Fia, and then I named my dog that because I love that name. She was from Belgium or something.

BEMIS: So I think my initial interest back in the day on AOL was exploring my sexuality and stuff like that. Our most famous song* is about that reality of kids having cell phones and kids having AOL, and the things that you would get up to. I took a lot of shit for what is sometimes considered misogynistic in terms of the lyrics of that song. That's the whole joke of it, but even if it wasn't a joke, those kinds of experiences are so surreal that they make everyone feel crazy.

SAPORTA: If you live in a town and you're the only person that listens to a certain kind of music in that town, you're going to feel alone. But then you go on the Internet and then you're going to find that there's literally thousands of kids like you, all spread out, that are looking for

---

* "Wow, I Can Get Sexual Too," is a knowingly creepy tale of Internet-enabled phone sex. It would prove to be both a hit single and, later, an albatross that Bemis would find himself frequently having to explain before he finally publicly decided to banish it from live performances.

community. So that idea of communities online, my feeling is that the pioneers of that were scene kids. Music kids, really. And when MySpace was first happening, it felt like it was basically just a place for scene kids, for music people. Now the idea is your favorite shampoo brand has their own community online, everyone has their community. Corporations hire community managers to manage a community. But that idea definitely comes from the punk rock DIY ethos. So it was novel at the time. Right now, everything is corporatizing.

DAVID: Those AOL chat rooms, it seems crazy that it could exist now, but they were so much fun. I was a big proponent of the Now Listening To feature, because your messenger could sync with your media player and display what you were listening to through that. So absolutely, that was something that would be used for posturing and for making a point of what you were listening to. It wasn't about listening to music while you were chatting to people, as much as it was about ensuring that the person you were chatting to knew what you were listening to or at least pretending to listen to.

HEISEL: AIM took a corner once you had Taking Back Sunday and Brand New hitting, that kind of third wave of emo. But if I was posting lyrics on AIM, it would be like Braid or the Get Up Kids, and that wouldn't translate at all with the new wave of people.

RAMONE: I actually had a pretty popular LiveJournal. It's incredibly embarrassing to think back on what I put on my LiveJournal; it's like the most embarrassing thing I did. But that being said, I actually had a pretty prominent following and I actually met somebody. I'm not going to say who it is, but somebody who's also a pretty big name in the indie rock world through LiveJournal. I've known this person since I was, like, sixteen. And then it turned out that we came to be peers in music.

MILLER: LiveJournal was a big deal. So, everybody that was on Makeout-club would link their LiveJournal and their Instant Message. So, LiveJournal was definitely the blogging platform for everybody on Makeoutclub, one hundred percent. I think what it boils down to is there's an underlying human need for attention and affirmation. I think that being able to post your work in a somewhat public space and have people comment on it, or look at it, really feels good. It can, of course, feel bad.

RAMONE: I've got to say that if you weren't an embarrassing teenager, then I don't trust you, because every teenager is embarrassing.

2

THE MY GENERATION

IN 2000, THE COMPACT DISC WAS KING. It averaged around $18.52 a pop and very often only had one memorable song on it. (There's no evidence that Len's 1999 album *You Can't Stop the Bum Rush* is *not* the single "Steal My Sunshine" twelve times in a row.) The CD was the most popular—and more or less only—way to consume new music. The vinyl diehard was then a much rarer breed, and there usually was no way to buy just the one song you wanted, as the record industry had begun phasing out the CD single in order to goose sales of albums. As Eric Boehlert wrote in *Salon*, "Labels insist they simply cannot make a big enough return if fans are buying $3 singles instead of $16 albums. Retailers, though, fume that they're suffering without singles, which have historically increased foot traffic in stores, especially among younger shoppers."

The music industry arguably wasn't giving the customer what they wanted. But it did seem to be doing something right, at least for a time. The year 2000 was when the Orlando song-and-dance boy band NSYNC released their album *No Strings Attached*. It sold 2.4 million copies in a week and eventually moved 10 million units by the end of the year, while "It's Gonna Be Me" remains an eternal jam and unkillable meme. That level of success would be all but unimaginable when the decade ended, give or take an Adele. And the reason for that is Napster.

Before Napster, downloading music on the Internet was a shadowy operation, the sort of thing that only a select-few-obsessives were able to figure out, one of them being Andrew "Noz" Nosnitsky, a teenage rap obsessive who would eventually start Cocaine Blunts, one of the most respected hip-hop blogs of the '00s. "I used this software called Hotline which was peer-to-peer, but you basically just hosted a server, and you would get other people's IPs, and you could go in. It wasn't searchable at all, you just had to know people," he says. "That was the big deal. It was just like random dudes with an FTP. I remember pulling the leaked Nas album *I Am. . .* off of an FTP. Probably like rec.music.hiphop or something. That's kind of legendary in the rap world."

Napster made the search a lot easier for people. Developed by nineteen-year-old Northeastern University student Shawn Fanning, the file-trading service Napster hit the world like a bomb. That's the way the music industry and its lawyers viewed it, anyway. And it's not like the nervous executives were incorrect, given that their ability to sell a million copies of a CD in a week was about to go bye, bye, bye. Napster debuted in 1999 but caught fire in the summer of 2000 with dorm-bound college kids and people whose parents had just gotten high-speed Internet. (Or people with the fortitude to spend an entire evening downloading, via dial-up Internet, a garish bluegrass cover of Snoop Dogg's "Gin and Juice" that has been mistakenly and frequently attributed to Phish but was actually a group called the Gourds.)

A few months into the summer of 2000, heavy metal legends Metallica, upset that a demo of their single "I Disappear" had leaked onto the network, filed a lawsuit against Napster and the company's cofounders Fanning and Sean Parker. Lawsuits from Dr. Dre and A&M Records followed, and Napster went bankrupt. It would later be sold to a series of companies that would try to monetize it with mixed results. Similar file-sharing applications LimeWire and Kazaa would spring up in Napster's wake, usually sticking around for a few years until the copyright lawyers had their way.

By the summer of 2000, people desperately needed new ways to find music. A few years earlier, President Bill Clinton signed the Telecommunications Act of 1996, the first major change to telecommunications law in sixty-two years. Previously, no company could own more than four stations in a given market, or more than forty stations overall.

The Telecommunications Act of 1996 massively deregulated the radio industry by all but removing these limits. The idea was that removing these limits would foster competition. Two years later, nearly a quarter of America's radio stations were purchased by a handful of companies. By the early 2000s, Clear Channel Communications was the biggest name in radio. A 2002 report from the Future of Music Coalition found that in the wake of the deregulation, Clear Channel owned "1,240 stations—30 times more than congressional regulation previously allowed."

In 2000, Clear Channel was forced by law to sell ninety-nine stations in twenty-seven markets so it could merge with rival AMFM Inc., to comply with federal ownership limits. The sale of those ninety-nine stations didn't really do much to increase the diversity of the airwaves. As noted in the research paper "The Effect of Clear Channel Radio" by Abby Berendt, published in 2002 in Colorado State's academic journal *Talking Back*, "though more than 30,000 CD's are released each year, national radio playlists are slimming down. The top stations add around 16–20 songs per week, and spin the top songs more than 85 times each between the hours of 6 AM and 6 PM, Monday through Friday."

As Clear Channel and other companies began gobbling up outlets, the number of songs in rotation on any given radio station's playlist tightened to suffocating levels, and MTV followed suit. (As Poe fans learned, women were the first to be shown the door at rock radio.) Repetition was the goal, as it was imperative to flog the latest hit until it was inescapable and therefore easily resented. It might not be technically accurate to say that by the summer of 2000, the only songs you would hear on the radio or MTV were Creed's "With Arms Wide Open," Papa Roach's "Last Resort," and Britney Spears's "Oops! . . . I Did It Again." But I certainly don't remember hearing anything else on the airwaves at the time.

It's here that I will take a moment to say that, unfortunately, I have achieved some level of emotional maturity and come to the realization that "not liking things" is not a solid basis for a personality, and being on some hater shit is for the young. People can dig what they dig, and not everyone is cut out to be the type of person for whom deep music fandom is their *thing*. But a musical ecosystem that can only offer you that which is already popular, as well as nominal variations on that which is very popular, is stultifying indeed.

By the time a new avenue opened up to discover music, a certain type of bored music head was quick to take advantage. The monotony was suffocating, but the Internet was about to give you far more options than you could ever possibly listen to.

"My girlfriend lived in a different town, so our early twee high school courtship was sending mixed CDs back home in the mail, and she had older brothers and was really plugged into cool music. So I was just constantly downloading music," remembers Graham Wright. "It is maybe slightly shameful to admit it as someone who nominally makes my living off intellectual property, but there's a website called Indietorrents* where you could get free music. Oink's Pink Palace was a membership where you had to maintain a certain share ratio or they'd boot you off. It's funny to think that, like three years after this, I was getting frantic phone calls about how our album leaking was a disaster. I could never get too worked up about people pirating our music because I've done so very much of it in my younger days."

While the Metallicas and Dr. Dres of the world were livid over Napster, upstarts much lower on the food chain were grateful for the free exposure that file sharing, message boards, and LiveJournal provided, even if they found it a bit confusing at first.

Eddie Reyes was a guitarist and longtime fixture of the Long Island punk and hardcore community who spent the end of the '90s trying to put together a band that would elevate him beyond his local scene. But he couldn't help but notice that something was going on when his new group Taking Back Sunday started catching on much quicker than he anticipated.

Chris Carrabba also found himself caught off guard by the Internet's sudden bump in importance. In the late '90s, he was a South Florida musician who was quietly writing acoustic songs that he knew didn't fit with the bombastic bands he was fronting at the time. But his friend Amy Fleisher Madden knew he had something that was too pure to remain a secret. While she was still a high school student, she signed

---

* Torrents were peer-to-peer files that became popular in file-sharing forums.

him to her record label Fiddler and accompanied him on tour for his 2000 debut *The Swiss Army Romance,* acting as his unofficial business and spiritual advisor.

CHRIS CARRABBA (DASHBOARD CONFESSIONAL): I started going to cities that I'd never been to and people were singing along to every word, and they clearly had lived with the record for some time without me having been there to sell it to them or play the songs for the first time for them. It was kind of befuddling.

SCOTT HEISEL (*ALTERNATIVE PRESS* EDITOR): My freshman year of college, Napster was a thing and everyone was like, "Have you heard Dashboard Confessional? And everyone's passing around Dashboard Confessional tracks, and it was lighting up my dorm, because it was something totally new.

CARRABBA: Of course, I asked. The thing was that they all had the record and then they'd come and buy the record, anyway. That would give me my chance to discuss with them, like, how did they know about it, and why were they buying it if they had it? Well, they wanted to buy it, but they had no way to get it. I was able to find out how, and it was message boards, and it was Napster and LimeWire.

GEOFF RICKLY (THURSDAY): We played a pre-record release show; the record wasn't out yet. It was supposed to be our release show, but they delivered us the records late or something, it was one of those screwups. So we're playing with Midtown at the Wetlands, and it was packed, and we started playing new songs off *Full Collapse,* and people were singing along to them. And I just couldn't figure out what the fuck was going on.

EDDIE REYES (TAKING BACK SUNDAY): I wasn't the online-savvy guy in my band. But Lars Ulrich from Metallica was right when he said that this is going to fuck up the music industry and everyone's going to take your music. We were like, "Fuck you. That's not punk rock." And then . . . yeah.

LIL JON: Napster was where everybody just got everything. I don't think I liked it too much. I could see when I went into a market, I actually ran up on bootleggers and snatched all my shit, like, "Motherfucker, this is me. Give me all this shit, no more."

AMY FLEISHER MADDEN (FIDDLER RECORDS): Chris and I would tour in various capacities. At a certain point, people started coming up to the merch table and being like, "I want to buy this CD because I downloaded the songs on Napster." It was so cool that kids were buying it and downloading it.

RICKLY: I really had no idea. I really couldn't figure out why there were hundreds of people singing along to songs that weren't on the old record. Speaking to fans afterwards who were like, "We downloaded the record." And I really was like, "What? What does that mean?"

RON WASSERMAN (FISHER): The public was sick of it. I hated it. When I go buy a CD and I'm like, "Well, the rest of the album is not nearly the same as the single. It almost sounds like a different band than the single." And along comes the thief, the Internet, and it says, "We can completely destroy your business model."

COURTNEY HOLT (MYSPACE MUSIC PRESIDENT): When I went to Interscope Geffen A&M, I met with Sean and Shawn. I was the one label person who was meeting with these people, not with a lawsuit in hand, but I wanted to understand what these businesses were doing. I was sort of the ambassador, even though I couldn't ever get the industry to take it seriously. I made a mental note that the world had changed, and that we need to be on the other side of this equation. I called it a consumer first strategy, as opposed to a business first strategy. Which isn't to say that their recklessness wasn't a fuck-you to the industry.

FLEISHER MADDEN: I didn't have any contempt for Napster. Every major label corporation was like, "We have to shut this down." But I was like, "This is great. This is free marketing if you really think about it." I think established artists hated it and younger artists loved it.

HOLT: I tended to be a friendly face, but I met with Sean and Shawn at some point very early on, and I knew what they were doing was wrong. But part of what I was trying to figure out is the psychology that was driving them to want to do this. I didn't look at these as people that were purposely trying to take down music. They were trying to solve a problem that consumers were having that we didn't know how to solve.

REYES: It's a double-edged sword. We were from the old school where we were making flyers at the Kinko's. But right on the cusp of us becoming bigger, the Internet blew up. It got the word out. We can give a lot of credit to the Internet, though we stopped selling records. But it doesn't matter because all those people came to see us play. It's good, and it hurts.

HOLT: So the problem is you had Walmart and Best Buy and the big-box retailers and Target essentially commoditizing music. We were not incentivized to put out singles. So you had basically this inflation that was coming from trying to protect the CD business. The industry was sort of blind to the realities of what was happening. The issue with piracy, it was really just about consumer control and choice more than it was about piracy. I think people want to pay for music. We just weren't giving them the products they wanted. They didn't want to have to go to the big-box retailer and pay eighteen bucks. They wanted convenience, access, and community.

MARK RICHARDSON (FORMER PITCHFORK EDITOR IN CHIEF): Modern rock radio was both huge and pretty shitty.

ANDREW NOSNITSKY (COCAINE BLUNTS): MTV by that point had gone to shit. I feel like it was in the early 2000s that it truly just became worthless to me. The Internet started opening up, and then suddenly that was my primary resource for music information. I feel like probably from the years of 1992 to probably 1999, I would just come home from school and watch TV, whether it was Rap City or MTV. At a certain point it was like, "There's nothing here anymore."

RICHARDSON: By the end of the '90s, I thought alternative rock was pretty awful. *Spin* kind of built that world, and then once it got to be the mainstream, they latched onto it. And of course, they had tons of great writers at that time, but *Spin* covers by the late '90s . . . I just wasn't really interested in it as much anymore. I was just too old for rap metal completely. I could recognize that Rage Against the Machine is a good band in some ways, but it's just not my kind of music.

NOSNITSKY: [Napster] made it easier to access a lot of stuff because prior to that point, I was just like, squirreling away my lunch money. I would hear about an album and I might not hear it for six months, but suddenly just everything opened up for me. It opened me up to older music a lot more easily. I had already been getting a lot of music off the Internet before Napster. There were already MP3 and tape trading communities for that stuff. I remember getting *Operation: Doomsday** on—I think it was called Cipher Divine? That was the big underground rap MP3 site.

HOLT: The most interesting feature of Napster for me wasn't the free music. It was the ability to browse someone else's library. Whenever I'd go on a date with a woman, I'd go into their apartment, I'd look at the records, like, "Who is this person?" And the most telling thing about any individual is what music they listen to. I think if you look at what percentage of the downloaded music was actually played, it's probably not as much as people were stealing.

WASSERMAN: I sat with Jimmy Iovine and Doug Morris† because they would ask, "What do you think's coming?" And I said, "I believe that your album days are done, and it's going to come down to ninety-nine-cent singles." They both said, "That will never happen in our lifetime. We will never allow that. Never, ever."

---

* The debut album from the cultishly loved, late rapper MF Doom, aka Daniel Dumile, known for wearing a metal mask and for his densely packed, abstract wordplay.
† Respectively, the former chairman of Interscope Geffen A&M and the former CEO of Universal Music Group.

CARRABBA: So my experience, I guess at the time, was that [the Internet] was this great equalizer. I had no distribution, but I had a record, so I discovered quickly that when I started touring, that I would get to new cities I'd never been to, and my record was already there. People had already downloaded it from Napster and were sharing it. There wasn't a social network at that point, but there was a network nonetheless. It wasn't a one-stop hub, but it was sort of already in the infancy of what would come to be. And I think it started with Napster and music fans.

Success isn't always about being first. Investor and engineer Jonathan Abrams launched Friendster, the first major social media platform, in March 2003. Mark J. Pincus, a Silicon Valley entrepreneur who provided Abrams with seed money, told the *New York Times* that Abrams started the service "as a way to surf through his friends' address books for good-looking girls."

By October 2003, the company was valued at $53 million, and the media became fascinated by this thing called "a social network." Friendster was written up by *Spin*, *Time*, and *Vanity Fair*, and Abrams appeared on *Jimmy Kimmel Live*. Abrams also, the *New York Times* noted, began "showing up regularly at parties with a strikingly attractive woman on each arm," so it seems his plan succeeded.

A year after its founding, Abrams was offered $30 million for Friend-ster by Google. Taking advice from Silicon Valley peers and inspired by myriad stories of self-made technology billionaires, Abrams declined the offer. Had he taken the offer in Google stock, he would have made $1 billion by 2006. Abrams became focused on growth rather than the day-to-day operations of his site. As Friendster grew more popular, its infrastructure buckled, and pages began taking "up to forty seconds" to load, an eternity in web time, and eventually it became difficult to sign in.

In April 2004, two months after Facebook launched and just a year and change after Friendster started, Friendster's board of investors replaced Abrams as the company's CEO. Three other CEOs followed in short order, each with their own ideas of how to right the ship. Abrams left the company in 2005. In 2009, Friendster was purchased by MOL Global, an online payments provider based in Malaysia. It pivoted to being a gaming website and eventually closed in 2015. Four years after starting, Friendster's failure to launch was being taught at Harvard Business School as an example of what not to do.

The genius director Steven Soderbergh once said that instead of playing it safe and redundantly remaking films that were already a success, Hollywood executives should look for films with strong ideas that didn't quite work and remake the flops, getting it right this time. Hollywood largely ignored this advice, as recognizable intellectual property became the only matter of importance in the twenty-first century. But at least someone listened to him.

Even beyond the technical glitches, Friendster wasn't likely to work long-term. You could only view your friends, or your friends of friends. But once you checked in on everyone, there wasn't much else to do. A few months after Friendster started, a social media site would come along to show everyone what social media could be. Sometimes, success is about being right on time.

Before he became everybody's friend, Tom Anderson was a reformed teenage hacker, operating under the name Lord Flathead. In 1985, he triggered an FBI raid after he hacked the security of Chase Manhattan Bank. Being only fourteen at the time, he wasn't arrested.

The "Keith Richards and Mick Jagger meet at a train stop, bond over Chuck Berry, and form the Rolling Stones" legend of MySpace is that Anderson, a student-debt ridden UCLA Film Studies student and the former lead singer of a band called Swank (*such* a '90s band name), answered a job advertisement for a product tester and copywriter posted by Chris DeWolfe.

Anderson's job was to test a product for Xdrive, a data-storage company where DeWolfe was head of sales and marketing. Anderson told DeWolfe that he hated the product. DeWolfe was impressed by the honesty, and they became fast friends, starting a direct marketing company together called ResponseBase. In 2002, it was sold to the marketing company eUniverse.

"One of the things that they sold were Razor scooters; they would import them and sell them for a hundred bucks apiece online over the holidays and make a profit," Ngọc Cao remembers of the pair's early hustle, which involved getting as many of the items on a plane as possible. "It was a very specific model."

Sean Percival would eventually become MySpace's vice president of online marketing in 2009 and an in-demand marketing advisor. But before that, he was just a guy who wanted to work at MySpace so badly that he created a company that marketed through MySpace, eventually earning himself a lawsuit for his efforts. He's been observing MySpace from the beginning, and he remembers DeWolfe and Anderson's early marketing efforts.

"The whole genesis of MySpace was that they had all these kind of junky products and they needed a lot of ad impressions. They looked at Friendster and they realized the page views per session were higher than any website in the history of websites," he says. "And every page view means an ad impression. 'So let's copy Friendster just to get those ad impressions for our products and our diet pills and our junk,' and basically build this massive ad network via a social network. Just clone Friendster to get the page views."

Anderson was a digital native before such a term even existed, and he had intuited that social media was about to be the thing. "I had looked at dating sites and niche communities like BlackPlanet, AsianAve, and MiGente, as well as Friendster," he told *Fortune* in 2006, "and I thought, *They're thinking way too small.*"

His FBI dalliances aside, Anderson wasn't a smash-the-state anarchist punk. He was instead a suburban pop-punk, up for a bit of comfortable rebellion. He didn't want to tear down the status quo and make the world a more equitable place. He just wanted everyone to have a good time and not be so concerned with the rules. It could also be argued he wasn't too concerned with appropriating ideas from minority communities.

The problem with Friendster, he observed, was that it was just too closed off and too square. There was no way to easily find fellow Weezer fans so you could defend or deride their latest comeback album. And

Friendster had a very unpunk humorlessness, as the company was quick to take down the type of jokey pages users might make for, say, their dog.

MySpace would take a more open, laid-back approach. You could look at anyone's page you wanted, and you could easily search for everyone who listed Rivers Cuomo and co. on their profile. And if you wanted to make a MySpace page for Sparky? You do you, man. Post away. Post whatever you want. (In response to MySpace's growing success and apparent cool factor, Friendster had plans to allow users to reach out to potential friends based on their tastes in bands, but the idea never got off the ground.)

Anderson and DeWolfe hit the Viper Room and other Los Angeles clubs, inviting local bands, club owners, and assorted hotties to join their site. The pair hoped that musicians and the nightlife butterflies you could only meet in Hollywood would sell the site for them. They did.

GIBBY MILLER (MAKEOUTCLUB): I was pissed off, man. I heard someone mention it, like, "Oh yeah, Friendster, blah blah blah." And I was like, "What is this? Where the fuck did this come from? This isn't cool. This is business-y. Who are these people? This is so corporate. This is just totally contrived and productized and commoditized." I think the first person who takes the first dance gets copied, you know?

NORMAN BRANNON (TEXAS IS THE REASON): I was sort of a late adopter to Friendster. Mostly because I still considered myself to be a semiprivate person, or at least I thought that artists should be private. And the only reason I joined was because I was getting to a place where my queerness was becoming much more part of my identity. And I wanted to see what kind of queer people were on Friendster.

MILLER: "Ooh, they've got this thing called testimonials? Ooh, that's a good idea. Fuuuck." And then I just started using Friendster.

HEISEL: A lot of high school and college kids are getting on Friendster and connecting. The biggest problem with Friendster is that you couldn't have nonperson profiles. You couldn't be a band. You had the fans there, but there was nothing to rally around. And that's one of the problems that MySpace solved, while also creating ten million other problems, you can give a band a gathering place for their fans.

BÍCH NGỌC CAO (MYSPACE MUSIC EDITOR): There are people who said that Chris DeWolfe had the idea for MySpace when he was in college, and this is straight up not true. Tom came up with the idea and pitched it to Chris, and Chris was very resistant to it, from my understanding, and then later was just like, "Yeah, do this little thing." It was a super corporate company in one regard, because MySpace was not started as a true start-up. It was a small mini start-up within a large company called eUniverse, that later had to change its name to Intermix because Eliot Spitzer* sued them for all kinds of nefarious practices. They sold all kinds of really weird, sketchy stuff. Tom and Chris were employed by them because they purchased a company that those guys had started where they were importing products and selling them online.

SEAN PERCIVAL (VICE PRESIDENT, ONLINE MARKETING): Friendster was suffering because they couldn't keep the site online. It was constantly going down. So every time Friendster went down, people started rushing over to MySpace. It would create a boom. And then eventually people got sick of the downtime. And then they went to MySpace, who, of course, had their own scaling issues, but they managed to hold on a little bit better.

NGỌC CAO: If you logged into Friendster and went to your profile and you looked at a page, it would say so-and-so is in your network and this is how you're connected to them. Every time that you loaded a page, it would recalculate those connections. And as people were loading those pages, before we had access to things like cloud servers and better technology, it kept crashing their site. So they had a junky experience.

---

* In 2005, before he became tabloid fodder, the former New York State attorney general sued Intermix, which owned more than forty websites, for hiding spyware programs inside downloadable games, among other charges. Said spyware could generate pop-up advertising and redirect web searches.

PERCIVAL: A friend of mine talked about social networks in the early days, and he said it doesn't matter what's on the social network. All people care about is, are my homies there? And there was this shift. You were on Friendster and then everyone is on MySpace. And it didn't matter how ugly the site was, how broken it was; if your friends were there, you wanted to be there. And we see this today, with TikTok and Snapchat, people move into tribes and wherever everyone is, that's where they want to be.

3

THE LONELY
HEARTS CLUB

EMO. IT EVEN SOUNDS GOOFY to say it out loud, doesn't it? No wonder every emo band hated the name.

Nearly all forms of music have *some* sort of emotion behind them, or are at least attempting to stir some type of emotion in the listener. The idea that there's a music scene that has an implied monopoly on sincerity and feeling is ridiculous and borderline offensive to all other artists in all other genres. So much about emo is silly, from the fashion to the incessant debates about what wave of emo we're currently in.

But emo is also deeply important and absolutely necessary for the people who need it. For fans of the genre, it can sometimes feel like the only true thing in the world for the listener. Maybe that's silly. But silly things can have a lot of power if you believe in them. And if emo didn't have any power, then it wouldn't have made so many people so deeply mad.

Consider the intensely polarized reaction to the breakthrough success of Chris Carrabba, front man, songwriter, and the only member of Dashboard Confessional who got to be on magazine covers. With his diamond-cut cheekbones and a voice purer than the driven snow, Carrabba was preordained to become emo's ambassador to the mainstream.

Carrabba fronted a Boca Raton, Florida, pop-punk band called the Vacant Andys, whose debut single was released in 1996 by Fiddler Records, which was started by high school entrepreneur Amy Fleisher Madden as an outgrowth of her zine *Fiddler Jones*. She remembers that even in the beginning, Carrabba was worried that people wouldn't like him.

"I put out a seven-inch for them. I was like fifteen, and he was probably nineteen or twenty. He was a little bit like, 'please don't hate me on the Internet,'" she remembers.

After the Vacant Andys ended, Carrabba started fronting the harder edged band Further Seems Forever, but it was an awkward fit. The sleeve tattoos that would soon become one of his defining images, along with his pointy, anime-esque "Chris-hawk" haircut, didn't fool anybody. Carrabba was at his core a delicate man, and a life of screaming over muted palm riffs just wasn't for him.

On the side, he began writing songs on his acoustic guitar after a tough breakup. It turned out that Carrabba was preternaturally good at tapping into an unguarded space that enabled him to write naked, openhearted explorations of hurt feelings that either instantly disarmed you or instantly elicited eye rolls.

Released by Fiddler Records, Dashboard Confessional's 2000 debut *The Swiss Army Romance* was one of the first LiveJournal and file-trading peer-to-peer hits. For the 2001 follow-up, *The Places You Have Come to Fear the Most*, Carrabba signed with the Santa Monica–based independent label Vagrant,* also home to Kansas City's hearty the Get Up Kids and New Jersey's cherubic Saves the Day, both of which were fast becoming emo institutions themselves, especially after the Vagrant Across America tour brought them into clubs nationwide with a ticket price that maxed out at fifteen dollars.

Even if you weren't inclined to make Carrabba's explorations of heartbreak and loneliness into some sort of lifestyle, it was clear the guy knew how to do a lot with a little, turning bare-bones acoustic

---

* The label was started in the mid-'90s by Joe Cohen and Rich Egan, the latter of whom would be the target of criticism within the punk community for business moves such as buying luxury tour buses for his artists, selling half his label to Interscope Records, and relentlessly focusing on merchandise. What some saw as business savvy, others saw as the commercialization of the emo and punk scenes.

arrangements into room-filling anthems. The single "Screaming Infidelities" started to become such a word-of-AIM hit that offline outlets such as *Elle* and *Teen People* took notice of him and his scene.

"Screaming Infidelities" was such an obvious anthem that Carrabba recorded it twice, hitting the rising action parts harder on the *Places* version like the seasoned professional he had become. The song's composition is a series of escalating, slightly deescalating, and then almost worryingly reescalating hooks, with Carrabba owning up to some truly dejected post breakup feelings ("I am alone/in my defeat") with a palpable honesty that, for some, quickly moves the reaction needle from "this guy needs to get over it" to "yeah, been there."

So, obviously the knives came out as soon as Dashboard Confessional started to break through. To Carrabba's detractors he was a wimp, a whiner, or worse. Many of the insults were homophobic and sexist in nature, implying he was less of a man for putting his vulnerabilities on display, but that's the Internet (and a society that needed to start unpacking its identity hang-ups) for you.

"I think I was a polarizing figure, 'cause my music's not for everybody, and it got really popular," says Carrabba. "And also, I'm one guy as opposed to a band. So it was really easy just to fling it at us. I was at the pinnacle of my success, so I looked at it as an even trade."

Even before Pitchfork had become a tastemaker, it was down on emo in all its forms, especially Dashboard (the review of *Places* deemed it music for "sensitive, gender-role-enlightened, bedwetting emo boys") while Buddyhead memorably said that Carrabba wanted the terrorists to win, among other insults. That emo was originally used as an insult in the punk community and would endure as The Genre That Dare Not Speak Its Name is a telling commentary on masculine insecurity during the Bush era.

What's so bad about having emotions? Don't deny that which makes you feel fragile; don't tamp down your inchoate longing. It's part of what makes you human. And because of ingrained ideas of how men should perform their masculinity that American society can never quite divest from—which are to just suck it up and pretend whatever is there isn't there—young men can often use the extra push to get introspective.

If you're of the opinion (put forth by left-wing thinkers such as author Naomi Klein, documentarian Adam Curtis, and other highbrow sorts who would be quite surprised to find themselves lassoed into a defense of emo) that much of the business of late capitalism is about manipulating people's insecurities to make them obedient consumers (and most masculine fears are so immediately perceivable that it doesn't take much to tweak them in the needed direction) and that much of mass media is about offering a cultural anesthetic, then any art form dedicated to at least trying to get people out of their stupor into something deeper is laudable. Noble, even.

What makes emo special, and what Carrabba was always smart enough to grasp, is that the genre took the vulnerability that's always been at the heart of the best rock music and made it the main driver. Rock music is always at its best when the rather silly binary cultural notions we have of the masculine and feminine are intermingling, raw power and all that bullshit swagger mixed with leavening grace. (David Bowie is the master of this, though all worthwhile rock stars play around with the proper ratio of strong, sassy, sensitive, and sweet in their work.) When it's really cooking, emo hits both ends of the spectrum hard, making the boundaries between them irrelevant in the process.

The whole argument with this music is to just drop your bullshit and accept, if only to yourself and the emo dude singing at you, that you're just a human being, which means you're often silly and sad and worried that you're not enough. It's just healthier if you admit it before you put up the sort of walls that will lead you down a bad path. And once you can connect with yourself, try to connect with someone else. We're all in this together, and you have to start cultivating an inner life at some point.

There are certainly worse underpinnings for a genre and a subculture. And if it didn't work for everyone? Well, even the haters felt *something*, which is still a win. Emo was a very messy genre, which would eventually make it the perfect fit for MySpace, where displaying messy emotions was value added.

———————————

The *e*-word was originally a pejorative term, leveled at D.C. hardcore bands Rites of Spring and Embrace, whose members grew tired of yelling about Ronald Reagan and decided to interrogate their own feelings; their live shows became legendary for band and audience members openly weeping. Onlookers, perhaps uncomfortable with such displays of emotion in this most masculine of genres, immediately dubbed such bands *emocore*. Each band released one self-titled, scene-defining album before breaking up.*

"Embrace, when I listen to that record now I'm still like, 'Wow. This took fucking guts,'" says Brannon. "Especially the guy from Minor Threat singing these words, his career could have ended right there. I think people listened to it and said, 'This is real. He's not faking it.'"

For the next ten years, emo was seemingly a cursed word, and for a while you weren't truly about that life unless you burned brightly and then burned out.

Jawbreaker front man Blake Schwarzenbach wrote the sort of lyrics that inspired many tattoos, many of them from the crush anthem "Chesterfield King." ("I left your house and kicked myself/I put those feelings on a shelf to die.") Sunny Day Real Estate singer Jeremy Enigk developed an intense following thanks to an ability to make anything he sang feel like mystical wisdom from a newly unearthed ancient scroll. Texas Is the Reason was a New York group that specialized in writing anthemic songs dripping with ennui ("Same old shit just a different day/ Well I'll wait around for one more day") over guitars that sounded as anxious as they were furious.

All three had little in common aesthetically. But they all played with an intensity that set them apart from the often aloof and intellectual indie rock scene of the '90s and had singers who seemed like they were telling the listener a secret they couldn't entrust to anyone else, and that was enough to qualify them as emo. The stylistic variety they collectively displayed showed that emo wasn't ever about one particular signifier; it was more of a "know it when you hear it" deal at first. They all became far more popular after they broke up.

---

* Their respective front men, Guy Picciotto and Ian MacKaye (also of Minor Threat), would go on to form the massively influential and respected underground institution Fugazi.

Sometimes you were called emo when no one knew what else to call you. Far was a Sacramento, California, rock group with soaring, whisper-to-a-scream choruses and intricate arrangements that Epic Records tried and failed to market as heavy metal and whose front man, Jonah Matranga, would go on to form a head-spinning number of projects in the '00s. The 1998 release *Water and Solutions* would later become a touchstone for the heavier emo groups.

Emo could even—somehow—refer to Weezer, a major label alt-rock band that went dormant after their second album *Pinkerton* (an account of front man Rivers Cuomo's sexual neuroses and the shame they cause him) flopped both commercially and critically in 1996, only to be reha-bilitated as a cult classic. Upon Weezer's return to active duty with 2001's *Weezer*, a gleaming album with loads of hooks and not much in the way of actual feelings, Cuomo would repeatedly insist he had no idea what the term *emo* meant, and he spent the rest of his career with Weezer mostly running away from introspective lyrics and sincerity as a whole. (Weezer's heel turn from one of the best bands in the world to, seem-ingly on purpose, one of the worst is a generational trauma to many.)

Jimmy Eat World are widely regarded as the first emo band to sign to a major label, as well as the first to have a number-one hit in rock radio and a video in heavy rotation at MTV. From Mesa, Arizona, the band started as a traditional pop-punk act and released a very ado-lescent self-titled album in 1994 they pretend never happened. Then, inspired by nascent emo groups such as Mineral, Christie Front Drive, and Sense Field (all of whom didn't have much recognition in their time but became better known after breaking up), Jimmy Eat World released 1996's promising *Static Prevails* and 1999's emo masterpiece *Clarity*, a grandiose report on waking up to the world, with all the joy and terror that implies, on Capitol Records. The opening song "Table for Glasses" lays out the album's thesis, "it happens too fast/to make sense of it/to make it last," as good a summation of youth as you'll ever encounter.

Perhaps Jimmy Eat World's greatest contribution to the genre was that they just kept going, even after being dropped by their label, show-ing emo bands in the process that they didn't have to die young to become legends. The band regrouped and recorded the 2001 album

Bleed American with producer Mark Trombino,* funding the sessions with hard-earned touring money. *Bleed American* was more direct, while no less sincere. Their hit single "The Middle," a sonic pep talk that would cement them as the reliable, down-to-earth Tom Petty of emo, was a long-awaited breakthrough, for both the band and a genre that Jimmy Eat World swore they knew nothing of.

"I look back on *Bleed American*, that's the record that pushed everything over the edge in a lot of ways. I admire Jimmy Eat World deeply," says Matranga. "I've spent quite a bit of time with them, and they're just much more a go with the flow, do their thing entity than I am."

There was a time when onlookers (and the press that was finally starting to catch on) thought that Kansas City's the Get Up Kids and Milwaukee's the Promise Ring would go all the way. The two had similar trajectories, as the Promise Ring made an early emo classic with 1997's vibrant, searching *Nothing Feels Good* and followed it up with the smart, wistful power pop of 1999's *Very Emergency*, both released via Jade Tree,† which brought them both backlash and mainstream attention from publications looking for someone to pin their "emo, it's totally a thing" scene reports on. In response, guitarist Jason Gnewikow once told a *Spin* reporter that their conversation would end if he even brought up the word during a 2001 interview.

The Get Up Kids made their debut in 1997 with *Four Minute Mile*, released on the label Doghouse. Their 1999 follow-up *Something to Write Home About* became a word-of-mouth and file-sharing hit on the backs of simple, sturdy, and sincere love songs such as "Ten Minutes." The album eventually sold more than 100,000 copies, making it the biggest seller for their label Vagrant until Dashboard came along. Light MTV exposure, slots opening for Green Day and Weezer, and a spot on their label's nine-week Vagrant Across America tour seemed to augur a mainstream breakthrough.

In a 1999 *Spin* feature profile on the Promise Ring and what the magazine dubbed the Emocore Scene, writer Jeff Salamon theorized that

---

* A pop-punk and emo superproducer who recorded *Clarity* and *Bleed American*, as well as Blink-182's *Dude Ranch* and Midtown's first two albums.

† A Delaware-based record label that put out many classic emo albums. Its message board was one of the most popular in the scene.

emo groups, which "are starting to look like the only way rock—as in verse-chorus-verse and guitar-bass-drums—can still function as both a subculture and a mass culture." That year found the gaudy rap-rock mooks Kid Rock *and* Limp Bizkit gracing the alternative rock institution's cover, so you could understand why editors were desperate for an alternative to what alternative had become.

Emo was still a dirty word by 2000. But a lot more people were starting to hear it.

CHRIS CARRABBA (DASHBOARD CONFESSIONAL): I was a little confused at first and felt like it didn't apply to my music, because it existed before I started my band. And I had such reverence for the bands that I called emo. They were from a generation before my band, like Texas Is the Reason and Sunny Day Real Estate. But I understood later that it just boiled down to the commonality between those bands and my band, which was this sincerity. I embraced it; I thought it was aptly named.

MATT PRYOR (THE GET UP KIDS/THE NEW AMSTERDAMS): It was a derogatory term, something that punk kids and hardcore kids would call "these pussies in these emo bands." I was already into bands that would go on to be called emo before I think I knew what it was.

JUSTIN COURTNEY PIERRE (MOTION CITY SOUNDTRACK): I was at a party in 1997, and somebody was asking me what music I like to listen to. It was right after that second Sunny Day Real Estate record came out. I mentioned that name and they said, "Oh, so you like emo music?" And then they kind of turned and walked away, and I was like, "I don't know what that means." That was the only time I ever heard that term until maybe five years later.

AMY FLEISHER MADDEN (FIDDLER RECORDS): When *Pinkerton* came out, it was like, is this emo? It feels like emo, but this is on a major label and Weezer's kind of pop; I don't know.

JOSHUA CAIN (MOTION CITY SOUNDTRACK): People were starting to see this new scene evolving out of the ashes of what had been the
alternative scene.

PRYOR: I listened to Embrace and Rites of Spring, and I already knew
Mineral and Promise Ring had already put out their first record, and so
I was aware of stuff. It certainly wasn't something that you wore on your
sleeve, something to be proud of.

FLEISHER MADDEN: For a really long time, when I had my label, I never
used the word *emo* with Dashboard Confessional. Not once. Because it
was like something that either people made fun of it or they didn't know
what it was. I would always call bands indie rock because emo was this
negative term.

GABE SAPORTA (MIDTOWN/HUMBLE BEGINNINGS/COBRA STAR-
SHIP): There was a crazy thing that was happening at the time. All these
punk and ska bands were kind of breaking up and doing emo.

PRYOR: I think somewhere in my bones, I knew instinctively that there
was nothing I could do about it. It is what it is, I'm gonna be called the
singer of an emo band for the rest of my life, and I'm fine with that.

SCOTT HEISEL (*ALTERNATIVE PRESS* EDITOR): You had the kids who
were like, "I'm just so attracted to the super, super, super over-the-top
heart-on-sleeve emotion," which I could relate to because, like, that was
what attracted me to like Braid* and the Get Up Kids and Texas Is the
Reason, then Rainer Maria. It all kind of starts with Weezer's *Pinkerton*,
that was the real Big Bang for that whole idea.

FLEISHER MADDEN: The first time I heard the word was when I interviewed the Vacant Andys for my zine before they were on my label. The
guitar player John Owens described their sound as emo, and I didn't
know what it was. I was too young to be like, "Hey, what's that, man?"

---

* An Illinois emo group whose 1998 album *Frame & Canvas* was considered a genre staple.

And then I remember not too long after I got a promo of *Static Prevails* from Capitol.

CARRABBA: I was long from being on the radio. I didn't even have distribution, so they couldn't go to a record store, it wouldn't be there on a shelf, no matter how small the record store was, or how indie it was or punk rock it was. So it was through word of mouth and e-mails and chat rooms and file sharing.

FLEISHER MADDEN: The guys in a band called Strongarm had broken up and started forming a new band that they kept calling an arena rock band. And we were all at a party, and I remember Chris being like, "The Strongarm guys are here, they want me to try singing." And that became Further Seems Forever. And then simultaneously, Chris started writing with an acoustic guitar, I think in hopes to bring music into Further. And those guys are very stylistically different musically. So the music that Chris was bringing was not their vibe, to put it gently.

SAPORTA: I remember I was dating this girl who lived in Long Island. She had a poster of it up and I'm like, "Who is this band?" Because they weren't from the scene. That was the thing about Jimmy Eat World. They were a major label band. But [*Clarity*] was so revolutionary, everyone in the scene started adopting it and loving it.

CAIN: It's got to be the spark of Jimmy Eat World.

PRYOR: They have been putting out good records, but then that one [*Clarity*] was just a studio masterpiece. If you were in the scene, it's just *Sgt. Pepper's* or *Pet Sounds* or something, like "Well, that's significantly more advanced than anything . . . any of us have ever done."

HEISEL: Say what you will about Jimmy Eat World, but "The Middle" is one of the greatest songs of all time. Three chords, it's fucking brilliant. I've heard it in my life a million times. I'll welcome to hear it a million more. That one song has given them another twenty years of their career.

PRYOR: There was never a piece of a press release that called us an emo band, and I think that would have been the same on whatever label we were on. I think it has probably more to do with the other bands that were kind of in the same circuit as us, like Promise Ring, Braid, Saves the Day, Jimmy Eat World, Mineral . . . even though all those bands are very different sounding, something about it clumped us all together. It wasn't an intentional thing of building a scene, it was kind of like, "Oh I like that band, I want to play shows with that band."

FLEISHER MADDEN: [Carrabba] would come over and play me these songs that I was like, "These are just awesome." And he was like, "Yeah, they're kind of good demos." And I was like, "They're not demos, this is the song. It's done. Let's put it out, let's do it." I put him in the studio with James Wisner to record what would become *The Swiss Army Romance*. And it was super quick, because it was just obviously him and a guitar. It was kind of awkward because Chris was still in Further Seems Forever. And then it was like, "We're just going to do this other thing also on our own, by himself; let's see what happens."

PRYOR: When we saw Jimmy Eat World play for the first time, we were just like, "Wow, fuck. That's what we wanna do." And so at that point, we started a new band. We're like, "I don't know, we wanna do something different that's still pop-y, that's still hook-y and loud and fast, but with a little more complexity to it," I guess.

FLEISHER MADDEN: I mean, I know all the bits and pieces and the songs and what they're about and it never even mattered. When something is art, it doesn't belong to you anymore because people take it and they make it theirs and it becomes about their experience. So by no means, and this is not a real name, but by no means was I like, "All of these people are singing a song about Barbara!"

PRYOR: I went to UNCP [University of North Carolina at Pembroke] for one year. And then when I was flunking everything there, I went to Penn Valley community college for one year. And then fed up with that, I tricked my dad into sending me tuition money for the following year and just kept it. [*laughter*] And made up a fake report card. Actually, I bought another van with that money instead of going to school. I was taking business classes and I was just like, "I think I could just do this on my own." He was pretty pissed. But it's fine.

NORMAN BRANNON (TEXAS IS THE REASON): I think that we were caught in the middle of the alternative rock shit show. I often say how there were three people in our first show. Our first show was in my living room. So, these were people that were friends of mine from the hardcore scene who had become A&R people. We were nervous and we were awful. It was shocking to me that basically all three of them almost immediately were like, "You realize this could be a thing." And when we went in and recorded our first demo, which turned into our first seven-inch, that's when everything just blew the fuck up. Every label alive was just on it immediately.

JONAH MATRANGA (FAR/ONELINEDRAWING): I moved to Sacramento in the summer of '91. We started a band, I was finishing university at the time. So the first couple of years, we were just big local heroes. I became a father in '94 and I went to the band at that time and said, "Look, I've been having fun and everything, but I got a kid to raise, and I grew up really poor, and I do not want her to grow up really poor. So, we've got to figure something out to have a little more money around." Then we got signed by Immortal Epic. We toured with rock bands like Monster Magnet and Korn that we did not fit with at all; the sort of macho thing was always the thing I really just didn't want anything to do with.

BRANNON: I think there were a lot of people who were constantly blowing smoke up our asses, constantly telling us what we should and shouldn't be doing, and constantly filling us with dreams that I think essentially tore the band apart. Because once you start feeling like you're more important than another person in the band, or whatever, this is not gonna end well. And unfortunately, that's kind of part of an A&R playbook really, is to cozy up with someone who you see as a primary member in the band.

So some people might cozy up with me and some people might cozy up with Garrett*, and then me and Garrett are at each other's throats.

MATRANGA: Just to go back to a perfect summation of how Far did not make sense in the world, at the same club in Florida within a span of a couple of months, we came through once opening for Monster Magnet and the next time opening for Promise Ring and Jets to Brazil.† So we were just incredibly in between worlds and we fit sort of on both bills, but we didn't fit on either bill. Far played with Jimmy Eat World, Far played with Promise Ring, Far played with a lot of entities like that.

BRANNON: Honestly, it was impossible for us to function as a normal band. I was surprised we got as much done as we did.

MATRANGA: Whatever kind of music it was we were making, which turns out to be sort of post-hardcore emo something, as that was starting to get more popular, we were breaking up. So that brings us to like '98. We broke up in the fall of '98, and then by '99 I was doing onelinedrawing because again my daughter was five at the time, and I needed to still figure out ways to have money. I was pretty deep into trying to do music for a living, so I at least had to try and make that work. So that's essentially the arc of Far.

BRANNON: We were really sort of entertaining this because we felt like it was the only way to keep the band going, because it was sort of impossible to live in the city otherwise, and if you listen to the lyrics to the song "Back and to the Left," that's exactly what that song's about—that song was about trying to survive in New York City. And hoping that you make it before you have to go back to wherever you grew up from. But in my case, I grew up in New York, so I had nowhere to go.

MATRANGA: Generally speaking, bands are comprised of people who started playing music because they weren't that good at communicating

---

* Guitarist and vocalist Garrett Klahn.
† The band Blake Schwarzenbach formed after Jawbreaker.

outside of music. It's their only way to really effectively communicate with the world and process their feelings. And then you add in ambition, fear, money, trauma. And then you add in spending more time with those people in a band for twelve hours at a time, and however many days straight.

BRANNON: We're thinking we're the shit. I think that was probably an experience that a lot of bands had at that time, but ours was definitely, I think, ramped up to the *n*th degree. There was no breathing room; that bidding war lasted over two years until we finally gave in, and when we finally gave in, we broke up.

HEISEL: Not everyone is going to be the Rolling Stones, and I would argue that's true of the vast majority of most of those bands that were formed from '93 to '99, starting with Sunny Day Real Estate and including Mineral and Christie Front Drive. The Promise Ring is a great example. These are bands that were not trying to make a career, and so then they had this kind of natural underground buzz because they weren't trying to make the leap. And furthermore, making that leap was career suicide. You look at Jawbreaker as a perfect example, right? Making the leap to DGC, I mean, they were going to break up anyway, but it just absolutely killed their band. And that was when labels mattered a lot.

MATRANGA: I guess the first time I really remember seeing it in writing, I think it was *Kerrang*, they'd have writers in L.A., like, reporting on little club shows that we were doing. There's a picture of me and it said JONAH MATRANGA, EMO KING. That was maybe '96 or '97, something like that. All of my friends outside of our little music scene, our little world, are like, "What the fuck is this thing that you're supposed to be the king of?"

HEISEL: I remember the Promise Ring getting a music video on *120 Minutes*. That was a huge shock. I think you had all these bands that were coming out that were clearly inspired by Jimmy [Eat] World, clearly inspired by Braid, the Get Up Kids, the Promise Ring. This whole kind of next class of bands that thought, *Well, how do I make this into a career? How do I take that step?*

Whenever a movement reaches a certain level of cultural saturation, the main artists and animating ideas will become obscured by musical carpetbaggers, the wheels of commerce, and innumerable things that are not related to art, and it will be hard to remember why anyone ever cared, and audiences will look for something that represents the antithesis of the wave. You couldn't ask for a more direct pendulum swing than moving from the aggressive, wounded anger of nu metal to the bracing sensitivity of emo.

Dashboard Confessional and Jimmy Eat World had led the counterattack, but they were soon to have company. Taking Back Sunday was Reyes's ticket out of Long Island, a band that would become as well known for its lineup changes as its anthemic songs and playful titles like "You're So Last Summer." Their first and classic lineup was formed by Reyes, a post-hardcore lifer looking to level up. He recruited front man Adam Lazzara and covocalist and guitarist John Nolan. The band's dynamic felt like an ever-escalating conversation between two intense dudes who needed to reassure each other that it's OK to sing lyrics like "Boys like you are a dime a dozen." After touring hard behind a demo for a year, they signed to the Chicago hardcore label Victory Records, a label that was as notorious for the hard sell it gave to up-and-coming bands like Thursday as it was for its allegedly "creative" approach to paying bands.

"I've always been a fan of two guys singing, one could be grunty and screamy. One could sing. Both can sing. So that was my main goal with Taking Back Sunday was to get two people to sing," says Reyes. "It really is like a disagreement, or John's backing him up."

It's an "I've got your back" dynamic they'd also adopt with their fan base after the release of their 2002 debut *Tell All Your Friends*, which did indeed become a word-of-mouth hit, attracting the attention of people who weren't strictly of the scene, including Jillian Newman, a young woman with enough years in the industry to already seem like a seasoned vet after working at A&M Records and Vagrant. After catching a gig at South by Southwest, Jillian began managing the band, splitting time between her job at the online marketing firm Fanscape.

That many of the bands that would go on to break emo wide open came from the tristate area isn't a coincidence. It was a scene that had long since created a network of self-booked shows in basements and VFW halls, a self-contained loop that incubated acts that weathered the rough early shows and developed the hardened skin required to take a crack at New York City.*

"There had been quite a tradition already by the time I was doing it, of romanticizing those shows," says Rickly. "It was about as anti-corporate as it gets . . . it was pass the hat around for donations, and it was all word of mouth. It was just teenagers doing shows for teenagers. It was very community oriented. We had a door that we took off its hinges. It was like the merch table, but it was mostly to trade zines." That teenager-led community was about to grow too big for America's basements, thanks to a few exceptional bands.

From New Brunswick came Midtown, an emo-punk quartet that formed at Rutgers and played alongside Taking Back Sunday and Thursday. Front man and bassist Gabe Saporta was a New York City punk kid turned Jersey boy who got his start playing in the high school band Humble Beginnings. Midtown went the major label route before most of their contemporaries, upstreaming to MCA Records for 2002's *Living Well Is the Best Revenge* after conflicts with California indie Drive-Thru Records over their 2000 debut *Save the World, Lose the Girl.*

The state of New Jersey incubated Saves the Day, a band very concerned with the politics of young adulthood, and Thursday, a band very concerned with the weight of the world. After getting their bearings in the late '90s, Thursday and Saves the Day would release their breakout albums *Full Collapse* and *Stay What You Are*, receiving rotation on MTV's more adventurous sister channel MTV2 for the singles "Understanding in a Car Crash" and "At Your Funeral."

Thursday and Saves the Day don't sound that much alike, which was a sign that emo was increasingly becoming more about a feeling (and

---

* The hardcore act Lifetime, on its 1997 album *Jersey's Best Dancers*, saluted this tradition with "Theme Song for a New Brunswick Basement Show."

"feelings") than a sound. Thursday's songs were dense but explosive, filled with jagged riffs and dense bass lines cribbed from '70s post-punk, topped off by the almost feral sincerity of singer Geoff Rickly. Saves the Day held onto their youthful energy but opened their arrangements up just enough to make it clear that Chris Conley was a bit of a pop softie at heart.

Rickly and Conley would have gotten cut on the audition rounds on the about-to-launch *American Idol*, as neither fits the classic definition of a "good" singer. But good singing can be a bit overrated, the type of thing only the gormless need fret about. David Byrne once said that good singing can make it hard to trust the sincerity of the singer, and since Byrne is the smartest man to ever become a rock star, it's best to believe him.

It's very hard to doubt the sincerity of Rickly, who sounded like he was willing himself into becoming a front man on "Understanding in a Car Crash," which was inspired by the death of one of his high school friends. The song chronicles Rickly's shock that life, innocence, and your entire world can end very suddenly. He digs deep into the struggle to move past a terrible moment when the terrible moment seems to be the only one that now feels real. The refrain "The spinning hubcaps set the tempo/for the music of the broken window/The camera's on and the cameras click/We open up the lens and can't stop" would serve as a declaration that Rickly was already the scene's most vivid, literary writer.

But while these bands were getting ready to take on the world, they would soon be joined by a band that didn't understand why it was being called emo, as well as a once and future emo king.

Minneapolis's Motion City Soundtrack considered themselves a power-pop band. But genre tags aren't something you get to choose for yourself. The group had too great of an awkward dispossession about them and too many hooky songs about getting dumped not to get adopted by the emo scene, starting with their 2003 debut *I Am the Movie.* "The Future Freaks Me Out" stands as one of the era's best articulations of always feeling like you never understand what's going on.

After breaking up Far in an attempt to shed any association with the mook-beloved heavy metal that was gaining popularity in the late '90s, Matranga teamed up with Brannon to form the short-lived emo group New End Original, which broke up after releasing the cheekily titled album *Thriller* in 2001. He'd find more success with onelinedrawing (an anagram of New End Original), which was basically him and an acoustic guitar, occasionally performing with a beeping R2-D2 toy. He released two albums capturing the intimacy of his live shows, 2002's *Visitor* and 2004's *The Volunteers*, before retiring the project's name.

"My little world was made up of sensitive misfit people who didn't fit in other rock scenes, and they found solace at Far shows and they found solace at onelinedrawing shows, because it was a place that there wasn't the super strict scene rules," Matranga says. "I think at its very best, the emo culture was a culture of actual misfits who didn't really want to put on the uniform of any particular scene. Now, of course, emo ended up having its own uniform, which is when I became less interested in it. But there was a time in which it was a legit kind of response, a kind of opting out of more traditional mainstream rock culture."

And somewhere along the way in 2002, the heady Year That Emo Broke, Carrabba started to become a fashion icon. The thrift store T-shirt and jeans (both tight, if possible) look had long been the default emo uniform, but now the emo posterboy's preferred haircut—a spiky, anime-like, safe-for-the-dinner-table spin on the mohawk (alternately called the *Chris-hawk* and *faux hawk*)—had become the look du jour for a while in contrast to the eye-covering side-swept bangs. No one was more surprised by this development than Carrabba.

———————

CARRABBA: I had a pompadour forever, and then I shaved my head. As it was growing back, it stuck up in the middle. I went with it. And so I had a faux hawk for a little while. I didn't know that was a thing until I saw the name of it somewhere. I just thought it was what it looks like when your hair is growing back and you're doing the best you can. I did notice that people were cutting their hair to look like that, and I thought, *Wow, I'm trying to get out of this haircut and they're getting into it.* I found that to be . . . not exactly funny but illuminating.

MATRANGA: Yeah, I was totally on Makeoutclub. And I remember starting to see more coalescing social interaction situations on the Internet, and I also remember touring through people's homes and seeing these stacks of burned CDs and having people come to me with a burned CD of our record and asking me to sign it, and me being like, "Uh-oh, the industry's fucked."

BRANNON: Dashboard was a phenomenon, that was an organic phenomenon that no fucking marketer could have conceived or created. New End was on tour and we were playing in North Carolina, but we had a day off and Dashboard was playing at the Cat's Cradle that night, and I went to the show. He was alone actually, and the shit just completely fucking blew my mind.

CARRABBA: The bands just dressed like the kids in the audience at that point. Later, they started dressing with more intention and then the audience started copying them. But in my era, we just dressed like the audience, 'cause why should we change our clothes from having been in an audience watching another band to when we go on stage?

MATRANGA: Initially, we were booking things like house shows just through an e-mail list. We had like three thousand to five thousand people at that time. It was a pretty big network of people. I leaned into it because I didn't know what else to do. And so all those people were like, "Hey, just release your demos, all this stuff you're putting up on Napster, just release CDs of that." And it was such a revelation to me because it's like, "Wait, you don't have to go into the studio and make it fancy?" I literally used the Sony CD burner towers to burn fifty CDs and used their promo packaging and made a little Xerox of like a handwritten sleeve cover thing. That was the first *Sketchy* EP.

BRANNON: Dashboard was almost made for the social Internet. It was a community of people around this person. They knew each other, they traveled together, they were friends. They saw each other almost as a traveling family, the people who went to go see Dashboard shows. They were almost creating a social Internet, offline, until it finally appeared online.

MATRANGA: I guess I don't know how many people are getting it off Napster, but the neat thing about me and where I exist in the universe is that I wasn't really popular enough for this critical mass of like Napster people to want my shit. I cultivated a relationship with people wherein they liked to get it directly from me. So they completely funded me.

HEISEL: Chris Carrabba is a fucking genius. He was singing for Further Seems Forever, an amazing band that was never going to make it because all their songs were so purposefully obtuse. They would put all these bizarre time changes and shifts in the song so you couldn't tap your foot or sing along. They were amazing songs, but they weren't meant to be consumed by a mass audience. And Chris realized, "Yeah, I need to do something different." So he just started writing a bunch of acoustic love songs in Drop D and then kaboom.

MATRANGA: R2-D2 was purchased on tour with Far and was just a late-night clearance special. The little R2's chest cavity opens up and then you can play tapes on it, and there's a little speaker on top of R2's head, and then there's four buttons across that do different iconic artsy noises. So I initially would basically just play '80s hip-hop in it. It was just tour insanity. I remember these incredibly drunk Monster Magnet fans coming up to me and being vaguely curious, and I would point the R2 at them and press the noise that made the R2-D2 scream noise, so Monster Magnet fan repellent.

SAPORTA: Growing up in the area that I grew up in, in Flushing, was pretty rough. We couldn't ride our bikes around the corner. We found a switchblade once when we were little and brought it to school. So it wasn't the worst, but it was pretty rough for me. I haven't really evaluated it that much, but I think I was a pretty disillusioned kid. I came from a small community in Uruguay where I had my grandparents, my cousins, and everything. We went to Flushing by ourselves. You're not really aware of what's happening, but I think it has a psychological impact on you. So I definitely gravitated towards angry things.

MATRANGA: I specifically remember getting an offer on a deal for one-linedrawing where the guy was like, you know, "I love the way you play the robot. We're going to make a big deal about it, the kids are going to love that concept," and I was just like, I don't want a big marketing plan around this goofy idea I've got, that doesn't sound fun to me. Whereas, to most people, they'd be like, "Yeah, hell yeah, do it, you know, sign me up." And I, for better or for worse, had an allergy to that stuff. I think I've got a little bit of a shoot-myself-in-the-foot gene.

CAIN: There used to be a website called Book Your Own Fucking Life,* and I would use it to reach out to basements and book like two-week tours, and we would just go out with whatever version of the band that existed. It just had lists of cities, and then anybody who wanted to put on shows would put in their e-mail and explain what their situation was. We were just doing that and playing whatever shows I could grasp.

SAPORTA: We had a few years where things seemed like they were going well. And then my parents got divorced when I was fifteen. So it was pretty tumultuous the whole time. It's kind of the thing about music . . . the people that become lifers don't have a support system, so they look for support in the community of music.

PRYOR: Eventually, we got to the point with Doghouse Records where they couldn't keep up with the demand, and they started prioritizing their distribution over us having records on tour to sell, and that pissed us off something fierce, so we decided that we needed to get away. That was a big part of why we desperately wanted to get off of that label, even

---

* The website was an offshoot of the long-running punk zine bible *Maximumrocknroll.*

though we had one record left in our contract. We entertained the idea of signing to a major label, so that's when we started actively pursuing it, in early '99. It's a weird time. If I think about it objectively now, it's kind of like post–Green Day, post-Offspring, just at the very beginning of Limp Bizkit and Korn.

SAPORTA: I was into pop-punk, my first band before Midtown called Humble Beginnings. We started booking shows at the VFW, and that's when the Jersey scene was happening. We tapped into that, and a lot of things started happening from there. There were a lot of shows suddenly being booked. I remember taking out the phonebook, before the Internet, and going through every town and calling every VFW hall and Elks Lodge and Rotary Club, like, "Hey, we want to do a show for our friends' bands. Could you guys rent out the place? Could we bring a PA?" There's no stage. Just bringing a PA, three hundred kids from all the local towns would come. Sometimes the people liked it and we'd develop relationships with a few key places. Sometimes people would be like, "You're out. Never again." And that's how The Scene happened.

CAIN: We saw the Get Up Kids play in a basement with Braid at this punk rock place. We had these six-minute-long epics, and something my brother said to me, he's a mean critic: "When we've heard it once, we've heard it." And then I said to Justin, "Let's write songs that are so poppy to us they almost make us wanna vomit." 'Cause here's the deal. They won't be, because we're not poppy; we can't write that kind of music. I think that was the biggest shift in our writing styles, and then Justin said, "Well, I'm going to write really sad lyrics, so deal with that." That was the piece of the puzzle that we figured out.

PRYOR: It was like as soon as we took it to the suits, they're like, "What if you re-recorded the song from your first record on your new record?" And we're just like, "If you think we've peaked and that's the best song we can write, then there's no point in moving forward with you." A couple of the major labels that we talked to always wanted us to re-record "Don't Hate Me."

PIERRE: I think we all felt a version of "Yeah, we have a lot of self-hatred and self-death. We're all seriously depressed people." There's different ways to deal with that, whether it's pretending you're not, or just acting the complete opposite, whatever. But that juxtaposition just seemed to work for all of us.

PRYOR: Doghouse wanted to get paid for us to leave, which is reasonable, and Mojo didn't wanna pay Doghouse, and it was kind of like, "Then we can't sign to your label unless we get bought out." And that's the same thing that happened at Sub Pop. I think it's 'cause we were expensive, and it was kinda unproven, as far as when you're looking around at what's on K-Rock or whatever—it's just not bands like us, 'cause it was before Jimmy Eat World broke. Jimmy Eat World had kind of a string of artistic brilliance that were commercial failures. I remember going to Geffen, and the first thing we said was, "Where's the closet full of free stuff?" And then once we got all of our Jawbreaker vinyl, we said, "So, what happened with Jawbreaker? And they're like, "What do you mean?" "Yeah, so they signed to your label, put out one record, and then broke up. Why did that happen? That record is amazing, why wasn't it huge?" I think they were taken aback by that. They blamed the band.

GEOFF RICKLY (THURSDAY): I was living in New Brunswick. I was doing basement shows in a house that I lived in with a bunch of punk, hardcore kids. One of the roommates and I, when we still lived in the dorms our freshman year, we joined the student arts council so we could put on shows at Rutgers. And so we started doing basement shows, and Thursday really started [because] we just wanted to play those shows.

EDDIE REYES (TAKING BACK SUNDAY): When I started Taking Back Sunday, I wanted to go out of the box and start something that was really insane and out of control, with the music and the people, and I got lucky.

RICKLY: I remember being really nervous, and I didn't really drink or anything at the time. I think one of our roommates had been gifted a bottle of amaretto for Christmas. And so I was sitting on the stairs trying to drink some of that, to not be nervous. That's most of what I remember about the show. But we also didn't play like a full set. We had three or four songs.

PRYOR: So then in an act of desperation, 'cause we wanted to get off Doghouse, our manager offered to put our record out on his tiny little record label. And so we kind of did it as a means to an end of just like, "OK, you can get us off Doghouse, we'll put this record out on Vagrant, and then we'll keep looking around for major labels." But the great thing about Vagrant is that we had absolutely complete artistic freedom. They never told us one thing to do, ever.

SAPORTA: I think the first basement show I saw of them, there was a pole in the middle of a basement. And I remember Geoff just going crazy around the pole. I have great memories of going, "Wow, this band's unbelievable."

RICKLY: I grew up in North Jersey, and so the thing that was really cool about moving to New Brunswick was, it wasn't about trying to aspire to get to be big enough or good enough to go hang out with the cool kids in New York. It was just like, "Who gives a shit about cool kids? Fuck cool kids. Let's just be our own thing and make it very antimaterialistic."

SAPORTA: So at the beginning, I started booking the shows as a way to help Humble Beginnings do shows. And New Jersey is the most densely populated state in the nation. So you literally drive thirty minutes, it's a whole group of other high school kids. That formula of booking shows at local Elks Lodges and stuff was really the move. When I went to college, I did Humble Beginnings. I took a year off to do it, and we went on tour and then I ended up getting kicked out of that band. And that's when I was like, "Oh man, I have to have more control. I need to learn how to sing. If I can just get kicked out by the singer, that's a problem."

REYES: I was personally getting to the end of wanting to be in bands anymore, because I'm like, "I'm fucking going to be thirty and I'm playing in backyards and in bars and I work at a deli." Not that there's anything wrong with that, because I still do that. But I remember telling myself that if it just didn't work in a year, I was done. And it blew up in the year. So I was like, "OK, I guess I'm not going anywhere."

RICKLY: People didn't feel like Limp Bizkit. That wasn't reflecting the weird thing that was happening and sort of like the sad postmodern, overly analytical thing that was starting to happen, and that was much more reflective of what we were doing.

———

By early 2002, emo had become such a *thing* that *Seventeen* magazine felt compelled to publish the instant punchline "Am I Emo Quiz," featuring a vintage sweater–clad male model who was clearly in his late twenties (who had to have further increased the target demographics' insecurities) and such can't-miss pickup lines as "Do you blog here often?" and "Your hair is everywhere. Mind if I brush it out of your face?"

Carrabba sheepishly started to quasi-apologize for how big "Screaming Infidelities" was getting during his shows, telling his fans it was still *their* song. Dashboard Confessional, which by this point featured a full band backing Carrabba, opened a summer amphitheater tour for Weezer and filmed *MTV Unplugged*, backed by an impassioned army of fans turned backup singers.

"I didn't feel like I wanted to apologize, but I did feel self-conscious," Carrabba says. "That thing of being on the radio wasn't my goal. I didn't really know how to grapple with it—I still don't. It just felt like this weird *Twilight Zone* moment."

After signing Dashboard to her label, Fleisher Madden served as Carrabba's music industry Sherpa for many years. She guided him when he almost signed with Drive-Thru Records, which had signed her friends New Found Glory,* but the deal fell apart, as would later happen with

———

* Also discovered by Fleisher Madden, New Found Glory is a South Florida pop-punk band known for their sugary pop hooks. They are often considered emo, but really they're just childish. Fiddler would release their debut EP *It's All About the Girls* in 1997, a title that

the label and Midtown. After helping him sign to Vagrant Records, she would later begin working at the label, though she admits it was often a difficult transition for her after years of her and Carrabba working closely as a pair.

"It's not a sellout thing by any means, because what's the point of having a company if you're not going to make money? I'm sure Ian MacKaye would disagree with that one hundred percent. But I knew my weird feeling was not any sort of major label ickiness or anything like that," Fleisher Madden says. "I think maybe it was jealousy that I was not the only cook in the kitchen anymore."

Even without Dashboard, Drive-Thru Records did fine for itself for a while. The California-based independent label, started by Richard and Stefanie Reines, would become synonymous with the mainstream popularity of emo and shiny pop-punk, in the process blurring the distinction between the two in the public's mind. In addition to Dashboard and New Found Glory, it would eventually find a great deal of success with pop-rock acts such as Something Corporate and the Starting Line, and the screamy pop-punk group Senses Fail—all acts that would get called emo but were missing the genre's essential *je ne sais quoi*.

Drive-Thru's head of marketing at the time, John T. Frazier, was an early Internet music head as well as an early emo adopter and message board denizen. He began working at Drive-Thru right around the time most of the world would take notice of emo. But even well before that, back when he was just a hungry young music fan, "there was an actual scene. There was actually something going on," he remembers of the time. "The word *emo* has a stigma, you could place that on any number of different things. You could argue all day that all music is emotional and all this stuff. But it's appropriate, and you had to label it something."

---

serves as an apt summation of their artistic focus and also one that aged horribly after guitarist and cofounder Steve Klein was kicked out of the band in 2013 and arraigned in 2014 for multiple felony charges, including "two counts of lewd conduct with a minor under the age of 14, three counts of lewd conduct with a minor aged 14 or 15, one count of intent to commit a lewd act with a minor and one count of possession of child pornography," per *Billboard*. He was sentenced to a two-year formal probation and is now a registered sex offender.

Some called it emo, others called it a rebranding opportunity. *Alternative Press* was a Cleveland-based magazine founded by Mike Shea, a goth kid and Kent State filmmaker, as a zine handed out in local record stores. In the '90s it grew into an independent magazine that featured cover stories on alternative radio and Lollapalooza favorites like Nine Inch Nails and Smashing Pumpkins, as well as hipster reference points Portishead and My Bloody Valentine. *Alternative Press* mostly covered hard rock bands that had enough arty flair that you could try to justify liking them to your cooler friends, and Brannon even wrote cover stories on Rage Against the Machine and Tool. But by the 2000s, it had become all nu metal, all the time.

Shea would later tell the *Repository* that "whatever the suburban rebellious music is at any time, that's what we're featuring. Our secret has been that we don't grow older with our readership. We stay consistently in that high-school to early-college demo. Tribalism is at its purest as a teenager."

But by 2002, nu metal was waning and widely derided, and *Alternative Press* took baby steps into finding a different lane, with its 2002 "Bands You Need to Know" issue featuring dual covers of Saves the Day and AFI.* That same issue featured one of the earliest pieces of press that Dashboard Confessional ever received, written by Leslie Simon, a former hippie who had recently begun working at the magazine and would go on to be one of its most important voices.

"I started interning in May of 2001. At the time, the big 'if you put [blank] on the cover, it was an automatic sell' would include Trent Reznor, Insane Clown Posse. Marilyn Manson always did really well," Simon remembers. "It was sort of the death rattle of nu metal. Your Limp Bizkits, your Puddle of Mudd, that sort of era. And the charts are still reflecting all of that JNCO† jeans, backwards baseball hat–type rock.

---

* Fronted by the heavily mascara'd singer Davey Havok, they got tagged as emo, largely because they did the Warped Tour in the early '00s, toured with Thursday, and influenced the eventual scene look. Though they shared emo's aesthetic of treating connection as the highest possible goal, sonically, it's kind of a lazy grouping. No shade though, as "Girl's Not Grey" slaps.

† A Los Angeles jeans company whose name stood for "Judge None Choose One." Its wildly oversized pants, which were big enough that you could hide a chihuahua in them, gained popularity with teenage nu metal fans in the '90s.

"Once we started embracing more of the Dashboard Confessional, Saves the Day, AFI, there was maybe a slight cross section, because what all of these bands had in common was Hot Topic," she continues. "And if you could find a band at Hot Topic, even if it was unrelated, it was still somewhat in the same vein as everything else."

But not everyone caught the wave. In 2002, the Promise Ring released *Wood/Water*, a collection of moody, lightly psychedelic ballads, and the Get Up Kids dropped *On a Wire*, a collection of acoustic guitar–heavy numbers. Though neither album was a completely successful reinvention, both were an attempt by the bands to grow up and leave emo behind them right as emo was booming.

"*Wood/Water* by the Promise Ring is my favorite Promise Ring album. I think it's so good," says Heisel. "I think slowly it's getting that critical reappraisal. The Get Up Kids tried it with *On a Wire*, a big swing and a miss. They were trying to grow, and they were getting rejected for growth. Look at *Dear You* by Jawbreaker, this isn't a new pattern, right?"

While "typical emo self-destruction" wouldn't be the right way to put it, both albums saw the former scene stars bow out gracefully, if perhaps inadvertently, so the next generation could take it home. The Promise Ring would disband shortly afterward, but the Get-Up Kids slugged it out for a few more years. "It was split right down the middle. People either immediately hated it and didn't give it a chance or people went, 'OK, I see what they're doing. I guess as long as they still play 'Action and Action' every night, then that's fine,'" Pryor says. "It was the first record we ever got that actually got good reviews. *Rolling Stone* gave it a really great review. And I was just like, 'OK, this is so confusing, we can either put out a record that reviewers hate that our fans like, or we can put out a record that fans hate and reviewers like. We can never seem to find that sweet spot."

———

HEISEL: You had some really smart people who were clearly influenced by the past five to eight years and wanted to see their name in lights, they wanted to get out there to pursue stardom, a little bit more than I think their predecessors probably wanted to.

RICKLY: We got called emo right away. Right away.

REYES: I'm not against emo. I mean, it means emotional punk. It's just, I hate when people talk about Taking Back Sunday and say, "Oh, they're an emo band." It's like, hey, bud, we're not a bunch of wimps, we came from a pretty tough scene. But we're all wimps and nerds at the same time.

BRANNON: So when you think about this vanguard of new emo at that time, Dashboard, My Chem, Thursday, Taking Back Sunday, it's humorous to me, because none of those bands sound alike at all to my ears. I don't think of those bands as one genre. Emo was a very . . . I don't want to say that it was a cynical way of marketing, but we have to sort of just assume whenever these words take hold, they take hold for two reasons. They take hold because one, either the media needs to create a story about a new sensation and they need to call it something. And then obviously, from the cynical marketing perspective, it's important buy-in to certain record stores. Then yeah, fair play, *emo* it is. Obviously language develops over time, and I have to submit to the social contract that we have, which is that once a certain number of people seem to agree that one word means a thing, it means that thing.

PRYOR: It just got to be this thing where it was just all-encompassing. Just everything was "emo, emo, emo," and then it was like . . . *Teen People* wrote an article about how to dress like an emo, and it was just like, "The fuck is this?"

REYES: The bigger we got, the more interviews we had to do, and it was just like they kept bringing up emo, and we were like, "Why are you doing that?" It got to the point where we wouldn't do an interview if that was in there.

HEISEL: If you look at the whole trajectory of it, part of it was the right place, right time. Part of it was that those bands were legitimately good bands and wrote legitimately good songs, but also there was a need for something new.

JILL NEWMAN (MANAGER FOR TAKING BACK SUNDAY AND MIDTOWN): With Midtown, I was friends with the Drive-Thru folks, and I just really fell in love with their record. There was a lot of stuff that was going from the underground to the aboveground back then. I started helping them. Gabe was Gabe; he knows what he wants. I'm sure he's just as demanding as a manager as he was as an artist, and we just tried to try to get him there.

SAPORTA: So I went to college. I'm like, "Fuck this, I'm going to start trying to make a career." I started playing with other kids who were in other pop-punk bands locally. We had an EP ready to go before we played our first show. Midtown picked up from right where Humble Beginnings left off. Humble Beginnings was starting to get interest from labels, and Midtown took that interest as well.

REYES: I started the band and named the band [Taking Back Sunday], but I'm not in my band anymore, funny how that works. Our bassist quit the day before we were supposed to go to North Carolina to play three shows. So my buddy Phil filled in on bass and then he said, "Hey, I got a friend, he's really good on bass. He's a little young, but he's a really cool kid. We're going to meet up at Waffle House." And then we went and I met Adam, and he was just some skinny, pimple-faced kid who was like, "I'll do it, I'll do it."

NEWMAN: So Gabe was friends with a woman named Cathy at Victory, who was the publicist, I think at the time Midtown was recording a record in L.A., and this is back before the Internet really, and so he had her send a package of CDs to my office. Victory is mostly a hardcore label. So he's putting these CDs, and then he put on the demo for *Tell All Your Friends*, and I just immediately stopped what I was doing. I just was hooked from the first song, just the melody and Adam's voice. He reminded me of Bono. I still have that demo. It's sitting on my desk right now.

SAPORTA: I remember there was some kind of online bulletin board posting things on the Jersey scene. And the girlfriend of the dude from Humble Beginnings called me a scene hopper that went from pop-punk to emo. I think we definitely considered ourselves that. I mean, we dressed like it, too. There was a big thing on the back of the first Midtown record, we're dressed up wearing turtlenecks and scarves. And to us, that was emo at the time. That dark, kind of rainy New York look was a very emo thing. The punk rock thing was so big at the time, everyone wanted to look like skate punk or whatever. So to us, that was rebellious. We got a lot of shit for that, which is interesting.

REYES: So Adam moved up to Long Island, stayed up in my apartment, slept on my couch, and he learned all the bass parts. And then our singer at the time, Antonio, didn't want to do it anymore, and he moved on. I heard Adam singing backup vocals on a demo and I said, "You're going to sing."

SAPORTA: It felt like something was happening. It felt like it was going to a national level, and like everything that was happening in Jersey went to the next level. So it almost felt like, OK, this thing happening in Jersey is happening in Chicago. It's happening in Florida. Something is bubbling all over the country.

REYES: Adam is the epitome of punk rock. The guy doesn't shower. He doesn't change his clothes. He doesn't give a fuck about authority. The guy's constantly being chased by cops or arrested when we're on tour. He just had this attitude that reminded me of when I was fourteen, jumping on trains and going into the city to see these shows.

SAPORTA: I met Drive-Thru because they were interested in Humble Beginnings. So when I created Midtown, I was like, "I really want to work with you guys. I have this new project. We sent them the EP, and they loved it. Midtown were in our first year of college, kind of doing it on the side of school. I think we signed to Drive-Thru that spring, drove to L.A. that summer, and we recorded our first album.

REYES: I remember our first show. Adam was like, "I don't know what to do with my hands. Like, What the fuck do I do?" I was like, "Well, what would, like, Roger Daltrey do, what would Cedric* do? Go nuts, break shit, throw that mic around." And he did. And like that the crowd was like, "What the fuck is this?" And then we just blew up from that. It was just the right decision.

SAPORTA: And so our second album came in the midst of that. On that album with Mark Trombino it was not the same experience as in the first album. Our first album was a little more punk rock. It was a kind of run and gun. It was organic. On the second album, I don't know if the label was pressuring Mark, but the second album was very slick. Listen back to it now, it sounds fine. But I was fighting to try to keep the rough edges of Midtown, the things that were important to me, front and center. And because we were young, cute kids, the machine kind of wants to put those things front and center, and it's a hard thing to fight when you're young. Especially at the time, there weren't resources for that. It wasn't like on the Internet you could read about this stuff.

NEWMAN: When the record came out, the SoundScan came out the next week and they sold 250,000, which was really good for a new band. Victory was good at their marketing, putting the sampler CDs and all that together. But Adam was on tour at that time, You know, you're not paying your phone bill, so your cell phone gets shut off. And so I can't call him. I'm calling his friends, trying to get messages to him to get a hold of him.

REYES: We didn't get signed until I was twenty-nine, dude. So I wasn't that young. I learned how to be a better musician. I learned how to be more patient instead of always being like, "Come on, let's go. Let's go, let's go." We were just living together, starting something. We didn't like each other all the time, like right now, things aren't so great between us, but I still love them. They're my brothers.

---

* Cedric Bixler-Zavala, front man of the Texas post-hardcore, emo-adjacent group At the Drive-In, who broke up just as their 2000 album *Relationship of Command* brought them mainstream attention.

SAPORTA: What happened with MCA is, not only were we having complications with our label, but then the label got completely absorbed. The label didn't exist anymore. MCA was bundled into Interscope and Geffen, and that whole thing happened. And a whole bunch of people just lost their jobs. And when that stuff is happening, you're not trying to develop bands. You're trying to make sure that the company is making money off the stars. It was a whole mess.

NEWMAN: Then I was at South by Southwest. This was in March of 2002, right before *Tell All Your Friends* came out, and I saw them play someplace way off the beaten path, and I just thought they were great. I thought Adam was amazing. He actually had a mic injury that night. So after the show, he was sitting on the curb out front, and he was bleeding. Literally our first conversation was like, "Hi, I'm Jillian, I loved your show. You're bleeding. I'll talk to you another time." He had hit himself in the teeth with his microphone, which was not uncommon back then.

SAPORTA: The other thing [that] was happening at the time, too, was a lot of bands were getting signed to major labels, like Thursday and Thrice* both got signed to major deals. And they had to get bought out of their contracts, like seven figures. And that money goes on their P&L. So they're in the hole right away. Which is why the label is more reticent to invest in those acts long-term. I don't know what their experience was on majors, but I think it was not the best experience.

NEWMAN: When I saw them play that show, I didn't care that there were twenty people there, I knew it was the right band. Even back then, when Adam was a little more shy, he was putting on a show like there was an arena full of people.

REYES: There's a shady side to running a music label. And then there's the honest good side that wants to sacrifice and actually believe in you. There were people there who believed in us that we loved and worked

---

* A hard-edged California emo band that often toured with Thursday.

so hard for us. And then there were other situations, other people that didn't. I never like to dig deep because it was always personal. Victory worked very hard for us and did so much for us. But then there were other things that didn't work out, and it goes like that with every label you're on. For a brief moment, I was a little pissy about it, but honestly, I'm grateful for Victory.

NEWMAN: I wasn't there in the early days when no one else would sign them and Victory gave them a chance. They don't know if they would be where they ended up if Victory didn't do what they did, with their strong-arm tactics or whatever you want to call it. So that's all they have to say about it at this point; they always praise them when they're in. Victory was the first label that took a chance on them.

SAPORTA: There were a lot of things that kind of happened. I feel like I'm over it now, but looking back, I brought New Found to Drive-Thru. And as a kid, you bring your friend to your label and you want them to get signed. What you don't want to happen is that you bring someone who's then going to be the focus, and they're not going to focus on you anymore. So I felt like that happened a little bit. New Found were definitely taking off more than Midtown was, so that was hurtful for me. I also felt Drive-Thru made a ton of money from New Found, and as a person who brought that to them, I felt I wasn't fairly compensated for that or thanked, you know? I feel like I'm over that, because I learned.

HEISEL: You had the door kicked open by Jimmy Eat World. You had the door kept open by Thursday and then Saves the Day. So this is kind of like the last remnants of the second wave, and now we're launching the third wave, right? And so you had these really intelligent songwriters who were writing really well-written songs, who would put out a couple of records and had gotten really good at what they were doing. And then you had all these young kids who are like, "I want to do this," and then just grabbed onto it.

RICKLY: Suburban kids loved Thursday. I think it spoke to them in a way that more metropolitan bands didn't speak to them. It wasn't because we were writing great songs; I think it was just more that we had somehow captured the feeling in the moment. It wasn't that it was some great song that everybody wanted to sing along to. There is a certain level of post-modern angst being explored in our music that hadn't been explored in the bigger bands before us.

PRYOR: The day that [*Something to Write Home About*] came out, we started a seventy-five-day tour. 'Cause we were just like, "We're gonna go everywhere and anywhere, all over the US. And then after that, we're gonna go back to Europe, and then after that we're gonna go to Japan, and after that we're gonna go to Australia, and then we're gonna do the US tour again." And then by the time we were exhausted with all of that, a year and a half later, the Green Day and Weezer things come up, and [we were] just like, "Oh god, fine." It's of course an excellent opportunity, but it was just sort of like, "Why didn't anybody ask us at the beginning? Why does this stuff come up when we're exhausted?"

RICKLY: I wanted to be a high school English teacher. All my classes were poetry; it's what I cared about. But I'm not from a rich family or anything, so it was like . . . "You're gonna have to have a job." It was always, "We'll do this for a couple of years." When we put out the first record, *Waiting*, it was just literally like, "Wow, this label wanted to put out our demo tape as a seven-inch." So we talked them into doing the whole record because who the hell's ever gonna pay us to do a record? So we were just thinking, *We won't take off any time but in the summer, maybe we'll go play a few shows, we'll drive around in this minivan. . . .* And that was kinda it. And then when Victory started asking about *Full Collapse*, it turned into, "Well, maybe we could take a year off and tour for real."

PRYOR: Weezer is the only band I've ever toured with for an entire month and never met. I can still listen to those first two records, but it's changed it for me. That was the first time that I was having a hard time separating the artist from the art. I was just like, "I love these records so much, and I really had an unpleasant experience with you guys." That's a bummer.

RICKLY: I don't know when the video started getting played, but that's when Victory started buying end caps and putting our names in Best Buy circulars, and all the kind of stuff that keeps it going. People are hearing the name and they're seeing the record everywhere, and also then there's ads. That's very easy to screw up. But they didn't; they really went for it.

REYES: Thursday helped us out a lot, and I just knew that they [had] already blown up, because you had all these buses showing up with fucking EMI and Warner Bros. representatives. The greedy suits started showing up, and that's when you're like, "Oh shit, they're getting big." And then next thing you know, you got people coming up to you handing you a card.

RICKLY: The next time you go on tour, you go to a bigger place and you sell it out yourself. That was really weird. It didn't feel real, and it also very much felt like we had skipped so many steps. We had never gone on our own little headlining tour, and it was like, "Oh there's a couple hundred people here that care." It just went from, like, "You're opening up for somebody" to "People think your band's huge, and why can't you sing better?" Nobody cared about the band until like two weeks ago. What are you talking about?

PRYOR: I'm not proud of this, but we were getting kinda irritated, I think, when we started writing our record *On a Wire* in 2001. We were starting to get disheartened with what was going on around us—not the bands, but that we were starting to feel artistically stagnant, in that it seemed like everything that we were doing followed a formula, and we wanted to break away from that. I was getting more into singer-songwriters, everybody in the band was getting more into rock of the '60s and '70s. We were very comfortable at the level that we were at, we were doing very, very well, and it was like, "OK, let's keep challenging ourselves and let's keep moving forward."

RICKLY: And then all the major labels were flying in to see us and our label . . . . I didn't know what negging was at the time. I wasn't at all familiar with the psychological benefit of being bad to somebody that you liked. Things got really weird. They had a Thursday-branded whoopee cushion that they were gonna give out on Warped Tour. And we were like, "Hey, this isn't what the band's about, we're not like NOFX."* They were like, "We got a great deal on these; people will love these." I just saw the dove† on the whoopie cushion, [and] I just felt this couldn't be more offensive to me.

LESLIE SIMON (*ALTERNATIVE PRESS*): I definitely had a super embarrassing screen name that I can't believe I allowed viewing of the public. It was Ldogg—with two *g*'s, of course—479. And I originally got into the portal of Internet music because I was a really big Dave Matthews Band fan in high school, and I got into tape trading and tape trees and sending Maxell—I even remember the tapes, Maxell XL 2s—all over the country, and getting different soundboard show recordings from Dave Matthews. I applied for an internship at *Alternative Press*, which was one of the few entertainment-slash-media companies in Cleveland. Within about four years, I would say, I went from editorial intern to managing editor.

RICKLY: "I poured my heart into this band, and this is what you think of it." Just the way that they picked up the phone, the way that they talked to us, they told us about like how unimportant we were compared to the rest of the bands on the label and stuff like that, which I just didn't understand, I was like, "Wait, we're doing great for you guys." They'd never had a hit like *Full Collapse*. Even when they signed Taking Back Sunday, it was very much like same producer, same kind of vibe, same kind of artwork. They were definitely trying to capitalize on Thursday's success with Taking Back Sunday. Taking Back Sunday happened to be great on their own, and it's a whole separate thing. They never should have been marketed as the next Thursday.

---

* A long-running Los Angeles skate-punk band, whose "everything is a joke" sense of humor has aged poorly, though at one time they were one of the unofficial house bands for the traveling punk music festival the Warped Tour.

† A political emo group when such a thing was largely unheard of, Thursday's logo is the dove of peace.

SIMON: When I started at *Alternative Press*, I was not a reader of *Alternative Press*. I started off at the magazine as a huge pseudohippie. And it wasn't more than a couple of months that I recalibrated my musical interests and the aesthetic. I went from patchwork pants to pegged jeans. And then it was like nothing ever happened. You never saw me with those homemade clothes.

FLEISHER MADDEN: It seems like it took years for things to get like big, big, big. But every single day that he and I did something together, it increased exponentially. Like, we would drive to Orlando and sell twenty-five CDs and it'd be like, whoa, we sold twenty-five CDs. And then the next day we drive to Gainesville and we sell fifty CDs. It just kept going up.

SIMON: I never had a cool opinion on the first generation of emo bands, and I didn't pretend to, because they weren't my gateway. I came in when things were sunnier, in a way. And I know a lot of that initial audience dropped off around the same time and screamed, "Blasphemy. How dare you? This isn't what I'm used to." I appreciate what they did. And I know their importance and their legacy. If we did not have bands like them, we wouldn't have bands that I got into. Maybe Sunny Day Real Estate would probably be what I like. Jawbreaker, probably better than anybody.

CARRABBA: It was hard work, and word of mouth, and then some luck, and some people sticking their necks out here and there. Bands that would give me tours that I, on paper, didn't belong on, because the bands were so, so heavy and I wasn't playing distorted guitars. [Former MTV producer] Alex Coletti getting us on *MTV Unplugged*, even though no nonplatinum band had ever done a *MTV Unplugged*, and it went platinum, thanks to his belief in us. And the network of people that were sharing our music with each other, were also not being so precious about it. Sometimes you don't want a band to get so popular that you can't identify it as yours anymore. That didn't seem to be the case with my fans. This is a scene for counterculture kids, kids that don't fit in other places, and they're inviting their square friends to come, and when they see squares at the show, they don't feel like it's less theirs. They feel it's more ours.

SIMON: We would have to see what the reaction was in person. That was always the best judge of how well a band was doing and what potential they had to increase their level of success. When I did go to shows, most of my time was watching the crowd. How many people are singing the songs? How many people are standing at the merch tent?

FLEISHER MADDEN: The second wave of emo was very proprietary and small and "these are our bands," and that's where that whole world of "selling out" and "don't trust the major label" came from. By the time things happened in the third wave, my generation of bands were like, "Hey, if we could do this instead of going to work at a car dealership, isn't that a better living?"

SIMON: I walk in, and it is packed and everyone is scream-singing every word. I had no idea. I couldn't even see the band because Chris is a smaller person. And I honestly don't even think he was actually singing them for most of the show. I believe that he was away from the microphone, play-ing his guitar and just singing along. But he was not leading the chorus. And I have very strong memories of seeing one girl in particular out of the corner of my right eye, and she was wearing a black-and-white striped sort of French naval boatneck shirt and a silly-looking haircut. And she had her eyes closed and she was screaming, and it was as if we were in her bedroom. But we weren't. There were hundreds of people there, but she did not care. She just was having a sort of . . . it wasn't even like a religious experience. It was as if she was purging all of her feelings. I couldn't walk away without being just hugely impressed, but like, "What did I just see? I don't understand what I just saw, and how is it as huge as it is?"

FLEISHER MADDEN: The only thing that was a factor, it got very con-voluted with who was signing with who and who got what money for what and people screwing people over. And it did become Wild West-ish. It got real messy.

MAX BEMIS (SAY ANYTHING/MAXIM MENTAL): There was a bidding war-ish thing when I was fourteen . . . I wouldn't even call it a bidding war, because I still felt like we couldn't get signed. All I wanted was to be on tour. I would go see the Vagrant [Across] America tour at the House of Blues in Sunset, and I'm like, "Why can't we just be fucking doing this right now? Saves the Day was on tour when they were seventeen, and I'm seventeen, and I'm stuck fucking in this high school. I have to go to college; I hate this." Because our parents wouldn't let us drop out.

SIMON: When "Screaming Infidelities" came out, I remember sitting at the front desk for *AP*. The offices at the time, there was a TV for anybody waiting, they could watch. And the videos I saw on nonstop repeat from, I would say, the fall of 2001 through the summer or the spring, at least . . . there was Thursday, "Car Crash," Saves the Day, "At Your Funeral," and Dashboard Confessional. Once an hour they might as well have been played. So it wasn't just a secret for scene kids anymore, or whoever was becoming a scene kid. This was a full-on mainstream, play-for-chart supremacy. Nothing could stop him. He was such a nice guy making such sad music. But music that everybody could relate to. And I think it's what everybody needed at the time, to purge themselves from the testosterone-fueled nu metal bro fest.

JOHN T. FRAZIER (MARKETING DIRECTOR FOR DRIVE-THRU RECORDS, TOOTH & NAIL RECORDS): There was no rules back then. There were a lot of enthusiastic young people who would spend time at the office. It was just sort of this crazy environment. But after high school, kids come over to the Drive-Thru office, and then we would have them do stuff with AOL profiles. One of the most vivid things I remember is—and we do stuff like this now through, like, targeted Facebook advertising and all this stuff—but back in the day, if you had a record by some pop-punk band or whatever, and you wanted to find other people who might like it, we would just sit these kids at these little iMacs or whatever, and you knew that if you could just harvest their username and just add @aol.com to the end of it, and you can just amass this mailing list of people who might really be interested. Now you can't just take people's data. But we amassed a mailing list of like tens of thousands of kids.

BEMIS: The real crazy thing of it was that I cold e-mailed Richard and Stefanie Reines from Drive-Thru, having never played a show, having never played my music for anyone besides my friends and the girls they were about, I went in there like a total geek with, like, my Atari sticker on an acoustic guitar. I had never thought that I could be a professional musician. Never once.

FRAZIER: We did something with this site Makeoutclub. This was just like ultimate chicanery. We worked with a band called the Starting Line, and they went on to sign to MCA, through the Drive-Thru relationship, but we—this is so weird—one of the contests we did, we gave away a date with the lead singer of the Starting Line. And at this point, the singer must have been sixteen or seventeen? Kenny* was checking out all these little fan girls' profiles and stuff, from Makeoutclub to LiveJournal, figuring out who he might want to go out on the date with. The date never happened, for whatever reason. So, it was just like it ended up just being like a marketing thing that never got followed through with. I don't remember why.

BEMIS: I think that maybe the difference with us, and it was very obvious, was that because of my background, we had the hindrance and the blessing of knowing how full of shit the entertainment industry was, coming from Hollywood and the showbiz stuff. If I grew up in such a genuine environment as Thursday, like New Brunswick and these amazing basement shows . . . I was so jealous of it because I was going to school with like Bow Wow or whatever. But then it was a good thing because when they started to say stuff to me that was like sketch and definitely dubious, I was like, "OK, just let me do what I want. I wanna sign at Equal Vision."†

---

* Kenny Vasoli, lead singer of the Pennsylvania pop-punk group the Starting Line, known for the single "The Best of Me."
† A New York–based punk and hardcore label.

RICKLY: Thursday made me a more social person. Before that, I was a much shyer person. And the thing that really rubbed the shyness off of me was people coming up to me at shows and telling me their life story. Just early on, even before the Saves the Day tour, coming out to me at the Fireside Bowl and being like, "Yeah, I tried to kill myself, and then I got *Full Collapse.*" And then showing me scars of where they cut their wrists. I was just like, "Holy shit, the moment I met you, I found out one of the most painful moments of your life. Wow."

CARRABBA: I'm really cognizant of the fact that this music is personal and revealing, and so people tend to wanna share things with me sometimes when I meet them that are kind of heavy sometimes, and I listen. That's their thing. If they wanna share it, I'm not gonna tell them not to.

RICKLY: If there's an opportunity to try and get him some help, I have to do my best, was the way that I saw it. I also had a weird talk with his mom where I was like, "What are you gonna do?" So I started keeping resources with me, so that I could give them numbers to call. There was a kid that was really into the band. He was suicidal, and his mom came to the show with him, basically being like, "You gotta talk him out of killing himself."

PIERRE: It must have started with MySpace, but the one-on-one started getting more confessional about, "Oh, this song really helped me. I wanted to kill myself, or I was going through this thing and that thing." And that felt very heavy, but awesome. And I would often respond with something like, "I am not a doctor, so please don't listen to me, seek real help, but thank you, and also . . . I didn't do shit. We're just a catalyst, you heard it at the right time, it spoke to you, something made sense, it clicked, and then you did the work."

One way of viewing emo is that it's a way to define not just who you are, but who you are *not.* Emo gave sensitive young people in the '90s and '00s (and onward) a way to make it clear that they weren't listening to plain old rock 'n' roll or punk, which is what their parents had—they were listening to *emo*. They didn't need a suffocating, retrograde culture. They had their own. This was *theirs*, and it was *their* time. The distinction seems silly from the outside, but it means everything to those in the scene.

By early 2003, Emo America was on its way to becoming the defining sound of the '00s, but the Nirvana/*Nevermind* level of success that some onlookers dreamed of hadn't quite materialized yet. Publications such as *Rolling Stone* and *NME* were far more interested in the garage rock and "New York Is Back" story line of artists such as the Strokes, and the inroads made by Thursday and Dashboard weren't exactly making pop hitmakers such as Justin Timberlake sweat.

The fashionable crowd and greater critical community was largely ignoring this stuff. Emo still wasn't cool, and it never would be, which would eventually prove to be one of its saving graces, as there are far more uncool people than cool ones in the world.

But if emo hadn't conquered the airwaves or silenced the haters, the genre most certainly had conquered the Internet, which was easier to do back then, as the LiveJournals and AIMs now seemed like publicity outlets for the movement, and even the music message board denizens who hated this stuff had to reckon with it. The community was growing online; it just needed a bigger home. Fortunately, one was right around the corner.

4

TOP EIGHT

MySpace was founded in August 2003, and the world was introduced to Tom Anderson via an instantly iconic photo of the cofounder looking over his shoulder with the surprised grin of a college sophomore who is *so* psyched that you came to his house party.

MySpace quickly surpassed the slow-to-load, bug-ridden Friendster, by moving faster and offering far more to do. Even if you'd never felt the need to post the lyrics from "Screaming Infidelities" to a LiveJournal, MySpace came with a built-in status update box so you could blog your heart out. You could list your interests on your profile at length, in hopes that your fellow Death Cab for Cutie fans would find you. You could also add a song to your profile, so you could force your refined taste on visitors whether they liked it or not.

And then there was the Top Eight.

MySpace's defining feature was that you could display eight of your best friends, crushes, favorite bands, or vanishingly clothed Internet hotties in any order you like. Anderson was every new account's top friend by default, but you could remove him if you felt ungracious.

Deciding the order of your Top Eight was a panic-inducing endeavor for the teenagers and college kids who began flocking to MySpace in droves, an activity you could lose entire afternoons to. "I really liked the Top Eight feature. Mostly just to keep tabs on my enemies and my crushes. Which I still love doing, by the way," remembers Cassie

Grzymkowski, who was a Ridgewood, New Jersey, high school student when she joined MySpace, though she would eventually use it to promote her noise-pop trio Vivian Girls.

"I had this crush on a guy who later ended up being my boyfriend for a while," she elaborates. "I remember looking at his Top Eight, and his number one, I assumed, was his girlfriend. And I was so mad at her," she says. "I just looked at her profile all the time like, 'I hate you.' But then it turned out that she was just his best friend, and they never had anything romantic going on. I felt really stupid. But it was a good lesson."

––––––––––

JONAH MATRANGA (FAR/ONELINEDRAWING): I've had just impossibly beautiful interactions through the Internet, and I still treasure them. That's one of my North Stars: "Keep that vibe." And I would say MySpace was the last stop on that.

LESLIE SIMON (*ALTERNATIVE PRESS*): If you were mainstream, you went for Friendster. If you were edgy, you went Makeoutclub. Then MySpace emerges, and Friendster very quickly becomes the Walmart of social media. Everyone dropped Friendster like a bad habit and migrated over to MySpace.

GEOFF RICKLY (THURSDAY): Right away, I saw MySpace was doing something. I had a song on my profile; I had it all done up, customized profiles and all that shit. I got some hate mail about not putting my top fans in the Top Eight. Or I'd put them in for a day and switch them back out, 'cause I was like, "I gotta have my friends in the Top Eight. That's my crew."

GRAHAM WRIGHT (TOKYO POLICE CLUB): The gentle intraband negotiations were like, "Hey, can we bump someone out of the Top Eight so I can pull my buddy's band in there for like a week or something? They have a new song coming out." I have no idea if being in our Top

Eight was worth a damn at all to anyone who was in there. But it just felt really important.

BÍCH NGỌC CAO (MYSPACE MUSIC EDITOR): I was not there from day one. I was in college when MySpace started, and I was probably one of the first users because I was just an Internet kid. So I found everything really, really early. I actually signed on and I found that the community was too insular and too small, and I deleted my account. And then later I was asked to rejoin by the company that I was working for, a marketing agency called Buzztone.

CHRIS CARRABBA (DASHBOARD CONFESSIONAL): Our scene was based on community, and we were young. So those two things made us well suited to embrace MySpace, hugely.

WRIGHT: We had a MySpace as soon as we had songs. We met other bands there. I was just doing an Instagram Story about how we met Born Ruffians, who are still our good friends. They just MySpaced us out of the blue, like, "Oh, we're a band from the suburbs of Toronto as well. We should play a show together."

CASSIE RAMONE (VIVIAN GIRLS): I was pretty hardcore into underground obscure music since I was fourteen. I was very much into indie rock. I mostly found out about bands word of mouth or just seeing them play in Brooklyn. But that being said, I would also look up a lot of these newer bands on MySpace after I saw them live or after somebody told me about them or whatnot. It was like a great place to find music for free.

NGỌC CAO: Tom just wanted people to be who they were, and we weren't judgmental about it. We didn't want people to have nudity, but people could just post photos of themselves in scantily clad outfits, and it didn't matter. By the time I left, we actually had a pretty big moderation team that was looking at everything, at every single photo that was being uploaded one-by-one.

GABE SAPORTA (MIDTOWN/HUMBLE BEGINNINGS/COBRA STAR-SHIP): Especially at that point, the only people really online were scene people. So it felt like it was the whole world. It was such an amazing time, because it's almost like the Internet just existed for the scene.

GARETH DAVID (LOS CAMPESINOS!): I think I got heavily into it the summer before I went to university, having a three-year relationship end and trying to meet new people and make new friends through MySpace. I remember that little orange and green logo. I think it was an image meant to be a human to indicate people were online now.

NGQC CAO: Rivers Cuomo was one of the first musicians to use MySpace personally, and he was obsessed with it. He was also obsessed with Asian women, which were bountiful on MySpace in the early days. So he became obsessed with a girl named Ann Poonkasem. Ann fancied herself a musician. She was more like a go-go dancer who had some demos recorded.

JOSHUA CAIN (MOTION CITY SOUNDTRACK): We were lacking music discoverability at the time. People made their Angelfire websites or whatever, but there was no straightforward, like, "Here's where you go find music with your friends and they share it with each other and whatever."

NGQC CAO: And so he ran across her profile and saw that she was into supposedly transcendental meditation, which was his new obsession. And he became obsessed with Ann, and Rivers started uploading songs with the word *Ann* in them, that were cover songs to his MySpace page. If you look up this woman, she had pictures of herself in different types of outfits that she was, quote-unquote, "modeling." But one of them was her in a traditional Chinese dress with an oriental umbrella, the sort of fetishizing of Asian women that makes me ill.

FRANK IERO (MY CHEMICAL ROMANCE): At that point you weren't really putting up stuff on YouTube, you were just putting up MP3s on MySpace. It was so centralized. The audience was there, and the bands were there, and you could just click through and find out about bands that you liked.

MAX BEMIS (SAY ANYTHING/MAXIM MENTAL): I think I got on MySpace pretty quick, mainly because of dating. I wanted to fall in love. I hadn't really been in love; I'd been in unrequited love and was just meeting girls on it probably and talking to my friends. It wasn't to meet people, or to promote my band, it was completely personal. But my profile was like my personality, which is sloppy at best.

DAVID: Searching for people with Pavement in their profile who were online . . . it just seemed like such a cool thing to be doing. It didn't seem strange or like there was any ulterior motive to trying to meet people; you literally did just want to talk about bands and trade recommendations and that sort of stuff.

CARRABBA: We understood we were utilizing this technology in a way that the generation before us hadn't. I think we all felt like it was like this wild and vast new frontier. There was this weird adventure to it, which is unusual, since it has become commonplace, and before you couldn't conceive of just feeling adventurous by sitting at your desk or sitting in your room, but that's what it felt like. I remember at the time, someone in my family would say, "You just sit in there, and you're walled off from the world, come out and interact," and I was thinking to myself, *This is more interaction than you could believe. This is true human interaction. I'm not walled off; I'm opened up to the world.*

DAVID: Back then I was probably most into Pavement, Neutral Milk Hotel, Modest Mouse. If somebody has those three and then a fourth band, I'd be like, "Oh, who's that? Who are the Decemberists? I have to listen to them." I guess there was an element of posturing to it because you'd have a list of fifty-odd bands that you wanted everyone to know you liked.

CARRABBA: When it shifted over to MySpace, I remember wondering if I was gonna lose this sense of community and having a little bit of hesitancy until I discovered that it was a better interface to be with fans, because you could also find people that weren't going directly to find you.

Or they could find you without going directly to find you. It was laid out in front of them for them to use. You could mess with the layout, make it yours. You could find people like you, if you were searching. People were looking for you. It just felt like a community.

MATRANGA: MySpace was the first one where basically there started being a concentration of people. I've never been a big numbers person, but I remember I would check the little graph of the visitors to the site, and I could send out an e-mail thing to this long, curated e-mail list. And at one point, sending out a MySpace bulletin would do more for my traffic in one day than the whole e-mail list. And I remember thinking, *Oh shit.* I'm so sad that artists have basically lost control of the Internet. MySpace was the first time I was like, *Uh-oh, I'm kind of beholden to this platform. This platform is doing a better job of reaching people than I can do in my little world.* And that was exciting, but I immediately was like, *Well, OK, so how do I keep in touch with these people outside of MySpace?* And that was the whole thing.

AMY FLEISHER MADDEN (FIDDLER RECORDS): I can tell you that MySpace one-hundred-percent changed the scope of marketing overnight. It was like every time there was an update, it was a big deal. And then when there was the Top Eight, it was a huge game changer. It was like a decade prior, being in a band's thank-you notes. If a band thanked you in the liner notes, you knew every kid that read the liner notes would then look at your band name and be like, "Who's that?" I could see bands who were teeny tiny and never left Las Vegas. All of a sudden it was like all the little dots were connecting and you have a thousand fans. It was completely organic and natural. You couldn't buy them.

NATE HENRY (SHERWOOD): MySpace was like, "Hey, I think you can promote your band on this webpage." You can network with other bands, but you can also promote yourself to people who are out there looking to find out about new music. Our guitar player figured out that he could open up several tabs and send messages to people who were friends of other bands. So we started doing some of our own guerilla marketing:

"Hey, you like the band Copeland, check out *our* band." I think that was before people were kind of spammed out. So most people were, I remember, being open-minded. Our numbers started to grow.

MATRANGA: I think the Internet has always been the place of nerds, and of course, *nerd*, like everything else, is sort of this brand name now, and everyone wants to be nerdy and everyone wants to be a misfit. But of course, everyone being a misfit is an oxymoron. So at the time, there were people who I think, like me, just really wanted to communicate, didn't really think they fit in the world, but all of a sudden there's this little place that's made of people who are kind of nerdy.

HENRY: To this day we joke about it because we sort of hacked the system with PureVolume. They reset their charts at midnight every night on their top ten bands. So we would go to our college library and go to every computer in the college library and get our plays going so we would kind of creep up on the top of the charts and then we would stay number one all day long because people were like, "Oh, I'll check out this band." There wasn't a ton of bands on there, so all you have to do is kind of give yourself a little head start and you'll stay in the top.

GIBBY MILLER (MAKEOUTCLUB): When MySpace came out, I had kind of already been softened to the blow of a website being better than mine. With Friendster, I was like, "Oh, this is technically better and has features that I didn't think about." The idea that you could inject code, you could edit your MySpace page that needs HTML code to fuck with the page. Like, goddamn it, why didn't I think of that?

HENRY: MySpace was the first time we were talking to fans directly like, "Oh, I heard you guys on PureVolume and this is rad, I'll check it out." Then we started creeping up the sales on SmartPunk* and started thinking to ourselves, *Hey, maybe we could tour, maybe we could get signed.* But it all revolved around those first interactions on MySpace with fans, for sure.

---

* An online record store.

DAVID: Los Campesinos! had a MySpace before I was even in the band. They were Los Campesinos but without the exclamation mark, but that lasted six weeks. That was with a different guy singing. They took a candid picture on a really crappy old phone camera—that's on their MySpace. They didn't really have anything else to put except maybe influences. I heard the demos they recorded on their phone in the bedroom jamming and thought they were really good. With a lot of bands, you had a MySpace page before you had a song even. They didn't play a show or anything like that. It was just jamming, and then one week, the other guy couldn't make the practice, so I showed up with a glockenspiel.

NGỌC CAO: I think that the earliest people on MySpace were Asian. Well, particularly very heavily Korean club kids from Los Angeles, the hot import night–type of models. And as it got bigger, other subcultures sort of picked up. But one of the reasons that happened is because Tom specifically went onto Friendster and invited people who had gotten popular on Friendster to join MySpace. Because Friendster had a rule that you were supposed to know all the people who are friending you in real life. He wanted them to build the following on MySpace, because he just wanted numbers. He was finding dates, too.

HENRY: We were one of those grit bands. We were determined to do it. And some of the guys were like, "Hey, do I enroll for classes next quarter or do I *not* enroll for classes next quarter, what are we doing?" Half the band was still going to school. So MySpace became this thing where we could promote the band 24/7. If somebody didn't have class that day, they could go to the library for three hours and message people on MySpace and try to get the ball rolling. I think we were so eager to tour, we were gonna make it happen, and MySpace was definitely like, hey, this is *how* we can make it happen so much faster, because we have this tool. I mean, looking back on it, I wish we spent more time writing better songs then promoting what we had on MySpace.

IERO: I never ever in my life had a conversation with another band like, "Oh, what's your social media presence like?" You'd sound like a fuckin' narc.

NISH (FAR EAST MOVEMENT): We would put flyers in every store in Melrose and then posters. James would hang up posters in every bathroom in K-Town. Probably they don't allow you to do that anymore. Marketing our albums back then was definitely like hand-to-hand combat. You're just trying to make every person that supports you appreciate it, especially because we were so new. When we started doing shows in Asian clubs, they had never had any live shows in their history. So when we were doing the first shows, people were like, "What the fuck is going on?"

NGỌC CAO: Far East Movement, they were one of the first bands I ever saw on the site. They really built their career from the ground into having a massive hit.

NISH: We were such fans of hip-hop, like El-P* and all that fire music, that when we got on the mic, we knew we weren't the guys we looked up to. So we're like, "I think the only approach is to take the influence of the rappers and the scenes we loved and figure out a new approach." So we made this really, really pop-rap song that we put in this really underground forum. We were surprised at the good feedback in the comments. And that AsianRaps.com community grew, then boom, we hit MySpace. It's a way to floss and to talk to your fans. And to spam and troll. I feel like MySpace created the spam and troll-y comment culture of today.

PROHGRESS (FAR EAST MOVEMENT): They didn't stop us back then. We were cutting and pasting. We would spend whole three-, four-hour blocks just doing that. Sometimes you're going to hit some people that don't appreciate what you're doing, but in the end, it's marketing, it's a numbers game, so you just kind of keep rolling.

NISH: There's nights where we'll be up to like 6:00 AM, 7:00 AM. And it's just nonstop. So it's not like, "OK, let's dedicate two hours and just spam." There's always a new community to hit. There's always a new artist or model or promotion crew that we could send a message to.

---

* Rapper-producer Jamie Meline was a fixture of underground rap in the '00s and later cofounded the group Run the Jewels.

———————

By June of 2004, MySpace had more than one million unique users per month. *Unique* is the operative term here, since people just couldn't stop using the site to express themselves. While MySpace's capacity for endless customization would eventually be one of the many headaches that would lead to the site's downfall, for a while it was one of its most attractive features. As an added bonus, it gave many young people a crash course in how HTML worked, which likely cemented many a career path. Was MySpace's default royal blue and white layout not doing it for you? You were free—encouraged even—to download code from sources such as Pimp-My-Profile.com and customize your page to your heart's content.

We would soon achieve new levels of transcendent tastelessness. Do you want the background of your page to be the brightest hue known to man? Or are you more into stoner-friendly pictures of aliens? Do you want to make it so that your five favorite Avril Lavigne videos play at once when someone visits your page, resulting in an avant-garde cacophony of mall pop? Well, no one is stopping you, though someone probably should have.

Before he began rapping as Sir Michael Rocks, Antoine Reed was a Chicago high school student who wanted his MySpace page to look as fresh as the music he posted on it.

Eventually, he would cofound the group the Cool Kids, a group that symbolized the way MySpace and blogs were overtaking, for a time, radio and MTV when it came to minting new hip-hop stars.

"I had a couple of different layouts. I was switching it often, depending on what the vibe was. For my background I had some stupid like stock samurai kind of images and then some little ninja guy," he says. "I found out how to code a top 16 and a top 32 because too many people started feeling left out. It was starting to cause real friendship problems, man."

One of MySpace's greatest innovations is that it made finding new friends, new bands, and new scenes a real-life roleplaying game quest, with the hope that the end goal might be a favorite new song, a hookup, or increased social currency. Or all three, if it's a good night.

There was a "Browse Users" function at the top of the page, so you could roll the dice and see if there was anyone else whose favorite book was *Catch-22* or if there were any single people at your school who liked Radiohead and didn't smoke. You could head over to the MySpace.com/music page to see what was popping in your favorite genre. Or you could wait for Sherwood to hit you up directly because you seemed cool.

There were plenty of musicians *on* MySpace from the beginning. But only some of them were *of* MySpace, a crucial distinction that your ears and heart could discern quicker than your higher cognitive functions. Only some artists embodied the confused, shy, horny, excited, lonely, weird, desperate-to-connect, throw-out-the-rules ethos of the era. At first, a lot of those artists and their fans were naturally from the emo world, because emo has always been concerned with both the need and struggle to bridge the insurmountable divide between you and the rest of the world, or even just you and the person next to you (very often the most difficult gap to close).

The emo scene and MySpace formed a connected loop. As one grew, so did the other. The more people who joined the site, the more they saw emo bands everywhere they looked, the more emo fans who joined because they'd heard the homeland had been discovered, and the bigger the site got. After years as a punch line and untouchable underground scene, emo was crossing over by the fall of 2003. The scene ran the Internet and quickly made MySpace its home base.

After releasing a series of cheaply recorded EPs and embarking on DIY tours, Motion City Soundtrack finished an early version of their debut *I Am the Movie*, which caught record label attention when a few tracks were posted to the industry music blog The Scout. Eventually, they would choose to go with the California punk label Epitaph. Founded by Brett Gurewitz of punk institution Bad Religion, the label broke huge in the '90s thanks to the breakout success of the Offspring and Rancid, becoming the rare indie with a reach competitive with a major label.

"We had no management, nothing like that. I'm getting calls from Virgin and RCA and just endless people talking to us about our band," says Cain. "We were seeing a shift that was driving this hunger for these bands. It was viewed as 'this is going to blow up.'"

Released in the summer of 2003, *I Am the Movie* showed Pierre's flair with nagging hooks and wordy nerd-play that tried to obscure some heavy shit. The album established them as the scene's neurotic under-dogs, an image cemented by the single "The Future Freaks Me Out." Along the way, he adopted his signature punk Marge Simpson look, asking a friend "can you just fuck up my hair? He took the razor, he was just whacking at it. He was like, 'Huh, none of those pieces look the same.' And I was like, 'That's it, great.'"

Dashboard Confessional, Thursday and Saves the Day were all at make-or-break points in their careers by 2003, as emo was being touted as the biggest rock-based youth movement since rap metal, and these were considered the three most likely bets to go mainstream (or to collapse under the pressure and instead break up. Always a possibility, especially in this genre.). Some artists fared better than others during emo's cultural moment. The Get Up Kids released the more energetic *Guilt Show* in 2004 and opened for Dashboard Confessional on a sum-mer tour before going on extended hiatus. And after going through the major label ringer with MCA, a dispirited Midtown regrouped for one last try. It, uh, didn't go so great.

Following a drawn-out fight with the Chicago-based hardcore label Victory Records and its owner Tony Brummel over money, creative con-trol, and whoopie cushions, a financially damaged Thursday signed with Island Records, impressed with the label's deep catalog (which included U2 and Bob Marley) and then copresident Lyor Cohen's artist-friendly touch.

"Lyor Cohen was running Island and Def Jam together, and signed Jay-Z, Kanye West, and DMX and all these huge people. He suddenly became a huge fan of the band and was like, 'You guys are what's next. And whatever Victory can do to you, we're gonna protect you from them, and if you think he's powerful, wait till you see how powerful we can be,'" says Rickly. "Well, if we're gonna be screwed by this guy, we better get more powerful friends that are gonna protect us from him."

War All the Time pushed the soaring choruses even higher, but the dense song structures and Rickly's poetic tales of America suffo-cation betrayed no signs of compromise. If anything, Thursday used their mainstream platform to go even deeper, doubling down on the complex arrangements and minor-major dynamic shifts that set them apart from the pack, hitting with a force that showed these sensitive boys could subsume any meathead band out there. The title track was a panoramic view of Rickly's childhood, recounting a friend's death to suicide, finding salvation in music, and the generational loss of innocence after September 11, delivered over a heady guitar swell that shimmered with wounded strength.

The album was met with overall positive reviews, a solid *Billboard* debut, and decent airplay for the single "Signals Over the Air," though it didn't quite break as big as everyone was hoping for. "The label was telling us, 'Yeah, you sold 80,000 records. But we have a monitoring service and they told us it was downloaded 325,000 times the first day it was on LimeWire,'" Rickly says. "So if there was no downloading, you would have a number-one record.' I don't know what they knew. It could also be just a really nice thing to say to a band."

Saves the Day signed to DreamWorks Records and recruited Elliott Smith producer Rob Schnapf. *In Reverie* found Chris Conley taking his foot off the gas a bit to explore classic pop songcraft à la the Beatles and the Zombies, baffling an audience perhaps not familiar with the reference points and not at the point in their lives where they wanted to broaden their tastes just yet. (Maybe they should have waited until those fans were in college.) *In Reverie* would later become a fan favorite, but that's cold comfort for an artist in the moment who just watched their ambitious step forward brick. They'd later return to a more mature version of their early sound, but mainstream rock stardom just wasn't in the cards for them either.

Carrabba didn't even have to sign to a major label to break through. Instead, Interscope increased its stake in Vagrant Records to 49 percent. Carrabba teamed with Foo Fighters and Counting Crows producer Gil Norton for *A Mark, a Mission, a Brand, a Scar*, a confident step forward that paid the haters no mind, as Carrabba was determined to be as sincere as he damn well wanted to be. It was an exercise in both smart songwriting and smart brand management, embracing just enough polish and full rock-band songs to earn new fans, but keeping enough brokenhearted ballads such as "Ghost of a Good Thing" to appease day-ones worried that Dashboard Confessional might soon be everyone's favorite band instead of *their* favorite band.

The hype around emo and Dashboard Confessional was so loud in 2003 that Carrabba appeared on multiple magazine covers, including two separate appearances on the cover of *Spin* in one year. The album debuted at number two on the *Billboard* chart, and bigger opportunities kept rolling in, including an MTV special wherein Dashboard Confessional covered R.E.M.'s classic album *Automatic for the People*, Michael Stipe dropped by to guest on a performance of the hit single "Hands Down," and Honda Civic sponsored a headlining summer package tour. In the summer of 2004, Dashboard Confessional were recruited for the *Spider-Man 2* soundtrack, trading in the acoustic for beefy modern rock guitars. "Vindicated" was the band's biggest hit yet, and Carrabba's ascension to stardom was complete. Mainstream rock stardom was in fact in the cards for him. But he quickly realized that he didn't like being famous all that much.

Meanwhile, the future world conquerors in My Chemical Romance wondered how people kept getting their phone number.

———

CARRABBA: Losing privacy was really fucked up for me. Losing the ability to go to shows anymore and just stand in the audience without having to wear a baseball hat and a sweatshirt to cover my tattoos and stuff like that. I stood out like a sore thumb. And the demands on my time, and the lack of sleep, and the whole year with eleven days off, total. It was just breakneck speed.

FLEISHER MADDEN: How did fame affect [Carrabba]? I don't think it affected him. I think he stayed exactly the same. He's always been a really smart businessman, and the only thing that I think was affected by his success is he became even sharper of a businessman.

MATT PRYOR (THE GET UP KIDS/THE NEW AMSTERDAMS): By the time Dashboard happened, it was just such a phenomenon. I've known

Chris since 2001, and I can just shoot straight with him and just be like, "This is weird, dude." And he's like, "Yeah, it's crazy." And I'm like, "Do you want this? This is like a lot."

CARRABBA: I really tried to make sure fame didn't change me. I hope it didn't make me worse in the moment. It was so exhausting that I wasn't always at my finest, but I really had this strong intention of not letting it change me. If you're trying that hard, it's gonna have some results.

FLEISHER MADDEN: Chris and I . . . it was really confusing for us because we were best friends and tour buddies, and I was the label and he was the artist, which was no big deal when it was Fiddler and Dashboard. And things got very confusing when it was Vagrant and Dashboard, because there are a lot of things happening at Vagrant that I wasn't really allowed to tell my best friend about. We took a decade-long break, I'd say.

MATRANGA: I remember being around Chris as he blew up. At one point, he was on one of the Vagrant Tours and had a big bus, and there's a big AT&T ad on it. He's like, "Oh yeah, they just gave us the bus as long as we wrapped it in this banner." I totally get that, and I would never, ever, ever, ever go in a fucking bus wrapped in an AT&T logo. Like, I just wouldn't. And it's not that I thought badly of Chris for doing it, I just realized that's not me. I've always been a person that if I'm not going to make that choice then I shouldn't expect to have that success.

PRYOR: When we were on tour with them in 2004, I remember sitting in the parking lot by the bus and he and I were just sitting and talking. And a bunch of kids had kinda gathered. We were in a recessed parking lot, and they were like above us on the street. And they just started taking pictures like a paparazzi almost kind of thing. And he seemed really annoyed by that. I was just like, "OK, if this is what you get when you win, I'm pretty happy with where I'm at."

NORMAN BRANNON (TEXAS IS THE REASON): I mean, it's funny because my rubric is still the same, which is just: "Are you real?" That's the only thing I care about. And I can fucking sniff it a mile away when I listen to a band that's not real. And it bums me out. But [Carrabba], he's real. He's grateful. He knows where he comes from, and he always pays it forward. That to me is the sign of a real one.

IERO: We had this lock-out practice studio where one of our friends was living there illegally and he had this phone put in and a bunch of bands just shared it, and they were calling this practice studio looking for some sort of representation to talk to for our band. It was like, "This is ridiculous, how is that even possible? There's something way bigger than we could've imagined." Is it someone's job to troll MySpace and listen for new bands?

SCOTT HEISEL (*ALTERNATIVE PRESS* EDITOR): My wife worked for Victory Records. She was there the day the lawsuit came in from Hawthorne Heights.* I mean, Tony Brummel found creative ways to not pay bands who were the ones paying for everything else. You had your Taking Back Sunday, which is paying for the next fifty releases on that label. And then all those bands are all generating a little bit of money, but he's constantly billing out and saying, we spent this money on promo, this money on marketing, so that nobody ever saw a royalty statement. It's creative accounting, which Victory was masters of.

IERO: I definitely think that in the beginning, putting the band up on a social platform, having people listening to it and coming to shows and checking it out from there, that was the jumping-off point. I think there was a good three years of the band where we didn't really have anybody else—it was just us, a few people at the label, our manager, our lawyer, and our booking agent, and that was it. Maybe seven people pushing the band.

RICKLY: We've got Victory telling us, "We're gonna sell your contract, we're gonna make sure you never put out another record again." They're

---

* The Ohio band released their debut *The Silence in Black and White* on Victory and later sued the label.

very aggressively like, "We're gonna ruin you." Which I just couldn't understand. We're the biggest band on their label?

HEISEL: I never want to discourage anyone from exploring their creativity. I mean, the music industry's been predatory since its inception. You look back to the 1950s and see examples of that. It's always been about "how can we take advantage of these people and make as much money as we can?" And if you're lucky, you're creative and successful enough to then control your career down the line. That's why bands would still sign to Victory Records, even knowing that every fucking band that succeeded on Victory Records sued them to leave. "Well, maybe we'll get lucky enough to make enough money to sue them." Which is insane. But that's the music industry.

RICKLY: The head of Warner Bros. is flying to Albany to see us, all these A&R guys are coming out to every show and saying things, bringing cocaine, trying to get us drunk, just really trying to inundate us with the rockstar lifestyle, which was very anathema to what we're interested in. But at the same time, we were only human, so we were like, "Yeah, I'll try cocaine with you."

SIMON: Thursday was of definite value to *Alternative Press*. Geoff Rickly provided a lot of credit to any artist or act he produced or did a feature with. Even when Thursday was up-and-coming, they still had this sort of wise air to them, that they were older and wiser than their years. And Geoff also was brutally honest about everything, for better or for worse. Which made him a great person to ask for any sound bite, because he had something to say about everything. When they signed to Island, and then Island started signing more up-and-coming bands, Thursday shepherded a lot of core values and ideas and—I don't want to say strategies, but—approaches, maybe. The way that they did things would become a blueprint for how future bands did things.

RICKLY: Gary Gersh tried to sign us, and he was like, "You're gonna be the next Nirvana. I know, I signed Nirvana." And that was the only time we almost didn't sign the Island Record shit. The guy who signed Nirvana says we're gonna be the next Nirvana, that's a big deal. And the A&R guy at Island had a very smart response: "He also told Jimmie's Chicken Shack* they're gonna be the next Nirvana." That's just your line. Of course, you use it on anybody you wanna sign up, come on.

BEMIS: He did that to me too. We had smoke blown up our ass about being the next Nirvana.

IERO: All these bands were doing something and tapping into what the kids wanted to hear. I think it happens every ten years or so, someone says, oh, fuckin' Minneapolis, Minnesota, is the new Seattle. And at that moment it was New Jersey is the new Seattle. And for such-and-such subgenre of whatever rock 'n' roll music, and they put a fuckin' tag on it, which eventually became *emo* or whatever the fuck they wanted to call it that week. It was like, oh this is a hotbed, so people just kind of went for it.

RICKLY: I was still a very innocent suburban kid, but there would be dinners where I realized later like, "Oh, was that person trying to set me up with Rihanna?" I hadn't heard any music by her yet or anything, but I sat next to them at a table. I went to dip a dumpling in sauce and eat it, and the waiter was like, "That's a finger bowl." Whatever pop star that you're bringing to introduce me to is not interested in this idiot who doesn't even know what a finger bowl is.

IERO: I would say within a month . . . . I'm not sure if it happened to other bands around us, or just in that genre of music at the time, but we were playing basement shows. I remember we had a basement show in Philly one day, and Mike Gitter, he was the A&R for Roadrunner, showed up. It was like him and maybe ten other people, and one of them was a homeless guy with a tape recorder around his neck trying to sell us a bootleg of our show after the show. Those were the kind of things that were happening. It was very surreal, very weird, and we were aware of how strange it was and ran away from it as fast as we could.

---

* A forgettable late '90s funk-metal band from Annapolis, Maryland.

JUSTIN COURTNEY PIERRE (MOTION CITY SOUNDTRACK): We were about six to eight years older than most of the bands we were touring with.

CAIN: There was a lot of impostor syndrome going on in our lives. We would take ourselves super seriously, but we end up joking about stuff. Maybe it's a defense mechanism. We think it's funny when we're self-deprecating, and maybe it's not. When Brett took "The Future Freaks Me Out" to K-Rock,* they said we were a novelty band, because our lyrics were funny.

PIERRE: I had something missing. There was a lot of self-hatred going on. I would prefer to get drunk and hide from everyone as much as possible whenever I could.

PRYOR: We had gone through this *On the Wire* experience, which was divisive both publicly and internally. Then it's kind of this thing of like, "Should we double down on this or should we go back and make *Something to Write About Home Part Two*?" I was starting a family and I didn't wanna go on tour, and then I got into a pretty good-sized darkness that I now know that I'm prone to do. [Guitarist Jim Suptic] referred to that record as our adult record, because there's a lot of stuff about divorce, there's a lot of stuff about death, there's a lot of stuff about redemption. I can hear me wanting to leave in that record, not in the music, but in the words. And then around that time too is when things started falling apart for our band, just internally.

HENRY: I think most local bands, they can't figure out how to get out of town. I remember at the time us standing back and hanging out in the van and going, "Whoa, people in Seattle know who we are, this is crazy!" A year after our first EP came out that we had been promoting on MySpace and PureVolume, we ended up getting onto Warped Tour that summer in 2004.

---

* The Los Angeles radio station 106.7 KROQ was the main bellwether for alternative rock radio.

PRYOR: I think going into *Guilt Show*, we were like, "we gotta make a rock record, we're a rock band." But at the same time, we were done with each other. I mean we weren't fighting, but that whole record is assembled, we never played in the same room at the same time on that entire record. We started a band when we were children. Ultimately, we should have taken a year off or more, and because we weren't mature enough to know that that's something we could do, we broke up, and then took three years off, and then just got back together again. Which is why we all admit it was stupid.

SAPORTA: We're just hitting reset. We're twenty-two years old by then. We started Midtown when we were eighteen. It's like a generation, when you're that age. We were in a protracted legal negotiation to get off of Drive-Thru. And I think that actually strengthened our bond and made us think, *We're just going to make a record for ourselves. We don't give a fuck. Our career is basically over unless we do this. Let's just do something because we love it.* And that was very inspiring for us and motivating, and we all worked really hard to make it happen. We're literally rehearsing in my dad's basement in Springfield, New Jersey, just recording and doing this stuff.

PRYOR: I remember having a conscious decision, sitting on the couch in my living room with my wife, who was very pregnant at the time, watching Saves the Day play on *Conan* or *Letterman*, and making a conscious decision not to be jealous and to be happy for my friends. I don't want this to be a competitive sport. I'm very happy doing what we are doing and where we're at, and if they surpass us, then I will be happy for them.

―――――――――

Like emo, MySpace was growing fast. Anderson and DeWolfe started bringing in new talent over the next year or so, never forgetting the music was the site's heart. They hired Ngọc Cao as a producer and the DJ and party promoter Roslynn Alba Cobarrubias (aka DJ Rose) as the head of Artist Relations and unofficial hip-hop guru, both to get artists to sign up and to highlight the site's undiscovered talent.

Key to this initiative was the vertical MySpace Music, an editorial, curated section of the site where Ngọc Cao and Alba Cobarrubias highlighted artists both established and new, many of them unsigned and just getting started in their career, from country superstars Dixie Chicks to the pop-punk band Alkaline Trio, to the San Diego indie rock group Pinback, to whatever else the team felt like highlighting that day.

"I will always love that original team. And Tom, to me, was the heart and soul of MySpace and heart and soul of MySpace Music," says Ngọc Cao. "In the beginning, he came up with MySpace Music, and I want people to know that it was him and that we were there because of him."

Josh Brooks, who worked at the artist management company The Firm, was brought in to help with advertising and marketing partnerships, eventually working his way up to the vice president of programming and music. Isac Walter was a former music journalist for the skateboard magazine *Heckler* who later worked at Capitol Records and the indie Big Wheel Recreation before taking a job as senior marketing director and editor in chief for MySpace Music. Nate Auerbach was a touring manager for the funk-rock band Ozomatli before he came on board as a marketing manager.

Intermix Media changed its name to eUniverse. While the company nominally owned MySpace, the site very much felt like its own entity. "The company was owned by Brad Greenspan," says Ngọc Cao. "Those guys were very absent from MySpace. They will try to take credit for MySpace. They had nothing to do with MySpace."

Anderson was also keen to bring in as many artists and genres onto the site as possible, even if he didn't really understand who they were half the time. "I remember one time Wyclef Jean came to the office, and Tom didn't really know a ton of artists outside of the rock genres," says Alba Cobarrubias. "So I said, 'Hey, Tom, Wyclef is here.' And he was like, 'Hey, are you an artist?' I was like, 'He's from the Fugees.' And he's like, 'Oh, OK, nice to meet you.' And then Wyclef asked for a photo."

MySpace was quickly becoming the biggest talent incubator the world had ever seen, and Anderson wasn't going to let that go to waste. MySpace Records was a joint partnership with Interscope Records that launched in 2005. Jon Pikus,* a former A&R man for Interscope Records and Columbia Records, served as the senior director of A&R, and J Scavo, former executive director of Hollywood Records, served as the general manager of MySpace Records.

MySpace was a for-profit-business that made money for its parent company Intermix Media with ads. But it was also a tool that independent artists could use as easily as pop stars to find new fans. It was corporate from the start and as DIY as it gets, a strange tension that gave the site its unique frisson, at least for a while. Even if one has the punk inclination to always be wary of the gears of big business and its tendency to turn everything into a product, it was hard to argue with how useful it was to have a site where you could book tours of DIY houses or reach potential fans who didn't even realize they liked your sort of thing because they'd never been exposed to it.

Like an indie auteur making a daring, big budget Hollywood film or an agitprop act signed to a major label, sometimes you need an established infrastructure to smuggle vital new ideas into the greater world. And that's important, because people need these ideas. They save lives. Anderson had world-conquering ambitions for MySpace, but he nonetheless helped nurture the underground, as his site linked music scenes across the country and gave small artists a chance to compete in a way they never could before. It helped that MySpace's rampant half-naked (at best) selfies and garish personal pages made the site feel pleasingly chaotic and unprofessional.

All the while investors, titans of industry, and other manifestations of The Man were beginning to circle. Things were happening fast, and the major labels that fought Napster kicking and screaming were getting pulled into the future.

NGQC CAO: I was told by my employer that I had to rejoin MySpace and I had to invite all of my friends to it. I noticed that the site had

---

* A former member of the alt-rock group Campfire Girls, he also recorded the demos that earned Weezer a record deal.

gotten bigger, and Tom had fleshed out his profile. So I started chatting with him on MySpace and talking about music and what I wanted from a site like MySpace, because I felt like there was a lot of potential for it to grow as a music space. So we just started hanging out and going to shows together, and I was giving him a lot of advice about what I wanted the site to be and my vision for it. And one day he said, "Why don't you just come work here?"

ROSLYNN ALBA COBARRUBIAS (HEAD OF ARTIST RELATIONS, MYSPACE): There was Friendster, Asian Avenue, BlackPlanet, as well as the Okayplayer message boards. I was an early adopter of those platforms. I was a DJ and a club promoter and events producer. So my main objective was to promote my underground hip-hop radio show, Third Floor Radio. It stands for three levels of hip-hop: past, present, and future. When I was living in Pasadena, I worked for a networking organization called NARIP.* I met Chris DeWolfe, and he started asking me, "How is this room full? Are you on these sites?"

NGQC CAO: We called it sixty-sixty.† The office was very corporate looking; it's one of those giant high-rises right by the Howard Hughes mall on the west side. It felt corporate when you walked into the building. But the way that people worked was really not corporate in a lot of ways because we were still a really small team.

ALBA COBARRUBIAS: He told me that they wanted to create a similar version of Friendster, but as a creative platform. And my boss knew Chris and set up a meeting. So we sat outside and he was like, "So what are your ideas of how you would market MySpace to artists?" And at that time I helped put together a music video for the Black Eyed Peas, and we were having an after-party screening, and I said, "Why don't you have parties with artists involved?" And in order to get in, you had to have a

---

* National Association of Record Industry Professionals.
† Between 2004 and 2005, MySpace was located at 6060 Center Drive. From 2005 to 2006, it was located at 1333 Second Street office. It would later be located at 407 Maple Drive.

MySpace profile. And so that became like the very first MySpace party that had artists attached to it. We have photos with Fergie and all the Peas with MySpace swag items.

NATE AUERBACH (MARKETING MANAGER): Music was intentionally infused into the site at the beginning. When I came, the foundation was already there. Tom set the foundation with the culture and the music aspect of it. He's the one who decided to have music pages.

NGOC CAO: I was still a post-college kid, I was wearing like tube tops in the office, people are running around wearing outfits that they were going to go to the club in later, because a lot of us also went out at night. I went to from one to three shows a night, every single night, for the entire time that I worked there. I did so much work there that I actually got incredibly sick because I wasn't sleeping. I was working from like 10:00 in the morning until 6:00 AM every day for about two years because we were building a beast that could not rest.

AUERBACH: Friendster is, and this is what I would say about Facebook, too, it's where your friends are the people you went to high school with. MySpace was where you could be friends with the people you wish you went to high school with.

ALBA COBARRUBIAS: Chris asked if I could join full-time. And at the time, I said, "No, I'm going to be a big DJ, so I'll be a consultant and work part-time." I think it was like $750 a week or something really small. But I wound up loving it. I was the first one there, the last one to leave. At night I would just go out to all the clubs and meet all the DJs and the artists and get them on. And that just became what I was doing twenty-four seven; it became my identity.

NGOC CAO: It also got really big in very weird places. Very early on in 2004, almost the entire population of Hawaii had a profile on MySpace. One of the reasons Tom lives in Hawaii part of the time is because he would go there and they would treat him like a VIP everywhere he went.

AUERBACH: There were one hundred employees when I started. It was still very much like a start-up. We had companies like HP throwing happy hours for our employees once a week. It was ridiculous. We were by the beach in Santa Monica, which was crazy for an Ohio boy.

ALBA COBARRUBIAS: When I first met Chris, he was super sweet, super humble, and honest about not knowing exactly where they wanted to go. Their marketing plan at that time was, like, girls in bikinis in college newspaper ads. It wasn't very strategic.

AUERBACH: People would hit up Tom on his inbox, and I would read through Tom's inbox, when people wanted to throw MySpace parties and I would send them out MySpace Parties In A Box. You basically get a banner and some T-shirts or some swag.

NGQC CAO: I was often the only person awake when it crashed in the middle of the night. I had a list of names that I could call to reboot the site until somebody picked up the phone and basically turned the site back on. So there was a lot of that going on where people were doing things that were not really their jobs and I took on way more than a single human being should have taken on simply because I was young. I was ambitious. I had no real structure because I was hired first in marketing and then I told Tom I didn't want to report to anyone but him, and I just wanted to work on what I wanted to work on. And he just let me do it.

ALBA COBARRUBIAS: Tom is automatically everybody's friend; they wanted to make it seem like it was a personal site rather than just being a corporation. Artists and celebrities would always come in wanting to take photos with Tom or at our parties. It was just this mystery of Tom. He's super humble, too. Even when the company sold, he's still wearing the same T-shirt and jeans and he didn't change his car. He drove this old Jaguar; I would say the other founders got new cars, but he didn't. He still had the same hat.

NGQC CAO: He didn't really have much of a life outside of MySpace, and I don't think he felt like he needed a lot.

ALBA COBARRUBIAS: Tom still sat with all the engineers, not even in an office, he was there the latest. He didn't drink, he just had a good time and he enjoyed being around people and hearing how cool MySpace was. He was just there for the experience.

AUERBACH: Every club in L.A. wanted to do something with MySpace. It was like the biggest thing culturally that was happening. I was twenty-four, and I would go to a club in Hollywood and ask to speak to the manager and show my card. He'd be like, "Oh, anything you need."

COURTNEY HOLT (MYSPACE MUSIC PRESIDENT): We were sort of lost in this idea of radio, which is really one-dimensional and was heavily playlist driven at that point and heavily regimented. It became way, way harder for discovery to take place. I think more artists were broken on the back of MySpace rolling out and more communities built around it. That actually was the way that both scaled. MySpace scaled, but artist fandom also scaled.

JOSH BROOKS (MARKETING AND PROGRAMMING CHIEF FOR MYSPACE): It sort of democratized the online web world for people. This is the first time that you can actually create a page in which you put up videos, books you like, movies you see, things that represent you, right? So it's almost like decorating your dorm room, if you will. Back in the day you could also have a "webmaster," which is a nutty word to say these days, but the only other way you could actually have a website is if someone built it for you.

NGOC CAO: What people don't understand when they get kicked off a site is that they cite the First Amendment, but that just means they don't know what the First Amendment means. You have free speech for the government, but we were not the government. So you do not get to be racist or be homophobic toward people. The racism thing was always a given, that you couldn't be racist on the site. But the homophobic thing, I think, was a little bit early because society had not quite reached the point where being gay or being queer could be cool.

Gay marriage was not yet legal and would not be legal for another ten years. So that's why that particular moderation really stood out to me because I was a gay rights activist from the time that I was a teenager. Not because I was queer, but because I felt like it was the next civil rights movement to be a part of, and that it was the right thing to be a part of. I brought that to MySpace, and Tom stood by me because he also felt like it was wrong.

HOLT: No one knew what to make of MySpace. I saw it as a real viable opportunity. In fact, I tried to get Universal to make an investment in MySpace at that time, being like, "This is going to be a thing. And it's very powerful." And ultimately we did cut a record deal with them. So MySpace Records was an actual label output deal that we did with them when I was there. Luke Wood, who ended up becoming the COO of Beats, he and I kind of crafted that deal.

JON PIKUS (SENIOR DIRECTOR OF A&R): I was looking to move on from Interscope, and my manager said, "MySpace wants to start a record label. You're the guy for this, but you have to go interview with Tom and get him to say yes." What I thought would be a quick half-hour meeting turned into three hours of him and I sitting together behind his desk surfing from one artist's Top Eight to another. So they hired me and pretty much gave me a laptop and a cubicle and said, "Start the label," with no real parameters.

J SCAVO (GENERAL MANAGER, MYSPACE RECORDS): In the '90s, I managed bands, and then I went to Hollywood Records to run their artist development department, and then I sort of saw the digital revolution on the horizon, and I sought out a job that would give me some experience in that realm. I got the job to run MySpace's joint venture label with Interscope. It was housed at MySpace, all the employees were MySpace, but if and when things went well, Interscope could upstream them.

BROOKS: Older people didn't understand the platform. And this is cyclical, by the way. So, younger people, no problem, got it and it was intuitive.

Older people were sort of perplexed by it. And so a lot of the marketers' jobs were to evangelize and partner with people so it actually started making sense.

SCAVO: When I was at Hollywood [Records], somebody walked in with their marketing plan for a new band: the entire plan was to get on MySpace. I think that it is a unicorn in the music space. There was never any place—and has never been since—a single destination where almost everybody in the world went to find out and interact with music. It's a lot harder now, right?

NGQC CAO: In the beginning, Tom came up with MySpace Music, and I want people to know that it was him and that we were there because of *him*.

ISAC WALTER (MARKETING DIRECTOR AND EDITOR IN CHIEF, MYSPACE MUSIC): So one of my first jobs was just calling every label I knew, every band and every manager, being like, "Are you guys on MySpace? No? Let me build you a page and I'll put some music up, and then you can see how it goes from there." There was, I would say, some apprehension at first. They were definitely more likely to give you the newer bands they're trying to break, because they're doing everything they can, but Neil Young wasn't putting up a MySpace page at that point. Those old-school people, it took time. But there were certainly bands like Nine Inch Nails who adopted it early, and I think really made some success off of it because of that.

NGQC CAO: I helped launch MySpace Music. Bands were joining before, but there was nowhere for them to place the music. We had to make the music player. We had to make it so that there was a section where you could actually get featured and there was a chart. Everything that I wanted out of it wasn't quite there when I first got there. So all of that had to be built. It wasn't a huge portion of the site at the beginning. It was just this new section and a lot of it was just, "We think this is good music." We were working on building up and trying to get bands to sign up. There were people who would tell me that they got record deals off of getting a feature, there were bands that got to do tours.

WALTER: It was some random band that Tom or Bích picked to put on the home page. It was always, I thought, some really obscure shit, but I think they liked picking this obscure shit.

NGQC CAO: It wasn't looking and saying, "They need to reach so-and-so plays before we will feature them." What we were looking for was if something just popped out of nowhere. Why is this artist all of a sudden in our chart?

PIKUS: Tom had great taste in music. He certainly loved Weezer, and that was one of the first things we bonded on, our mutual love of Weezer. He definitely loved the poppier side of alternative/indie rock. Each artist that we signed, we had to run by Tom because Tom had to love it, and in the two-and-a-half years or so I was there, I was able to get about ten artists signed and around ten employees hired. MySpace Records was an incubator for Interscope, but it was also a stand-alone indie label with Fontana, which was Universal's independent distribution arm at the time. We were autonomous until Interscope said, "Hey, that one's good, we'll take that."

NGQC CAO: As we got really big, people from all over the company were sending me stuff and trying to get like their cousin's band to be featured. "Oh, so-and-so really needs so-and-so to be featured on the site," and well, that's really not a good band, so I'm not going to feature it.

PIKUS: We had a top artist chart that was segmented into major, indie, and unsigned. So if you were an A&R person, you could just look at the unsigned top artist chart, which was the top 100, and anyone could look at that and see. One of the reasons I believe MySpace Records was dreamt up in the first place was because we wanted to take advantage of the data that MySpace was generating and find artists that way, but also of course make sure they were great. You can't just rely on the data, you have to also rely on your ears. But the data can certainly be a good indicator of what stuff to pay attention to. It became the go-to place for finding bands.

NGQC CAO: It felt like they started MySpace Records without a real plan in place. Tom had just decided he wanted to sign some bands and partner with Interscope, so the first project was to put together a compilation. And Tom wanted the compilation to be a bunch of bands that he liked. It didn't really flow as an album. I didn't love it, but he loved it. And in order to try to sell it, the gimmick was that if you purchase the album, you got a little code that you can enter into MySpace and add eight more photos in your profile page. Because back then it was really expensive to host photos, so we had to limit people to a certain number of photos. Some people bought multiple copies of the album to try to get more photos. It was just kind of a ridiculous experience. Tom had forgotten one of the songs, and he was in a very expensive recording studio across town, and he didn't want to drive home and drive back, because he said it would cost an extra $800 if he took the time to do that, because we were paying by the hour. So he asked me to break into his apartment. I jumped through a window, logged into his computer, logged into my FTP, and dumped the file onto my server so that he could download the file from the studio and get that record done. I told Tom that he had to put me on the liner notes of that album as the MySpace Ninja, so that's what I became known as at the site, and people are writing to him, asking who the MySpace Ninja was.

AUERBACH: We had a pool going, for when we hit number one. We thought that we had so much more to go.

5

ENOUGH SPACE
FOR EVERYONE

In April of 2005, MySpace boasted nearly twenty-seven million members and was beating Google in monthly page views, becoming the top site
on the Internet. The average user spent an hour and forty-three minutes
on the site. This engagement far surpassed Friendster and Facebook, the
latter of which was then still only for college students with a .edu e-mail
address.

Emo fans brought MySpace one of its first user bases, which then
helped the genre grow in reach greater than could have possibly been
expected. Was the default image of a MySpace user a scene kid with
emo bangs? Well, you certainly saw a lot of them there.

But while emo kids may have gotten to MySpace first, once their
tears warmed the water, everyone wanted a space of their own. Emo and
MySpace are forever paired in the sense that if the latter hadn't existed,
the former very likely would have hit a ceiling of "thriving subculture"
rather than rising to the level of "what teendom sounded and felt like
in the 2000s." But if emo just wasn't your thing, MySpace offered plenty
of other soundtracks for your feelings.

If hip-hop, pop, and dance music aren't as synonymous with
MySpace in the cultural imagination, it's because everyone understands
these genres would have remained popular even if Anderson's band

had taken off and none of us ever heard of a Top Eight. But MySpace infused new blood into the game. Though the genre was slow to adopt the Internet, hip-hop was naturally suited toward MySpace and social media, as it's a genre with hustle in its marrow.

And there was no one at the time who hustled harder than Lil Jon. Born Jonathan Smith, Lil Jon spent the late '90s as an Atlanta-based DJ, record producer, and A&R man for the So So Def label. Back then, the national hip-hop scene revolved around New York and Los Angeles, and their respectively all-powerful radio stations, WQHT/Hot 97 and KPWR/Power 106, which could break an artist by adding one of their records to rotation. Those stations rarely deigned to play Southern rap artists for most of the '90s. So Lil Jon improvised.

"All of that shit just made me work harder," he says. "I learned to just take over markets. I started in Atlanta, ran Atlanta, with the record banging in Atlanta. Then I go to Birmingham, fuck with Birmingham. You just go and take over different cities."

Lil Jon's mission was to evangelize on behalf of crunk, an Atlanta-based subgenre of hip-hop at its most debauched and bass-heavy, with the low-end turned so loud that any thought beyond the desire to take another shot was driven sternly from the mind. Lil Jon & the East Side Boyz began to break through with the 2001 album *Put Yo Hood Up* and the single "Bia' Bia'." A flurry of work followed, including "Get Low" (with fellow Atlanta rappers Ying Yang Twins) and "Lovers and Friends" and "Yeah" (collaborations with Ludacris and Usher, both huge hits).

Along the way, he'd make a home for himself on MySpace. "It's basically a street team without you having to be on the street," he says. "I was used to hand-to-hand, you go see the DJ, you got to go to the club, and this made it where I can do it right here from my computer. It was a damn near revolutionary change for connecting with your audience. There's never been nothing like that before."

Hip-hop loving teenagers were increasingly spending their entire afternoons on MySpace, and party/fight-starting anthems such as Cam'ron's "Hey Ma," Ying Yang Twins featuring Lil Jon & the East Side Boyz's "Salt Shaker," DJ Unk's "Walk It Out," Dem Franchize Boyz's

"Lean wit It, Rock wit It," and anything dropped by the human mixtape factory Lil Wayne were all omnipresent profile songs.

It would take a little while to achieve full fruition, but already MySpace was starting to breed a new variation of hyperonline rapper, one fundamentally *of* the MySpace era. One of the earliest iterations was the Cool Kids. The Chicago duo formed almost by accident, after Sir Michael Rocks, aka Antoine Reed, bought a beat from college student, skateboarder, and producer Evan Ingersoll, aka Chuck Inglish. The pair pared hip-hop back down to '80s minimalism in order to push it forward, with a style that was as cheeky as their MySpace profiles. For a time, they were one of the hottest groups in any genre on the site.

"We made that song 'Mikey Rocks' towards the end of my high school career. And by the time I was about to graduate from high school, I was the most popular kid in the whole school," says Reed. "Everybody had that song on their page. Teachers would talk about the song. It didn't take very long at all for our stuff to catch fire on MySpace."

Though Far East Movement started as an alternative rap group, they slowly shifted to a more bottle service–friendly sound, heavy on the sort of keyboard trills that always seem to automatically trigger fog machines. This was not the edgiest thing around, but someone's got to make music to get the basketball arenas pumped, and Far East Movement was dedicated to the cause.

They recorded and gigged around downtown L.A. constantly, self-releasing 2005's mixtape *Audio-Bio* and their 2006 debut album *Folk Music*. Eventually, their MySpace popularity earned them a spot on *The Fast and the Furious: Tokyo Drift* and a deal with Interscope. Their hustle-all-the-time mentality launched their 2010 single "Like a G6" to the top of the *Billboard* singles chart, the first time Asian Americans achieved such a feat.

There are always going to be college kids, aimless twenty-somethings, and bar-hoppers who are just looking for kicks. But the mid-'00s were a particularly rowdy time. Perhaps it was a reaction to Bush-era cultural malaise, or perhaps MySpace made sure there was always a party to find.

LIL JON: I found an interview I did with Ros, and she said I was number 594 of artists on MySpace, and she said then we had two million hip-hop artists within two years as the top genre. So I came in that early.

ROSLYNN ALBA COBARRUBIAS (HEAD OF ARTIST RELATIONS, MYSPACE): When rappers would fight, they would take each other out of their Top Eight.

A-TRAK: Your Top Eight was a way to signal to the rest of the world who your alliances were. DJing has an ecosystem that's different from other forms of making music, where DJs support each other's music very actively. So there's this idea of mutual support that was very reflected in the Top Eight, where your DJ friends had you in theirs and you had them in yours. There was a reciprocity in the DJ friendships, that was a strong thing.

ANDREW NOSNITSKY (COCAINE BLUNTS): I started seriously engaging MySpace around the time when I was writing for *XXL*. And then it was incredible. The main thing that I used it for was contacting artists. You got to keep in mind hip-hop artists weren't really on the Internet prior to MySpace. It probably has something to do with the access to the Internet increasing. But, I mean, I also think it was probably seen as kinda like for nerds.

ALBA COBARRUBIAS: Lil Jon was the first one to use the URL myspace .com/liljon, he would wear that everywhere. He introduced me to E-40 and Pitbull. They were some of the early adopters of the platform. Pitbull even put it in a song, because he used MySpace so much and really built his platform. E-40 was the first hip-hop artist to premiere a record.

GEOFF RICKLY (THURSDAY): I could always tell who was crossing over with emo kids, if they were doing well in MySpace. I remember when Lil Wayne was blowing up on MySpace, I was like, "Emo kids love Lil Wayne." And I stand by that. Emo kids were huge, early supporters of Lil Wayne.

ALBA COBARRUBIAS: When we first launched, there were 126 hip-hop registered users and they wanted specifically to grow the hip-hop audience. So while they wanted Jay-Z and all these huge artists, I really focused on the underground, because I know that's who would actually utilize the site every day.

LIL JON: I would look up all of the fans, like, "Cleveland. I've got a show coming through. Make sure y'all come check me out," or "Everybody that follows me on MySpace, here's a sneak peek of my new single." It's a way of talking to your fans, getting direct interaction with someone. That's just where I come from in the sense of being an independent artist. We did it because we knew it was going to go a long way.

ALBA COBARRUBIAS: Diddy became a huge fan. He would call me all the time, every time he would do something. So it really, really grew fast. I think within a couple of years it was the number-one genre on the site.

A-TRAK: There's music projects that were born off of MySpace. I got into producing electronic music around those years, and sort of my sketchpad, almost, was doing remixes. And the first remix that I did that got a decent amount of notice, that got other DJs playing it, was a remix that I did for Boys Noize,* for the song "Oh!" And Boys Noize and I were friends on MySpace. I remember seeing him DJ in Miami for the first time and messaging him on MySpace afterwards and being like, "Yo, I was at your show. That was amazing." And then him asking me to do a remix. All this via MySpace messages. Again, everyone's used to doing business deals on Instagram DM. But in those years that was revolutionary. It was crazy in those years to hire someone for a real job on a platform that wasn't via e-mail or phone call.

LIL JON: It was just so fast, man. I was producing for Usher, Ciara, I did Trick Daddy, I had so many records on the *Billboard* charts. It was a crazy time, and it's kind of a blur, because it was so much stuff going

---

* A Berlin-based DJ and producer, born Alexander Ridha.

on so fast, plus my own records was still going and it just was a lot. It doesn't even seem like all that stuff was happening at the same time, but all of that stuff kind of happened right at the same time.

NISH (FAR EAST MOVEMENT): When you really think of the context of the Far East Movement, that's coming from a place as a foreigner. I'm fourth generation American. We grew up American. So when we think about that name now, we felt the need to represent our community in music because it didn't exist. We were always told that this industry . . . I don't want to loosely word this, but the idea was like, "Wow, Asians in music? That's so strange."

CHUCK INGLISH (COOL KIDS): I would friend everybody I was fans of. And I remember the first night, I friended Ciara and JoJo. I remember sending JoJo a message telling her how much I liked her music. She even responded back.

SIR MICHAEL ROCKS (COOL KIDS): Me and Chuck, we were both weird mutual friends with this guy, and he eventually told us about each other. He showed me Chuck's page and I was like, "Oh, damn, this dude is on all the same stuff that I'm on." Nobody in the entire neighborhood or city was thinking how I was at the time. I would definitely say that I was a lot more alternative when it came to music and fashion, and so was Chuck at that time, and I think we were like the only two that really felt how we felt. And yeah, we just kind of found each other through MySpace, listening to each other's beats. I was like, "Oh, damn, like, we should do something, man." I was trying to buy a beat from him.

NISH: I think something clicked, where we thought, *If anyone in the world can hear this record in a club and not think about race, did we do our job?* And is *that* the true Far East movement? We chose this path. At the time, there was Black Eyed Peas. We have a lot of friends that do gangsta rap, street rap, backpack hip-hop, that did it so well, and we were like, "Why feed what's already there?" We knew that going left was going to get a lot of hate. But I think that it was a business decision that we decided to run with.

INGLISH: I had two coding classes when MySpace came out, so it just all was a perfect storm, and I discovered how to make my own page with music. I was using a lot of the skills from the HTML class I had and adding it to what I was doing on MySpace. I made a custom picture that had Inglish on it, and it had me as a baby in a white suit standing on top of my name. So it was a way to stand out a little bit early.

ROCKS: He had this illustration that he drew of a record label, it was a cake with a chain on it. I thought that he was already established because of how his page looked and how his beats sounded. And there's no way this guy's even going to respond to me because he's probably like seven beats for five thousand or something. And I ended up talking to him and it was completely the opposite. He had no clue about anything. Once I started talking to him, I was like, "Oh, damn, OK, he's just like a kid like me."

NISH: Even before the radio play, "Round, Round" got featured on MySpace. We saw the plays just shoot up, and it was attached to the movie [*The Fast and the Furious: Tokyo Drift*]. We just saw our followers, everything, just go up after that. Which kind of motivated us to keep doing that fun sound. That's when we did "Girls on the Dance Floor." We started seeing it on *America's Best Dance Crew*, the TV show, which at the time was the staple for every dancer and Asian American. We started getting meetings early, but maybe they didn't want to sign us. But a year later, we got booked to do the Powerhouse Stage,* which was at the Arrowhead Pond in Anaheim. And that's when we got a call back from Interscope and Cherry Tree saying, "We really want to sign you." They took a meeting with us, and they didn't feel it. We were all dressed like backpackers. We had flannels on. And then six months later, we had this whole look, we had sunglasses, we just looked like an electro band. And the A&R just really loved that. We got the record deal offer.

---

* An indoor hip-hop concert hosted by the hip-hop station Power 106.

ROCKS: Chuck had that cool, like, Pharrell, Neptunes* sound that I was looking for and nobody else was making. That minimal, futuristic kind of skate music. So I hit him up about buying a beat. And he was really nice and he was just like, "Oh yeah, man, I don't know how much to charge for a beat or anything like that, but you can come over my house and we can, like, listen to some beats and you know, we'll pick them out and figure it out." I was like, "Damn, you got your own apartment. That's sick." I was still in high school living with my parents.

INGLISH: I was making beats for like four years at that point, and at that time, there was just a skinny road, which is: you gotta get around the A&R, you gotta have label meetings, you gotta play your beats, you gotta do all this very prehistoric shit just to kinda exist. Being slightly delusional and knowing that I had this value to what I was making, I saw this as, "Fuck that, I'm gonna just put up my best shit." And I remember putting up stuff and coming back home with nine hundred plays, one thousand plays.

ROCKS: He was like, "So what do you want to buy beats for? I thought you were just a producer." I kind of slowed down on rapping because I wanted to make more beats, but I said "yeah, put the beat on." I ended up rapping for like two hours straight, beat after beat. Then Chuck came up with the idea of, he was like, "All right, scratch that exchanging beats thing. How about I just make the beats and then you rap on them? And that was the beginning of the Cool Kids. We would be kind of like the Eric B and Rakim–type of duo. But after our second song, he came with a verse on one of his songs, and he's like, "Yo, I want you to check this out," and I was like, "Damn, that's crazy. Why don't we just both rap and make the beats? Like, let's just both do it." And from there, that was really when the Cool Kids got started.

---

* Known at the time for space-age productions with lots of empty space and swirling keyboard tones, Pharrell Williams and the Neptunes were some of the most popular producers in rap.

Once computers began including built-in microphones, a generation of songwriters discovered they could easily record demos using software that was either preinstalled or readily available online. While a full-band demo recorded on a laptop's mic would likely sound cruddy, and not in a cool way, these computers could capture a voice and a guitar reasonably well, with the rough edges adding a sense of intimacy. Once you had a few demos sitting on your computer, taking the next step to put them on your page was so easy that it would feel silly *not* to.

Kate Voegele and Colbie Caillat were both high school students when they began posting songs to MySpace. Well, in Caillat's case, her friends made the page and posted her songs for her. "[They] kept telling me, 'Look how far you're starting to chart on the Unsigned Artists chart,'" she remembers. "I didn't even know what to think."

Both quickly found fans, with the Cleveland-born Voegele hearing from Anderson himself, and Caillat's soft-rock gold anthem "Bubbly" eventually earned her the top unsigned artist spot on MySpace. Joining them soon was Melissa McAllister Sheppard, a songwriter who'd moved from the small town of Roberta, Georgia, and began performing as Meiko at Hollywood's songwriter incubator The Hotel Café when she wasn't busy working there as a waitress.

COLBIE CAILLAT: I never went on music websites. I really wasn't on the computer much. We lived in Southern California and we were more outdoorsy, like hiking and going to the beach. I was really new to all of it.

KATE VOEGELE: I grew up in Cleveland, Ohio, in a suburb. Not the type of place where you would think you're going to get discovered and become famous in the entertainment business.

CAILLAT: I had just started recording some demos after I had written my first few songs ever in my life. One of my best friends from high school told me about the website. I thought that was a bizarre out-of-this-world thing. I think, the end of 2005 my friend put a few of my songs up on MySpace, including "Bubbly," and that was my introduction to that website.

MEIKO: I moved to L.A. in 2001. I graduated high school and I didn't really know what I wanted to do with my life. I didn't really know why I would go to college. I knew I wanted to play music, but I didn't think that there was a college pathway for me to be a professional singer. I didn't have a computer until right before MySpace came out. So that was the first thing I did. I had a personal page for a few months and then switched to an artist page.

VOEGELE: It started when I first learned to play the guitar, I was fifteen, and my dad taught me. I was a freshman, and I just wanted an outlet to describe how I was feeling about teenage-girl issues and boys. I really fell in love with writing songs, but I was also a very introverted kid. So I was not the kid who went back to high school after that spring break with a couple of new songs in my back pocket and shouted from the rooftops to all my classmates like, "Hey guys, I'm going to be playing a coffeehouse this weekend." I was almost mortified at the thought of people even knowing who I wrote my songs about.

MEIKO: I was always a bedroom musician, but I had really bad stage fright. So it took me living in L.A. a few years before I played my first open-mic night. I was pretty terrified. There was like two people in the audience, but I was really proud of myself.

VOEGELE: I ended up going to New York for the first time because I was a finalist in this contest and got to make a music video, and it aired on MTV and VH1. All of it was based on a song that I had written. I think in that moment I knew, if I had my way, this is what I would want to do with my life, hands down. They called it the Pantene Pro-Voice Contest. I think I was like sixteen or something, and that was pretty wild.

BÍCH NGỌC CAO (MYSPACE MUSIC EDITOR): Meiko's actually one of my dear friends. I saw the very first time that she ever picked up a guitar and played in that club, because it was in the middle of the night. I used to stay there till 4 AM sometimes. So she had finished her shift. They cleaned out. We were just hanging out there with a bunch of our friends, and she just picked up a guitar and got on stage and started playing.

MEIKO: I guess I got kind of competitive, but with myself. "OK, let's see how many people I can get for the next show," and I guess that correlates with MySpace, because then it was like, how many fans did I get today?

NGỌC CAO: [Meiko's] funnier than a lot of singer-songwriters, she's very self-deprecating. She is horribly frightened of being on stage, and I remember her sister used to have to sit in the front row just looking at her so that she would be able to stand up there. But she's a natural comedian. I think a lot of those guys, you know, who get up on stage and play really sad songs, have to have something that counterbalances that. And she's one of those people.

VOEGELE: I put together an EP of some music in high school, and that led to a manager reaching out. So half of my time was spent like a regular high school kid in a totally typical Midwest suburb. The other half of my life was spent, like, flying to New York City and playing my songs for these record labels.

CAILLAT: My parents were aware of it. They were like, "Something might be happening, and we should get you a manager to prepare you if your music takes off," which I thought was the most bizarre thing. I had never played any shows live besides like two acoustic shows and school talent shows, and I really didn't expect that I could get a career from this website.

VOEGELE: I got a message from *the* first friend, MySpace Tom. And I thought it was for sure spam or something 'cause by this time, there were a bunch of people sending weird messages on MySpace, spammy-type random stuff. But I opened it, and he was like, 'Hey, I love your music. Are you signed yet?' I was like, on the off chance that this is real, I've gotta respond, you know? But I didn't really think anything of it until I got a pretty prompt response back. He was like, "I really want to have you come out and showcase for my new record label."

MEIKO: I thought when I first moved to L.A. I was going to find a lucky break. But what I realized was I learned how to hustle and work my ass off and bartend and waitress and play anywhere and everywhere. When I first started playing, someone gave me this advice like, "You have to, like, put your ego aside, and when someone asks you to sing or play, you do it."

VOEGELE: It was just wild to me that Tom was even a real guy. He kind of had this *Wizard of Oz* vibe where he was your first friend, but you're like, "I don't know if this is a real guy or if this is just a stock-photo picture of some dude." Literally a few weeks later, I was here in Los Angeles, in Santa Monica at their offices, talking to Tom and his A&R guy Jon Pikus, who was a guy who had heard of me when I was in high school showcasing in New York

CAILLAT: Once I hit number one, my manager instantly got calls from record labels, and we had bidding wars. Honestly, it's so hard to even explain, because I wasn't prepared for any of it, it just happened. I was this twenty-year-old. I just wrote some songs for fun.

VOEGELE: This is a big deal for me, because I had never been to a big city before outside of Cleveland. So it was this crazy dichotomy. I ended up deciding to go to college, right before the MySpace thing. I had decided I needed to do a year of being like a regular college kid. I think I need that experience for myself. I decided against moving straight to New York and trying to become famous after high school. And literally, months after I made that decision, that's when I got the message from Tom on MySpace. I don't know if you want to call it a message from the universe.

CAILLAT: I know that it was particularly my song "Bubbly." None of us even thought that was a single. It just so happened to be the first few songs that we ended up recording, so those were the first songs that went on the page. It wasn't like we strategically chose which songs to put up. In a way, I really had nothing to do with it.

VOEGELE: It was an indie label that had complete and full jurisdiction and control over this powerhouse social network that they owned. I'd been offered some kinda shitty deals from major labels in high school that never felt right, and I decided to go to college, take a breath, and figure it out. When I got offered the MySpace deal, that's why I knew it was the right one, because they said these people love music. They're music fans, they're not jaded, they're not about the bottom line as much as they are about making something cool. And they happen to own MySpace.com.

Like a can of Sparks or a VOTE FOR PEDRO T-shirt, the MP3 blog was so omnipresent in the '00s it was destined to become shorthand for an era. Platforms such as WordPress and Blogger made it easy for anyone to set up a rudimentary website, host an MP3, and write breathlessly about the day's latest paradigm-shifting masterpiece. By the middle of the '00s, everyone had an MP3 blog—or an MP3 blog they checked daily. Or they made a big show of rolling their eyes at the word *blog*. And very often, MySpace was one of the main feeders for new songs and artists.

"MySpace had the player, but you could make tracks downloadable," says Mark Richardson. "And so if a band made a track downloadable, then it would get posted on every blog."

A loop to find the latest hot thing would quickly form between an artist's MySpace page, message boards, and music blogs such as Stereogum, Said the Gramophone, BrooklynVegan, Gorilla vs. Bear, and Cocaine Blunts and established publications such as *XXL, Vice, Spin*, the *Village Voice*, and the increasingly dominant Pitchfork. "I still will cringe if anyone calls Pitchfork a blog," says Richardson, who after years as a writer became the site's managing editor in 2006, helping to make the coverage more professional. "But since breaking artists was so important to it, blogs were absolutely seen as competition, even though it's often just one person in their bedroom or whatever."

For fans, it was an exciting time, with many having memories of rushing to their dorm's computer labs to scour the blogs for the latest greatest band in the world, who sometimes even lived up to the hype, at least for a few minutes. Everything was beautiful, and my back didn't hurt.

Among the artists who found themselves in the spotlight were Gareth David and his mates in Los Campesinos!, a seven-piece pack of excitable Scottish college students who loved to write about the experience of loving indie rock. Graham Wright and his schoolmates formed Tokyo Police Club, a quartet of wide-eyed Ontario high schoolers who went from reading Pitchfork to worrying if Pitchfork would like their band.

Once Cassie Ramone quit lurking on LiveJournal, the guitarist-singer teamed with bassist Katy "Kickball Katy" Goodman and drummer Frankie Rose to form Vivian Girls, a trio that drenched classic girl-group pop-hooks in waves of distorted feedback, giving a hint of menace to their melancholy. Cloud Nothings was just one of many band names that Ohio college student and fellow feedback lover Dylan Baldi used on MySpace, posting song after song of tunefully distorted power pop, but that name was the one the world finally noticed. All four of them would earn careers as indie rock lifers, and MySpace was their launching pad.

CASSIE RAMONE (VIVIAN GIRLS): When I was a sophomore in college, I would use MySpace to go and find out who the cliques were in Brooklyn. I probably sound like a psychopath stalker right now. But sometimes there's nothing better to do than to stalk people online. If I made a friend or something, then I would go on their MySpace and see who their friends were. I would find out how the social cliques ran in Brooklyn. So I eventually befriended this group of people that were older than me. They were in their mid-twenties. I was nineteen, and they all lived in a loft in Greenpoint. I would spend the night there on the couch a lot. I was always there.

MARK RICHARDSON (FORMER PITCHFORK EDITOR IN CHIEF): We didn't really have a system in place for just combing random MySpace pages. But we certainly made it a point for the news team to be checking MySpace pages for big bands that frequently posted new songs there.

RAMONE: So Frankie Rose, the first drummer of Vivian Girls, lived in that loft at one point, and we weren't really close at all. And then one day we were at brunch at this Mexican restaurant called Acapulco in Greenpoint, and Frankie was like, "Hey, do you want to start a band?" And I was like, at first, kind of taken aback because I was like, "Whoa. I don't know this girl. That's random. But I'm kind of a yes man in a lot of situations. So I was like, "Sure, why not?" And then we jammed together once. It sounded cool and we're like, "OK, we need a bass player." So my friend Katy, who I've been friends with since I was like fourteen, I knew that Katy was between bands. She was living in New Brunswick at the time. She was going to Rutgers and I was like, "Hey, I know you're not in a band right now, so do you want to be in my band?" We just got motivated to, like, keep going and shoot for the stars, if you will.

DYLAN BALDI (CLOUD NOTHINGS): MySpace had a four-song limit for each page. But I'd be like, "I just made more songs. I don't want to take these songs down yet." So I made a new MySpace page for another fake band for my songs. I kept cycling through these imaginary bands that were all just me. I think there were probably four or five. Cloud Nothings was the final one. That was the one that, randomly, people actually liked.

RAMONE: Our first show was in this little punk house in Bed-Stuy that had a lot of shows. It was kind of like a go-to spot back in those days. And Tobi Vail's* band was playing. We had only been a band for two months. We hustled and we got together a set, and it was very short—it was like fifteen minutes long, as a lot of our sets were in the early days. Then afterwards, we were all hanging out and our friends were like, "Our friends did this festival in Chicago of indie, DIY punk bands. Why don't you come play?" This is literally an hour after we played our first show, and then we're like, "Huh, OK." So we went on this ten-day tour. It was so ridiculously last minute. But you've got to start somewhere.

GARETH DAVID (LOS CAMPESINOS!): None of us went into the band thinking, *Right, we're going to form a band, and we are going to be a band*

---

* Drummer for riot grrrl legends Bikini Kill.

in fifteen years' time or even in two or three years' time. It was literally, *We will form a band, we'll play some shows at university, get drunk, and meet people. And that will be it.* I must have had an inkling that it was worth being a part of. If I hadn't pushed myself into the band, I'm not sure that they would ever have even played a gig.

BALDI: I think I just happened to add the right MySpace friends to that page, because I found the band Coasting from New York. I still talk to those people today. They happened to be roommates with this guy Todd P,* who booked a lot of indie rock shows. He happened to be in the room when they were listening to the Cloud Nothings page, because I just added them as friends. And that was how this band started, basically. That was the start of everything. That was the only reason anybody wanted to do anything to do with us. We got to do the show, playing with Woods and Real Estate, who were both pretty new bands at the time, you know. So it was our first show ever, all thanks to this random MySpace friend.

DAVID: I couldn't overexaggerate just how quickly it went. So the day that we completed the demo, we uploaded them to MySpace. We went out to an Indie Disco Night and took a copy of the demo for the DJ. There was nobody there, so he played one of our songs and we were there dancing to it. And these days, you'd be checking Twitter or whatever to see the reaction, and there wasn't any of that. But we get home, and it's like, "Oh, wow, this is crazy." Like, the message boards that we posted it on were going nuts for it. The play counts on MySpace were way higher than we could have anticipated, our followers shot up.

BALDI: It was surreal because Cleveland, where I grew up, has no analogue to that level of DIY scene that existed in New York at the time and probably still does. It was at the Market Hotel, which was a venue built from the ground up by some bands basically, and I didn't know

---

* Todd Patrick organized, booked, and promoted DIY, independent concerts in ramshackle New York and Brooklyn venues such as Death by Audio, Market Hotel, 285 Kent Ave, and many others, giving countless bands crucial early shows. The respect he carried in indie scenes verges on the religious.

anything about that. It felt like a movie to me, going in and being like, "This is something people really do." It was just kind of a blur, and it was eye-opening in a way, because it made me realize, like, "Oh, I can take this super DIY MySpace page into this realm." And that could be something that is a viable path for this band. I remember we actually got paid a decently significant amount of money at the end of the gig, and Todd P said, "Don't get used to this." He was right; the next three years we didn't make any money.

DAVID: I looked at the specific date we uploaded our songs to MySpace. It was the 29th of June, 2006. We recorded the four-track demo in the local community center, which I think cost one hundred pounds to record four tracks and mix them all in the space of eight hours. We recorded "You! Me! Dancing!," "Death to Los Campesinos!," "It Started with a Mixx," and "Sweet Dreams, Sweet Cheeks."

BALDI: We played that show and immediately we met this guy who was like, "I'll book your band." And you're like, what? We met a guy who was like, "I'll be your lawyer." We thought, *Whoa, why do we need a lawyer? What does that mean? Do we owe you money? What's happening?* He ended up being our lawyer. A couple of things happened immediately at that gig. That was kind of a lucky break.

DAVID: By the end of the week, we had somebody from an Australian record label saying, "We want to release your album." But we don't have an album. We have like seven songs. And, you know, within two weeks we're getting people traveling down from London to meet with us, be it managers, record labels, booking agents. It was insane, and this was right at the end of the school year. So at the point of putting the MySpace demos up, we've done a maximum of six gigs.

GRAHAM WRIGHT (TOKYO POLICE CLUB): We just applied for Pop Montreal on a whim. Actually, it's a fucking miracle that we actually put together the package and nobody forgot to mail it—the way that we were conducting ourselves at that point, it was much more likely that we just would have talked about it and then never done it. We'd all applied to universities at that point. We were all sort of on the rails of that version of suburban middle-class respectability. So me and Josh, the guitar player, were taking a gap year anyway, that was when we played Pop Montreal. Right after that, we got label interest and, with the slightest provocation, we were like, "OK, everyone quit school. Let's do this for real."

BALDI: The other thing I particularly liked about that era is that a lot of the bands, the recording quality was questionable at best. A lot of stuff that just sounded wildly bad was getting pretty popular, at least like, you know, indie music world popular. And that is the kind of thing I gravitate towards anyway. I like stuff that sounds bad. So it was fun for me during that era to be like, "Oh, this band sounds like they made their record in a shoebox. I love this."

WRIGHT: MySpace was very much in step with our rise. Being the featured artist on MySpace, which sounds so quaint now, was one of the biggest-deal things that happened during that period of our life. We were playing on *Letterman*, and being the featured band on MySpace was treated with the same amount of "holy shit" big reverence as *Letterman* was. We had always tried to be engaged with the fans, and then being like, "There are too many messages, we can't respond to them all, we don't have time." Being the feature band on MySpace was indeed a big deal in terms of how many messages you received.

RAMONE: *Blog rock*, I've heard it before, but I'd have to say I haven't thought about that term in a very long time. I know from personal experience that my band, and a lot of bands that I know, worked their butts off, and they didn't do it just to be on a blog. They did it because they believed in their own music.

DAVID: We had different managers show up. One guy came from London and brought a lookbook with him, illustrating how he'd have us dress and stuff like that. We were gonna be wearing leather jackets, that sort of thing. We knew this was a once-in-a lifetime opportunity, so we had every record label come visit us and take us out for dinner and bring us gifts. We truly milked it. The last one we went out for, Virgin came and brought us out for food, and I think they brought a lawyer to come meet with us and we left that meal, phoned Wichita, and said, "Yeah we're gonna sign with you guys." Seems like a lifetime ago.

While hip-hop, indie rock pop, and everything else in the record store was migrating over to MySpace, there was no mistaking the fact that the site was still very emo at its heart. And thanks to MySpace, emo's unofficial sound was reaching heights in the summer of 2005.

But this was a very different iteration of emo from even 2002, to say nothing of the '90s wave. Dashboard Confessional, Taking Back Sunday, Jimmy Eat World, and Thursday had done their part, but it was My Chemical Romance, Fall Out Boy, and Paramore that truly brought it all home, and their cultural impact was immediately apparent.

The clothing mall chain Hot Topic had become infamous for sending employees to shows to see which fashion trends were emerging (and has been frequently accused of copying artists' designs), and it was going all-in on the emo look, which had mutated from the sweater and horn-rimmed glasses look of the scene's college phase to eyeliner, swoopy bangs, and tight jeans.

Alternative Press had reoriented its coverage to basically become the print version of MySpace, almost exclusively covering emo and pop-punk. "*AP* had been doing the nu metal thing for a couple of years and then they were alternating in 2003. It would be nu metal band, emo band, like, Coal Chamber, Thursday," says Scott Heisel. "Back and forth, and the other issues are blowing them out of the water."

The changing of the guard was most notable on the Vans Warped Tour, a traveling music festival started in 1995 by Kevin Lyman, a touring industry lifer who worked on the original Lollapalooza. He spent the second half of the '90s focused on promoting the sort of shout-along punk that had long fueled epic skateboarding afternoons. But by 2005, emo was driving the show, as My Chemical Romance and Fall Out Boy were the year's main draws.

Like any good superhero, Gerard Way has an oft-referenced origin story. A graduate of New York's School of Visual Arts, he planned to be a visual artist after all his adolescent bands went nowhere. He was interning at the Cartoon Network when he watched the September 11th terrorist attacks. After witnessing the previously unimaginable, he called his brother Mikey Way and friends in the New Jersey punk scene and got to work. He would later remark on social media that the band was his way of processing collective post-traumatic stress that affected society. "The world changed that day, and the next day we set about trying to change the world."

Rickly produced the band's 2002 debut album *I Brought You My Bullets, You Brought Me Your Love*, which was released on the New Jersey indie label Eyeball. For their absurd (in the best possible sense) 2004 album *Three Cheers for Sweet Revenge*, the band signed to Warner Music Group subsidiary Reprise Records and swung for the fences, creating a glammy, hilarious, and often poignant arena-sized album that made them rock stars via singles "I'm Not Okay (I Promise)," "Helena," and "The Ghost of You." In the process, they became a woke-before-woke millennial analog to Guns N' Roses, with the sleaze swapped out for progressive punk politics.

"It was watching him go from just a nerdy but intelligent kid into Gerard from My Chemical Romance. I watched it happen in front of my eyes," Rickly says. "We were working on 'Early Sunsets over Monroeville,' sort of a ballad. And I was really pushing him to go more and harder and more, commit harder.

"And then I heard the magic, and I turned to Mikey and I said, 'Dude, your band's gonna be huge. Huge.' And he was like, 'Do you think it's gonna be Thursday big?' And I was like, 'Nah, man, you're gonna be like Good Charlotte big.' I had no idea that they would eclipse everybody."

Way tended to complain in interviews that his band wasn't emo, and we all know how helpful that is. The Rickly connection was probably enough to get them lumped into the scene, but Way's particular genius was to honor the genuine sense of isolation and sadness in the genre and then to blow it up well past the point of parody until it reached a level of poetic truth.

"I think all you have to do is listen to the lyrics to understand the heart of the band, and if you really dig into the song structures," says Carrabba, "they are arena rock, but they are steeped in this counter–arena rock song structure and musicality. It's this weird duality. I don't know if they would consider themselves emo, but I think that they are absolutely emblematic of what emo is."

Three Cheers for Sweet Revenge was nominally a concept album* about a hitman who is allowed to leave hell to be reunited with his love if he brings the Devil the souls of a thousand evil men. But really, Way would admit in interviews, the album was his way of dealing with the death of his beloved grandmother, a loss so painful that it felt akin to a supernatural horror, thus reframing the grieving process into its own heroic undertaking. That grief, as well as stage fright, found Way turning to cocaine, Xanax, and alcohol abuse to cope. After he wandered under the stage during a gig in Kentucky and refused to perform, he began attending AA meetings.

"It was pretty clear that they weren't gonna be able to be a successful band if he was gonna keep drinking," says Rickly. "I hated that they were a big band, so people were talking about it, because that's not anybody's business, really."

With his penchant for mascara and tendency toward onstage costumes such as bulletproof vests or all-black suits and blood-red ties, Way treated his band like a superhero team, even telling *Blender*, "You're not in it for money or fame. You're in it to do some good. Becoming more popular, it's like people are granting us superpowers and we have to use them to fight evil," and adding, "We're saying it's OK to be messed up. There's other people just like you. And if we stick together we'll get through this." It would be nice if more rock stars realized their job is to be big siblings to the fucked-up children of this world.

---

* Way read a *lot* of comic books and was a big fan of DC's mature imprint Vertigo. Neil Gaimain's *The Sandman* and Garth Ennis's *Preacher* were big for him, and he would later author a run on his all-time favorite *Doom Patrol* for DC. He also created the series *The Umbrella Academy* for Dark Horse and oversaw a Netflix adaptation.

My Chemical Romance was ahead of the curve on a variety of cultural issues (or, you know, telling people to grow a fucking heart already), in ways that truly felt heroic to their fans. Way would regularly introduce "Headfirst for Halos" as a song about suicidal thoughts and would urge the audience to seek help if they needed it. He tended to kiss Iero onstage and often winked* at the band's queer fans, and would regularly call out sexism and homophobia from the stage during a time when those attitudes went shamefully unchallenged.

"They were definitely doing things that weren't cool, but they ended up pushing through pretty progressive agendas that then became the mainstream. And that includes mental wellness. That includes being an ally. That includes celebrating the things that make you different," says Leslie Simon. "All of the parts about you that maybe don't fit into the box, it's possible that you can change the box instead of changing yourself."

MCR's fellow world conquerors Fall Out Boy were named for a comic book character from *The Simpsons*. In retrospect, their dual cultural ascendency reads as a metaphor for the way comic book culture would soon completely overtake the film industry and most of pop culture.

The members of Fall Out Boy all met while playing in Chicago's hardcore scene, and joined together to a form a very unhardcore band with a very unusual creative arrangement. Singer Patrick Stump (whose songs on MP3.com convinced bassist Pete Wentz and guitarist Joe Trohman to recruit him) fronted the band and wrote the melodies, while Wentz wrote the wildly verbose lyrics. For years, emo bands had inspired LiveJournal outpourings and AIM away messages. Wentz smartly internalized this dynamic. Naturally attuned to the rhythms of the Internet, he wrote lyrics in the new cadence of the time, full of in-scene in-jokes and sharp vacillations between wild self-aggrandizement and self-pity, with a healthy dose of self-awareness to let the listener know he's aware they can be a bit much. On "Dance, Dance," Wentz straight-up calls

---

* The song "You Know What They Do to Guys Like Us in Prison" features the lyrics "We're just two men as God had made us/Well I can't/Well I can." While touring for his 2014 solo album *Hesitant Alien*, Way often took time to tell transgender people in the audience that they had his full support, and in interviews he noted that while he identified as cisgender, he'd never been comfortable with traditional masculinity.

himself "A joke of a romantic/stuck to my tongue/weighed down with words/too overdramatic."

A biracial man with a matinee-idol smile, Wentz toured with a straightening iron and mascara, and supplied the rock star charisma (lots of onstage jump kicks) that Stump never felt comfortable with. "With Pete, I get to be the anti-frontman," he said in the *Rolling Stone* feature. "I just get to sing. Pete loves photo shoots, and I fucking hate them." But underneath his rock star ambitions (in the same *Rolling Stone* feature, Wentz remarked that he wanted Fall Out Boy to "be a culture. You're going to eat, sleep and breathe it. I want it to be a way you think about the world") was an often troubled soul. He struggled with bipolar disorder and anxiety and was dealing with a tumultuous romantic relationship.

In February 2005, while sitting in a Chicago Best Buy parking lot, he overdosed on Ativan pills and was hospitalized for a week. While Wentz never referred to it as a suicide attempt, he told *Rolling Stone*, "I was isolating myself further and further, and the more I isolated myself, the more isolated I'd feel. I wasn't sleeping. I just wanted my head to shut off, like, I just wanted to completely stop thinking about anything at all."

After releasing their 2003 debut *Take This to Your Grave* on the Florida-based indie Fueled by Ramen, they signed to Island Records. Their 2005 candy-punk album *From Under the Cork Tree* would go double-platinum in two years, thanks to singles "Sugar, We're Goin Down" and "Dance, Dance" and Stump's ability to translate Wentz's clusters of neurotic word dumps into soaring anthems. Those overdramatic words didn't weigh him down *too* much, apparently.

"Pete's old hardcore band Racetraitor had played in my basement at one point, and then Thursday played a basement in Chicago with Arma Angelus, which was his sort of in-between, metally, hardcore bands. And he said to me at that show, 'Yo, wait till you hear my other band, Fall Out Boy, it's like what you guys are doing, it's pop-punk,' says Rickly. "And I remember, all I held on to at the time was, 'Does Pete think we're a fucking pop-punk band?'"

While Fall Out Boy and My Chemical Romance were getting all the attention on the Warped Tour in 2005, on the side stage was Paramore, from Franklin, Tennessee, fronted by singer Hayley Williams, who was fifteen at the time and was technically the only person in the band signed to Atlantic Records.*

"She fought very hard to not appear to be the focal point. But you couldn't deny that she was the focal point because that's just how talented and incredible she was," Simon says. "She could have been a solo artist, but she fought to be a part of something that was more than just herself. She's a tiny creature, but she is a massive personality and talent."

Williams moved around a lot as a kid, partly as an effort to escape from her deeply religious stepfather, whom she once called a "super Southern Baptist nazi," and turned to music for refuge. She was discovered at the age of fourteen and signed a deal with Atlantic Records, which wanted to make her a Top 40 pop star. But she pushed to be able to front a rock band with her friends, which included the brothers Josh and twelve-year-old Zac Farro, on guitar and drums, respectively. Atlantic acquiesced to Williams's wishes, releasing their debut *All We Know Is Falling* via the indie imprint Fueled by Ramen, home to Fall Out Boy and generally considered by the kids a bit cooler than a traditional major label. (At the time, Williams's commanding voice was the draw; the songs would later catch up.)

Due to a combination of factors including sexism, a major label affiliation for a group of teenagers, and an overall radio-ready shine, there was a great deal of suspicion toward Paramore when they began, remembers Jonah Matranga, who caught them on their initial Warped outing when he was touring with his new band Gratitude.

"They were a little bit of a joke to everyone just because they were on the sponsored stage. A lot of us experienced them as like this heavily packaged-to-be-kind-of-emo thing. I remember watching them, and I loved it," he says. "I think Hayley's fucking amazing, and I've always loved female singers and performers, at least as much as male

---

* Paramore was one of the first bands to sign a 360 deal, which meant that their label got a cut of merchandise and ticket sales in return for greater promotion. This arrangement was criticized as exploitative at the time but became more commonplace as record sales continued to decline.

performers. I can kind of relate to them in a lot of ways. I thought they were rad and all that. But I do remember that the perception was like, 'Who is this kind-of-industry emo band?'"

Paramore would have quite a bit of band member turnover over the years, a condition shared by Taking Back Sunday. (There's just a lot of emotions in play in this scene.) The fraught tensions of male friendships were one of Taking Back Sunday's main lyrical concerns. But the sudden success of *Tell All Your Friends* was a stress test for the friendships at the heart of Taking Back Sunday. Burned out due to nonstop touring, infighting, and a general vibe of young dudes being young dudes, John Nolan and bassist Shaun Cooper left the band in 2003.

"Adam was dating John's sister. And then, as the story went, he cheated on her with, I believe, a friend of mine," says Heisel. "These people are all like twenty years old, right? So that's a huge deal. You just broke the heart of your bandmate's sister. That was the number-one flashpoint for that band detonating."

Taking Back Sunday almost broke up, but Reyes recruited vocalist/guitarist Fred Mascherino and bassist Matt Rubano and released *Where You Want to Be* a year later. The forward momentum kept the band going, though they evolved a bit, opening up the choruses in a bid for crossover success without losing their mess-is-more nature. The lyrics hinted that Adam Lazzara was still working through a breakup more fraught than his usual heartaches. Every fan assumed they knew what was meant by the line "I know you didn't mean it" from "This Photograph Is Proof (I Know You Know)."

Also on that fateful '05 Warped Tour was Motion City Soundtrack, who just released their second album *Commit This to Memory* and scored a hit with "Everything Is Alright." Though Justin Pierre would come to regret his tendency to lean on jokey pop-culture references, the album was ultimately a mature work that found him ruefully recounting coming home drunk to eat breakfast, trying to stay clean, and then bottoming out on "L.G. FUAD" (short for Let's Get Fucked Up And Die). The album earned not-bad-for-this-sort-of-thing qualified raves and is the sort of smart new wave–influenced pop that could have won admiration from doubters if they hadn't preemptively written it off as kid's stuff. But Pierre's struggles with addiction intensified before the making of the album, leading to an intervention.

Gabe Saporta had joined up with the manager Jonathan Daniel. After signing with Columbia Records, Midtown recruited the producer Butch Walker for the album *Forget What You Know*, which Saporta hoped would be received as a mature step forward. The scene felt differently.

The boom was convincing more and more emo and pop-punk bands that if they ever had any dreams of making it, *now* was the time, so they'd better start writing songs and getting their social media game up to snuff, college be damned. Led by singer-bassist Will Pugh, Cartel was a wide-eyed pop-punk group with emo-ish tendencies from the outskirts of Atlanta, Georgia. They specialized in making the type of songs meant to be placed in teen-centric movies wherein the good-hearted but doofy boy realizes he's in love with his best friend. Eventually, they'd sign with California indie The Militia Group for their debut *Chroma*.

With a hustle Lil Jon would admire, Sherwood kept grinding, releasing their debut *Sing, but Keep Going* through the indie label SideCho Records in 2005. Songs like "Lake Tahoe (For My Father)" demonstrated an obvious grasp of songcraft, even if the album was a document of a bunch of young guys who couldn't quite decide what kind of band they wanted to be.

There's likely no one who wanted it more than Max Bemis, who started Say Anything in high school and began writing what became the band's proper debut while attending Sarah Lawrence. After dropping out and a listless period, he signed with Doghouse, because of the Get Up Kids affiliation, recruiting emo standby Tim O'Heir and Stephen Trask* for his grand coming-out.

Bemis began having depressive episodes as a teenager and was later diagnosed with bipolar disorder, which he treated with a massive intake of cannabis. "I had this incident that I'll always remember," he says. "My mom gave me a photo collection of pictures of me when I was a baby. I looked so innocent that even at age like twelve, I was like, 'I've lost

---

* A composer who's had great success with the rock opera *Hedwig and the Angry Inch*.

this. This is gone now.' And I felt the crushing weight of mortality and nostalgia, and I cried. I also have severe OCD, coupled with trauma. I'm a pretty fucked-up guy."

Say Anything's 2004 debut . . . *Is a Real Boy* chronicles his early battles with depression and mania, as well as the intense creative pressure he put himself under to live up to his idols. He commented on and wallowed in the narcissism and posturing he saw growing up in Hollywood and in the music scene. An audacious and hilarious mixture of Broadway pomp, visceral emo, and "did he really just say that?" lyric bombs,* *Real Boy* found him creating an outsize persona of himself as a loquacious, horny, shit-talking over-sharer, and then on songs like "The Futile" he undercuts the bombast to reveal an insecure boy who desperately wants to be loved.

But during the making of the album, his mental health struggles came to a head. He entered a manic period, beginning to think that a mockumentary film idea he had proposed was actually taking place, and that he was secretly being filmed for a documentary no one else could see. He later entered a long depressive episode and was hospitalized in a rehab facility in Texas.

Emo bands had begun to embrace a big-gesture, rock star flash that was previously alien for a genre that thrived in small rooms and shared secrets, as mystique had never really been this scene's stock in trade. Plenty wondered if any of the new guard really were emo, and if the term was being thrown around willy-nilly. While that would certainly prove to be true later, thanks to a series of carpetbaggers writing embarrassingly childish music, these bands all brought an openness and vulnerability to their work that seemed to whisper to the audience that "You might think I'm a big deal, but I'm a mess also. But if I can keep going, so can you." For a generation that was quickly adopting online as a state of being and using the Internet to often live as an entirely different person, a fantastical genre rooted in real, tangible confusion and a messy, all-prevailing ache was a necessary ballast.

---

* On "Admit It!!!" he says, "I worry about how this album will sell/Because I believe it will determine the amount of sex I will have in the future." Most bands don't say the quiet part out loud.

SCOTT HEISEL (*ALTERNATIVE PRESS* EDITOR): That Warped Tour was the first time they had four bands with songs in the *Billboard* Top 20 that summer. It's incredible to think about.

CHRIS CARRABBA (DASHBOARD CONFESSIONAL): [My Chemical Romance] certainly came up in our scene, and maybe they were the last connecting bridge between my class of emo and the next one. I think their ethos, their attitude towards their fans, their sincerity of their lyrics, the song structures, they reveal the nature of emo to me. They do relate to Sunny Day, they do relate to Promise Ring and Texas Is the Reason and so on. I see a strong connection with that band. I think they're probably the best version from my period.

GABE SAPORTA (MIDTOWN/HUMBLE BEGINNINGS/COBRA STAR-SHIP): I remember I gave the Thursday tape to my friend Alex at Eyeball Records. Then Geoff gave Alex My Chem. So if we had a pyramid scheme, multilevel marketing, I'd get a piece of My Chem.

RICKLY: I had met Mikey many times before Gerard. He would always say, "Oh, you're into comics too? You're gonna love my brother G." We both liked really Placebo and shit like that, and he'd be like, "You're supposed to be the singer of this cool hardcore band. You like Placebo?" I fucking love Placebo,* but it was kind of not a super-hip band at the time. He brought him out to a party and, yeah, immediately we got along like a house on fire.

LESLIE SIMON (*ALTERNATIVE PRESS*): I discovered My Chemical Romance through a friend of mine from high school who had met Mikey Way at a bar in Brooklyn, and they had started dating long distance. She was telling me how she met this new guy and he had this band and

---

* A London band at the exact intersection of goth and Britpop. The song "Pure Morning" is still a banger, and Robert Pattinson ripped off singer Brian Molko's look for *The Batman*.

they're coming to Cleveland, you should go see them. So I go to the show, they were openers and they weren't great. Emphasis on the *w-e-r-e-n-t*. But they had a spark and they seemed really hungry, and also, watching them, it felt like their skills just didn't catch up to their vision yet. They were super raw and rough around the edges, but the core of it and the core of some of the songs were just really good.

RICKLY: It was an extremely illuminating experience, because both of them had been pitching to me that they were gonna do a band for a while. At a party they'd pull me aside and grab a guitar with three strings and try to play me a song. I'd be like, "These guys are clueless. What are they playing? There's nothing to this. It's not in tune; it sounds terrible." I thought Gerard was a super talented artist. I wanted to do a comic book with him. But they took me to a practice space and played me their demo. "I don't know, it sounds like a NOFX thing." I just wasn't into it.

SIMON: So after that show, I introduced myself to Mikey to say, "You know, I'm a friend of your new girlfriend." And we just started chatting and he introduced me to Gerard. And it was just friendly. Every time they came to Cleveland, I would go see them, and because I knew them from more than just their music, I knew more about them. I remember when their grandmother Helena was sick, and I remember when she passed. Things like that, which helped build a real connection. I wasn't just looking to use them for the magazine.

RICKLY: It was a practice space and bad equipment, and I couldn't hear Gerard singing, which, to be fair, it's like, you put anybody else singing on My Chemical Romance, it's probably not gonna be that special. It's just a good rock band. It was before Ray* was really letting himself be too ambitious songwriting-wise, so I didn't see, "Oh, this guy's gonna be a guitar legend someday." So I was just kinda, "Yeah, you guys are getting there, your drummer sucks, and this sucks, and you gotta learn how to do this, but you're getting there." I went on tour, and they gave me a CD-R of "Vampires Will Never Hurt You." By the end of that tour, my

* Guitarist Ray Toro.

band was so sick of me playing that song. It started getting in my head: *There's something here. This singer has got a cool voice. He's writing cool, weird lyrics.* So then when I came back, I was like, "All right. I'll work on the record with you."

SIMON: Gerard, he's a very particular person. He likes things a specific way, he is very methodical and organized. And when he was not sober, he was loose. He didn't care as much about the details. It just couldn't keep his attention. Typically, he was not a person who enjoyed small talk and strangers and schmoozing, but he could get there a lot easier when he had the aid of substances. He was always the same person who was always introspective and curious and artistic and interesting. But he was also insecure and unsure of himself. So for all the characteristics that made him an aspirational person, those weren't always seen as strengths.

RICKLY: One of the things that I kept hammering into Gerard during the first record was, "Your visual identity is gonna be more important than your music. You write comic books, you know how important that cover is. It's all about your image. Write yourself like a comic book character, your lyrics, everything. The idea of the band has to be special and big."

FRANK IERO (MY CHEMICAL ROMANCE): I think MySpace was integral to spreading the word about the band. That was the initial jump-off point, but then once people heard the band and heard what we were doing, it started to be this word-of-mouth thing. That's the thing too, every band that put their songs up on MySpace didn't end up doing great career things. So, it didn't happen for everyone.

SIMON: The first time I heard anything from *Three Cheers* was after a show at the Grog Shop. I want to say it was "I'm Not Okay." And Brian Schechter, their manager, handed me this Discman. I remember thinking, *Holy fuck. This is next-level incredible. They didn't just take a few steps forward, they took a running leap and high-jump Olympic javelin.* Just insane. I knew that the record was going to be incredible. In regards to MySpace, I feel like their online persona at the time, much like the visuals that accompanied the first Marc Webb* video for "I'm Not Okay," was very drenched in fandom. It was showing how much they loved pop culture and music and movies and books and all sorts of nerdy things that are not usually deemed cool.

IERO: At a certain point very early on, we did decide that this bubble was needed. That's the fine line with social media, between being accessible but keeping the mystique of being an artist and having your own time to do your thing and not have everyone know every single little thing about you. The MySpace thing was coming to a head and being so prevalent, and bands were doing this thing where they would get up on stage and say, "Hey, there's no difference between us and you guys in the crowd." And yes, I do agree with that, but that faux-y mystique is missing, there's no pageantry anymore if there is no difference. We made a very conscious effort to be like, "Hey it's cool to be there for people, but let's be there for them through our art, and not have to correspond with every little thing and have to show pictures of us grocery shopping."

SIMON: They were just so open with their brand of misfit toys, and then also being the ones who ended up getting the last laugh against all of the more quote-unquote "normal" people. I don't know if that could have been possible without the support and more importantly the access that a site like MySpace gave them, in particular. Because they were able to reach areas of the country that didn't have rock clubs, that didn't have VFW halls, didn't have venues, didn't have record stores. We're talking small towns, Middle America, where you still have a bunch of outsiders, but they can't get out. There's nowhere to go. And MySpace opened up an entire new world of "Insert passion here," where you could be as close to a band without seeing them.

IERO: It got you only so far, and then you had to have the shit to back it up. I think that holds true through many generations. People can smell bullshit. If it's good, it's gonna take off; if it's not, it's gonna die in the

---

* A music video director that went on to direct *500 Days of Summer* and *The Amazing Spider-Man*.

water. But that was the thing, it was accessible, it was easy to find, and once you did, people started talking about it.

SIMON: And there's so many times I would overhear, either in the crowd or at meet and greets, "I drove ten hours," "I drove six hours," "I drove twenty hours." Fans were willing to do whatever it took to experience them live, but you wouldn't have that same level of almost a bloodlust, if they hadn't spent hours and hours and hours of time exploring the world of the band on MySpace, and just going into rabbit hole after rabbit hole. That was also the start of what the scene aesthetic was. It was the flat iron, big hair, the cranberry eyeshadow, the pouty lips, the selfies. Before Instagram, selfies were invented for MySpace. It was people holding their Sidekick as far away from their face as possible and trying to look sad but sexy. And that's still true to this day.

RICKLY: I don't think it's any coincidence that bands like Fall Out Boy blew up in that time period. Where other bands maybe would have been a little slower, a band like Fall Out was just like . . . boom.

SIMON: While I was writing the cover story on My Chem, we did go to Odessa, Texas, the same town that inspired *Friday Night Lights*. They played a venue that had a rodeo in the background. People sat at picnic tables. It was very different from what they were used to playing. But you saw the same kids there. And the only reason that they knew about them was from MySpace and from the Hot Topic that was maybe in a mall forty-five minutes away. That was the cultural epicenter. If you could find a Hot Topic, that was your key to discovering a whole new world outside of your own walls. So those together, MySpace and Hot Topic, really gave a passport to a lot of kids who would have been unreachable and unable to discover all the possibilities without it.

RICKLY: When [Fall Out Boy] signed to Island, the people that were there were like, "You gotta come to this show, welcome them to the label." The next time I saw them was after they had a smash hit, they were headlining Roseland, and I was there with Jay-Z and Beyoncé. We were both on the label and we were all in the balcony together in the label's VIP section. Jay was maybe the president of Island Def Jam. I was talking to him and he was like, "Oh yeah, they're gonna be huge. You know how I can tell?" And he points to Beyoncé, and she was there in this amazing green sequin dress, and she was religiously singing every word of Fall Out Boy's set. She was already fucking famous, she was already Beyoncé. And she fucking knew every word. Every word. That definitely made an impression. "If Beyoncé knows every word on your album, you're gonna be fucking huge."

SIMON: I had heard of [Fall Out Boy] for a while because they were friendly with other bands. I did a phoner with Pete and we got along really well. They were coming to Cleveland on the same day that Kelly Clarkson was coming to Cleveland. I was telling him, "I'm really torn about going to the show." And he's like, "Well, great news. We're doing a matinee show, so it's during the day." "Great, I can go to both you and Kelly Clarkson. That's awesome." And I think he must have said something like, "I want to go to Kelly Clarkson." And I was like, "Really? Do you actually mean that?"

RICKLY: When Thursday got really big off of *Full Collapse*, I almost had . . . it wasn't totally imposter syndrome. I think on some level, there was a part of me that was realistic enough to be like, "What? What the fuck is going on here?" I think just if you were to play "Cross Out the Eyes" next to "Sugar, We're Goin Down," it's pretty obvious which one of them is a hit song.

SIMON: So the day comes and I go to the matinee show for Fall Out Boy. It was overwhelming, just the energy and the theatrics. Because this was when everybody was doing those guitar and bass swings and jumping off of amps, and there was a lot of gymnastics involved. And the crowd was just swirling and dancing and running and jumping, and it just looked like when you put popcorn in a pan and it just starts popping up. That's what it felt like to see them.

HEISEL: I think what it comes down to is Thursday didn't have the songs. They did for me, but not for Joe Schmo programming the radio.

I love Thursday. I think they're a brilliant band, one of the most important bands of my lifetime. But when they did write a song that was good
enough, like "[Signals] over the Air," they wouldn't play it anymore. I
remember seeing them with Thrice, they both signed to Island, they're
opening for Deftones, who were drawing three thousand, four thousand
people a night. Neither one of those bands played their radio singles. I'm
like, "Who are you trying to impress?" You had that tidal shift where these
bands that were coming out of the DIY scene were still concerned with
cred to some degree, whether they meant it or not. And they thought,
*Well, I don't want to be a sellout. I don't want to be the band on MTV,
even though I do want to be the band on MTV, because who doesn't want
to be on MTV? Who doesn't want to have their video on rotation?* And
so they were self-sabotaging their careers.

SIMON: After the show, I went back and I said hi to my friend who
was tour managing, and I go see Pete. We went to Kelly Clarkson. We
talked about the band, and I think we talked a little bit about each other
and he told me about his family. And that's also where he told me the
story about the parking lot and the problems he was having with his on-
and-off girlfriend at the time, which was well documented in a lot of his
songs. He went into a parking lot and was thinking about some drastic
steps. And I was like, "You keep kicking ass and I will keep evangelizing
the band, and hopefully we'll end up together for a cover story at some
point in the near future." They weren't a favorite of the *AP* editors at
the time, mostly because their personal affinities just didn't mesh with
Fall Out Boy's music. But everyone understood, whether you like the
music or not, if a band is resonating with fans and blowing up . . . it's
not something you can really ignore, especially if you're a writer and you
have any semblance of objectivity.

RICKLY: It was weird when every third person in the audience gave
me their demo CD and it sounded like Thursday, and when everybody
looked like Thursday. I walked by Story of the Year, who was playing the
main stage at Warped Tour the first time I ever heard them. My friend
goes, "Yo, they're covering, 'Cross Out the Eyes.' That's weird." And it

wasn't a cover. They had just rewritten "Cross Out the Eyes." It was like, "That band's platinum. Why are they ripping us off? We still haven't gone gold! What's wrong with these guys?" But I didn't know how the music industry worked back then.

HEISEL: Thursday was real, authentic emotion, passion and tragedy. The Used* were a bunch of stoner burnouts from Utah who were cheesy as fuck but also understood the culture they were coming from. So there's still some level of authenticity there, even though there were pains in the ass to deal with. But then bands like Story of the Year were musical carpetbaggers.

SAPORTA: I remember being in the studio uploading things to MySpace. We were in the studio making this record. We weren't on a label. So this is where MySpace comes in. We were updating people that we were in the studio, and we booked two shows. Industry people were coming, and what we did is we put up one of the new songs that we did on MySpace a week before the show. At the Knitting Factory, we were like, "Hey, we're going to play a new song for you guys." It was a song called "Is It Me? Is It True?" So we start playing it, and every kid is singing every fucking word, I remember. In the video, I'm even shocked, like, "What the fuck?" Because this didn't exist then, that you could put a song on the Internet and kids would listen to music on the Internet.

HEISEL: It was crazy to watch that scene explode. And in a way, it was a bummer to watch bands just be completely eclipsed so quickly. In my mind, the epitome of what emo was—in terms of commercial emo— was Vagrant Records from '99 to 2003, and that's like the Get Up Kids, Dashboard. Within like a year, none of that stuff mattered, except for Dashboard. Fueled by Ramen became huge. The scene was so quick to dispose of the building blocks.

---

* An alt-rock group often lumped in with emo, they scored an MTV2 hit in 2002 with "The Taste of Ink." Singer Bert McCracken's attempts to appear intense just seemed goofy, but they could write a hook. McCracken and Way were close friends who even covered Queen's "Under Pressure" for a charity single, but they fell out for undetermined reasons after Way became sober.

MATT PRYOR (THE GET UP KIDS/THE NEW AMSTERDAMS): I think by that point with Get Up Kids breaking up, I think I had just given up on it all completely. When that was all happening, I was just like, "Yeah, it's not for me." But I totally understand why if you were sixteen, this would be the most important thing in the world to you. To be honest, I think My Chem is a really fucking good band. I'm just like, *I'm not gonna put on makeup and a marching band uniform every night. That's just me.*

SIMON: I was never the biggest Jimmy Eat World person, but they always just seemed very well adjusted, and they had their stuff together. They were adults when everybody else was in middle school—figuratively speaking. We used to say at *AP*, "There are the bands you want to listen to, and then there's the bands you want to read about." And there are a lot of bands that people want to listen to that they just don't care what their story is. They just want the song. I think that that also could apply to Get Up Kids. I think that could apply to a couple other bands that were like big brother bands to those who ended up being really popular.

HEISEL: A lot of those bands weren't savvy enough to get on the Internet. It's the same problem that a lot of like old punk bands had, which is like, how do we play the social media game?

MAX BEMIS (SAY ANYTHING/MAXIM MENTAL): I went into high school being like, "I want a girlfriend, and I wanna do art," and I was a really sincere, sweet kid, I think. And then by the end of high school, I was already doing drugs. It was dark in L.A.

SIMON: I always thought of Motion City Soundtrack as a band's band. Justin is such a master of wordplay and storytelling. And the way that he writes and the way that he sings are not easily duplicated or imitated. They come out with the first record, *I Am the Movie*, which is just littered with fanboy and -girl references and nods to musical inspirations. It's just all bangers. Front to back. Then you've got *Commit This to Memory*, which was primed to be their breakthrough record. They had slots on all the right tours. They were friends with all the right bands. But they were five guys from Minneapolis. And I'm not sure that they fit the mold of your typical *Teen People* cover stars at the time. The superficial part of the scene may have held them back from really achieving the massive success that probably could have been sparked by these bigger songs with bigger choruses. I think the band was maybe a bit more cerebral than what the fans were consuming in the scene in such mass quantities.

JUSTIN COURTNEY PIERRE (MOTION CITY SOUNDTRACK): At a certain point, people started saying, "Oh, I have OCD, too" and "Oh, I have anxiety, too." And I was like, "What do you mean *too?*"

JOSHUA CAIN (MOTION CITY SOUNDTRACK): The audience was growing so large and so insane for when we were playing, they would have to bring additional people to catch the crowd services up. We played Chicago on that tour, they had put us on as the last band of the evening. So we're just like, "Oh frick, we're in Chicago, we're playing after Fall Out Boy, this is not gonna be great." We started playing the set and the place just filled up. The entire Warped Tour came. Then you turned around and the entire staff and all the other bands from Warped Tour were surrounding us on stage.

BEMIS: We signed with Doghouse, but that was after I had to go to college. I just became an empty shell of a person briefly. I had never really gone through the motions in life like that and felt like I was held back, so I dropped out. And I couch-surfed a little bit and eventually moved back in with my parents and just became increasingly weird and alienated. There was some conflict over me leaving college, and then it was just a quest to find my niche, which I felt like I knew what it was. I knew we would be the next Taking Back Sunday or the next Brand New.

PIERRE: There were a lot of moments with the band where it was just super shitty. In the *I Am the Movie* years, I would just do these fucked-up things, and I don't think the other band members realized how bad I was, and it was really bad in 2004. I flew to Brett's house when we were about to record *Commit This to Memory*. We were supposed to be writing, but instead I flew there and Brett made me go to ninety AA meetings in ninety days. This punk rock dude was like, "I don't care if these words don't make sense, and they're stupid, they work for some people so just shut up and do this." I liked that he had a punk rock attitude about AA.

CAIN: We had had plenty of instances prior to any success to know that like, "Hey Justin, you really shouldn't drink." It was basically like the secret life of Justin Pierre at that period of time. So we wouldn't know that he was doing this until we came to pick him up, and he's trying to sober up in his house and he's not coming out to the van. That was an existing thing before the band existed; we were trying to get him out of being that person.

BEMIS: Working on *Real Boy* technically goes all the way back to Sarah Lawrence. I think I wrote it in order, basically, and the first song "Belt" is about wanting to leave college. Feeling like morally I need to do something to change this world, even on a small level. I've always felt that way. There are times where I have to suppress it because it's hard to live with that, and so it's a codependent reality of thinking that you have to save the world.

PIERRE: I was either hell-bent on fucking my life up or like hell-bent on trying to put it together. Somewhere in 2005, I was trying to be sober and then that didn't take. Between 2003 and 2007 were some really up and down years, and I was more focused on, "Oh shit. These people are all telling us things about how our music is affecting them. Whatever I'm doing, I don't really understand, because I'm just writing words based on how I feel. I have to figure out how to keep doing that so that I don't let people down."

BEMIS: I had to go back to L.A. to do the last of the vocals on the album. I smoked the most weed ever. I was like Seth Rogen level. It was just such an emotional time, and that's what sets me off, especially when I'm not on my medicine. I don't even remember what it's like. After two days of not taking my meds now, I'm like, *Oh, give me the meds!* It's bad, it's scary. I felt like myself before puberty and then I stopped feeling like myself for about five years. I was depressed, I was angry, I was up and down. That was probably the apex of me being paranoid that everyone hated me or thought I was like a brat and thought I was a bad person.

SAPORTA: Basically, this Midtown album [*Forget What You Know*] comes out. The scene *hated* it. They wanted another Midtown pop-punk record, and we made kind of this darker record that was more rock. They fucking hated it. So we had no place in this scene.

BEMIS: MySpace in general and social media, it was the advent of that and Napster and LimeWire and torrents that helped our first record . . . *Is a Real Boy*, and helped us become a big band, period. We would have just been a quarter as big, and who knows if a major label would have wanted to sign us if a fan base hadn't just appeared. Because you get on the right tour, and then anyone can get your music, it's not hard to find, no matter what the distribution is, even though at first we were on a smaller label, it just happens organically.

SAPORTA: We did almost a year of touring after the album. Literally, two months after the album came out there was a regime change at Sony and we got totally shelved. Jonathan Daniel* says, "Every band likes to say they got fucked by their label, but you guys really got fucked twice." I was on two major labels that both folded within a year after me signing there. No one paid attention to us there. Our music wasn't fitting with anything. Also, we were getting jaded.

EDDIE REYES (TAKING BACK SUNDAY): Mark left the band too, and I called him up and convinced them to come back, and I sent a message to Fred. He already knew the songs, and then when Mark came back, he goes, "I have another bassist," and that was Matt Rubano. And then that was that chapter of Taking Back Sunday. When those two came on board, we blew up, next-level shit.

JILL NEWMAN (MANAGER FOR TAKING BACK SUNDAY AND MIDTOWN): I was there for all of that, it was awful. I remember trying

---

* Midtown's manager. His firm Crush handled Fall Out Boy and Panic! at the Disco.

to talk to them about changing their mind, spending a lot of time with Adam, helping him decide what he wanted to do. Mark was back and forth at the time. John and Shaun, honestly, and I told them this, I thought it was very brave. A lot of people wouldn't have had the courage to leave. But I also told Adam that John can decide what John can do for himself. He can't decide what you do.

SAPORTA: There was the huge merger of Columbia and Epic. There's a huge change in ownership structure. Everything just came to a screeching halt. No one is trying to break a developing band. They're trying to make sure that they hit their numbers and they're making the most money possible for the company. And that means really juicing up the big artists. So that really fucked us. So we had a release come out with not the level of excitement that we had had when we were getting signed. The label, the whole promotion, the marketing of the record loses steam. And then also the scene fucking hates the record.

NEWMAN: We were booked on *Jimmy Kimmel* and had to drop off—and a couple of radio shows. One of the radio station people was like, "You really fucked me by dropping off my show," and I'm thinking, *Well, I don't fucking have a band so like, who's more fucked, dude?*

NATE AUERBACH (MARKETING MANAGER): Warped Tour was just a no-brainer of a partnership for MySpace, just based on the demographics. We got a tented space, and the idea was every day we would have different artists do meet and greets and acoustic performances in our tent. I took Tom to see our Warped Tour activation at Dodger Stadium, and there was a big line for whoever the band was that was about to do the meet and greet. I walk him into the tent and I start hearing people say, "Is that Tom from MySpace?" and all of a sudden the line shifted to meet him and get his autograph, and more and more people started lining up for Tom.

SAPORTA: When we made a record that was more rock, what happened is the entrenched Midtown audience was different from the audience at the very beginning of our career. So there was a lot of hate on that record. Everyone was like, "What the fuck? What is this?" Our feeling was, "Who cares if no one likes it?" But it did start to wear on us. We would go on tour and didn't have an audience. We're trying to open for different bands, it just wasn't working. You just felt it in the band. There was just not that energy anymore.

WILL PUGH (CARTEL): We all graduated in 2001, 2002. Everything else about our personal lives was centered around the band because you kind of have to sell out to it entirely. Otherwise, you're not going to do anything. I mean, PureVolume was a big thing. I think once MySpace actually kicked up, then all of that just amalgamated into one thing and that helped us consolidate our focus. And nothing was immediate because we had to go home and use whatever crappy Internet we had to do something. A stranger on the Internet giving me some sort of validation, it's a hit of dopamine.

NEWMAN: We were doing those Verizon campaigns. We got a free phone with a phone number, and we would just give it out. Whenever people were bored on a bus ride, they would turn on the phone and it would just ring nonstop and they would talk to fans. That became unintentionally a very good tactic when the labels were all flying out to try to sign them. We'd be at a meal, and they would just put the phone down in the middle of the table and it would not stop ringing.

NATE HENRY (SHERWOOD): We were all on MySpace messaging people. It was literally a twenty-four-hour job. You're young, you're eager, you wanna get on the road. We got influenced by the Warped Tour scene. The big bands were All-American Rejects and I think Fall Out Boy was just kinda becoming a thing. We were looking into this world thinking, *Oh, if we wanna be successful, this is what we have to do.* Our first album had a bit of a Beach Boys–Beatles kind of pop thing going. Looking back on it, if we would have perfected more of *that* sound, I think we would have been different than all those bands in that scene. If we spent all that MySpace time and wrote even better songs, I think when the time came for us to get launched into the mainstream, there would have been better songs to connect to the masses. Maybe we didn't have that talent to write those great songs, but every band thinks they do.

PUGH: Jimmy Eat World, I would say, is probably the one main influence that we all agreed on. Biggest one by far. Not even close.

HENRY: On our off days when we would tour, we would go to malls with headphones and CD players and walk up to kids who look like they went to shows, they had Converse shoes on or they had a band shirt. We'd be like, "Hey, we're in a band from California, do you wanna check out our band?" We would sell anywhere from twenty to fifty CDs within a couple hours, and we would get kicked out of malls all the time because security would get on to us. But that's where I say if we would have written better songs, we wouldn't have to force our mediocre songs onto people.

SAPORTA: What happened to me was twofold. One was that the last tour Midtown did was opening up for Fall Out Boy. Fall Out Boy got signed to Crush after we were signed there, and I remember we didn't like each other at the beginning. I felt like this next generation of bands were just driving down the highway that we paved hand by hand, brick by brick. A lot of artists feel that way. I completely empathize with that, and I understand that. The only problem is if you're going to feel that way, the only one who really suffers is you.

PUGH: In 2004, we really started going on tour. We're booking shows before we have a booking agent. We're sort of talking to these other two bands that are from different parts of the country. We all put each other in our Top Eight, and that just circulates some plays around. Because that was really all it was. How many plays do you have on MySpace? That was like our indicator of success at the time.

SAPORTA: For me, it was inspiring to see kids who were doe-eyed and bushy-tailed. You're excited and everything is new, and it's fun, and you're not judging things. Then you start judging things. You get betrayed, you get skeptical, or you get cynical. Things aren't exactly how you dreamt it would be. And that really wears on a lot of people. And I had to make a conscious decision to not let it destroy my psyche and my outlook on stuff. And honestly, being on that Fall Out Boy tour helped me reconnect to that, because I saw these kids who were four years younger than me—it's not the biggest age difference, but it's a huge age difference, it's a generation of music. It's a totally different generation of kids than I would have seen in high school.

HENRY: So late 2006, someone texted me or called me, and they were like, "Dude, you're on the front page of MySpace," and I logged in and shortly thereafter Tom from MySpace had messaged us. "Hey I see you guys are climbing the unsigned charts on MySpace." We knew they were doing something because obviously we're always on MySpace. We thought it was spam, and then we looked and realized, "No, this is the real Tom." So we started booking some shows through L.A. a couple months later, and then we hung out with Tom and everyone at the label and Tom takes us on this MySpace tour and he was like, "I wanna sign your band." We were just like, "Man, there's nothing like MySpace. Why *wouldn't* we?"

SAPORTA: Bands will play pranks on each other at the last show of the tour. And something happened with Midtown, which is basically, they threw flour on all of us. Two of us in the camp thought it was hilarious, and two of the guys got so pissed off they almost got into a fistfight with Fall Out Boy. That really was, to me, "OK, that's the end. You guys are just not having fun anymore. It can't work. It still needs to be fun. Music can be great, it can be serious, but it still needs to be fun. And it just wasn't fun anymore." There became a schism. And it just didn't really last after that. It was kind of over.

HENRY: Looking back, it was a bad association. It'd be like a band getting signed to Coca-Cola Records. It's just in the band's best interest to keep the corporate part out of it. At the end of the day, people look to bands and arts and music, they want it to sort of be . . . I don't know if *punk rock* is the right word, but they don't like it when it's corporate. But we were young and hungry, and we also didn't wanna tell Tom no, because at that time he had three hundred million friends. So we took the good with the bad, but I think that the bad was we were gonna be lumped in with the MySpace brand from then on out, and when it died, we were gonna go down with it.

6

TOP OF THE WORLD

By 2005, EVERYONE WANTED A PIECE OF MYSPACE. Bands and fans checked in daily, if not hourly. Television networks and movie studios used the site for trailers and sneak peeks. MySpace soon gave rise to what would later be known as the social media influencer, as model Tila Tequila (born Nguyễn Thị Thiên Thanh) and makeup blogger Jeffree Star (Jeffrey Lynn Steininger Jr.) amassed huge followings, with Tequila using it as a springboard for an MTV reality show (*A Shot at Love with Tila Tequila*) and an attempted music career. (Her 2007 single "Stripper Friends" failed to launch, a rare demonstration of the public's good taste).

"There were people who were trying to make a living online like Tila Tequila. She was posting nudes on her website but trying to build a following on Friendster so that people would go to her website. She kept getting kicked off of Friendster, so Tom told her, 'You can join,'" says Bích Ngọc Cao. "'MySpace will not kick you off.' Her profile ended up getting huge on MySpace. Because she was getting so many hits, she decided to release music, which, you know, was awful. There was nothing we could do to keep her off the top of the music charts because she simply had so many fans who liked her pictures."

A few years after his time in the limelight, pictures of Starr surfaced of him posing with pink swastikas on a website called LipstickNazi.com, and journalists like Kat Tenbarge of *Insider* uncovered multiple stories of him engaging in violent and abusive behavior, "including multiple allegations of sexual assault" and attempts to pay off his accusers. After Tequila's star faded, she revealed herself to be a white supremacist and conspiracy monger; at one point her Twitter bio read "Alt-reich queen! Literally Hitler!"

Everyone loved MySpace. But no one wanted a piece of MySpace more than Rupert Murdoch, the world's most conservative man. The Australian-born media mogul's signature product Fox News had become a cable TV behemoth and would later prove to be the reason many Americans stopped talking to their grandparents. The then seventy-four-year-old Murdoch wanted to reach (and to lucratively help advertisers reach) MySpace's young audience, who largely eschewed traditional media such as newspapers and, increasingly, television. (Around this time, Tom Anderson asked the *New York Times*, "Who cares about MTV* anymore?")

Murdoch bought Intermix Media for $649 million,† beating rival Viacom (owner of MTV, CBS, BET, and Showtime) to the punch. Viacom digital executive Jason Hirschhorn had been negotiating with MySpace, but the deal dragged on, leaving an opening for News Corp. "Murdoch only wanted MySpace, but he was not allowed to buy the company on its own," says Ngọc Cao. "Intermix knew that the only thing that was really worth something was MySpace."

As reported by the *Wall Street Journal*, News Corp negotiated the deal directly with Intermix CEO Richard Rosenblatt, who took over the position in 2004, and the site's founders were left "out of the loop until the last minute." To smooth over hurt feelings, Murdoch "immediately sought to mollify the founders with lucrative two-year pay packages of $30 million each, but DeWolfe and Anderson still chafed at the fact that MySpace ad sales were taken over by executives at Fox Interactive Media, according to people familiar with the situation."

By 2005, Fox News and Murdoch were enough of a boogeyman to raise concerns among anyone who paid attention, and fake profiles with names like FUQ RUPERT and EVIL BILLIONAIRE TYRANT! began

---

* Ironically, MySpace was where Michael "The Situation" Sorrentino got his start, before starring in 2009's *Jersey Shore*. This was arguably the last time MTV had a TV show everyone knew about, even if many disdained it.

† MySpace was purchased for $580 million, and the remainder of the purchase was for the rest of Intermix Media.

to proliferate. But by and large, users seemed OK as long as they could still post away. DeWolfe and Anderson stayed on as CEO and president, respectively, with Anderson noting to the New York Times that "we get to keep doing what we're doing, and have more money to do it."

BÍCH NGỌC CAO (MYSPACE MUSIC EDITOR): When they sold, they didn't own as much of the company as everyone thought. They made millions. Not hundreds of millions. I don't think that anybody who has a company that blows up that big and makes millions and not hundreds of millions is happy.

SCOTT HEISEL (*ALTERNATIVE PRESS* EDITOR): In retrospect, it's like, "Boy, you fucked that one up." But there was no massive "we have to leave this website because Rupert Murdoch owns it." I don't think any of us knew what that meant or anything. As long as I can still get my bulletins and my notifications, who cares, right? That was the average teenager's mindset.

NGỌC CAO: The rest of us who had stock options, Murdoch's company paid us out a few dollars per share, which would not have been the case if we had IPO-ed an actual start-up. I really didn't understand that when I was younger. I think when they started, they probably didn't have any real sense it was going to blow up the way that it did until a little while later. I got some stock options, but it didn't make me rich. I was mad at them for that, because if they had had an IPO like Facebook, I would have been a millionaire.

ISAC WALTER (MARKETING DIRECTOR AND EDITOR IN CHIEF, MYSPACE MUSIC): In my head I was thinking, *They're going to close this place down*, because in the late '90s and early 2000s I had started at, I want to say, three companies doing marketing. Literally the day I got hired, they shut down and closed the doors, because they ran out of money. This was at the very end of that dot-com bubble. So when they said they got bought by Fox, I thought, *I'm going to have to go look for another job again*. It was the opposite—they then got a lot more money to push into everything and hire more people. It also turned out to be great for everybody that worked there who had stock options, except for me. I would have gotten them had I been hired a week earlier.

COURTNEY HOLT (MYSPACE MUSIC PRESIDENT): I joke that MySpace was in some ways a virtual world. People like Tila Tequila and The Situation on *Jersey Shore* existed because of MySpace, because they wouldn't have been those people on Facebook. You got to be whoever you wanted. But that led to chaos. I'm not sure Rupert Murdoch knew he was buying into chaos. And that chaos had all of these other implications beyond the investment. You need to make it work. But then it's like, what is it? Is it the next MTV? Is it a place for youth culture? You could say, if Viacom had bought it, it probably would have done better. I don't know if it would have made it work.

NGQC CAO: When we moved to the Santa Monica office, I moved myself directly outside of Tom's office so that I could be close with him. It made me look like I was his assistant, even though he didn't have one. When Richard Rosenblatt and other executives from Intermix would come by and try to schedule a meeting with Tom through me, I would just tell them that I didn't know where he was, because I knew Tom didn't care to talk to executives. So none of those Intermix guys had anything to do with the success of the site.

HOLT: You would have thought that film and TV assets would flow through it, and you build this thing that becomes an amplifier for what all of Fox did. What ended up happening was Chris and Tom just alienated all the executives because there's only so many pictures of you hugging Murdoch and walking in and out of private planes that are going to make people that have been working at Fox for fifteen years happy.

JOSH BROOKS (MARKETING AND PROGRAMMING CHIEF FOR MYSPACE): The first year really was a honeymoon phase, and it was great, because we had access to some real interesting stuff; there was so much knowledge sharing. I think where the machine changes is when you're further into the relationship and then things like quarterly numbers and targets become much more important.

NGOC CAO: It stressed them out. Chris knew that his success would be tied to Tom's success. I don't know all the facts of their deal, of course, but my understanding is that when he renegotiated with Murdoch to stay at MySpace, that their deals were tied together as one—that one would not work there without the other.

Why worry about the iceberg when there's so much entertainment on the *Titanic*'s deck? By 2006, MySpace's musical and cultural dominance was hard to ignore, thanks to the success of Arctic Monkeys, the begrudging British Kings of MySpace, and Lily Allen, the cheerful British Queen of Online.

Before the Arctic Monkeys even released a debut album, their early fans were happy to act as their online emissaries, creating a MySpace page for the Sheffield band and uploading their early demos to message boards and file-sharing services. Their debut single "I Bet You Look Good on the Dancefloor" debuted at number one on the British singles chart, and their 2006 debut *Whatever People Say I Am, That's What I'm Not* became the fastest-selling British debut of all time in January 2006, a multiplatinum success and a symbol of the Internet's power to quickly build an artist's fan base. When Arctic Monkeys returned in 2007 with *Favourite Worst Nightmare*, their publicity team sent journalists a list of questions the band was tired of answering. Turns out that talking about MySpace was one of their worst nightmares.

"I hate to say it, but my favorite artist that I discovered through MySpace is Arctic Monkeys. I was at Interscope and we went and tried to sign them," says Holt. "Jimmy Iovine said, 'They're a rock band, but they write like rappers,' which was an interesting approach. I remember that level of exposure, because that was before they were signed. It was such a moment."

Allen already had a deal, but her label Parlophone was more focused on Coldplay than developing an unknown artist. So she took to MySpace in November 2005, posting singles such as "LDN," a peppy, ska-influenced breakdown of modern life in London. Parlophone had neglected her to the point that, when a reporter called to set up an interview after Allen's songs began attracting attention, no one had heard of her, so the reporter reached out to Allen directly via MySpace. Eventually, the buzz around Allen grew so great that *Alright, Still* debuted at number two on the UK albums chart.

The future music biz impresario Scooter Braun also discovered future pop prince Justin Bieber through MySpace, Alba Cobarrubias insists, even though Braun's official story is that he found him through YouTube.

"Scooter Braun called when Justin Bieber first came out, so I wound up having him at the office, and he did his first livestream interview with me. He brought his mom. And then he was playing basketball with the staff for like two hours, and he put on a MySpace sweater. We couldn't really get him to leave," she says. "He didn't even really know what he was doing there. Scooter Braun, because of his relationship with YouTube, the story has changed. Like Scooter couldn't get a hold of Justin on YouTube, so he found his mom on MySpace. In the documentary, he talks about YouTube, because YouTube sponsored it. But I have an interview with Bieber saying that it was MySpace that helped him get started."

But while MySpace was breaking artists all the time, Anderson's attempts to directly play kingmaker didn't go as smoothly. MySpace Records, which was completely separate from the MySpace Music editorial project Ngọc Cao oversaw, officially launched in 2005, partnering with Universal Music Group and Interscope Records.

For a while, Anderson and the team were having fun scouting new talent by clicking through the unsigned artist charts. In addition to Sherwood and Voegele, MySpace Records signed a few other artists, including the debaucherous L.A. rapper Mickey Avalon and the alt-rock trio Nico Vega, and Jordyn Taylor, a beauty pageant contestant from Riverside, California, with ambitions to be a pop star. She attracted attention for her strummy ballad "Strong," and when she was contacted by MySpace Records, she already had enough of a following that she was immediately upstreamed to Interscope. She recorded hundreds of songs with a variety of producers, but an album was never released. She's now a New York-based realtor.

On the opposite end of the spectrum of MySpace artists, Hollywood Undead dressed like a crew of Batman supervillains and made a gnarly, disreputable take on rap-rock that repelled most of the adults in the room. But underneath the masks were a group of Los Angeles kids who knew the word *no* better than their own name. Led by front man George "Johnny 3 Tears" Ragan, they masked up and began posting songs such as "Young," chronicling the rough, hopeless lives they feared they could never leave behind.

On paper, it seemed like a can't-miss prospect, a gigantic record company and experienced executives teaming up with the largest collection of unsigned talent the world had ever known, all overseen by a true-blue music fanatic. What could go wrong?

NGQC CAO: When I first started going to shows with Tom, he was working a ton and had not been outside his house or the office in ages. We were initially going to just have a good time. This is before I started working there. Later, when I was going to shows, I was scouting bands. Not to try to get them onto MySpace, but trying to figure out who I wanted to feature. There are artists that I featured very early in their careers, like Lily Allen, people that had not actually broken yet. We were on the forefront of showing them to everyone.

NATE HENRY (SHERWOOD): Dude, Tom was super cool. He was a little shy, he was a little reserved. I wanna say that Tom is actually a pretty upstanding guy. I think he's a pretty moral dude. He would debate stuff with us and make sure that we were kinda thinking things through and we had a good vision. But he was a really nice guy, and he didn't come across like corporate or too cool for us or any of that.

WALTER: I wanted to make MySpace as broad as the music collection I had at home. I didn't want it to be something that was too homogenous. Pitchfork, to me, was very snobby indie rock. MySpace, I just wanted to be a record store when you walk in and there's twenty-five million records. You're like, "Oh my god, this is a lot." But I was on Stereogum, and I was an avid reader of Pitchfork and all that shit. Before I worked at that magazine, I worked at a record store for four years, and I was a buyer of music there.

NGQC CAO: The sales team started selling features on MySpace, and they were trying to pass it off like artist features. I was not going to allow that to happen, and I actually fought them, and I won, in that they had to put a sponsored logo on those features. I got into a pretty heated argument with Chris over it, because, obviously, as a CEO he wanted to make money. And I understood where he was coming from, but I was not letting a feature for a major label band that was manufactured and put together be featured in that same way. It was the Pussycat Dolls. I yelled at him. Chris was very level-headed and very cool, and I think he knew that I was very passionate, and he took it fairly well.

NATE AUERBACH (MARKETING MANAGER): With MySpace, every-one knew it was about the culture, like the salespeople were DJs or were music fans.

NGQC CAO: What I want out of the music industry is when people are able to democratize how music is distributed, and more people have access to getting their music out to fans and more people have access to making a living as a musician. I don't necessarily care as much about making superstars.

J SCAVO (GENERAL MANAGER, MYSPACE RECORDS): MySpace at the time had all the music and data any record label would ever want, as far as what's happening early on. MySpace had a finger on the pulse— what was happening, what was hip—and bands were breaking off there. The other part was Tom's interest in music. The site was clearly music focused, and he was a fan at heart. He wanted to sign bands and use the platform to really make the case for being the major spine in record campaigns that were successful. There was a genuine interest from Tom and the MySpace team in music and the ability of the platform to really develop careers out in the real world. "IRL," as they say.

KATE VOEGELE: There's a long history in the entertainment business of people trying to see what they can get away with, with an artist who's unassuming, especially when you're from Ohio. People who prey on young artists, they're just hoping that you're desperate enough to sign whatever sketchy contract they put in front of you. I was really lucky that my parents were super involved. They were definitely not stage parents whatsoever. They were always telling me, "If you want to quit tomorrow, that's totally fine." But definitely there were development deals and deals that felt like they were just going to put me in, for lack of a better term, artist jail.

HOLT: Then they hired J Scavo, who is an excellent A&R guy, and he started to sign real artists. But he was operating a label and thinking Interscope cared.

VOEGELE: There were certain prospective managers who flew to Cleveland to see me play and who I met along the way, and I was very adamant: "I have to be the one writing the songs." I was so rigid about wanting it to really be my vision. But I definitely experienced a lot of people trying to see how much they could kind of puppeteer the situation.

NGỌC CAO: Tom and I didn't always agree on music. He loved Hollywood Undead. I understood why people liked them, but I hated their music. Tom would say, "This band is going to blow up." And I was like, "I don't really care. I just do not like their music."

GEORGE RAGAN (JOHNNY 3 TEARS/HOLLYWOOD UNDEAD): When we started, we didn't want anybody to know who we were, because we'd already been in all these bands. So we wore cheap hockey masks. I love the artwork and the presentation we can make with the masks.

The other part of it is, though, if you're a thirty-year-old and you live in New York, you're going to be like, "Dude, what the fuck is this?" But to a sixteen-year-old in Ohio, I think our anger appealed to a lot of them. And it still does.

LESLIE SIMON (*ALTERNATIVE PRESS*): Hollywood Undead were big for a minute, because they became part of this MySpace mythology of "we don't need traditional record labels. We don't need A&R scouts. MySpace can make and break bands." And the first band that seemed to rise to the top of this crowdsourcing environment was Hollywood Undead. I remember being at *AP* when they came out, and no one understood it. It was very much billed as, "This is emo Slipknot. And no one knows who these guys are, and they wear masks."

RAGAN: We had very tough shit that we had to go through. Suicide was a big one for us. . . . It's weird talking about this. But we all had very troubled backgrounds. I think instead of skirting around it, you have to admit at some point what the reality is inside. We didn't have therapists where I grew up. You're asking to get put in a trunk if you talk about going to a therapist. That was our one outlet. We didn't think anybody was going to give a shit. We've already been told no for ten fucking years. So, we just go, like, "Well, fuck you, too."

NGQC CAO: The thing with Hollywood Undead and some of these other bands was that they took off virally in a way that could not be controlled. They came at a time when there was a particular look that really resonated with kids. They felt a little dangerous. They were making a type of music that was resonating at the time. They were perfect for the screamo era.

RAGAN: It was MySpace proper that wrote us first. We thought it was fake. And then Tom messaged us, saying, "I really like the band. Would you guys like to meet me for dinner?" And I was like, *Get the fuck out of here. We're going to meet Tom for dinner?*

The Warped scene skewed heavily toward young women as it became more popular. But as is often the case, it was rare for these fans to see themselves represented onstage, as radio programmers and many magazine publishers had long upheld the mistaken impression that the appetite for female rock stars is limited, and Heisel admits it was a struggle to get any women besides Williams on the cover of *Alternative Press*. This hasn't changed much in the decade since MySpace's prominence, as a 2018 *Billboard* story found that there were only five songs in that week's Alternative Songs Top 40 featuring female singers. Misogyny is so fucking predictable.

But the success of Paramore and the ease with which MySpace made discovering new talent opened the door, at least a little, and in particular Ngọc Cao remembers hearing a demo from a young Florida teenager named Juliet Simms. "She had a big voice and this really crappy demo. The recording was awful," says Ngọc Cao. "I just felt like she had something, and I gave her a feature to try to see if something would happen. And the next week she was in record label boardrooms playing for people. She was just this little kid I found while looking around the site."

After landing on the MySpace frontpage, Simms signed with Epic Records and formed the emo-pop group Automatic Loveletter in 2005. Epic spent the next three years throwing cold water on Simms's plans, rejecting songs and entire albums that she submitted, pushing for more pop hits, and at one point firing everyone in the band but her. She carried on, playing Warped Tour and releasing EPs until the band's debut *Truth or Dare* came out in 2010.

Sierra Kay Kusterbeck was a high school student at a St. Petersburg magnet school who wanted to be a theater major until she fell in love with the scene, particularly the Philadelphia post-hardcore group Circa Survive.* She discovered the high-energy Port St. Lucie group Versa-Emerge through MySpace and auditioned to be their new singer when the previous dude's parents wouldn't let him tour. Half of the band

---

* Fronted by the singer Anthony Green, who left the band Saosin due to his substance abuse struggles and began looking for a more stable situation, they found an audience of people just a bit too young to catch Thursday and My Chemical Romance when they were breaking.

quit immediately after she joined, leaving her and multi-instrumentalist Blake Harnage as the core of the group. They were quickly signed by Fueled by Ramen, played the Warped Tour, and were even featured in an MTV documentary. Kusterbeck brought to the scene a playful yet determined energy. Given the options, back then she'd rather you just thought of her as one of the guys.

Drummer Jess Bowen served as the musical backbone of the Scottsdale, Arizona, emo-pop group the Summer Set, which recorded a few EPs for The Militia Group before signing with Razor & Tie. They became *Alternative Press* and Warped Tour favorites after the release of their 2009 album *Love Like This*, a collection of eager-to-please pop.

All three of these women would grow up in the music industry and on the road, which likely wouldn't have happened without the MySpace Effect. But looking back, they have mixed feelings about landing what seemed like a dream opportunity at such a young age.

Though they sonically didn't have much in common, the experiences of the women of the Warped Tour weren't dissimilar from those of the younger singer-songwriters who were scooped up via MySpace. By 2007, Voegele had released her debut album *Don't Look Away* through MySpace and Interscope, earning a hit with "Only Fooling Myself," and Colbie Caillat had released *Coco*, scoring a hit with "Bubbly," but generally she was not enjoying herself at all. After years of hustling, Meiko finally had the funds to self-release her self-titled debut in 2007.

———

NGOC CAO: MySpace was so bizarre. There was so much going on; one day I might be tasked with, "Hey, we want to build a video section on the site, can you be the lead on that?" Another day I might be writing Tom's newsletter that went out to tens of millions of people. I would write it in his voice. But throughout it all I was listening to music. People sent me thousands of CDs. I just had stacks and stacks and stacks of CDs that I would listen to. I had this idea that I really wanted to be fair to people and really give them a shot.

JULIET SIMMS (AUTOMATIC LOVELETTER/LILITH CZAR): Growing up in a small town in Florida, it was go to the beach with your friends and drive down the strip and drink, or sit in your room alone for hours on end playing guitar and writing songs. I chose the latter. I dove pretty much headfirst into music at a very young age.

SIERRA KAY (VERSA/VERSAEMERGE): The band I was in, I discovered on MySpace. They were obviously based in Florida, just on the other coast. I actually had them as my MySpace song. And so I put them as my song, and then it wasn't long after that, I saw they posted, what was it, a bulletin or something? They're auditioning for a new singer. And at the time, I'm in high school. I am in a magnet art program that's pretty rigorous, you have to audition three times to get into. And I'm working to be a singer. My goal then was to be in theater, but I'm starting to wane because I started going to shows, and every time I see a show, I'm like, "I want to be on stage. That's exactly what I want to do." So when I saw the opportunity, I was like, "I'm definitely going to audition for this band, even though it isn't quite popular for women to be fronting bands like this." It's almost like a movie, this band's having an audition in town and everybody in town is trying out and everyone thinks they're going to get it, and it's this weird competition.

SIMMS: I was a solo artist. I caught my big break because of MySpace. I was fourteen, fifteen in Florida and spent every single day, at least a couple of hours a day, adding people to my MySpace page, with little song demos that I had up there that I had recorded in Florida. And I essentially got asked to come out to L.A. to showcase some of my music. So I drove with my mom from Florida to California, and we'd play little coffee shops along the way. This indie label decided to sign me, so I went back home, packed up as much as I could, and moved out to L.A. at fifteen, sixteen years old. What I got out of it was this really great EP that I was able to put up on MySpace after the label and I parted ways. I was basically couch surfing for about a year.

JESS BOWEN (THE SUMMER SET): I remember, at this time I hadn't come out yet. I was still dating guys. And so I would—my parents would kill me if they knew this—talk to random guys on MySpace. You just, at the time, assumed that everyone was being honest, because I had my own picture up. You just thought this must be safe. I'm doing this the right way. Everyone should be, right?

SIMMS: The EP of mine that I had done with the indie label was up on my MySpace page. I woke up one morning, and I logged into MySpace. I called my mom, and I was like, "Holy shit, Mom, I don't know what's happening. I have millions of streams all of a sudden. Last night, I only had like a couple thousand," and my mom said, "Honey, look at the front of MySpace." And I went onto the front of MySpace, and I was the featured artist on the front of MySpace. And they kept me up there for two weeks, and the same day I got contacted by every major record label, essentially.

BOWEN: I remember getting into a fight with someone, because she wasn't on my Top Eight anymore. And looking back on this, it's like, "Oh, my god, can you believe that this is stuff that we went through?" From freshman year to senior year, you've got a new friend group, so your Top Eight changes. And I was also in a band, so it was like I had to have the guys in my band in my Top Eight, and that already took up four of the spots. So, there you go. There's half of the Top Eight already taken up.

SIMMS: Once I signed with Epic Records, I decided to go with Allison Hagendorf* as my A&R. She was very much a huge part of the beginning of my career, her and I joining forces and sort of creatively collaborating, we decided to come up with the band Automatic Loveletter. Michelle Branch and Avril Lavigne were the references when I first signed with the indie label. Record labels as a whole, I feel, are bandwagon hoppers. They see what's working, what's sticking. They follow that trend until it's dead in the water. So at the time, when I first signed with Epic Records, one of the biggest female-fronted acts was Paramore. So the head of Epic was like, "We need to put a band together, and that's what's hot right now. Blah blah blah blah blah." I was down. I mean, I grew up playing

---

* A music journalist, record executive, television host, and the head of rock at Spotify.

in bands. It didn't feel like I was sacrificing my integrity at all. So that's how Automatic Loveletter started.

BOWEN: So, Stephen and John Gomez, they're two brothers, we were actually in elementary school. Stephen was like, "We're going to start a band. Do you want to be our drummer? We're going to do Blink-182 and Green Day covers." I was like one of the only drummers in the school. We found Brian, who was our singer, through MySpace.* We had posted a MySpace bulletin, and he happened to be someone that knew about our band through MySpace and through the Arizona local scene. He messaged us, "Hey, I've heard of you guys before. I'd love to come try out." And we just never even questioned that; he was the first person, and we were like, "Yep, you're the guy."

SIMMS: I actually years ago thanked [Bích Ngọc Cao] profusely for opening the door for me. I don't know where I would be if she hadn't decided to go, "I'm going to help this girl out." I was literally living in a closet. I'm not even kidding. I was living in my friend's walk-in closet on a little cot, and she helped me get a bedroom.

BOWEN: We literally got signed to our first record label because of MySpace. But we knew that could happen because we saw it happen with other bands on MySpace. It was like, "Oh, all these bands, what did they do?" They just worked pretty hard to get their music out there and to get their numbers up on their MySpace. Whoever was getting millions of plays, it was like, "Oh, clearly they're going to get signed. They're like the new hot thing, right?"

KAY: I actually missed the audition deadline. They said, "We're done taking audition tapes at this time." But I went and I got a recording last minute, and two days after the deadline I was like, "Can I still submit this?" And they were like, "Yeah, sure. I'm interested to hear." And then

---

* The Summer Set first played in a band called Last Call for Camden and opened for Motion City Soundtrack. When their singer left, they started over with a new name and front man.

I'm working at a hair salon, doing hair in high school. And they're like, "I really would love it if you would come over to my studio and we could talk." And it hit me. I was like, "Did I just fucking make this band?" I was this underdog, sending it in late. "Am I actually being considered?" It went pretty quickly from there.

BOWEN: We made it like office hours. We would get on MySpace from 8 AM to 5 PM, and we'd sit there and just add as many people on MySpace as we could and send them messages or comment on their page and be like, "Hey, thanks for having us. Check out our music." And that's essentially how we ended up getting signed, because we happened to add the head of a record label—it's called The Militia Group and his name is Rory Felton—we just happened to add him, unknowingly. We were all just pressing buttons a million miles an hour, just being like, *add add add add*. He saw our page and listened to the music and saw the pictures and sent us a message within a few days and was like, "Hey, I would love for you guys to come out to Long Beach, California, and meet with us." We were on The Militia Group initially. And then it got acquired by Razor & Tie.

KAY: I may or may not have misled them. Technically, the reason why they needed a new singer is because his parents were like, "We're not going to let you tour." They were all quite young. So they wanted that security of having somebody to go on tour, because they were determined. "We're not going to be some hometown heroes. We want to get signed, we want to hit the road, we want to do this for real." So I wanted to let them know I was committed. My mom was really supportive. She knows that I will do anything to sing in a band. I was so obsessed about it at the time. I said I was seventeen and my birthday was coming up soon. But really, I was sixteen, about to be seventeen. I think two of them quit because I joined. They did not want a female.

BOWEN: We had started the Summer Set officially at the end of me and Stephen's senior year of high school. While we were in college, we were still touring. This is 2007. We would play shows on the weekends. I went to the University of Arizona. I got picked up in a van, at the end of a

Thursday night or something, and then dropped back off on Monday morning after we had just gone on a mini weekend tour, playing shows and having to go to class at like 7:30 AM. It got to the point where it wasn't really manageable anymore. I wish I had completed a full year, but I dropped out in March right before I would have completed my full year in May. But it was because we were getting tour offers, and they just had to put us out on the road.

KAY: I think Blake was like, "I see something else happening. And her voice is interesting." The other guys were like, "No, this is a male-fronted band and screaming," and this and that. And Blake stuck to his guns, and he brought me on board. A guy who had heard about us and wanted to manage us actually flew in and saw my first show ever, which was fucking horrific. The energy was there. The vibe was there. Everything was good, but I couldn't hear myself. I was flat. I was all over the place. I hadn't quite performed with the band like that before. But he just trusted the process of it and believed in us. And then he brought in a booking agent. It didn't take very long. I think we put out our first song, and we'd already had some labels offering. It was odd because I was like, "Oh wow, this is pretty easy, huh?" But it's really an anomaly of a thing to happen.

BOWEN: I remember sitting down with our managers when we first signed, and they asked us what our goal was as a band, and we were all teenagers between seventeen and eighteen years old. So, our goal was to just play Warped Tour. And then, sure enough, the album came out, and that was one of the first tours we did. So, I think it all feels like a whirlwind, because I just thought it would take so much more time. And then when the album came out, it just felt like, "Oh, it's all happening this fast?" We got the offer to play the *Alternative Press* tour, opening for other bands, and then we played Warped Tour in 2010. But it was pretty weird to deal with, because all of a sudden you have all these people that you don't know being so nice to you.

KAY: So when we put out that EP, a lot of labels were approaching. I was in la-la land; I was young. I was excited to play shows. I was on the road, and I just love to sing and write songs. Fueled by Ramen seemed like the best bet. Also, John Janick is personally signing us. He personally signed Paramore and he took really good care of them. And not that we wanted to follow in Paramore's footsteps, but they're like, "Look at the past and what has already gone down. Why wouldn't the same be done for us?"

SIMMS: The major label machine happened. I signed with Epic in 2006. The head of Epic Records changed a year and a half into me being signed with them. Charlie Walk* came in, and he was like, "Actually, we don't want this anymore. We want *this*." So I probably made the writing rounds and wrote over 130 songs. He wanted Katy Perry. It's the references and the comparisons. I mean, it still happens to this day, and it is so fucking annoying. Allison was always very, very pro what the artist wanted and what my vision was. That's why Automatic Loveletter, sure, there was pop influence, but it had rock in it; it had electric guitars. The songwriting stayed true to who I was as an artist and who I was when I was fourteen years old and whining and being emo in my bedroom.

KAY: It did get kind of insane. The moment that we got invited to MTV it was like, *What?* It seemed unstoppable. It really did. But I feel when stuff gets that big, that popular, you have everybody jumping into it, there's a lot of money being poured into it, it's bound to explode. We got the shit end of the stick. We're the perfect example of gaining success in this era where this thing is really popular and then the rug is pulled from under us.

COLBIE CAILLAT: Me and my manager, we flew to New York, and we had meetings with nine different labels. We lugged my guitar all around town and sang my songs for them and then had to narrow it down to which label I wanted to sign with. I signed that winter or early spring, and then I got offered to go on tour with the Goo Goo Dolls and Lifehouse that following summer. So it basically was go-time of finding a band and getting a stage coach, because I didn't know how to perform, and I didn't open my eyes on stage. People wanted me to go on a diet, because I was

---

* A music executive and television personality who once worked at Columbia Records.

a little thick, and I didn't wear makeup and I didn't do my hair. So they brought in a team of people to kinda help me be more marketable. So having a stage coach was actually really helpful. Her name was Nancy. She helped me get out of my shell a little bit and learn ways to move on stage and how to talk to the audience. And so, yeah, it was all just interviews and TV and travel.

NGỌC CAO: Meiko actually asked me if she should sign to MySpace Records, because I left by that time. And I told her no, but she did it anyway.

MEIKO: The real start of it was when I got a song on *Grey's Anatomy*. I didn't have a television at the time. When I knew that it was playing that night, I would just refresh my MySpace page over and over again. And by the end of the night, I'd had a million plays of my song, "Reasons to Love You." And at that moment, I realized that MySpace had a huge impact on the music industry. That changed everything.

VOEGELE: It was pretty wild. When I look back on it, it feels like it was over the span of several years, and then I look at the calendar—I remember, "Oh wait, no, that happened within the course of six months to a year." So it was definitely intense. I went from living in a dorm room to living on a tour bus and in hotels. But I was ready for it. There was definitely this big push that I needed in order to sort of take the jump officially, and signing with MySpace really solidified that for me.

MEIKO: Alexandra Patsavas* found me. It was through The Hotel Café, because there was a woman that was always there. She would always go to see shows and find new artists, and her name was Lynn Grossman, and she had a company that would help people get into film and TV. She was one of the few people in the audience at my show and said afterwards, like, "Oh, that song 'Reasons to Love You,' I really like it. Do you mind

---

* The music supervisor for *The O.C.* and *Grey's Anatomy*, among other shows. Fond of breaking unknown artists, she's the reason why the Scottish band Snow Patrol headlined Madison Square Garden.

if I put it in one of the shows that I'm working on?" I was like, "I don't mind at all."*

CAILLAT: It made it more difficult for me when I did get signed and I did go on tour, because I wasn't prepared in any way for the stage fright and not having the desire to go and be an artist and get signed. I was really shy and uncomfortable. I didn't want to perform; I didn't want to do TV performances. I didn't know how to talk to people in interviews, because I was too quiet.

VOEGELE: I remember one girl blogged about my music career and me being on TV and was talking shit about it. I think that happens to everybody; just the randoms cropping up in the DMs are a fact of life, I think, in this sort of social media era. I had a great group of friends who I'm still very close with in high school, but I was not popular. I wasn't cool. I didn't party. But then something that happened a lot was people from high school who never spoke to me would be like, "Girl, we have got to hang out." You just have to laugh and be like, "OK, that kind of comes with the territory."

CAILLAT: I wish I had the desire years before because, I could have been preparing myself and getting myself ready for that situation. But instead I had to learn already in the spotlight, which was bizarre and terrifying.

VOEGELE: I definitely felt I heard a lot of clichés that I don't know that anyone would have said to a man. In terms of being taken seriously as a songwriter as well, people say, "Well, did you really write these songs by yourself?" I have been pitched so many stupid song ideas and so many stupid titles.

CAILLAT: From that summer for the next two years, I was never home. I was just constantly gone and traveling. I don't think I had fun hardly any of the time, unfortunately. Because I didn't enjoy performing, I didn't

---

* Eventually, every song on her first album would be licensed to a TV show. Her hometown took out a billboard to congratulate her.

know how to perform. I remember almost canceling every show right beforehand, because I was on the side stage crying, because I didn't wanna go out there.

MEIKO: I'd gotten the number-one spot on a chart that MySpace would do of unsigned artists. That brought a lot of interest, which was pretty damn cool. I independently released my record in 2007, and I think I sold like forty thousand copies or something before I had a record label. So there was a lot of different labels interested, and I went with MySpace, because I just thought it was a no-brainer. They had such a huge reach to everybody.

CAILLAT: It sounds so bad to complain, but it wasn't anything I set out to want. My childhood dog died when I was traveling, so I didn't get to say goodbye. I felt all this pressure: "Don't be a baby, you're gonna let so many people down because you're uncomfortable with this."

MEIKO: I was recording with the two sound guys from The Hotel Café, and I had no money, and so I was paying people in whiskey. A lot of people say, "Why can't you make music like your first record?" or "Why does your stuff sound different?" It was because I was hungry and drinking a lot and just being up for being creative with lots of people. And it was a party time, and it was such a nutty experience of recording.

VOEGELE: I had been upstreamed to Interscope at the beginning of 2008. It was kind of bittersweet, because obviously that was my goal when I signed with MySpace, to sell so many records that they upstreamed me to Interscope, and we hit it with flying colors. And it was great that we all made that happen together, but I really didn't get to work with anybody from the MySpace team at all after I was upstreamed to Interscope. It was not the same as working with these people who were running an indie label that had more heart and more enthusiasm for music than any company I've ever worked with since. At the end of the day, it's sort of like your favorite mom-and-pop coffee shop versus Starbucks. And both have their great qualities. But I was kind of a Starbucks gal then, and I had to kind of go with it.

MEIKO: Tom would come to my shows. And he was always just so nice, and I was always like, "That's Tom! I see that guy's face every day!" So I was like, "Hey, can you put me in your Top Eight?" And then he did, and I felt like I'd won the lottery.

CAILLAT: I would try to be like, "You know, this is too much, I need to tone it down a little bit," and then everyone would tell me, "You can't, this is your first album, you have to do all the promo, you have to go to all the radio visits, you have to do all the shows," and "After this it'll get easier and you can do less stuff." So I kept getting told, "You gotta tough it out so that your album is a success." I always felt guilty that they wanted it, and I didn't want it, and I had it. I always wished that I could have given it to someone who would have enjoyed it more.

Voegele was upstreamed to Interscope for her second album, *A Fine Mess*, for which she worked with Fiona Apple producer Mike Elizondo. It was a just-grown-up-enough effort, scoring hits with "99 Times" and "Manhattan from the Sky," which would have worked well in the sort of romantic comedies Hollywood would soon stop making.

While the industry was crumbling, Voegele scored a recurring role on the CW drama *One Tree Hill*, on which she would often perform her latest singles. Though the transition to a bigger label in the time of crisis was an uncomfortable one, as Interscope had acquired the rights to *American Idol* and basically began giving up on organically nurturing an artist's career over a period of time. Voegele would later sign with the indie label ATO for the stripped-down 2011 album *Gravity Happens* and would self-release *Canyonlands* in 2016.

Meiko went through an endless series of delays while trying to work on her follow-up *The Bright Side*, eventually leaving the label after Interscope declined to pick up her contract and signing with the

indie Fantasy Records/Concord Records in 2011. She's been independent since the release of her 2016 album *Moving Day*. Caillat would
release a series of albums, including 2009's *Breakthrough* and 2011's
All of You, though the playful spirit that captured MySpace fans' attention with "Bubbly" was often subsumed underneath mounds of slick
adult contemporary production, and it took her many years to feel
comfortable in the studio, on stage, or in the industry as a whole. In
2016, she self-released the easygoing *The Malibu Sessions* and finally
started to have fun.

CAILLAT: I didn't know how to handle it, and then it wasn't until the
past couple of years that I actually really learned to love being on stage
and love touring and performing. If I had found those tools when I was
younger, I could have enjoyed it so much more. But I wasn't the right
personality type to just instantly enjoy it.

VOEGELE: With Interscope, ultimately, we put out two albums. At the
end of 2010, they acquired *American Idol*. I think that became their entire
focus. I was able to just get out of the deal relatively easily. It was like,
"OK, all of our resources are going into *American Idol* now, and everything we're doing is basically trying to create a splash with the people
from that show." I felt like I was steadily building something great, but
it was not a flash-in-the-pan, super-gimmicky type thing. I was lucky. I
was able to just get out of the deal relatively easily.

MEIKO: There's so many positives about that experience, and I'm not
trying to be Negative Nellie right now, but the one bummer about it is
I had such a large following of people. I can't even tell you how many
people. Millions of fans. And then when it started kind of fizzling out,
there was no way to just pick those people up and move them onto
Instagram or Spotify or anything. It was just like, I hope they find me.
It was like being lost in the woods, just trying to figure out, like, the
next—the next shelter.

CAILLAT: A lot of times I would say, "Why am I still doing this?" I honestly think the reason why I was is because so many people had helped me get there, and I didn't want to let anyone down. My manager put in so much time, and my parents wouldn't have been upset if I didn't want to do it at all. My label took a chance on me, and my band and crew had a job, they were out there touring and traveling because of me. Now I'm working on a new project with a group of people, actually. I'm not a solo artist this time around, and it just feels really nice to have no pressures and just start to enjoy it again, because it really did turn into a business only, for a really long time.

MEIKO: I remember finding out that MySpace was dismantling, and I really wasn't sure what was going to happen. I'd hoped to be upstreamed to Interscope, but that didn't happen. I was just an independent artist again. I was working very hard to keep in communication with people and use the social networking aspect as a job. It inspired me to just figure out how to keep it going.

VOEGELE: Essentially labels needed to start looking for things that look like guarantees. But there was no "let's develop this artist's career so that they're touring when they're sixty-five and making millions of dollars for us." That was what I had hoped for in a major label, but it just isn't really who the major labels seemed to be anymore. I think that the era of music that I grew up in is over. I think I got in right at the tail end.

––––––––––

After completing rehab, Say Anything signed with J Records, an imprint of RCA, and rereleased . . . Is a Real Boy with a bonus disc of material. The band had begun fielding major label offers for a while, but the sudden mainstream attention was a bit disorienting for Max Bemis, as was rubbing shoulders with bands he idolized.

"I didn't have a drug problem. Codependency is way worse for me than drinking, for instance, and I was in NA [Narcotics Anonymous] and even Love Addiction," says Bemis. "I basically learned, 'This is all about taking my pills.' Because my ideas are pretty out there . . . especially given that I have the propensity to hallucinate without seeing weird stuff. So I came out of it, and then we became a normal band. We started to tour; we just went right into the cycle as if nothing happened."

After some tours and working MySpace and PureVolume hard, Cartel signed with the California indie label The Militia Group. After main songwriter Andy Lee quit, Will Pugh panicked and then got to work, helming 2005's *Chroma*, a peppy, purehearted, and eager-to-please effort that would eventually land them on the mammoth 2005 Warped Tour. The album got them upstreamed to Epic Records and even landed a Top 20 pop hit and *Total Request Live* appearance with "Honestly."

While Geoff Rickly watched his friends in Fall Out Boy and My Chemical Romance conquer the world, Thursday toured hard, playing the prestigious Coachella music festival in 2004, and Rickly was especially excited that one of his favorite bands, the Cure, was the headliner that year. But the relentless pace his band had been on for years took a toll on his voice and health, and he was prescribed Nexium, as doctors assumed he had stomach problems. He turned out to be allergic to the medication.

"I was losing my voice and I couldn't catch my breath and I was coughing up blood," he remembers. "We cut the song short and the medics took me to a tent, and I remember listening to the Cure from the tent. The Cure, growing up, were one of my favorite bands, so that was a pretty depressing moment. It's supposed to be 'We're opening for the fucking Cure, like, holy shit.' Instead, you're in a tent, feeling like you blew it."

———————

MAX BEMIS (SAY ANYTHING/MAXIM MENTAL): We have a really weird age dynamic with a lot of the bands that are seen as our peers. We were there for the exact point where it changed over into the Fall Out Boy era. So even a band like My Chemical Romance were older than us. I remember we played Skate and Surf Festival, it was our first big festival ever, and my booking agent was like, "This is the stage where one year it was Taking Back Sunday, and then they blew up, and now it's you." And I'm like . . . "Aaaaah!"

GEOFF RICKLY (THURSDAY): My Chemical Romance took six months to surpass everything we had done. We had kinda stalled out, six months after *War All the Time* came out. The tone sort of shifted; it was pretty easy to read the writing on the wall right away. But there was just so much going on at the time. I was having health problems; I was losing my voice all the time. The band was sort of fighting. I got married. It was really hard to pinpoint one way or the other what the thing was.

WILL PUGH (CARTEL): It was kind of a daunting first year. So when we lost Andy, that was kind of like, "All right, well, somebody's got to step up to the plate." When you're in it, when you're young, everything's life or death. I was in a major writing period between January and April of '05 before we ultimately went in and recorded, starting in the end of April or May, for *Chroma*. Those four months pretty much made or broke the band. We just didn't have a choice. It was either that or quit when we just got signed.

RICKLY: I had had major psychological damage done, because I had gone on *Conan* not being able to sing. We did "War All the Time" on Thanksgiving. All my friends who were singers, years later, went like, "Yeah, dude, after that, I just never wanted to play on TV, because that was so painful to watch. I could just hear that your voice was gone, and you were trying to hit notes and they were just squeaking out." It was just brutal. And we had been on tour for like three hundred days at that point. It's sort of the most prestigious thing that you could possibly do, and blowing it that bad, it fucks you up.

BEMIS: Another misperception is that the whole first era of the band was really rocky and crazy and turmoil and me going crazy all the time. I was sober, like literally from . . . *Is a Real Boy*, maybe with one mess-up or two, all the way through a tiny period at the last Say Anything record, and I'm sober now. I drank for a time, but it's not a good thing to have in our family.

PUGH: You see other bands: Panic! at the Disco were getting tons of radio play and [so was] Fall Out Boy. And then we were the third band getting radio play at Top 40. If you could cross over the Top 40, then it's like, "Oh boy, there you can really take off."

RICKLY: I certainly think that there were people in the extended Thursday camp that were like, "Look, the reason you're not bigger is because your singer can't sing." And they were all really, very, extremely cool to me about . . . "Well, you're also the reason why people listened to us up to this point, like there's something that you have that people seem to relate to." I think on some level they understood like, "Fuck, we're not gonna get further with him, like this is the ceiling. But also like we did pretty good with him." Nobody was turned to the dark side where they were like, "Yeah, fuck this guy, let's get a real singer."

PUGH: People would just know so much personal information about you. When you barely got any money, and really the only thing you got going for you is the catering tent and Warped Tour, and then somebody's coming up to you, they'd see like pictures of my mom and be like, "Oh, your mom's so cute, she looks just like you," and you're like, "What the hell is going on?"

RICKLY: I think good singers often get in the way of good performances. I think people who are naturally talented don't yearn to connect in the same way. I think not being able to sing and wanting to be able to sing can be really powerful, but there's people who you don't think of as traditionally the best singers who can really fucking sing that I love, like PJ Harvey. We had the same vocal teacher for a while, and he was very clear about like . . . "No, she's a good singer. You don't know what you're doing." The guy who produced *Waiting* and *Full Collapse* and *War All the Time* would always just say, "Look, if you're gonna sing fucking rock 'n' roll, the only thing that matters is believability. I always believe you when you sing." I don't consider it rock 'n' roll, but I get what they're saying. But then they're like, "But you do need to do it again, 'cause that was just too far away from the pitch."

PUGH: "Honestly," that had like, god, I don't know how many millions of plays on MySpace. That was blowing up on top of being on tour and doing all this stuff. We felt like it was almost bound to happen, just because of how quickly things were ascending. And, you know, Fall Out Boy had already basically done it. When we got off Warped Tour, the label sent us in to do a MTV interview. So all of that together was where you start to realize that things aren't the way they used to be.

RICKLY: It took me long enough, and I really had to train myself, but now I love the way that I sing. And now I look back at *Full Collapse*, and I'm like, I'm glad I couldn't sing back then, because the charm of it is how innocent it is. Like, the kid doesn't know what he's doing, he's just trying his best. That's a big powerful part of why people like that album.

———————

Halfway through the '00s, MySpace wasn't just a website, or even a music platform. It was a state of being. MySpace Nation was always on, never alone, and ready to share. Everything felt like it was getting dialed up far past ten. Emo was the biggest genre in rock. Hip-hop had achieved new levels of cultural saturation. While indie rockers had long viewed the mainstream with skepticism, they discovered that MySpace and the blogosphere allowed them to make their own little enclave away from the mainstream, one bigger than they could have ever imagined. At least for a little while.

Lil Jon split with TVT Records (which would go bankrupt in 2008) after the release of the single "Snap Yo Fingers." After winning a Grammy for "Yeah!" alongside Usher and Ludacris and getting lovingly parodied by Dave Chappelle on *Chappelle's Show*, he suddenly went from a "famous rap force" to "widely beloved cultural figure."

DeAndre Cortez Way was a high school student who kept uploading music to his MySpace page and YouTube. The video for his single "Crank That (Soulja Boy)" became a viral dance craze in the summer of 2007 (the dance is mostly a lot of flailing your limbs about), leading to the rush release of his critically maligned and awkwardly titled major label debut *Souljaboytellem.com* via Interscope in 2007.

As a show of force, Fall Out Boy recruited Jay-Z for a guest appearance on "Thriller," the opener on their 2007 album *Infinity on High*. Wentz had become the defining rock star of his era and a bit of a tabloid fixture, marrying pop singer Ashlee Simpson, feuding with the Killers' frontman Brandon Flowers, and having his nude photos leaked after his Sidekick was hacked. "He was always famous. Pete was famous in Chicago, then he became famous in the US. He was built for a spotlight." says Simon. "Patrick figured out how to be the best front man, and everyone figured out how to be a star version of themselves. Pete was probably famous in the prenatal wing. He's charisma for days, that guy."

But his rock star life didn't knock Wentz off his hustle. Before his rise to fame, he received a LiveJournal link from a Las Vegas high school group named Panic! at the Disco, a former Blink-182 cover band. He visited their rehearsal space and signed them on the spot, making them the first artist on his Fueled by Ramen imprint label Decaydance Records. Wentz began hyping Panic! at the Disco in interviews, putting the band in the previously unimaginable position of sensing an impending backlash before anyone had heard their music, and they wrote much of their debut album *A Fever You Can't Sweat Out* to head off haters at the pass.

"There's a lot on the record about proving our detractors wrong," guitarist Ryan Ross told MTV News in early 2006, a few months after the debut of *Fever*, "because we had two songs online and people were already making assumptions about what kind of band we were and what our album was going to sound like. And that's what a lot of the album is about. It's directed at all those kids that talk on message boards." On the strength of the Top 10 single "I Write Sins Not Tragedies," which upped the ante of Wentz's LiveJournal style of lyrical maximalism, the band's debut went platinum, and the single's central refrain, "haven't you people ever heard of/closing the goddamn door," become a bit of rallying cry for the kids. (Though the song's repeated use of the word *whore* was ugly then and is ugly now.)

Panic! served as a generational dividing line, winning the hearts of the new guard of MySpace teenagers and baffling anyone old enough to remember when bands didn't start complaining about fame and the media until at *least* the second album. Pitchfork used the album as an occasion to bash the contemporary state of emo ("Where does one begin to describe this steaming pile of garbage?"), while frontman Brendon Urie told the *NME*, "Emo is bullshit! People always try to stereotype us, but we don't fit the emo stereotype."

After Midtown's 2004 *Forget What You Know* didn't hit on the level of his peers, Saporta briefly retired, pursuing an interest in real estate and managing bands such as Armor for Sleep. But in the wildest heel turn of the MySpace Era, Saporta instead decided to form Cobra Starship, a keytar-wielding, proudly goofy synth-pop act that dressed and sounded the way an overly tweaked out MySpace page looked. This is not a slam; it was genuinely his intended artistic goal, one he succeeded at wildly.

This pivot proved to be one hundred percent what some people wanted, as some scene kids got in on the shameless fun while others wondered if they were being punked. After Saporta posted the Gwen Stefani parody "Hollaback Boy" to his MySpace, the song went viral enough for Wentz to sign him to Decaydance Records. Saporta was determined to never be ignored again, and Cobra Starship's first big mainstream moment was their naggingly catchy contribution to the 2006 film/social media fever dream *Snakes On a Plane* titled "Snakes on a Plane (Bring It)." Never one to let you make the joke first, Saporta was wildly self-aware about the whole thing, and the band's 2009 album *Hot Mess* featured a song titled "Pete Wentz Is the Only Reason We're Famous."

The mid-aughts were a weird, heady time, and as a cultural malaise set in further, many sought refuge in distracting nonsense, delivered with maximum panache. And one website was right in the middle of everything.

ROSLYNN ALBA COBARRUBIAS (HEAD OF ARTIST RELATIONS, MYSPACE): Soulja Boy was super fast. They would call him the King of MySpace. And usually those artists found a way of getting to me, because I was that little Asian girl from MySpace. That's how they describe me. If you got locked out of your profile, if you wanted to try to get into your girlfriend's profile, you would be messaging me. I wouldn't say yes to the girlfriend thing, though. Soulja Boy had reached out and said he wanted to do a lot with MySpace. The song blew up and everybody was doing the dance. Me, like college-radio, hip-hop-underground me, would not even listen to a Soulja Boy or Justin Bieber, I'd be like, "They're commercial." But I was able to adapt and change and appreciate them. Any new kid that comes up, there's going to be negative talk.

HEISEL: Panic!'s first big tour was the Honda Civic Tour opening for Fall Out Boy. They were one of five. And every kid in that crowd, five thousand kids, knew every word. That rise happened so fast, to the point where the following spring they were already booked to be the opening act for, I think, the Xbox tour with the Academy Is . . . . They had to be bumped up to main support, and they were given an equal set time as the Academy Is . . . , but they're only getting like a hundred bucks a night, because they were still this opening band, but they were so hot, they had to play them later in the show, otherwise, kids will leave after the first band. And then they just torpedoed their career by doing *Pretty. Odd.* They thought, *Oh, we're artists now*, you know?* And it was wild to watch that fan base collapse in real time. There were still plenty of people who were obsessed with them, and there are some good songs in that record, too. But it was just the perfect example of pride comes before the fall.

LIL JON: Dave Chappelle helped me to reach people that I never would have reached by my music. And he also basically put me in history as

---

* The band's 2008 second album was a hard and awkward pivot from emo pop to psychedelic classic rock, with the band quick to claim influence from the Zombies and the Beach Boys in interviews.

a cultural icon by doing that sketch. [*Chappelle's Show*] was the biggest show on television, and that's one of his most memorable characters, the Lil Jon character. That he would even think about doing a sketch on me like this is crazy, and it blows up.

GABE SAPORTA (MIDTOWN/HUMBLE BEGINNINGS/COBRA STARSHIP): I had a friend named Kelly McCauley, who worked at Diesel, and she was the music person who would hook up all the New York bands with Diesel gear. So she told me after one show, she goes, "Gabe, I go to a lot of shows, I work with a lot of bands, and I'm just telling you, I never see the heads of labels come out to talk to these artists. These people are coming out because they believe in you and they see something special in you. If you just get out of your own way, you could really make something happen." That really resonated with me: *I'm completely sabotaging myself.*

HEISEL: Members started dropping off the band. Ryan Ross quit and started his own band called the Young Veins, who are really cool, kind of like a Beatles-like garage rock band. Ryan Ross wrote everything for that band. And so then they had to start resorting to bringing in songwriters, and that's what happened with John Feldmann,* who helped them rehab their career. Now it's Brendon and whatever songwriter they can find.

SAPORTA: I definitely started going into the deserts and getting into having vision quests, which has been one of the things that has impacted my life. I'm very much an ayahuasca purist.

LIL JON: People would scream "Okay!" at me, one thousand percent. Like, oh my god, shut up. People used to hang out with me and be like, "How are you not sick of that shit?" I just tune it out.

SAPORTA: So, OK, Midtown is done. I kind of have a blueprint of what I want to do next. I want it to just be fun. I want to get out of my own

---

* Front man of the California ska-punk group Goldfinger, as well as a producer and professional songwriter.

way and not be judgmental. I want people to have a good time. I wanted
it to also have elements, from a music perspective, production elements
of something electronic. It was a hundred percent trolling.

But the Emo Boom was so huge at this point that Saporta wasn't the
only (sorta) old-school type to give the major label world another go.
Matranga formed the band Gratitude with his friend Mark Weinberg,
releasing a self-titled collection of heartland rock–influenced punk in 2005.
But hopes for crossover success ended with a destroyed friendship and
threats of a lawsuit.

Saporta's reinvention was more successful, as he used MySpace to
tap into the changing tastes of the kids who loved emo, or anything
that sort of seemed remotely emo, while also totally being into hip-hop,
dance music, or whatever—as long as it was delivered to them in a
package they could understand. Matranga's reinvention was ill-timed,
as he attempted to go for rock radio glory just as the Internet and file
sharing were finally destroying the music industry, starting with . . .
rock radio.

The reputation of Texas Is the Reason as an important emo influence brought the band a new generation of fans. Brannon agreed to
a Texas Is the Reason one-off reunion, as their MySpace page had
attracted legions of fans both old and new.

"We had announced the reunion in the summer of 2006, and we
started a Texas Is the Reason MySpace page. And the first thing I noticed
was just that we got a shit ton of MySpace friends overnight. It was clear
that people were using this platform and it was a type of conversation
with our followers we'd never had before, which had its pros and cons,"
he says.

"We were sort of a reunion band, it was almost like this medium
was made for nostalgia. Here are these pictures of us from fucking
ten years ago, how crazy is it? We would post ticket stubs and flyers
and tour stories, I mean, it's a visual medium, it was perfect for it. So
those are like the pros of it. It really energized our follower base in a

way that kept a sustained interest in the band. . . . The cons were that everyone had an opinion. I went on AlternativePress.com and said that 'I wanted to make it clear that these are the only shows for this foreseeable future.' We definitely got blowback from fans. That sort of hurts. So it's the first time you really get that, because the only time you ever get blowback from your fans is if you see someone after a show and they say, 'You sucked.' That was a little bit of a learning curve."

Meanwhile, Motion City Soundtrack couldn't help but notice that while they had blown up, their friends had blown up much bigger. Sherwood was still hoping to blow up even a little, releasing *A Different Light* through MySpace Records in 2007, filled with crunchy guitars and go-for-broke choruses, particularly on the soaring "Song in My Head." They had the right sound at the moment, and the full weight of MySpace. Surely, Fall Out Boy–level success was all but preordained, one would think at the time. I mean, everyone's getting huge, why not them? You can't say they didn't have the work ethic.

By this point, we had bands that stretched the definition of emo past the breaking point, or that only counted by legacy and association, or that had no qualms about changing their sound to win the favor of emo fans. It was no longer a shared secret, and some of the performers were so self-assured you wondered if they even took the time to let themselves have a good cry.

So what the hell was emo by 2006? Popular. It was really goddamn popular was what emo was. MySpace had somehow made this most awkward of genres into the sound of the times.

————————

HEISEL: With *AP*, I can tell you that every issue we did was our biggest issue ever. The whole scene was on steroids. Radio wanted it. MTV wanted it. Fuse became MySpace: the TV Channel. The industry hadn't completely collapsed yet, and even though file sharing was super, super, super prevalent, teenagers were still motivated to go buy CDs by these bands.

JONAH MATRANGA (FAR/ONELINEDRAWING): I broke up my solo project, because I was like, "People are starting to expect me to be a part of this scene that I had kind of helped to create." But the whole thing I had helped to create or whatever, the point was not having the uniform. So when there started being a uniform again, emotionally speaking, sort of a mopey, "I'm lost in the world" guy . . . it was being much more commodified. I dropped onelinedrawing and started performing under my own name.

SAPORTA: If you listen to the last Midtown record, there's a song called "The Tragedy of the Human Condition." That's just a program thing that I did while we were in the studio. The idea of creating music inside your computer was very novel. So I really wanted to take that approach to making music. I felt like starting off with beats and doing something that could open you up to doing different things than when you're just writing songs on guitar. My goal was to have music that could play at the party and people would dance to it, which is a very different goal from where I started.

MATRANGA: I was touring with a band called Gratitude around the time this is all really going on. Gratitude came out in 2005. So right when I should have just put on the eyeliner and flat-ironed my hair and done the thing, I joined a band that was like this very clean, down-the-middle pop-rock band. That record actually sounds pretty good and it holds up pretty well. But it could have been a much more overtly emo record. Slick, that might sound derogatory, but it's just a different aesthetic. [Atlantic] wanted us to make fucking serious money, and I'm sure that Jimmy Eat World was on their minds, for sure.

SAPORTA: Basically, I did the "Hollaback Boy" thing, and I put it on MySpace, and I called it Cobra Starship. I was friends with someone who worked for *Elle* magazine, Sophie Schulte-Hillen. She was really big into supporting underground bands in New York. She got me into Gwen Stefani's fashion show and got me credentials. And I made a video where I went and I talked to Gwen Stefani, and again, I'm like, twenty-three. So I snuck into that show, I'm backstage pretending to be press. I got her on camera and asked her what she thinks about the "Hollaback Boy" song. I'm like, "Have you heard it?" She's like, "Oh, the song? Yeah!" But at the same time, she was like, "Is that you?"

MATRANGA: I was deep into onelinedrawing when Gratitude started around 2003. I was getting a little sick of the emo scene. And my friend Mark was like, "You want to write songs together?" We started writing these songs, and he was really into the idea of "let's get signed." My only rule was like, I'm just not going to do this big dog and pony show to get signed. The band was getting pushed at Atlantic Records, making a video that cost $100,000, records that cost $200,000. And at the same time, the music industry was imploding. So we did like a radio tour where me and Mark went around with guitars and played for different radio stations, and we'd get added to a radio station. Then two weeks after we got added to the alt rock radio station, the whole station would close down and be turned into sports radio or talk radio or something else. The Internet was coming and radio was dying. And so this whole thing, we were watching the infrastructure collapse around us. It was a wild thing in real time to experience.

HENRY: We started kinda writing music that was a little less timeless, a little more of the moment. You listen to it, and you're like, "That's very 2007."

SAPORTA: I wrote that song "Bring It" that summer. It had a completely different chorus, which was interesting, and had a much cooler, more Le Tigre vibe. My manager at the time had put me in touch with these producers who he thought were going to be really cool to work on the stuff. I was still signed to Columbia technically. Columbia didn't want to put out the record.

HENRY: MySpace had so many opportunities that record labels didn't have. They got Slacker Radio to buy us a tour bus. We got sent to Europe like four times. They gave us good recording budgets, like

$50,000 plus to make a record. My only regret is we had a song on our second record called "Song in My Head," and at the time it'd sold like fifty thousand downloads just on iTunes, and for some reason they didn't pull the trigger on radio. I think they thought they were gonna be around a while. So they kind of slow-played us and some other bands. And then Facebook just kinda creeped out of nowhere and just killed it. So that's my only regret, but other than that, man, I almost wanna say they weren't very smart with the money. They would just spend money, and sometimes we were just like, "Man, that's stupid, but we'll take it."

SAPORTA: The opportunity for *Snakes on a Plane* kind of landed on our laps. Because I already had the name Cobra Starship. I had a little bit of hype for this "Hollaback Boy" thing. I had these songs ready to go, and the *Snakes on a Plane* people talked to Crush about helping put together the soundtrack. And basically, Jonathan had this idea of like, "Oh, let's make it a scene all-star thing." All of a sudden I was a part of a new scene.*

JOSHUA CAIN (MOTION CITY SOUNDTRACK): At that time, we're fighting to get on MTV's one to ten spots or whatever. We're still on a little indie label; our friends' bands have moved up to their majors, and they're just blowing up, and we're here going like, "What's not happening? What are we not doing right?" Instead of being like, "Look at how awesome this is."

HENRY: All of our friends, I could tell they didn't wanna hear us talk, because at the time we had a hundred-and-something thousand people that were friends with us on MySpace and we could just tell Tom like, "Hey, can you send a message to all those people?" And he'd be like, "OK, done." That's just insane, insane marketing. Other bands would

---

* The Cobra Starship song "Snakes on a Plane (Bring It)" featured William Beckett of the Academy Is . . . , Travie McCoy of Gym Class Heroes, and Maja Ivarsson of the Sounds, and Wentz cameoed in the video. It's both a parody of a grandiose, dumb theme song for a dumb action flick, as well as a prime example of one.

find out that we were able to do that, and they were like, "You guys suck; we hate you guys." That's why I say if we would have written better songs, I think we would have maybe had a name like Fall Out Boy. Because we had all the pieces in place; I just think the songs weren't as good as theirs were.

7

WARNING SIGNS

As Percy Bysshe Shelley mused in his poem "Ozymandias," empires are awesome, so sit back and enjoy the ride.

By August 2006, MySpace had become a nonstop, worldwide party, with more than 100 million registered users and 230,000 new ones a day joining in on the fun. It regularly had prerelease streams from superstar acts such as Black Eyed Peas, Queens of the Stone Age, and Nine Inch Nails, and in each case the artists had their biggest one-week debuts.

At the start of MySpace, DeWolfe and Anderson took care to protect their baby. They knew that if it felt too corporate, users would flee, so DeWolfe resisted the urge to flood the site with too much advertising. Murdoch was letting them run the website their way at first, and DeWolfe was adamant that they would never charge bands to join the service or post their music. But things were starting to change. News Corp struck a multiyear deal with Google that would make the search engine giant the official search tool for MySpace and would guarantee MySpace and other News Corp websites $900 million in advertising revenue through 2010.

"Intermix sold to Fox for something like $580 million, and then Fox immediately flipped a deal to Google for almost twice that to operate 50 percent of its ad inventory," says Auerbach. "I remember thinking MySpace should have sold for a lot more and Fox was really smart, because they just got their return on investment."

MySpace moved from Santa Monica, just a block away from the beach, to Beverly Hills, and more than doubled its staff. Companies had been reluctant to advertise with MySpace, as they didn't want to be associated with the often racy material users would post to their pages. So MySpace began launching separate verticals (i.e., spin-off websites) such as MySpace Film (launched at the 2006 Sundance Film Festival) and MySpace Comedy, where advertisers could feel comfortable that their products wouldn't be featured near the ambient pantslessness that often defined the MySpace experience. The platform also began charging companies to create and promote product pages, including a page for *X-Men: The Last Stand.*

Suddenly, MySpace couldn't stop launching verticals. It started a classified section to compete with eBay and Craigslist, and also launched MySpace offices across the world. A MySpace News pop culture video show and mobile phone access were in the works, and there was a short-lived video feature that MySpace introduced after temporarily removing YouTube. There were verticals for comedy, books, sports, fashion, and social justice issues, and it even purchased a service where brave users could record themselves singing karaoke tracks and post them to their profile.

MySpace was flexing its strength in any cultural arena it could, even offering a sneak preview of *The Office* before it premiered in 2005. But while it was conquering the wider world, it wasn't taking care of its problems back home.

————————

(Content warning: The following section includes descriptions of suicide, self-harm, and sexual assault.)

MySpace had a policy that no child under the age of fourteen could sign up for an account, but it wasn't rigorously enforced. Parent and teacher groups became concerned when stories began to circulate about high school and middle school students posting pictures of themselves partying or bragging about dubious sexual conquests and alcohol consumption. Parents worried that college admissions officials might see this—and not unfairly.

As Heisel noted, when the Internet first began catching on, the first few micro generations of young people who flocked to it were largely unsupervised by adults, for better and for worse. But while the stories about the darker side of MySpace and social media were often sensationalized by the media, they did bring attention to the long-term repercussions of the Internet's Wild West era, which were often harmful and horrifying. While reasonable supervision might not be the most fun concept imaginable, it's often necessary.

In October of 2006, Missouri teenager Megan Meier hung herself three weeks before her fourteenth birthday. She had been conversing with an older boy via MySpace when he eventually began harassing her. The older boy's account turned out to be fake. It was created by the mother of one of Meier's former friends to attack her as payback for the sort of falling out that most rational parents know is, unfortunately, just part of growing up. The resulting trial against the mother, who was later acquitted, was one of the first national cases about cyberbullying.

Meier is the most famous example of a young person harmed by MySpace's ability to facilitate cyberbullying and other forms of harm and exploitation, but there were untold numbers of others, as it would be a continuing problem throughout the site's existence.

Hope Witsell was a thirteen-year-old middle school student attending Shields Middle School in Ruskin, Florida. Some of the bullying she received was old-fashioned name-calling, as some students were outraged that she had sexted a "picture of her breasts to her boyfriend," according to CNN reporter Randi Kaye. "Another girl from school . . . got her hands on the photo and sent it to students at six different schools in the area." Local bullies created MySpace pages called the "Shields Middle School Burn Book" and a "Hope Hater Page." After Witsell committed suicide by hanging, bullies continued to attack her MySpace page, with her sister noting, "There were people putting comments on there: 'Did Hope really kill herself?' 'I can't believe that whore did that.' Just obscene things that I would never expect from a 12-year-old or a 13-year-old."

In 2008, MySpace was sued for "facilitating communication," according to *Wired* reporter Kevin Poulsen, between fourteen-year-old Kristin Helms, of Orange County, California, and twenty-seven-year-old Kiley

Bowers. Helms reached out to Bowers after finding his personal website, and he persuaded her to create a MySpace account. They "began a
sexual relationship over online chats and webcams." Her parents tried
to prevent the relationship from escalating, taking away her computer
and shutting down her MySpace profile, but she later snuck out of her
home and met Bowers, who had traveled from his home in Dallas, for
sex. After Bowers later broke off their relationship via instant messenger,
Helms hung herself. "In her suicide note she referenced Bowers, the
'man who raped me,'" according to *Wired*.

Bowers was later convicted of child molestation and sentenced to
nine years in a federal prison plus six years of supervised release after
completing his prison term. MySpace was generally shielded from most
lawsuits, under the Communications Decency Act, which protected
Internet companies from lawsuits pertaining to user-submitted content.
But the company did begin using a computer program that detected sex
offenders on its site using a national database.

MySpace's hands-off approach to social media was one of its initial
selling points, but parents grew increasingly concerned about the site
as it grew in popularity, as it seemed that the issue of cyberbullying
and the grooming of children were problems it had no idea how to
begin to tackle, and some schools began to ban students from using
it. In response, MySpace posted guidelines for safe online conduct and
employed teams to scroll through users' pages and delete pornographic
and inappropriate content and fake profiles.

It wasn't enough. At this point, MySpace was moving too fast to
slow down. Instead, it was trying to grow as fast as possible, in hopes
of leaving any bad press in the rearview mirror. But as MySpace got
bigger, it slowly began to buckle under its own weight.

The problems were there from the very beginning, as MySpace had
been built on Microsoft's .NET technology, which was rarely used by
Web 2.0 developers and had led to a weak interface that started to strain
as the site grew. One former executive admitted to Reuters that "it took
literally 10 to 15 times longer to build code on the MySpace system than
it would on any other technical platform." The site crashed for half a
day in the summer of 2006, and the loading speed wasn't what it used

to be. Critics and technology bloggers kept pointing out that the site's underlying code needed a serious upgrade, but there was always a new feature or vertical to work on or a traffic goal to hit. Because so many of the users had customized their pages (often adding Flash players that slowed load time), there was no easy solution at hand that wouldn't break a lot of people's pages, angering users. So the company kicked the can down the street, figuring it could solve the problem some other time.

Employees would later lament that the site was too focused on the wrong things while the problems piled up. But a reliable way to distract yourself from your problems is to go see a show.

In 2006, MySpace launched the Secret Shows program (*who* launched this program is a source of debate), in which A-list artists played a free Secret Show that was only announced via the site a few days beforehand. The program kicked off with the solo debut of Rilo Kiley's Jenny Lewis and her bandmate Blake Sennett at The Hotel Café in Hollywood, and it would soon take place all over the country, with everyone from Lil Wayne to Slayer to Gnarls Barkley. MySpace also launched the Secret Transmission live-in-studio programming, capturing an early Vampire Weekend show right before they broke big, and Isac Walter also started the Hey, Play This! series, in which artists filmed shows wherein the setlist was all audience requests . . . kinda.

BÍCH NGỌC CAO (MYSPACE MUSIC EDITOR): One of the downsides of all of these networks blowing up the way that Facebook did, is it's really hard to moderate and police bad behavior on something that big. When we had something much smaller, we could really set rules on things. Tom and I decided very early on that homophobia was not tolerated on our site. And if people were gay bashing in any way, they would get deleted off the site, and we got death threats for it. He was constantly under threat. We didn't have any sort of corporate structure that was making those rules in the beginning. We just decided we do not allow people to be abusive toward each other. If we had stayed longer as MySpace got big and corporatized, that would have been really hard to do.

NATE AUERBACH (MARKETING MANAGER): People started discovering what everyone could do on social media, the good things and the bad things, and that show [*To Catch a Predator*] was big. Parents heard their kids were getting bullied or in trouble on MySpace. So the police would come [to the office] and be like, "I got another call from some parents, but there's nothing that we could do here. Do you have any T-shirts for my kids?" And so I would give T-shirts to the police for their kids.

ROSLYNN ALBA COBARRUBIAS (HEAD OF ARTIST RELATIONS, MYSPACE): So the child pornography stuff would get reported on Fox News, my mom would call me, like, "What are you working for? What is this site? There's all these child predators?" I think when you have any sort of platform, people are going to do bad with it. I remember trying to explain to my mom that it wasn't bad, but the way that the news made it seem was really bad, like, "Flashy new site MySpace is trapping kids!"

NGOC CAO: MySpace never ran smoothly, OK? It didn't come up in a world in which it could have run smoothly. I think there are a lot of things that made it sort of nonfunctional from the start. It was initially built, I believe, off of Pearl. Then it was built on Cold Fusion, which crashed a ton. Then they moved it to .NET and bought a ton of Microsoft servers. But they never were able to fully stabilize the site. And I think part of it was that the technology wasn't quite there yet to allow us to scale it well.

GIBBY MILLER (MAKEOUTCLUB): MySpace was completely built on .NET, which didn't do it any favors. I dated a coder that worked there, that was the head of the code team in 2006. She would bitch at me about the code. They'd have to update all the servers concurrently whenever they wanted to change anything. They couldn't do it in an agile or nimble way.

NGOC CAO: Also, the things that created huge problems included a lot of hacking. The Flash issue was a really, really big problem. And there was a Christmas when the entire engineering team was offline, when somebody phished a bunch of users on the site. And we're hosting all of everyone's usernames and passwords in a text document on a random website. And in order to get that website taken down, I had to do a trace on the URL, and I ended up accidentally taking down most of the Internet in Brazil, because they were all hosted by the same host that I had shut down in order to shut down that hacking scheme. And so there are all these weird things that were happening because of the vulnerabilities of the site that couldn't be patched.

ISAC WALTER (MARKETING DIRECTOR AND EDITOR IN CHIEF, MYSPACE MUSIC): They launched MySpace Video. At some point I had to call labels and be like, "Yo, we need music videos. Can you upload them?" And at this point, they're like, "Oh yeah, we don't have a CD of the video." And I would have to get DVDs mailed to me, and then I would have to send them to a place to get encoded. And then I would upload the videos myself. Which you can imagine is a daunting job to populate an entire music catalog on the site. And then half the time there were errors and it didn't work, but that's MySpace in a nutshell.

JOSH BROOKS (MARKETING AND PROGRAMMING CHIEF FOR MYSPACE): I think we were probably an inch deep and a mile wide on a lot of stuff. We probably didn't need an Evite product. We probably didn't need karaoke. We probably didn't need a dating-like thing.

SEAN PERCIVAL (VICE PRESIDENT, ONLINE MARKETING): Nobody was going to MySpace to learn about books. I joke that some people are maybe not even literate. But here's a good example: HarperCollins* said, "Hey, we want to do an integrated marketing deal with you. We'll give you half a million dollars or something. Can you build MySpace Books?" So these things kept popping up. And it's another example of like, "Oh, money can be made? Great! Let's distract the engineers. Let's have them build this when they should be more focused on the core." The more venues we had, the more integrated marketing campaigns we could sell. And then we never killed the darlings. We never got rid of them once they were done.

---

* The publisher HarperCollins later teamed up with the site for *MySpace/Our Planet: Change Is Possible*, a book about environmental issues featuring a forward from Anderson.

WALTER: They were so adamant on trying to beat YouTube to the punch. They probably saw, "Hey, there's a lot of people embedding these videos on our site. We should be embedding our own videos. What are we doing?" But that's how business runs.

NGỌC CAO: One of the reasons MySpace sucked so badly during that era is because they forced us to build so much advertising in, that it was obstructing people from actually using the site. The Google deal broke the site.

WALTER: At some point the salespeople are like, "Hey, we have people wanting to put money into events. Do you have anything that they can do?" I was like, "Well, I'll come up with something." So eventually I had conceived of this Secret Shows program. It was a concept that I ripped off from some fucking beer company in the Bay Area where they were like, "Metallica is playing at some club!" It just appealed to the people who, if you want to see the Cure at the Troubadour, you're going to go down and wait in line for twelve hours, you don't give a fuck. You love this band.

AUERBACH: We were breaking artists, we were the biggest thing in music. If an artist did anything with MySpace officially, if they got any promotion on the home page or on the music page, it was amazing for them. And so anyone who was doing marketing, whose job it was to reach fans, MySpace was the most important thing to them. But for the business affairs people, they were terrified, because they didn't know how to monetize it.

ALBA COBARRUBIAS: I noticed new cars in the parking lot, and all of a sudden we had all of these offices, because we were able to take over some of the Fox offices. Now there was pressure to make money. "How do we sell somebody a home page ad?" and "OK, you're going to do this show, but now Coca-Cola has to sponsor. Can we get a Coca-Cola in the artist's hands?"

NGỌC CAO: He couldn't convince them to let him even do one Secret Show. So I sold the idea to Chris. It later became a blockbuster part of the company, and it made him famous. And I did that for him. I booked the very first Secret Show at The Hotel Café, which was Jenny Lewis and Blake Sennett, as they were launching their solo careers off of Rilo Kiley.* That was a really, really special show. It was a magical thing. Kids lined up early in the morning and we gave them wristbands. I actually wrote the names of every kid who went to that show on the back of that poster I have. Isac numbered all the posters, and I have the number-one poster hanging in my house, and I saw those kids at Rilo Kiley and Jenny Lewis shows for years to come.

ALBA COBARRUBIAS: Ice Cube, specifically, his team had reached out. And then Isac would just choose all of these different states, because he wanted them in different areas. So we wound up doing it at a place called The Jewish Mother in Virginia Beach, and that was the first hip-hop Secret Show. And so after he did it, everybody wanted their own hip-hop show after that. And what was different about the hip-hop shows versus the rock shows is that they did it in a way to kind of show off who their Top Eight was. When I did a T.I. show, Rihanna came out. Kanye came out. You were as cool as any friends you could get to come to your MySpace show.

AUERBACH: Tom came to us and said, "Hey, I need help marketing MySpace Instant Messenger. What can we do?" And we had this idea to do an all-requests live stream through MySpace Instant Messenger. So the first one we did is Ben Folds Live from MySpace, where I was literally fielding requests from MySpace. I am sending them to the screen in front of him. And he would play requests and it was a live stream.

WALTER: [Ben Folds] basically just picked the songs he wanted to play anyway, but found somebody who had like, "Oh, play this song because it's a song I got married to." And he was like, "OK, this song's for Jack." At some point we did one with Velvet Revolver. So Scott [Weiland]—and mind you, we're broadcasting it live on MySpace—he's like, "Is this a

---

* Rilo Kiley was one of the most beloved indie bands of the '00s, fronted by former child actress Jenny Lewis. Guitarist and cosongwriter Blake Sennett would also release music as the Elected. The band wound down after the 2007 album *Under the Blacklight*.

joke? Is somebody fucking with me?" I forget what got sent through. It was clear that Scott didn't understand the song request format. There's a lot of times when you set it up through a label and you get there, and it's clear that the dude in the band has no idea what it is they're doing.

ALBA COBARRUBIAS: These kids would line up in the morning and sit there for eight hours until the show started. And Isac loved doing the first come, first serve, and I eventually said, "No, we've got to give them wristbands," so they could kind of go away and come back, because I felt bad. There were certain nights we had people sleep outside, like when we had the Jay-Z show and they're like, "We've never been able to afford a Jay-Z show." People would come and they have a Jay-Z tattoo. Their son is named Jay-Z, but they've never been to a Jay-Z show because it's a fifty-dollar ticket at Madison Square Garden. So, yeah, it was pretty insane.

AUERBACH: I think people just have to get that the culture has to come first, right? It's time and time again. You look at big, cumbersome tech platforms that won't spend a dime to create something until an advertiser has written a check for it. That gives ownership to the advertiser, not to the community. And the rub is that the platform has to be able to figure out how they can justify fiscally investing in what they believe is going to be the best thing for the culture. That will maybe a year down the line be something that can sell to an advertiser for a lot of money. MySpace Secret Shows are a perfect example of it. We built that, we made that the phenomenon that it was, and then everyone wanted a piece of it.

WALTER: I did the Cure at the Troubadour. The band comes out and they give you the expectation that they'll play like forty minutes and don't expect much more. The band starts playing and I'm with one of the girls who works at Interscope at the time, or whatever label they were on, she's like, "Oh my god." And I was like, "What? Is something wrong?" She said "Robert Smith is smiling. That dude never smiles. He e-mails me in all caps every time. I've never seen him smile," and I was like, "I guess he's stoked." And then they played for three and a half hours or something like that and literally did every hit they had. And it was one of the top five greatest shows I've ever seen in my life.

ALBA COBARRUBIAS: I was looking at the charts, and I saw that there was a kid in Toronto that was getting a lot of plays. I looked him up, and he was an actor on *Degrassi*, and it turned out to be Drake. I tried to reach out to do an interview. So I went to the show and then I wound up seeing Drake backstage and I said, "Hey, can I interview you for MySpace, because you use the platform a lot? He's like, "Yeah, I'd love to. I love MySpace." And so I think he didn't really have a manager at the time. And he was laughing the whole time. I still have the interview on my YouTube. It's really shitty, because I told them I wanted to interview Drake, and they're like, "Oh, the kid from *Degrassi*? Like, no way." So I had no budget. I had to hire my friend to shoot it.

WALTER: We set up this show, Serj Tankian's first solo tour after System of a Down. We do this show, and he comes out and he just tells the producer on the floor of the show, "I can't have Acuvue up there, they're owned by fucking Johnson & Johnson. They're a fucking conglomerate and they test on animals," I was like, "Man, I can't believe he found a fucking reason to hate on contact lenses." But hey, no shade on Serj at all. Then Ros would have a show sponsored by Bud Light or something like that. And she would be like, "They want banners on the stage like right next to the band." And I was like, "Yeah, good luck. Like, no band's going to want that." And it's like Method Man and Redman. They're like, "Yo, you want me to do some shoutouts for Bud Light? Where's the camera at?" The real dichotomy between like rock band and a hip-hop artist, is hip-hop is down to fucking promote and do whatever you want to get out there. And you know, bands like Spoon and Phoenix are all temperamental. They have every right to be, but they just don't want to be involved in that shit at all. And watching that go down was just hilarious to me.

NGỌC CAO: During my interview with Chris, before I got to the company, I talked to him about what was happening in Darfur at the time with the genocide and the work that I've been doing as a student activist. One day he came up to me and he said, "Why don't we do something about it?" And so we came up with a series of concerts called Rock for Darfur. I had met a guy named Brian Steidle, who wrote a book called *The Devil Came On Horseback*, who had been working with filmmakers, trying to show the world what was happening in Darfur. So MySpace did an event where Steidle did an auction of his work, and I actually bought one of the photos from that time. Murdoch was in attendance at that event at some fancy-schmancy Beverly Hills mansion. And I saw him at the event, and as I was walking up to him, Chris ran to catch up with me, because I think he thought I was going to punch him or something, because he looked scared as he ran up. But I was polite, because if he was giving money to Darfur, I was not going to insult him then. That's the only time I met Rupert Murdoch.

––––––––––––

Emo had become one of the defining cultural movements of the time, but not everyone was on board. With the exception of *Spin*, almost all the hipper critical publications either ignored the genre completely or treated it with outright disdain.

Pitchfork basically shrugged off the commercial boom of emo, not reviewing albums by My Chemical Romance or Fall Out Boy in their mid-'00s peak. But at the site's start, it panned the Get Up Kids and Jimmy Eat World relentlessly. "It was before they became kind of the taste maker de jure, but everybody shit on us," says Pryor. "But fuck 'em, there were people at the shows, so I didn't care."

While Pitchfork would get criticized (to some extent unfairly) for turning on acts it supported when they got too popular, it stayed consistent in its emo apathy, so at least the site couldn't be accused of being fickle in this regard. "At the very top of Pitchfork editorial, none of us really liked that music. Honestly, we were probably five years too old for it, in some ways. Older than five years, in my case," says Richardson. "I feel like these bands in general, they mean a great deal to you if they catch you at the right time. And it's harder to get into Fall Out Boy for the first time when you're thirty-two, and that's where I was with it.

"Plenty of bands picked up the torch from some of those earlier emo bands of the 2000s," adds Richardson. "And Pitchfork was already on record as not liking that kind of music, and the people that were higher up in Pitchfork editorial definitely did not like that music."

Just as the patriarchy is bad for men, Rockism, which is the idea in critical circles that "authentic" music (which is to say often classic-ish rock music written by white men that makes gestures at profundity) is the only music worthy of critical praise, doesn't just hurt the reputations of genres such as pop, hip-hop, dance music, and so on—it also hurts the vibrancy of rock 'n' roll.

When emo and pop punk are automatically discounted because they are just assumed to be inherently suspect genres, then vibrant, creative, honest, and fun bands are left out of the equation, making rock music as a whole less than what it could be. And it's probably not a coincidence that many of the emo bands that were immediately written off first found a fan base with teenage girls, a demographic whose tastes have been dismissed as inherently less serious since at least the '60s, when crotchety types dismissed the Beatles as a fad and the Monkees as manufactured pop. Now, that's not to say that plenty of these bands weren't bad, but writing off an entire scene by default because of a perception of a fan base is just short-sighted and limiting.

The best bands in this emo boom were as good as any other band earning accolades in the '00s, such as the White Stripes, Yeah Yeah Yeahs, or TV on the Radio. It's understandable for anyone who's not in high school to find some of this music, or its visual presentation (*so* much eyeliner) garish or adolescent, but bands like Fall Out Boy and Taking Back Sunday took youthful turmoil and popcraft seriously, and there's a reason why they connected so deeply with the kids, and why they still spark fond reminiscences about where all the time went.

There was no one more pissed about the ongoing snub than Bemis, who turned the chip on his shoulder into the 2007 double-album *In Defense of the Genre*, in which he set out to prove the validity of his chosen medium while also recounting a toxic relationship he could never escape. The album showed that he was a restlessly creative songwriter who was willing to play around with everything from industrial dance music to scalding hardcore to Tin Pan Alley–influenced classic pop. The album also showed that Bemis needed an editor. But sometimes you've got to overreach to get your point across.

———————

EDDIE REYES (TAKING BACK SUNDAY): Pretty much every other musician in the world hates my genre.

MAX BEMIS (SAY ANYTHING/MAXIM MENTAL): I despised them, and literally I have songs referencing how much I hate Pitchfork directly in the lyrics, and it's 'cause I have resentment, but I knew that it came from insecurity, my own insecurities. They didn't do anything fucking wrong, they were just being Pitchfork.

JOSHUA CAIN (MOTION CITY SOUNDTRACK): We were the reject band in a weird way, until we weren't. But I think the crazy thing is like now, if we do anything, Pitchfork will write something about us.

BEMIS: That's why we had the song "Admit It!!!" and that record was ostensibly making fun of . . . but more so *backing* the MySpace era. People were like, "Yeah, my neighbor has the swoop bangs and he goes to Hot Topic and he thinks he's really cool." I'm like, "No, he might be cool; just 'cause he likes the swoop bangs doesn't mean that he's not cool." Whether it was the right or wrong decision, we very much drew a line in the sand: "We go with the younger generation."

NORMAN BRANNON (TEXAS IS THE REASON): MySpace was part of a youth cultural movement that extended in a few different ways. Obviously, Warped Tour was something that was very symbiotic with MySpace in a lot of ways at that time. But I think there's also, at the root of it, something about the generation that MySpace became sort of synonymous with. I think every musical movement is a reaction to something, and I think that emo, as we know it from the 2000s, was very much a reaction to indie. When I say indie I mean the Strokes, sort of like the Too Cool for School . . . I mean, I hate to pick on the Strokes, but let's just use them as an example. The Strokes very much came in, and what made them cool was that they were effortless. They were very like, "I don't give a shit. I'm just gonna sing in this monotone way." There was no sense of emoting.

SCOTT HEISEL (*ALTERNATIVE PRESS* EDITOR): I have so many feelings about this because as someone who's been waving the flag for emo, for, god, twenty-five years, more than half my life, it was so infuriating to watch any outlet dog the thing that you love the most. Very few of those bands even got press on any level, and then to see someone like Pitchfork, which was a Wild West in terms of online reviews . . . everyone went there and saw them give *Clarity* a 2.4.* That album is fucking flawless!

BRANNON: And emo was sort of a reaction to that. "Hey, there's something that's cool about expressing yourself." And then you have this medium that is essentially an identity machine, it's asking you, in no obscure terms, "Define yourself. Tell me who you are." And so in order for a kid to put together a profile, to choose the right pictures, to post with the right pictures, to pick the right quote that says something about who they are, there needs to be a level of introspection. This was the beginning of sort of the age of identity and sort of understanding who you are and then being able to present that to the masses in a way that is authentic, and in a way that is culturally legible. So the attraction to emo comes from that, because it's basically saying, "I'm gonna put my heart on my sleeve now. I'm gonna show you who I am, and my way is going to be vulnerability." So, if there's a connective tissue between what Texas Is the Reason did and what Dashboard did and what Cartel did, even, I think what that is is the vulnerability part.

---

* For the record, the score was actually 3.5, but still. Pitchfork would later introduce a Sunday Review series where writers would tackle older albums. The writer Brad Nelson later rereviewed *Clarity*, deeming it a classic. It got an 8.6, which still seems low.

GARETH DAVID (LOS CAMPESINOS!): I didn't become aware of Fall Out Boy until "Sugar, We're Goin Down." I was a late adopter of emo. I think I was probably more aware of emo as a subculture than a musical genre. I would see somebody on MySpace. I didn't necessarily know what bands they would listen to as a result of being emo, but I would know that they were emo. Our drummer Jason has always been emo. When we met in February of 2008 for the first time, he was wearing a Fall Out Boy T-shirt and a belt buckle made of a NES controller, which I think is a very emo look.

GEOFF RICKLY (THURSDAY): What's interesting about Pitchfork is they were shitting on us, but if you looked at all the writers' year-end lists, we were on half of them. So, it was like officially the position of the website that we weren't one of the cool bands that they liked. But the writers actually all did like us, and that was the first time that I realized, you know what, they're aware of what their brand is and we don't fit that brand, that's OK. I stopped taking it personally.

DAVID: Instinctively, I would think that me at that time would reject it. But I have a very vivid memory from the time of myself and Neil being in our Student Rock Club Night singing along to "Sugar, We're Goin Down," waving our T-shirts in circles around our heads. It's a great song. And those My Chemical Romance singles from the time are great. Like, if you look at bands these days, there are probably more bands that would cite Fall Out Boy and Los Campesinos! as an influence than would cite Pavement and Los Campesinos! Our influence, I think, is felt in the emo side of things rather than the indie rock side of things.

8

FACE OFF

MYSPACE WAS A WEBSITE FUELED by the distilled essence of teenhood. So it was perhaps inevitable that it would have a hard time growing up.

By the summer of 2008, MySpace had fifty-one billion display ads, more than any other website. When you visited your friend's MySpace, five thousand distinct music videos would start playing simultaneously and you would see advertising for every consumer product in existence, all set against a background that posed the question: "What if hot pink . . . were hotter?"

Seemingly every positive piece of news for MySpace was met by an equally headache-inducing headline. MySpace helped all the 2008 presidential candidates create a MySpace page, complete with a fundraising tool, a demonstration of the site's social leverage. But when you went to visit Barack Obama's page, you were likely to get a message about hot, horny singles in your area who wanted to meet you right away, which wasn't part of the candidate's official platform. Spam messages on MySpace had become as ubiquitous as shirtless selfies, and one particularly egregious pair of spammers, Sanford Wallace and Walter Rines, were fined $230 million in a Los Angeles court, the strongest punishment ever handed out to a spammer in the United States. The pair had sent more than 700,000 messages to MySpace users, posing as their friends and tricking them into visiting gambling and pornographic pages, earning a small fee for every click.

MySpace teamed with the US Department of Defense's Armed Forces Entertainment for Operation MySpace, a live concert for service members that featured performances from Disturbed, Filter, Pussycat Dolls, DJ Z-Trip, and host Carlos Mencia. Certainly a cultural flex and a nice gesture, considering the military had banned soldiers' access to MySpace—supposedly in order to preserve bandwidth. But it didn't distract the news media from focusing on stories of the site's teenaged users being exposed to pornography or being preyed upon by sexual predators. Police in Connecticut reported that at least seven teenage girls may have been sexually assaulted by men they met through MySpace. In response, the state's attorney general investigated whether criminal charges could be brought against the company, which spurred MySpace to identify and remove ninety thousand convicted sex offenders from the site.

But there was no greater headache for MySpace's inner circle than the rise of Facebook. After launching on February 4, 2004, at Harvard University, Facebook gradually started allowing college students in other Boston-area universities to join, before eventually allowing anyone with a .edu address to sign up. After eventually amassing 9.3 million registered users by the fall of 2006, Facebook opened its doors to the public, allowing anyone over the age of thirteen to sign up for an account. It also introduced a newsfeed that let users see the latest activity and updates on their friends' pages; though users initially complained about privacy concerns (certainly not for the last time), it became one of the most popular features on the site, one MySpace would eventually try to copy. At Ngọc Cao's urging, DeWolfe and Fox Interactive Media President Ross Levinsohn met with Facebook cofounder Mark Zuckerberg about buying the company out, though talks never went anywhere. She later tried a different way to fend off the competition.

"I tried to buy Facebook. The first time I logged into Facebook, it wasn't even open to the general public. I figured out that because I have an alumni .edu address from USC, that Facebook wasn't filtering out the alumni part," says Ngọc Cao, who left the company in 2006, taking a job at the AIDS charity (RED). "I looked at their structure. I realized they were built better than our site. And I showed it to Chris and said,

'Let's go buy this thing.' He got a hold of Mark Zuckerberg and went to see him. Obviously, that deal did not go through; he just said that he wasn't interested," she adds. "But I think the world would be a much better place if I had managed to buy Facebook."

Facebook was less chaotic, but also less fun. For the first few years of its existence, Facebook focused more on product development than advertising; it was considered a big deal when, in 2009, the company began experimenting with five banner ads on a page, as opposed to three.

Vehemently anti-customization from the start, Facebook didn't allow users to tweak their profiles, instead offering a clean, arguably sterile, design that felt less adolescent, and thus was more reassuring to advertisers. Zuckerberg recruited outside developers to add products that gave the site an identity, such as the application iLike, which allowed users to play song clips, one of many attempts the social media giant would take to establish itself as a music platform that would quickly fade away, as the site never really put its back into competing with MySpace in that arena.

While MySpace felt like a person who lived and breathed music and had strong, if perhaps a bit overly strident, opinions about what was good and what wasn't, Facebook resembled the kind of (perfectly nice) guy who was happy with whatever was on the radio at the time. When you are a certain type of teenager, music is everything—or at least, it often feels that way. Music fandom can inform the core of your future adult identity, and it helps shape your values and how you see the world, hopefully in a way that nurtures empathy, curiosity, and openness. Maybe it makes you seem a bit much to others, but it can also make you feel vibrantly alive. MySpace was that fandom in Internet form, an easy way to stay engaged, and that's what made it great, for a time.

Facebook was more "adult" in a way that made fandom and your interests feel more tangential to your personhood, now centered around your college plans, relationship status, and other grown-up responsibilities. Perhaps Facebook's ascendance was a sign of an inevitable, if not always welcome, generational maturity, or maybe it was a symbol that some things can't be reduced to a code, such as the emotionally nourishing bond between fan and artist, fan and fan, and everything else that was essentially human about online culture that would fall by the wayside.*

CHUCK INGLISH (COOL KIDS): MySpace was everything until about '08, '09. Then the principal came in the room when Facebook came out. It wasn't as fun.

COURTNEY HOLT (MYSPACE MUSIC PRESIDENT): The day I signed my deal, I remember looking and MySpace was like ninety-two million monthly uniques in the US, and I think Facebook was like forty. It had still not broken through. I think people forget that literally twelve years ago, MySpace was still way bigger than Facebook. Facebook was not a mass market product.

JON PIKUS (SENIOR DIRECTOR OF A&R): MySpace started off simple, clean, and utilitarian. When the customizability features of each person's MySpace page grew, it became more cluttered. You were able to change your background, and that would cause the page to load more slowly. These simple, little things actually turned people off, and people seemed to like the clean interface of Facebook more. It was there that the tide began to turn.

HOLT: The other piece was that Google deal that was done. That was a very, very large ad deal to drive the wealth, it was for Google search and Google AdSense for a billion dollars. That was all about optimizing for clicks. So the goal was to take that money in and generate revenue off of that, as opposed to investing it in the platform. Most technology companies at the stage that MySpace was at would have been investing in scalability, not at the expense of user experience.

---

* In 2016, Zuckerberg built an artificial intelligence–enabled personal assistant named Jarvis to recommend music to him and his wife. Who says you can't buy taste?

SEAN PERCIVAL (VICE PRESIDENT, ONLINE MARKETING): These were Flash-based ads when Flash was a thing. It hails back to some other more scummy stuff they do to get you to engage, because it's moving and it has a little bait of interactivity. And then they send you on this endless loop of surveys. And before you know it, you're just in this rabbit hole of all these things. And they're making money every single time. Once you click the ad, they make some money there. So the click rates were insanely high. And they were shameless.

HOLT: It was just a lot of clicks to do basic tasks. So you had to log in and there were ads on the landing screen, the login screen, and you log in and get taken to another screen. And to really get into the heart of the site, you had to go through like three or four clicks. MySpace was so popular at the time that we would just make you crawl through barbed wires to get on the basic site.

PERCIVAL: There was a guy in L.A. that had a website called Plenty of Fish, which is a dating website. And he had actually proven this, that the uglier the ad is, the better it performs. He would make all these beautiful dating ads. He wouldn't get anything out of it, and then he would open MS Paint and make the ugliest ad you've ever seen and the click through rate would be three times higher. You'll notice the call to action button is usually like a very ugly purple or an ugly orange. I call it baby poo orange. The contrast draws your eyes. And if you can draw the eye, you might get a click.

BÍCH NGỌC CAO (MYSPACE MUSIC EDITOR): I was also kind of a jerk in that I tried to figure out how to get the major labels to sue Facebook for Wirehog, which no one ever used. It was a P2P network built underneath Facebook, where people were pirating tons of music, LimeWire-style. And I just picked up the phone and called major labels and said, "Do you guys know that this is happening?" None of them had any idea. And none of them followed up on it because they couldn't figure out what the fuck I was talking about.

HOLT: Tom kind of ran his own organization inside of MySpace. There was a conference room with him and his team. And they were in there working on the projects they wanted to work on. And there was one point where I pulled out all the headers of all the different sections of MySpace, just to show how chaotic it was. And every single section was its own tech. So when I went from books to comics to music, it almost was like different websites. It wasn't one seamless architecture. It was multiple architectures, depending on who was driving it.

PERCIVAL: The iPhone, it just changed everything. I mean, that was the first phone for the masses that had Wi-Fi. So once that happened and all you had to [do was] sit on the couch, and I know that's what we do all day nowadays. You could load a real website, not a WAP website, which is like this crappier text version of your website.

ROSLYNN ALBA COBARRUBIAS (HEAD OF ARTIST RELATIONS, MYSPACE): They didn't think mobile first. It completely hurt it that the site was built this way, just not being able to adapt to the mobile community, not realizing how much of an impact iPhones would have because we all had BlackBerries and thought that was going to be the last phone. Tom had a Sidekick. Our site wasn't even mobile-responsive.

PERCIVAL: We were so far behind . . . So we had a very crappy news feed and we also had a major spam issue, and the mobile app was centered around the news feed and messaging. So the core of the app [was] two things that were already toxic. If you look at Facebook, they got really smart. The news feed got better every single week, whereas the MySpace news feed was just a dump of toxic garbage.

HOLT: So to do MySpace in support of lots of these different smartphones, meant there were eighty or ninety different specs that had to be architected to support it. So there was a huge amount of technical debt in a pre-cloud-based and a pre-dynamic world. We're sitting on .NET. It was a very tricky architecture to build on. And a lot of the music components had scaled with crap technology. So it was built to scale in one way, but then to adopt it for a more commercial business would require a level of technical investment and support that I thought we were willing to make, that we really weren't.

PERCIVAL: The team was super small, and I remember we had an issue with the iOS app, and we couldn't fix it, because the one person that knew how to fix it was no longer at the company. So there was never attention to it. I think it probably comes back to monetization, because at the time, there wasn't really money to be made in mobile, but there was user growth. Twitter was proving that this is a powerful growth channel. Facebook was starting to evolve mobile as well. And we were already behind. When we finally updated the iOS app, it was probably like six months into when I had been there. And it just felt like it was too little, too late.

NATE AUERBACH (MARKETING MANAGER): I can tell you from a culture perspective and from a business perspective, it was very clear that Fox cared about advertisers, that they made deals with labels without considering what the product could actually do or what the audience actually wanted.

ALBA COBARRUBIAS: And I remember hearing engineers talk about it, they just kept building bad code upon bad code instead of just wiping it clean. There's too much flexibility. It just felt like, OK, your college dorm was MySpace, and then your house is Facebook.

AUERBACH: MTV was losing relevance, so we had this idea: what if, instead of spending all this money all over the place with different studios, we just had a storefront studio? So I spent almost a full year with commercial real estate and with studio engineer partners finding the right place in L.A. And I put together a whole business plan. That was supposed to be the big thing leading up to MySpace Music. It would have been the broadcast and cultural hub of content for MySpace. But no one on the business executive team greenlit it, because it was such a big cost.

NGỌC CAO: At that point I was just finishing up my time there, and I was mostly working from home, partly out of protest.

AUERBACH: It just felt like we were working for a cable company. In the first half of 2006, we were working in Santa Monica. We were getting the company-supported happy hours, we were getting all of these things to bring the company together, and then we got too big to be able to sustain that. They moved us to Maple Drive in Beverly Hills and showed us this plan, how we were going to have locker rooms and a gym and a cafeteria and all that stuff. And then we show up and none of that happens, the cafeteria wasn't really a cafeteria. They brought in to-go food in plastic containers. Some days a week, I think we got fresh sandwiches or something. But I mean, I wasn't complaining, but it's just like, that wasn't really what they promised. You get a discount at the Fox store, and you can get whatever *Simpsons* memorabilia and DVDs you want at a discount price. That was what employee perks were to them.

HOLT: In the interim, everybody looked to Tom for innovation, and then there are all these people that just ignored what he was doing. And I think under Chris, there was sort of like: Tom will do his thing, and everyone else does their thing. And that's why MySpace grew to look like a bunch of individual websites held together in a wacky masthead.

AUERBACH: Meanwhile, we had to compete. It wasn't always about marketing and culture; it was also about competing for the best developers and the best talent in tech. There was no tech scene in L.A. at the time. MySpace consciously wanted to be in L.A., because it was the cultural hub. You had to compete for the developer talent and get those people to move to L.A. But a cable company isn't paying them tech salaries. They're paying them in Fox lot discounts.

Rupert Murdoch wasn't happy. He had predicted, in the fiscal year of 2008, that Fox Interactive Media (the News Corp online division that primarily consisted of MySpace but also Fox Sports Interactive, the gaming hub IGN, photo-sharing site Photobucket, and movie review aggregator Rotten Tomatoes) would generate a billion dollars in revenue. Instead FIM generated a mere $900 million, which was considered such an embarrassment that share prices dropped by 5 percent.

In May 2007, Facebook had 24 million members, roughly a third the size of MySpace's 67 million members. But by April 2008, Facebook had caught up. While MySpace still dominated in the United States (with 72 million monthly unique users to Facebook's 36), both sites had 115 million monthly worldwide visitors. Sensing blood in the water, stories began to circulate, such as *Businessweek*'s "Generation MySpace Is Getting Fed Up," in which users described quitting the site or barely bothering to check their accounts anymore.

Since MySpace's top brass weren't allowed to pause and fix the site, they instead gave it a face-lift. The home page was relaunched in summer of 2008 with a cleaner look to attract more advertisers and to make it easier to navigate. Knowing the company's strong connection to popular culture and music fandom gave it an edge over Facebook (DeWolfe estimated to *Fast Company* that 20 to 30 percent of its "total traffic is music traffic"), fall 2008 saw the official launch of MySpace Music, a long-in-the-works project that would be headed by Holt, who had already worked closely with MySpace when he was at Interscope.

"I signed my deal the day before the economic crash in September of 2008," says Holt. "I signed a deal to go work at one of the largest Internet ad companies at the time, primarily rooted in search. And then it was a mess."

Jim Merlis, a longtime publicist at the music firm Big Hassle, was hired to help with publicity for music events. Also coming on board around this time were Kevin Hershey, a former MTV senior director who handled label relationships with MySpace Music, and Sarah Joyce, a former media relations person for Epic Records, who became senior director of corporate communications. Percival finally got to work at the company he long admired, becoming the vice president of online marketing in 2009, even as it barely resembled the company he once followed feverishly. A feeling of right place, wrong time was beginning to sink in.

Technically a separate company from MySpace and a distinct entity (or, sigh, "vertical") from the MySpace Music homepage that Ngọc Cao developed at the start of the company, the new site would offer streaming, downloads, and editorial features on new and rising artists as well as more established acts. It would also help keep record labels happy.

In 2006, the Universal Music Group had filed a copyright infringement lawsuit against MySpace for allowing users to post videos and songs to their pages. (The suit was later settled.) MySpace Music would allow labels and artists to share in advertising revenue and would hopefully remind users that MySpace was still the place to discover new artists and share your new faves with all your friends.

"MySpace, as a social networking entity, definitely started fading out. But MySpace Music was still persevering and still growing because it was a great music destination," says Walter. "I would even say since then, nothing has filled that space. That was a one-stop shop."

MySpace Music was keeping the lights on, at least in terms of cultural relevance. It had a separate office and continued to publish editorial content, overseen by emo lifer and *Alternative Press* freelancer Trevor Kelley, with some of it written by Brannon. But Brannon couldn't help but notice that Ngọc Cao's mission to give all artists a fair shot and elevate lesser known gems was falling by the wayside, in a way that foreshadowed the future of Internet music coverage in the '10s.

"So I was aware, during my tenure there, that we were losing readership. Facebook was starting to happen. And everyone likes the new shiny thing. So in terms of social networking, MySpace was losing the race. But in terms of music, that's where everything was. So the focus on MySpace Music was huge," says Brannon. "So I think there was this idea that as long as MySpace focused on music, they would win.

"The vibe from editorial for most of my stay at MySpace Music was partially conscious of the numbers and then partially conscious of wanting to break things and wanting to be a real mover in terms of music at that time," he says. "I think MySpace saw that it had power, and what greater way to flex than to be able to say we broke this band. We were always looking at bands. I wrote a fucking two-thousand-word story on Tokyo Police Club. And that was exciting for me, because I love that band, and I wanted to help be part of their story."

While Anderson seemingly had no life beyond his site and music, DeWolfe had become the sort of bold-faced name that tabloids reported might be dating socialite Paris Hilton—the walking embodiment of '00s hot-mess culture dating the man behind the messiest site on the Internet.

———————————

NGỌC CAO: All of those people who came later, really, what were they going to do? The site was not going to do well. And so the brand was tarnished.

KEVIN HERSHEY (DIRECTOR, PARTNER AND LABEL RELATIONS): I worked at MTV in the music department. So walking into MySpace, I was very schooled on the history of MTV, which essentially did the same exact thing that MySpace was doing, which was taking content they didn't own and making money off of it but not paying the creators or the owners of the copyright. In the beginning of MTV, the videos were all considered promotional. So no one ever got paid. It was like, "Here's this new hair metal band, Poison or whatever the fuck, please play it for us so that we can treat it like a commercial and sell all of our physical products and whatnot, and you're going to make a ton of money off of selling advertising." That's essentially what MySpace did in the beginning.

SARAH JOYCE (SENIOR DIRECTOR, CORPORATE COMMUNICA-TIONS): MySpace Music was born out of a lawsuit. So MySpace—being a company where obviously people were using songs and music on their own sites—the labels came after MySpace and were like, "You can't do this, we'll sue you for rights, you're not paying royalties," so what they did is they created MySpace Music, which was essentially this secondary company that was an equal investment from all the major labels, which allowed MySpace to post music, and there would be a split royalty.

HERSHEY: It was interesting, because they were still rugged MySpace. They didn't have to play ball with anybody. They just had this huge, huge platform, and to have people like myself come in, sort of like suits, they were not psyched about that. But conflict has sort of always been part of my job with talent relations; it's about knowing every side and understanding every side and not really choosing sides. It didn't bother me as much as it bothered some people. You can tell me to fuck off a million times. I'm still going to smile and wish you good morning.

JIM MERLIS (PUBLICIST, BIG HASSLE): There was very much a clash of cultures, even within MySpace. The corporate people are very corporate, and the music people were just like real music people. They were awesome people to deal with. God, you knew within a millisecond who they were, just by the way they were dressed. They didn't look like record executives, they looked like fans.

HOLT: At the beginning, it was a situation where MySpace had challenges with the labels. And so they said, "Let's go build this joint venture because we want to take the music assets of MySpace and allow for the labels to share in the revenue, and build a business around it." So when I first got there, the thing that I think was not one hundred percent clear to me was whether MySpace was committed to build a business in music, or whether MySpace was creating a system by which they could ring-fence music in a way that protected the core business, but isolated music to be a subset of that business so they could keep growing, but not necessarily use music as the catalyst for growth.

MERLIS: I will never forget one time they gave me a list of what was going on, like, "Oh, yeah, we're premiering Madonna's album," and I said, "You don't have to do anything on that. I guarantee you people are going to review it off of the MySpace premiere." And that was true. I remember all these papers, like the *Boston Globe*, writing, "I heard this album on MySpace." That sort of passive mention is more effective than a story on MySpace Music—you get more people reading the Madonna review than the corporate stories. And the corporate people were always amazed by how much press we were getting. And I was like, "God, you don't even know how easy this is."

JOYCE: I joined up for Courtney Holt at MySpace Music, and it was a really short run. All of a sudden they were doing the rebrand, and they kind of got confused, and Facebook was catching up. When I first came there, I mean, nothing was bigger than MySpace. They were doing Cure Secret Shows. I think they just ran the business down. MySpace Music was separated, but the identity of MySpace as a whole was so reliant on music.

MERLIS: It's funny, because it was a short period. We were there for eighteen months, and we saw it going from Madonna premiering her album on the platform and all those other bands doing Secret Shows and whatever to sort of becoming nothing fairly quickly.

ISAC WALTER (MARKETING DIRECTOR AND EDITOR IN CHIEF, MYSPACE MUSIC): I got moved over from MySpace to MySpace Music when it started. So nothing changed for me. They were all excited. There's four major labels, and they had gotten three of them, and I was like, "That's great. Did you guys contact any of the indie labels?" And they're like, "What? No." And that was the start of that. I was like, "You guys, this doesn't work unless you're inclusive to everybody. It's going to backfire. Go out and make deals with these labels." And they just ignored me. And then as soon as they launched, they got a bunch of fucking pushback from all these indies and these indie coalitions.

MERLIS: The other thing was that there was a really thriving blog community which doesn't exist anymore. A lot of the bigger bloggers are playlisters now, and that's sad. As a publicist, you could feel the passion from these young kids, and you're getting them tickets to the shows and whatnot. It's helped the ecosystem and the level of engagement from the smaller levels that I think is really the most important thing, the smaller places, that's where music gets recognized. The stuff they get stamped by a big music outlet really early on isn't as valuable as the stuff that's bubbling under and then gets huge.

HOLT: The original impetus for MySpace music was to incentivize the labels to not be on the wrong side of MySpace. So we'll take the music out of MySpace. We'll treat it as a separate company. We'll get a broad structure, we'll get leadership in, and then we'll operate it as a stand-alone music service. And then we'll figure out the associated revenue share, so the labels will see we're participating in the experience with MySpace Music, not participating in the general MySpace experience. But the goal was, let's make a dedicated music experience. But in reality, really what it was was just an architecture to constrain the rights and rules of music and the commercialization of it.

HERSHEY: Everyone had a different rate, and what counted as a stream varied per deal with the different record labels, so Universal proper might make an eighth of a cent of a three-second stream, whereas like Virgin might make a sixteenth off of the tenth of a ten-second stream. So the contracts were different for everybody, which I'm sure still exists in the streaming world to this day. But to me, that never really made sense, because I was sort of saying you're not as worthy as this person. One of the first red flags was when details started to leak from label group to label group. "We're not getting paid as much as they are, why is that happening?" And, you know, it was never done with the best intentions for art, in my opinion.

ALBA COBARRUBIAS: So you get high traffic when you have Rihanna, rather than this underground artist. I think a part of me lost that DJ in me towards the latter years, and it became more of a business, for sure. Because there's only so many slots. So if you think of us like a pop radio station, maybe we could play twenty songs. So if there were six slots and Universal has a big release with Justin Bieber, Warner has a big release with whoever. There's only three other slots. So are they going to take a chance on this smaller artist? Most likely not.

WALTER: After the first six months or a year, I get promoted to marketing director. And there are multiple people that come in above me that are SVP of marketing, and none of them really get super involved with what I'm doing. So I just keep going in my ecosystem, and they look at the numbers, and they're like, "You're doing great. Keep doing what you're doing." And it's not until, I say, like 2009-ish where they start butting in, and they're like, "You should be doing more promotions with Lady

Gaga and Justin Bieber." My response was like, "Everybody does shit with Lady Gaga and Justin Bieber. I would rather do promotional promos with these ten smaller bands that will equal just as much traffic—and are much more diverse."

ALBA COBARRUBIAS: We were asked to incorporate these brands, so that made an impact on the editorial discretion of who we chose. Before we were just choosing the coolest artist. Now we know that they have to be OK for Coca-Cola, and they have to be broad enough for Coca-Cola to say, like, "OK, yeah, we want to sponsor that show." You're getting these huge pop stars. It doesn't necessarily make for a better show. We're just fulfilling the brand's wishes by then.

AUERBACH: I've built my career on this artist-fan relationship, and it's a really precious relationship, and it's important to be authentic in how you cultivate that. You have to give the audience what they want, and you have to create something that maybe the audience doesn't know that they want but that will blow their mind when they get it. Once we started thinking about the advertiser or something, that wasn't the artist-fan relationship, it became very clear. You went to the MySpace music page to discover artists you didn't know about. You didn't go there to see a feature of an artist that you knew about already. But based on our deals with all the labels, we had to feature more mainstream artists.

NORMAN BRANNON (TEXAS IS THE REASON): So I think there was this idea that as long as MySpace focused on music, they would win. But I think the problem came when the buyout happened, and the redesign happened. I think people underestimated how much of a DIY community of music lovers MySpace was, because ultimately, the new MySpace was a lot more like the old media and nobody wanted that. When the changeover happened, I was like . . . "I'm completely not interested. What is this even?" I couldn't really tell what they wanted it to be anymore. And I could tell that was the direction it was going. I think that there was a level of panicking, if I'm being frank.

WALTER: It kept going as an entity for, I would say, probably till 2009. People still wanted to do promotions, but the kids were definitely dropping off. They were going to Facebook to send messages to each other and talk to each other. But on MySpace, they were still going there to listen to music and see who was in whose Top Eight and like, what's going on in entertainment.

BRANNON: MySpace still had a vested interest in breaking new artists. That was a thing. And there was a consciousness that every day, we'd have to write about one super big artist or another. I know there was a list that existed: "These are the artists that bring the hits." And we had to write about one of the multiple artists from that every day. We'd draw from that well. The Beyoncés and the Rihannas, the Taylor Swift, and stuff like that. I've never actually seen the list. I've only been told, "This is a list, man; you got to do it." It was actually getting to the place where I didn't want my name on it, 'cause the vibe was being dumbed down. I was being asked to write stupid. It was like, "This person gets views, so write this stupid story about Rihanna." It was getting to the point where the stuff I was writing didn't feel like news; it was the beginning of "MySpace for clicks."

WALTER: I was very just involved in putting my head down and focusing on music only. And they were launching, like, MySpace Maps, just some shit like that.

BRANNON: When you have the "list," you're setting yourself up because not everybody is going to be a lifelong lister. Some of those people, the traffic's gonna burn out, and are you really paying attention to the next big things or creating the next list? What's your hand in creating the people who should be on list 2.0? One hundred percent, I think that everyone has their lists at this point. I'm gonna guess that even Pitchfork has a list. Because at the end of the day, it's fucking capitalism. What can we do? I can begrudge it all I want, but I live inside of the system, and I too have to eat, so I get it. It's funny. I watched it play out on a print level. I wrote for *Alternative Press* mostly between 1994 and 1998. And when I left was kind of when they were starting to get into the whole nu metal worlds, which turned into the Warped Tour worlds for them, and they also have their list, clearly. There were bands that were just always on the cover, and Fall Out Boy was certainly one of them, just certain bands where you just knew these bands were selling issues and you have to do it, they have to sell issues, but I think the problem is that no wave is forever.

MySpace's other musical arm, MySpace Records, would continue to sign artists and release albums, such as the rerelease of Meiko's self-titled album in 2008, which was done in conjunction with the Interscope subsidiary DGC Record. The album contained a few bonus tracks, including the single "Boys with Girlfriends." Meiko would take breaks from her job at The Hotel Café to tour but was reluctant to quit the position. But for every artist like Meiko who would make it to market, bands like Nico Vega would remain in development limbo, seemingly endlessly recording their debut album. MySpace Records was Anderson's baby, and once he left, the label basically became an afterthought at the company, while Hollywood Undead was moved to another label in the Universal Music Group and told to record their debut. All while plans that DeWolfe had for Fox to place MySpace Records artists in Fox films and TV shows never came to fruition. It seemed that Fox was falling out of love with MySpace.

HOLT: We started a record label with MySpace, and unfortunately, nothing resonated in the way that that first Arctic Monkeys record did for me. Luke [Woods] and Jimmy [Iovine] no longer cared, and they were already on the way out of the music business. They were already focused on selling iPhones.

GEORGE RAGAN (JOHNNY 3 TEARS/HOLLYWOOD UNDEAD): So you get to this point to release the record, and you send it in. We'd worked with Don Gilmore,* and you think you have the best shit in the

---

* A producer known for his work with Linkin Park.

world. The funny thing is, in retrospect, the label was right. We turned in the record and obviously you've done all this work, and Interscope wasn't interested anymore. But Interscope also wouldn't let us leave. We signed a five-record deal. So A&M Octone, which is a different label, they were under the same umbrella, so they picked it up. But the delay was essentially they didn't think we had it. And to be honest with you, in retrospect, Jimmy Iovine was absolutely correct.

HOLT: The fact is, by the time I got there, the label was winding down, and I ended up having to shut it down. Because it was just not working. You have to remember that, at the time, every major artist got an imprint at some point. Walking around Interscope, Timbaland had Beatclub, Pharell had Star Trek, Dr. Dre had Aftermath, Eminem had Shady, Fred Durst had Flawless. If you had a hit record, you got a label. They wanted you to treat every one of those artists like they were the number-one artist. But in reality, MySpace Records was competing with all of those artists doing exactly the same thing. So it was one hundred percent a JV. None of those imprints lasted.

RAGAN: I never felt like Tom checked out. I think this was more of a transaction between Interscope and MySpace, more so than us. But Tom was never anything, from my experiences with him, anything other than supportive. They were fans of music. These guys were already loaded. They're doing their shit. They don't need Hollywood Undead. One of the reasons I always liked them was because I knew they didn't need us, and they still worked us into the project. So, what happened between them and Interscope, or however that world works? I'm not privy to that information.

JOYCE: So Owen Van Natta, who was one of the heads at the time, met Slash from Guns N' Roses at a party. And his wife was like, "Oh, I really need help with my MySpace page. I can't figure this out. I need some-body who understands social media." So we get the call. This young guy's name was Sean, and he was kind of a rock kid. We have to go to Slash's house, and I go with them just as the PR rep. I'm there to make sure nothing goes awry. We show up because we're there to help Slash's wife learn how to use social media, which is just so silly. And we're there, and [Sean]'s like, "OK, so like if you want, you can put your location on, and this is a great way to know where your friends are." And in real time, as we're showing her this, we find out that Slash isn't at the Guitar Center in Hollywood where he's supposed to be; he's like at some chick's house, and she could tell by the coordinates and starts losing it. We hightailed it the fuck out of there.

Despite the redesign and deluge of advertisement, Murdoch still wasn't pleased with MySpace's earnings. By 2009, the world economy was in the toilet following the stock market crash, and even the biggest corporations were fighting for survival.

"We were so dependent on these really large integrated marketing campaigns. So you have a movie, and you get the homepage, and you get all this other stuff. So I sense that slowed," says Percival. Murdoch recruited Jonathan Miller, the former CEO at America Online, to reportedly "fix MySpace" in March of 2009. Three weeks later, news broke that DeWolfe would leave the company, and Anderson would no longer be president. He stuck around for a brief time as a consultant before leaving as well.

"I remember thinking that *Well, that'll be the end of MySpace,*" says Carrabba. "There was no question of, 'Oh, I wonder if this will succeed or fail.' I just knew it would fail. I think I spoke to [Tom] once around that time, and it was really brief, and he was excited for new adventures, and he felt that he was leaving it in good hands. I was happy for him, but . . . I didn't tell him this, but I did think that that would be the end of something great."

DeWolfe would be replaced by former Facebook COO Owen Van Natta, while Chief Technology Officer Aber Whitcomb and many other members of the original MySpace team would soon leave as well. Former MTV executive Jason Hirschhorn, who had tried to buy MySpace for Viacom back in 2005, came on board, as did Mike Jones, founder of the start-up Userplane, a chat company. Van Natta quit a year later due to infighting and a general feeling that there were too many people who thought they were in charge.

Plans to move to a 300,000-square-foot facility in Playa Vista, Los Angeles, were squashed, and Fox Interactive Media dissolved later in the year. Anderson's MySpace page became the Today on MySpace page, putting a period on the end of an era. The tracking firm ComScore eventually confirmed what executives had long feared: Facebook had officially overtaken MySpace, growing to seventy-seven million monthly visitors while MySpace had dropped to sixty-eight million. It became clear MySpace wasn't going to hit its $300 million revenue target as part of the Google deal for the year, and digital revenues dropped by 26 percent from the previous fiscal quarter. In response, MySpace laid off four hundred employees, about 30 percent of its staff.

NGQC CAO: He was upset. I mean, we didn't talk for a little bit. But I never really could get mad at Tom for that long. We stayed friends over time. The main thing that we talk about is music still to this day. He wrote to me recently telling me that he loved the Linda Lindas,* and I told him that it was my staff that blew the Linda Lindas up, because I am the president of the board that oversees the library department for the City of L.A. and our social media staff filmed them at the library.

ALBA COBARRUBIAS: It was sad, and it was a surprise as well. Chris hired me. I know there was a time that [Chris and Tom] didn't necessarily always talk. We don't have to go into detail with that.

WALTER: After Tom left, nobody filled that spot really well, right? And they hired Courtney Holt to be the president of MySpace Music. He was great. He was cool. He was very supportive, and he just basically wanted to elevate what we were doing at that time. But that was like almost too

---

* A punk group of Los Angeles teenage girls that earned a deal with Epitaph after their song "Racist, Sexist Boy" blew up online.

little, too late. MySpace traffic was slowly migrating at that point. I would say in 2010, like, I'm the longest running employee at that company.

HOLT: I think a lot of people said, "Well, that makes sense, because he sold the company, made the money." Chris never signed up to be an executive at News Corp, but a lot of dominoes fell at that time. Rupert was caring less about MySpace; the sexiness, the shine had worn off. And so all those great stories about "Look how amazing this thing is" turned into, like, "What are you going to do with it now?"

ALBA COBARRUBIAS: We were just trying to keep it afloat. I remember we were frustrated, because the MySpace Music home page was going down to one point five million pageviews a day.

HOLT: I started at the beginning of 2009. It was probably around September of 2010 where I had to fire a lot of people and shut down a lot of the stuff. I told Jonathan Miller it was a fire sale. And now Mike Jones and I were the only people left. Mike had a very clear vision for what he wanted to do. And he was given a different direction than I was being given by the company. Because I was basically told, "You have to keep the labels happy and keep the music rights centered so we can sell this thing." And Mike was doing his best to make the site work in the hopes that News Corp would keep investing in it, but also keeping his optionality set up to say, "If I have to get rid of it, I'm going to play both sides."

AUERBACH: I didn't think I was growing. I worked on a studio project that didn't happen. We weren't allowed to do Rock for Darfur anymore. I think they just decided they weren't going to support it. The thing you're passionate about that you built up, and they're just like, "Hey, we can't do this anymore." I was ready to do something new, and I had an opportunity to be the head of digital at a management company.

PERCIVAL: It's not like we had an offer on the table. But essentially, Daniel Ek* came to the office, and he had a meeting with Mike Jones and

---

* Founder of the music streaming service Spotify.

all these other people. I wasn't in the meeting, but someone basically told me afterwards that he had—I thought it was an amazing line—they said, "Would you be willing to sell?" And his response was, "All I care about is killing iTunes, killing the idea of ninety-nine-cent songs. Can you tell me how you would help me do that? If so, let's discuss." But it was my understanding from after that meeting that we didn't have an answer or anywhere close to a solution for that.

HOLT: MySpace at one point, we called ourselves a social portal, and the idea of a portal was that everything can happen in one place. And then what I realized is most of the Internet over the last ten years has been really good at doing one thing really, really well. And if you try too many things, you lose sight of the thing that you do really, really well. If your center of gravity is one thing, do that really well. I haven't seen a lot of Internet companies do fifty things well.

JOYCE: You're beholden to the sponsors, and it got very corporate, and then you started to lose the audience. It was all in the matter of a year and a half where it's like we're on the top of the fucking world to all of a sudden you started becoming the butt of a joke. "Who's on MySpace anymore?" And I mean, it happened pretty fast.

9

BAD SCENE, EVERYONE'S FAULT

SOME PEOPLE CALLED IT POP-PUNK. Some called it emo. Some deemed it Warped Tour music, or MySpace rock, or scene music. Plenty of people called it whiny. The passionate may not have called it an energy source, but they certainly treated it that way. But by 2007, you could have simply and accurately called it The Sound of Young America.

Or, if you were of a certain age and a certain inclination, you could just call it The Scene. By 2007, The Scene was growing in a way that was just straight-up weird, becoming a catchall term for anything that appealed to the *Alternative Press* and Warped Tour crowd as well as to a large chunk of MySpace users. The Scene included emo and its brattier cousin pop punk, two genres that were increasingly blurring together. But The Scene also included bands in the metalcore and screamo genres, two offshoots of hardcore punk that have lineages almost as deep as emo. Screamo, a variation on emo that features serrated riffs, throat-bursting cries, and an underlying introspection, could be traced back to 1990s pioneers Heroin and Orchid. Metalcore was a mutation of the 1980s hardcore scene that found some punks adopting elements of Metallica-style thrash metal; common tropes included mid-song drum breakdowns and an on-again/off-again variation between screaming and clean singing, as typified by '90s groups such as Integrity and Earth Crisis.

But the kids in The Scene cared about those early pioneers about as much as they cared about any emo group that existed prior to Dashboard Confessional (or maybe before Fall Out Boy). By 2007, the MySpace Scene's version of metalcore and screamo referred to groups such as Bullet for My Valentine, Avenged Sevenfold, and the absurdly named The Devil Wears Prada. (The band members insisted they named themselves after the book, not the movie, mind you.)

At some point, The Scene became basically anything that MySpace teenagers liked, and this dynamic did not go unnoticed. Saporta turned Cobra Starship into a real band, including a keytar player named Victoria Asher he found by searching through MySpace. The band's look was as proudly gaudy as their music, very heavy on pastels and bold colors. "I'm just a contrarian person. No matter what, if you say one thing, I'm just gonna say the opposite," says Saporta. "When what everyone was wearing was very street punk and Hot Topic looking, Midtown dressed in turtlenecks and scarves. And then when everyone became really dark and eyeliner and all black, we wore the brightest things possible. We were doing things that were '80s throwbacks. I didn't want to be lumped into what everyone else is doing, even if that means doing something that people think is ridiculous."

Before long, the all-important Wentz cosign also brought the hip-hop group Gym Class Heroes into the fold. Led by the heavily tattooed punk rapper Travie McCoy, who guested on "Snakes on a Plane (Bring It)," the group became Warped Tour and Scene mainstays after the Patrick Stump–featuring 2005 single "Cupid's Chokehold" became a viral MySpace favorite. Gym Class Heroes were a band that knew who their fans were and had no compunctions about catering to them, as the single "Taxi Driver" name-dropped emo acts such as Dashboard Confessional, My Chemical Romance, and anyone else McCoy could fit in with breathtaking try-hard energy. ("On a Thursday/taking back Sunday for a refund.") They later dropped the would-be Scene anthem "New Friend Request," an ode to crushing on a girl's MySpace page, with McCoy rapping "My man Tom introduced us." The group were popular among Scene kids until their breakup in 2012, but they were always kept at arm's length by the traditional hip-hop consumer base.

The apotheosis of the "quasi-rap music for Scene Kids" moment was 3OH!3. The University of Colorado–Boulder students Sean Foreman and Nathaniel Motte earned a deal with Photo Finish Records, a division of Atlantic Records, due to their MySpace popularity, as we can safely say their lyrical abilities weren't going to make Jay-Z concerned for his throne. The group became unlikely Warped Tour mainstays (sometimes with Jess Bowen playing drums for them) thanks to their reputation for guaranteed get-stoopid dance parties, and the single "Don't Trust Me" from their 2008 debut *Want* hit the *Billboard* Top 10. The song was indicative of the widespread cultural appropriation of hip-hop by the mainstream that the Internet supercharged, as well as the "stop being so uptight" shock humor that was the cultural default of the era. Even before social media was in a place to shout down this sort of thing, there were widespread objections to the duo's lyrics, as "Don't Trust Me" alone featured the bon mots "Shush girl, shut your lips/Do the Helen Keller and talk with your hips," along with the chanted chorus, "Don't trust a ho/never trust a ho."

Motte says, "We have never had anyone beef with any of our music." He adds that "I think people are smart and understand a sense of irony. For sure, you don't write the same music when you're twenty-four that you do when you're thirty-four or thirty-five. And that's part of being an artist."

The Scene's mutation was a bizarre development, and one baffling for anyone who was even just a few years (or a few months) past the target demographic. But by now, the MySpace Scene didn't care what anyone thought—as is every kid's god-given right.

GABE SAPORTA (MIDTOWN/HUMBLE BEGINNINGS/COBRA STARSHIP): I'm starting Cobra Starship with a fucking bang. I go from "Midtown is nothing. I'm back to living in my parents' basement working on this music." Bang, the stars align. We knock it out of the park. I'm on the radio, unsigned. I get a big publishing deal, which changed my life, helped me move out of my parents' basement. And then I signed to Fueled by Ramen, which was Atlantic, for no money, but just to be with my friends. I didn't read my contract. I just literally wrote a peace sign as my signature. I've always kind of been like that. I'm just like, "Dude, I just want to do cool shit with my friends. I don't really care. Everything will work itself out." Sometimes that works. Sometimes that doesn't.

SCOTT HEISEL (*ALTERNATIVE PRESS* EDITOR): You got to give Gabe credit, man. That dude has always been a businessman, and he's like a millionaire now from real estate. Good for him. He was a nice guy. He was like Steve Aoki,* where it's like, they were brought up with the punk rock ethics, and they figured out how to juggle that with their desire to succeed, which is hard to do. So I have no issue with Gabe. Cobra Starship, I thought that was super cringe. But "Snakes on a Plane" was a hilarious song. And my wife loved the second Starship album. She listens to it all the time.

NATHANIEL MOTTE (3OH!3): MySpace was such a huge tool for us. I mean, really, for us it seems like it was the first platform of music that was purely democratic in the sense that every artist from U2 and Coldplay to us—just a couple of dudes in Boulder, Colorado—had the same forum and the same capacity to reach people. This was really just a one-step thing for anyone, anywhere to hear music from it. I know Sean would spend a lot of his free time between classes at CU in the Norlin Library on the Colorado campus, just adding as many people as you could get, sending a friend request to as many people.

SAPORTA: So all of a sudden, bam, we're doing red carpets. The song is everywhere, and I didn't really have a band yet. I have these songs, I had most of the record done. But I needed to put together a band. Basically, the biggest challenge we had in Cobra Starship is everyone thought, "Wow, this is funny, ha ha ha." And then when I'm like, "Oh, here's my band, I have a full record." People are like, "Fuck you! You're trying to

---

* A California punk promoter turned DJ, record producer, and label head.

leverage this thing to make a career? It was just a joke." I'm like, "No, I have this record done. This is just a great way to launch my first song. Take it or leave it."

LESLIE SIMON (*ALTERNATIVE PRESS*): I thought that [3OH!3] were trying to be the emo Beastie Boys. They were very charismatic and very fun, but also very crude and cheeky, and I wasn't sure if everyone was in on the joke or if *they* were in on the joke. I didn't know if they meant it or if they just said things because they rhymed. I didn't take it that seriously. They were good people, whether or not it was reflected in the music.

JESS BOWEN (THE SUMMER SET): They are so, so sweet. Their music does not represent at all how they are as people. When I'm on tour with them, I'm constantly laughing, and it's not any sexist jokes or anything. Nat was going to school to be a doctor. And then I want to say Sean was like getting his master's in creative writing or something like that. I mean, they were just so, so intelligent. But then their band blew up and they're like, "Well, I guess we're going to do this instead of doing that," but they've been incredibly successful even outside of 3OH!3. They're both successful songwriters and producers.

MOTTE: When we started our thing, as we started using MySpace, we're still both in school. We're at the university. And music was a hobby. Our approach to it was just, let's extrapolate a house party to a venue and bring that sense of collectivity. And originally, we'd know half the people in the venue because they were homies. Because even when we first went on Warped Tour, we stood out in a good way, I think, because we provided something different. We've played metal fests and we played hardcore hip-hop shows, and we played the gazebo at Six Flags in Chicago to nine moms and their twelve kids, and I think everywhere in between. Bringing people together is our central mantra to everything we do. I think it translates.

SIMON: Cobra Starship, along with, I think, Gym Class Heroes in a way . . . it was a very safe edgy. Oh, do you wear American Apparel? And do you like when they throw the beach ball into the crowd? And do you want something to play in the car as you're heading to the big party? Cobra Starship's got your jam. Much like Black Eyed Peas would just be the go-to party starter soundtrack, I think Cobra Starship became that for the Warped Tour crowd.

SEAN FOREMAN (3OH!3): I think we had this very mountain T-shirt vibe, we liked wolf tees and mountain T-shirts.* So I think we adorned a little bit of that and our hand sign, which is the 3OH!3 with the fingers and the O in the middle. I think we used all those as much as possible across our page, but it definitely wasn't custom.

MOTTE: I remember it must have been 2004, 2005, or something. But we got booked on a show locally at the Fox Theater, and they're "All right guys, you got thirty minutes or so." And we were like, "Fuck, all right." Where this is a week or two before the show. So we got to write five or six or seven more songs. We wrote the songs immediately, put them on MySpace, and then just played the show. That was also the arc of our band—there wasn't too much second-guessing with anything. But it's that first thought, best thought mentality where you just spew it. And it was adorning your MySpace with some dumb shit that's funny and don't think about it too much.

FOREMAN: We got discovered initially through the shows we were play-ing and the success of that, but also our MySpace success. I think at one point we were the second most popular unsigned [artist]. I remember we got a call while I was in a class, and I got the voicemail, and I was like, "Nat, you got to hear this voicemail."

MOTTE: I graduated a year before Sean, and then I spent a year in France. And it was funny, because MySpace was still a tool for us. Every six weeks I would fly back from Paris to Boulder, Colorado, and play a show in Colorado, and I remember we were making enough money for me to buy

---

* T-shirts with dramatic drawings of wolves howling became popular ironic apparel at the end of the decade.

an airplane ticket, which blew my mind at the time. And during that year, long story short, I ended up getting accepted to med school at the University of Colorado in Denver. It was tough, because on one side, there's a path in your life that's very much set. It's something that I had worked incredibly hard towards, for the four years of undergrad and years afterwards. And then you got this other thing that's just absolutely the opposite and the antithesis of a planned-out life for you. We partied and had fun, but I feel like we had a really, really pure and really innocent look into it.

FOREMAN: Something Feingold. [The voice mail] was like out of *Wayne's World*. It was like, "This is Feingold. I'm going to make you guys rich. You just give me a call, and we'll sign this stuff, and we're going to make hit records." I was just like, "Oh my." Because, you know, to Nat and I, it was just fun to us, and we were just like, "This is insane." Our manager at the time, he hit us up through [MySpace] as well. Long story short, those labels, which were some major labels, it just didn't feel right for us coming from where we were coming from. It just felt so top-heavy. And then we went out to New York and we met with Photo Finish,* and we were like, "OK, this has a more one-to-one fit, where it's more indie feel. It's in-house. We were like, "Let's get a million and just quit, whatever." But we were just joking, because we eventually went to Photo Finish, and that was definitely not a million dollars that we signed with.

MOTTE: There were honestly a lot of parallels between Warped Tour and MySpace. There were a lot of similarities in the way that we approached both those things, in that it was about inclusivity and it was about having fun and not second-guessing too much shit and just putting it out there.

SAPORTA: The positions I take on everything are so counter to trying to be successful. But the reason why I think I am successful is because you'd have to kill me to stop me. That's a punk rock ideal. You have to persevere. You want to do something yourself, and you want to be DIY, and you want to have your own path, and you want to be connected to what you're doing from beginning to end. We just have to not stop, and

---

* A New York independent label distributed by Universal Records.

eventually it'll work. We don't know how it'll work. You're not going to
have a timeline. Your contracts aren't going to fucking matter. But at
some point, you are going to get it right.

———————

The twenty-four-hour restaurant chain Denny's had a decades-long reputation as the place teenagers, as well as inebriated people, would hang out
after a show, as you could order a single cup of coffee and stay all night
if you pleased. Just don't forget to tip. But in 2008, the owners of the
Denny's chain noticed they'd had a drop-off in late customers coming
in to order a Moons Over My Hammy and not leaving for hours, owing
to rival fast-food chains staying open later.

In response, Denny's started the All Nighter campaign to bring the
kids back in, playing various flavors of alt-rock music in the restaurant,
hiring younger servers for the 10 PM to 5 AM shift, and allowing them to
shun the chain dress code in lieu of jeans and T-shirts, ever the standard
rock kid uniform. But the pièce de résistance was the introduction of the
Rockstar Menu, in which artists, mostly from The Scene, were invited to
create their own dishes. None of the artists were paid, instead receiving
free advertising via exposure on Denny's menus and website, as well
as free Denny's for a month, as long as they mentioned the visits and
posted about Denny's on their personal accounts at least three times a
month. Did Denny's create influencer culture? Kind of.

Plain White T's contributed the Plain White Shake, consisting of a
vanilla milkshake with cheesecake, whipped cream, and white chocolate
chips, a concoction as treacly sweet as their music, and the first band
to participate in the program was Taking Back Sunday, auteurs of the
Taking Back Bacon Burger Fries (was a Taking Back Sundae too obvious?), which consisted of French fries with cheese, hamburger, tomatoes, pickles, bacon, onions, ketchup, and mustard. Reyes gamely played
along with the free food requirements, posting a video about how after
meeting his future wife after a show, he'd taken her to Denny's for his
first date. (He ordered chicken fingers, undeniably the best thing on
the Denny's menu.)

In case that wasn't an obvious enough sign of how commercialized The Scene, as well as emo as a whole, had become, a year earlier MTV debuted *Band in a Bubble*, which combined two of the channel's main late-aughts focus points: Scene music and reality TV.

The conceit was that Cartel would spend three weeks writing and recording their second album in a 55,000-pound, 2,000-square-foot fiberglass and steel bubble located at New York's Hudson River Park's Pier 54. (It was based on an Australian show by the same name, featuring the Australian rock band Regurgitator, and the whole thing was inspired by a stunt by the magician David Blaine.) Fans could drop by and watch the band in person whenever they wanted, or they could buy a bottle of sponsor Dr Pepper and get access to a 24/7 viewing of the band by one of the twenty-three webcams scattered around the enclosure.

Cartel were planning to continue to promote *Chroma*, which had begun to break into the mainstream by the end of 2006, but a planned radio campaign for the fan-favorite single "Say Anything (Else)" was put forcibly on hold, and the band bubbled up.

"Hindsight being what it is, there's always that reputation that the bands have to really watch their back. The label's trying to screw them, whatever. That's a common thing that people have about the music industry, and they're not necessarily wrong," says Pugh. "But, we felt like we're riding this wave. The radio stuff is going nuts. The album sales are going nuts. This is Epic Records. They know how to do this."

Pugh now admits they would have been better served working on a promotions campaign for "Say Anything (Else)," an abject example of the sort of song that would play at the end credits of a teen rom-com. But it's rather hard to say no to a major label like Epic when you're still a baby band.

"We one hundred percent should have done that. We didn't have that choice. That was the thing, the label did bring that up. They were like, 'Yeah, like if we're going to do this, we're not going to be able to work on anything else,'" he says. "Doesn't that seem kind of stupid, considering we have a Top 20 single? And we got a bunch of radio people who are actually paying attention to us? Shouldn't we actually try to work that song?

"'Well,'" he remembered being told, "'we just think it's going to be a bigger deal with the MTV show.' They couldn't really promote the old album while trying to promote the new album is what I was told."

The show would, shockingly, not be a nuanced look at a young band dealing with industry expectations that they were about to become the next Fall Out Boy while working on their make-or-break second album. MTV goosed the drama by having random street musicians (including an accordion player) and the Knicks City Dancers crash sessions. One night, producers plied the members with copious amounts of alcohol only to later unleash a fitness instructor to force the severely hungover group to engage in 7:00 AM jumping jacks, which is just rude. Episodes were edited to make it misleadingly look like the members were fighting with each other, and ten days into filming, the front window of the supposedly indomitable structure shattered during a storm.

"So essentially what happened is they had a negative air pressure thing come through when they were having wind from a tropical storm that was going out in the Atlantic. Luckily it's like windshield glass, where it doesn't splinter and go all over the place. It sort of clumped up," he adds. "Nobody got hit. We were standing far enough away, because three of our moms were there. They had brought us dinner that night. I think they were a little spooked."

The result was the worst of both worlds. *Band in a Bubble* felt forced and contrived even by the standards of reality television, without providing the juicy drama that makes viewers turn in anyway, while the association didn't do much for the band's sales or street cred. Released in August just a few weeks after *Band in a Bubble* aired, *Cartel* debuted at number twenty on the US *Billboard* 200 but ultimately sold 100,000 copies, far fewer copies than the 250,000 for *Chroma*. Reviews were tepid, and it certainly *sounded* like an album that was recorded in a rush by a distracted band that had the talent to do better. They were later dropped by Epic. They released *Cycles* via the hard-rock label Wind-Up Records in 2009, a bad year for rock bands and everyone else. After their self-released 2013 album *Collider*, they went on hiatus.

"We made a pretty ambitious album. We were trying to be a little more exploratory. I think if we made the exact same record and just put it out normally, we would have probably gotten a lot better reception. But I don't think that doing the bubble necessarily had anything to do with anyone's negative opinions. I think mostly it was just them advertising it in a certain way," Pugh says. "We'd also never been on MTV before. So if we can get five people that had never heard of our band to like our band, because they don't subscribe to *Alt Press*, then that's worth the one fan that might be bent out of shape because 'Oh, they went with Dr Pepper and MTV and blah, blah, blah.'"

With the exception of Thursday and Dashboard Confessional, who were vocally against the war in Iraq, emo became more apolitical as it got more popular in the '00s, and as time went on, some of the most basic underlying tenets of punk—a wariness of capitalism, macho culture, and conservatism, and an intrinsic empathy for those exploited and maligned by the world—began to get watered down by the newcomers, who either skipped some crucial lessons in their attempt to skate to the top or never had much interest in anything besides popularity to begin with.

As CD sales began to further erode, licensing your song for an advertisement was beginning to lose its stigma, as it became one of the few ways for bands in any genre to get paid. (In 2010, indie darlings Vampire Weekend and the Black Keys participated in a "sellout-off" on *The Colbert Report*, goofing on themselves for the amount of ad licensing deals that they profited from.) It was perhaps unavoidable, and ultimately fans would get used to hearing their favorite indie bands in soda commercials.

Even then, it seemed that every day a younger band that didn't have any hang-ups about the whole art-versus-commerce bugaboo (and often didn't have any compelling ideas worth watering down) were only too happy to give the kids what they wanted as slickly as possible. The unofficial genre of MySpace was becoming just as corporate as, well, MySpace.

―――――――

WILL PUGH (CARTEL): We weren't like bumpkins or anything. But it's like, "All right, this is Epic Records, this is Pearl Jam. This is Oasis. This is Michael Jackson." They want us to do this thing where we're going to have a TV show on MTV. They're going to promote it. Dr Pepper is sponsoring it. And you're going to do this live webcam documentary thing about your next album. I mean, there isn't anyone in their right mind who would say no to that. You literally cannot buy that sort of exposure and press. We all grew up watching MTV, and now we're going to have a show on MTV? What the hell is happening?

JOSHUA CAIN (MOTION CITY SOUNDTRACK): MTV approached us for it. The biggest thing is that we didn't wanna say "F you" to MTV, which maybe we did in the end. Maybe that's hurt our career with MTV in the long run.

JUSTIN COURTNEY PIERRE (MOTION CITY SOUNDTRACK): We were getting to a point where we were like, "Oh shit, we gotta sign this thing and if we don't, we're probably gonna ruin our career." But Walmart got involved, and they said that we couldn't release a record with any swearing on it for like a year.

CAIN: So basically, Walmart was censoring us at this point, so we were like, "You know what, that's a big F-you, we're out." Our booking agent was the same agent as Cartel's. It got kind of thrown in their way and I feel so bad. I talked to them afterwards, like, "You guys literally stepped in front of a bullet for us. Thank you so much."

NORMAN BRANNON (TEXAS IS THE REASON): I think the *Band in a Bubble* thing was very unique, especially because it was so branded. I may have watched that show a little differently if it was coming from a place where Cartel got dropped and they needed money to make a new record and they didn't have it, and Dr Pepper came in. That would have been interesting. But the fact that they were still on a major label, and this was just, strictly, a marketing gimmick, on some level it just made me sad, because I actually like that record. I think there are good songs on it. But, at the time, it was just going to be tarnished as the Dr Pepper *Band in a Bubble* record.

PUGH: You're going to manufacture some drama. You're going to have some creative editing, you're going to do all these things to try to make a TV show entertaining to watch. They did supply us with extra alcohol that evening, but by no means did they have to convince us. Then of course, they do all that and some fitness personality shows up and tries to run us through the ringer. We tried to play ball, but then I think [former bassist Jeff Lett] got sick, and we all were definitely not in the mood after a while. She was having us run around, it was kind of like boot camp. We didn't necessarily assume that they were going to mess with us like that. But looking back on it, you're like, "OK, yeah, that makes sense."

CAIN: I think it was a pretty hellish experience for them, but there was a lot of publicity. They kept sabotaging the shower cameras, it was definitely a debacle in the end.

BRANNON: Now, obviously when somebody goes to Spotify now, they're gonna click on that record and there's no backstory. They're not gonna know about the *Band in a Bubble* unless they go onto YouTube. Again, I understand that was the period of time where selling out became the nonissue. But even that was pushing boundaries for that. A lot of people at that time were like, "Hmm, that might be too far." This is the thing of every movement or historical moment in music, where there's always the one guy who goes too far.

PUGH: There was one [episode] where we were just talking about the sequencing of the record, what order songs are going to come in. We were trying to figure out the first three or four, to really get the people into it, that sort of thing. And [drummer Kevin Sanders] was like, "I don't really like that song to be the third or fourth song." And then that turned into an edit that said, "Listen, I don't like any of these songs." They put in a shot of me. I was playing acoustic guitar and I remember the moment because one of them made a shitty joke, and I looked over and gave him the "pshhhh" look. They had a shot of that that they put in right after Kevin. So it was from two different days. And when I saw that I was like, "Oh, that's what they're doing. OK. Well, you know, like, fair enough." That was the thing for us. We didn't care. The album was going to be the album, as long as nobody had any sort of editorial privilege over that, and nobody made us seem like, you know, racist misogynists.

BRANNON: The idea of selling out basically had completely dissipated, into something that was, "Oh, you boomers and your selling out."

PUGH: That was probably the only thing that really pissed me off about the whole thing. We didn't record that thing in the bubble. We recorded some vocals and guitar and some piano, so we did plenty of things in there. But when they initially pitched us, they were like, "We only want you to do four or five songs, so we can really feature them." As far as actually tracking the record in there? Hell, no. They didn't really let us in on the fact that they were going to start promoting it like that. So that kind of caught us off guard. We're like, "Wait, you think that somebody can write and record an album in twenty days? You realize there's fifteen songs on this record, right? In between tracks, we have interludes, orchestras, and a marching band. Did you see a marching band come into the studio? A symphony? Did you actually listen to the album?

HEISEL: Great band, by the way. I do love Cartel. Their manager got written up in the *New York Times* for some fucking podcast he has now. I'm like, "This fucking guy ruined this band's career for the fucking *Band in a Bubble*."

PUGH: They didn't promote any single. I think they just sort of saw that some people didn't really like the bubble myth. They didn't really have a flat-out single to promote that sounded like "Honestly" or something like that.

EDDIE REYES (TAKING BACK SUNDAY): Our stuff circulated for a couple of years on the menu. We did get made fun of, and people did think it was stupid, cheesy. But then the same people who said that shit were the people at Denny's ordering what we made.

PUGH: I mean, Wind-Up [Records] was great. I mean, yeah, it was smaller for sure. We didn't get big quick enough into the "we sell actual records" part of the music industry before streaming took over. We toured, we did the whole thing and kind of just were like, "All right guys, we're kind of getting up in our twenties here. How are we going to continue on being in a band where it can make sense?" Everybody started to sort of see the writing on the wall, and it's like, you know, I've just got to make money. I was married, I had a family.

REYES: You show up to a Denny's after you just played a long show to sit down and sign autographs for a million people, and there's families trying to eat. That's a little awkward. I think once they asked us to perform or something, we were like, "No, we're not doing that." But some other bands did, apparently.

HEISEL: The Plain White T's and the Gym Class Heroes have to go there after a Warped Tour and eat at Denny's with like forty sweaty fifteen-year-olds who just came from their show. It was weird. Very weird. So they were drunk, is what they were.

———————

When they weren't helping Denny's devise milkshakes that boldly pushed the limits of vanilla, the Illinois band Plain White T's were bringing the MySpace sound to its absolute commercial zenith and artistic nadir with their single "Hey There Delilah." A bashful, largely acoustic song that was originally included as a bonus track to their 2006 album *Every Second Counts*, it doesn't have the heft usually expected of the sort of statement songs that define an era, but there was no song that evoked the essence of 2007 more, so it's fitting that it eventually became a number-one *Billboard* hit a year after its release.

　　The story of "Hey There Delilah" is that T's songwriter and front man Tom Higgenson met Delilah DiCrescenzo, a professional cross-country runner and Olympic hopeful, at a party and decided to write a song about her. That she had a boyfriend was immaterial. Employing a rhyme scheme that could not be made simpler, Higgenson proceeded to pledge his devotion, whether she asked for it or not, creating the MySpace Era's answer to Poison's "Every Rose Has Its Thorn" in the process.

In retrospect, it's too appropriate that a song about obsessing over a girl you met at a party, once, would resonate in a time when many people were using MySpace and other social media sites to nurture virtual crushes with people they would never once actually speak with, or creating online personas that had nothing to do with their real lives.

"Hey There Delilah" was proof of just how dominant MySpace Emo had become. But the song continues to rankle because it also showed how much had been lost along the way, as the jagged, specific, raw, uncomfortable, and downright embarrassing feelings that once made this scene crackle had been reduced to bland pop or inert hard rock, often serviceable but in no way special.

As cloying as their music was, at least Plain White T's had a legit connection to the emo scene, having toured with Motion City Soundtrack and Dashboard Confessional. But after their success, the thread linking emo to The Scene had been fully severed, and things were about to get wayward.

"We referred to bands as *schemo*, because it was a scheme to just cross over and make more money," says Heisel. "People saw it was hot." Soon, schemo would largely squeeze emo out of the marketplace.

Emo once was a movement so déclassé that underground bands wanted nothing to do with it. Two decades later, it had conquered the world. Expressing your feelings isn't an inherently antiauthoritarian act, unless you view the world through the prism that society represses genuine human emotion in order to make the machine of capitalism more efficient. (This is an accurate way of viewing the world, but tone it down, or you'll bum everyone else out.)

But any movement that has a tangential connection to Ian MacKaye, one of the most principled anticommercial artists America ever produced, was bound to have some concerns about selling out encoded into its DNA. Jawbreaker spent years insisting it would never sign to a major label before it did, and Sunny Day Real Estate refused to play California during its initial run for reasons that have never been explained but seem pointed. And then, a decade later, emo bands had chart-topping singles and signature Denny's menu items. Sure, everybody's gotta eat, and the fear of selling out was both silly and classist. (People whose main audience wasn't their fellow liberal arts majors often couldn't afford *not* to sell out.) But did emo's sellout era have to be so tasteless as to invoke association with something called the Hooburrito?*

Every time there's a popular . . . anything, there will be imitators. Capitalism demands that the market be satiated. So just as Nirvana and Soundgarden would eventually beget Creed and Live and Bush, it was inevitable that the popularity of Thursday, Fall Out Boy, My Chemical Romance, and such would produce copies, so dumbed down for mainstream consumption they couldn't really be considered emo in any real way.

It was remarkable just how quickly the formula calcified, where the eyeliner, swoopy bangs, and tight jeans were adorned just *so*, and the compressed-to-death guitars and sing-songy vocals arrived at predictable intervals with punch-the-clock efficiency. If the band were going for the Fall Out Boy money, they'd throw in the most annoying melody you'd ever heard. If they want to be seen as edgier, then they'd throw down an overly technical drum breakdown. Then they'd pick a name that's a three-to-four-word phrase that sounds like either a nondescript video game (Escape the Fate, Bring Me the Horizon, I Am Ghost) or the title of a dashed-off young-adult novel (A Day to Remember, the Early November, Rookie of the Year).

There were vampire-core bands that tried to ape My Chemical Romance via way of Kiss without the humor or genuine pathos, chief among them Black Veil Brides. Though it's a competitive title, the most embarrassing band of all was Attack Attack!, a metalcore group whose ridiculously intense stage posturing spawned The Scene slang term *crabcore*, as the performers squatted their butts nearly all the way to the ground while making very silly faces that they presumably thought conveyed intensity.

But it's also totally fine if you like any of this garbage. Life is short, after all. I would never look down upon a music fan, especially a young one, for liking something I don't care for, and in the case of the abovementioned terrible acts, well, half the time, what you're exposed

---

* The Denny's contribution of the nu-metal balladeers Hoobastank, who are just too easy to mock.

to when you're young is a matter of timing and circumstance. I'm sure plenty of Attack Attack! fans moved on and ended up becoming Mitski stans and Frank Ocean obsessives. When the tide truly turned is also totally subjective. Some might say emo should have ended when Sunny Day Real Estate did, while others might point to the emo-adjacent power-pop group the All-American Rejects as when it all went wrong. Still others might defend the sanctity of "Swing, Swing," a true banger.

All artists have their influences, and the Warped/MySpace industrial complex pushed far too many young bands into the spotlight when they needed a few years to get the bad gigs and bad songs out of their system while they developed an artistic sensibility beyond "people like this sort of thing, so here's a worse version of it." But ultimately, these bands made what they made, and history will judge them accordingly.

Authenticity is a dicey term, one often used to contrast "good" music with pop music, or to condescendingly dismiss music that teenage girls like, or anything not made with guitars and "actual" instruments and "serious" intent. All art is an attempt to create something out of nothing, and there's no way of knowing if an artist *means* what they say, and it doesn't really matter if they do, as long as the listener gets something out of it. So if any of these bands I just ragged on gives someone the feeling that they and their favorite song are one unit of pure joy, if only for a few minutes, then I'm truly happy for all parties involved. We all deserve to feel that. It makes life worth living.

It's also true that, while authenticity might be a pernicious concept, artistic integrity is holy. Artists should attempt to do *something* when they make music. There has to be an intention in the creative process. It simply *has* to feel like it matters to them. Otherwise, why bother? Bad corporate art makes the world worse, and there's enough mediocrity out there. And it's not a coincidence that schemo took over just as MySpace as the site began losing its cachet. The noise was drowning out the signal, and it was beginning to feel like this was a genre that would refuse to grow up.

If anything, it seemed intent on becoming even more aggressively childish. If you have a young fan base, then the only morally correct thing to do is to act like an older sibling, offering some perspective and encouragement, and a sense that it's OK to feel awkward, because everyone does, and even when you feel alone, you're not. The best artists in this genre did this. The worst artists in the genre fed into the entitlement that someone who doesn't want to fuck you must be lyrically burned at the stake.

"Girl, You Done Me Wrong" songs are as old as songwriting, and there's nothing inherently *problematic* with singing about heartbreak and thwarted lust. Everyone gets hurt by love, and everyone can relate. But emo was supposed to be more. The genre's underlying promise was that it would foreground rigorous introspection, owning your feelings, and trying to connect with another person on a meaningful level, which is a powerful and terrifying thing.

Instead, what was now being offered up was Scene music monomaniacally fixated with petulant whines and (often but not exclusively) male grievance. Those were certainly in the mix from the start, as both Hayley Williams and Daryl Palumbo, front man of the emo-adjacent post-hardcore group Glassjaw, would later apologize for the misogynistic use of the word *whore* in their songs "Misery Business" and "Pretty Lush." But this was balanced out by artists, even the oft-problematic artists, who also wrote about regret, shame, and owning your shit, or the ways in which finding the right person could help you find yourself. None of this was of much concern to the newer groups. In addition to competent songcraft and dignity, a lot more was being lost. On their darker moments, even the OG True Believers sometimes felt that if this was what the outside world viewed as emo, then maybe the haters were right all along.

MySpace was slowly being ruined, ultimately by a man with a mission to shift Western culture in a right-wing direction. And the music scene that had been fostered via the site he purchased was heading in that direction. The 2008 Warped Tour was the turning point for when you could no longer ignore how much The Scene had changed. But at least 3OH!3 were having fun.

GEOFF RICKLY (THURSDAY): It was weird, man. We would get people that would heckle us, like, "Just shut up and play some music" kind of stuff. I did get into confrontations with people over that stuff, because I just felt like I was already doing a pretty, to me, palatable, middle-of-the-road, deradicalized kind of version of what I actually thought about a lot of that stuff. So, if I got challenged on it, I was like, "Well, I'm the singer of a hardcore band." That's the way I thought about it. "I'm gonna get in your face and tell you that you're wrong." It's just how it's supposed to be. But you could sort of also relate to them and be like, "Yeah, I know, I look stupid being this serious on a stage that has a Monster Energy drink backdrop. I get it." But I'm still gonna try to radicalize the pop-punk kids.

SIMON: Well, you have the first wave of big bands that sort of set the pace of The Scene, that would include people like My Chemical Romance, AFI, Jimmy Eat World, Fall Out Boy. Then what happens is the labels, the managers, the agents that put a bet on these bands to be big—and it paid off—everyone around them sees a formula that works and hedges the exact same bet, hoping that they get the same returns. So everyone needs to get an "insert band here." So then you've got your first-generation Xerox copy of the band. With the caveat that all the bands I mentioned are collective Xerox copies, you know, they're inspired by bands that came before them. They did something unique and original, but not without fingerprints left behind from the bands that influenced them.

JONAH MATRANGA (FAR/ONELINEDRAWING): So what I would say about Fall Out Boy and that rise of branded emo was just that it was at a time when the music industry—heavy on the *industry* part—was trying to distill the qualities that were making this groundswell possible. So I'm not mad at the bands. I'm not mad at anyone. I'm just saying that's what happened. There were bands that were just sort of put into this mold of, like, "this is what the kids want," and they were willing to do that. They're willing to dress up in the clothes and put on the eyeliner and flat iron the hair and do the studded belt buckle, like all the looks.

BRANNON: There were bands that didn't care about anything. They were looking for energy drink money.

RICKLY: That was the part that made me the most sad, taking all the stuff that was just sort of idiosyncratically style-based, the result of our personalities being the way that we were, and taking out all the stuff that really mattered and could actually be a positive for people. Stuff that was extreme compassion or even discussing the political climate of the world, disenfranchising people and all that.

BRANNON: I'm sure they're very nice people, but we played a show once where Something Corporate opened, and I mean, first of all, the name itself was just like, "Oh my God." But it must have been like a showcase for them or something because all of their label people were there, and I just remember feeling just so oddly uncomfortable with the whole thing. And also just, it was that feeling of like, I no longer understood the connective tissue between what they were doing and where I came from. And that's not a judgment call on them. It's just saying I didn't get it.

RICKLY: I got into it a few times with people, and it's weird to me, that sort of revanchist, conservative undercurrent that actually is in a lot of hardcore, beneath the top layer. I do think that there is a subset of people who were in the hardcore scene that are Proud Boys now that I wouldn't have guessed twenty years ago, but now I know better. Now I know how conservative hardcore can be.

BRANNON: I don't know what Boys Like Girls sound like, but I just remember thinking that name is just whack. And that's fine. It's not for me.

HEISEL: I have a vivid memory in 2004 of interviewing Senses Fail. Their publicist from Vagrant flew to Cleveland to take us out to lunch at Chipotle, which is hilarious. Like, when a major label publicist comes to town, you get a steak. An indie label, you get Chipotle. They were playing a show that night at a local club in Cleveland called The Grog Shop. And it was sold out, and we were debating whether to put them on the cover. And we're at lunch and afterward, we're kind of standing outside, milling around and I'm like, I'm twenty-two. I'm older than every member of this band. They're all like eighteen, nineteen. We're standing there on the sidewalk and we're talking to their drummer. He wanted to buy booze. I was like, "How old are you?" He says, "Well, I'm almost sixteen." I'm like, holy shit, like, you are fifteen and you're playing in a band that's selling out every night." And it's wild, just the amount of incredibly young, incredibly malleable people who were put in a position of power and then potentially abused that power.

BRANNON: This is a pre-Internet observation, but I think that one of the things that I loved about the pre-Internet punk world was that what it meant to be punk really depended on what it meant in your zip code. Once I started going on tour for the first time and seeing all of these different scenes, and seeing how they expressed their punk-ness differently from mine, I loved it. I was so like, "This is amazing." And I hate that we've lost that to a large extent. MySpace was a big part of deregionalizing this music world.

HEISEL: But then it's the people who are abusing them, like their managers and their label, their booking agents were taking these kids who were in high school and telling them to just drop out, go on the road, make your money, right? And now we have this whole scene now of high school dropouts with neck tattoos who are either trying to keep their band together fifteen years later or they're working at Chipotle. That's where your career path is. So it was weird to watch the boom and the bust happen. It's not an issue of a high school band getting this opportunity, because there's plenty of fucking awesome bands that came out of high school. I'm not going to judge that—if you can make cool songs, great. It's more of an issue of the people that they surround themselves with. Are they looking out for their best interest or not? Are they trying to protect those musicians and help them grow, or are they trying to exploit them? And exploitation is what this industry is built and built on for seventy-five years, and that will continue, unfortunately.

BÍCH NGỌC CAO (MYSPACE MUSIC EDITOR): We created the Scene kids' look that became really popular, and that could not have happened on a message board when people couldn't see each other. Kids in Iowa and all over the country were dressing in very similar ways, because they saw their friends online doing it. And so that sort of phenomenon Tom and I noticed very early on.

JILL NEWMAN (MANAGER FOR TAKING BACK SUNDAY AND MIDTOWN): It gets a little cutthroat. I was at A&M when Soundgarden was signed there and grunge was the thing, and everyone was trying to sign the next Soundgarden, but they were signing these copycat bands, and there wasn't a lot of people in there knowing who the true talent was, so you get a lot of the watered-down version. So I think there was a lot of that going on.

SIMON: What I tended to notice was the longer down the line of, you know, this is version five of My Chemical Romance, it would just be further and further away from the original. But close enough that you could try and sell their fans on this bright, shiny new band. And I see that as something like when you get down to a Blood on the Dance Floor type, seeing spooky, ooky gothy vampires, like, "Hey, do you like Tim Burton? You'll love these bands that wear face paint and look like Tim Burton characters. You don't even need to listen to the music."

CHRIS CARRABBA (DASHBOARD CONFESSIONAL): This "fashion first, maybe fashion everything" kind of thing, that came from people imitating My Chemical Romance. I think My Chemical Romance is steeped in this great fantastic drama in their look that I think is high-minded, in the tradition of Bowie and others, but then I think there were bands that took that and upped it or downed it, depending on your angle on The Scene, and started dressing like that. There was a period where it was fashion first.

SIERRA KAY (VERSA/VERSAEMERGE): The last Warped Tour, I just remember these kids . . . I'm not hating on anybody, it just wasn't for me. But it was keyboards and this techno-y, screamy thing. But they're really not playing the keyboards. We've seen them set up. We know what the fuck's going on. It's backing tracks, and there's nothing authentic about it to me. I was just like, *Why is this? This is going somewhere that I don't even understand or want to be a part of.* I should have done a little deep dive and brushed up on names of bands that I hated. Blood on the Dance Floor is one.

REYES: All those bands in the 2000s emo scene where all the kids are dyeing their hair black, wearing like black eyeliner and makeup, all of a sudden they were gothic? Emo was never a gothic thing. It was always a wimpy, dorky Weezer kind of vibe. I don't associate myself with it.

SIMON: I did start to see things turn a little bit. Every time a band gets big, all the other labels take notice, and they think, "I got to get me one of those." And they do. And maybe that first-generation band, I guess lookalike band, is popular. "Great. Let's do it again." Maybe the second one has one hit. "Great. Let's do it again." It's like the endless Xerox of a Xerox copy. You stop being able to see what was there in the beginning. The font is impossible to read. It gets darker and it just becomes unreadable. Or in some cases, in this case, unlistenable. And I felt at the time that we were on our third iteration of the bands that had originally been famous. And at that point, I think I started to know that it was going to be time for me to leave *AP*, because I was not as excited to write or read about the bands that they were covering more and more. And I ultimately left in winter of 2008.

KAY: I'm a big fan of the OG bands that I loved. Every once in a while, a certain band comes forward that has something a little different, and it's so refreshing, and everybody loves it. I like to think that we were one of those bands, and I like to think that's why we had a moment, as well as me being a female singer. But yeah, the copycat thing also led to the drastic—in my opinion—downfall of the music. We started getting into weird electro emo, post-screamy stuff, which led to crabcore, where every band sounded like I couldn't tell them apart. All the same riffs, the same that. It definitely felt a little contrived. It started getting really inauthentic.

HEISEL: There was such an oversaturation; anyone who could buy a Casio keyboard and straighten their hair all of a sudden had a three-album deal with Victory Records. And that's a problem; it just dilutes everything.

NGQC CAO: The particular Scene look was a bunch of kids who were into a type of rock music who like had funky hair and heavy mascara, a Hot Topic sort of feel to it. And I was well grown out of that era as an adult at the time, but really appreciated it as well, because it made me think of high school. I loved it at the time, and I noticed very early on that there were kids who are writing to us all over the country who are sort of copying each other's looks and innovating on top of each other's looks in the same way that you—now, you see on Instagram, kids who are doing makeup as teenagers and becoming makeup gurus who learn off of each other.

HEISEL: MySpace was a huge reason for that, because your average punk band doesn't have an edgy look; they're just four dudes wearing board shorts. Five years prior to that, it was either you look like Blink-182 or you don't have a career, but then like by 2007 or 2009, it's like you have to have crazy makeup and big hair or whatever it was.

REYES: So many fake bands, like on the Warped Tour there were just like so many bands coming to me and being like, "You're my inspiration." And I'd be like, "Why? Your band is terrible. That's not at all complimentary for me."

HEISEL: You can sniff out the pretenders. You know who is real emo, which sounds so fucking stupid to say out loud, but you just know, right? You know, based on what they're referencing and what they pull from and the T-shirts that they're wearing. The bands that go to the trouble of sourcing obscure T-shirts, I'm like, "OK, you didn't have to do that, but I respect it."

REYES: Bring Me the Horizon, terrible band. I'll say it to their face.

HEISEL: But then once you had fucking metalcore, the worst shit on the planet, it's the garbage dump of music. It's terrible. I don't care how good the players might be. With a few exceptions, it's by and large awful, and it's faceless, and it's just disposable. And I describe it as a persistent wet cough. It's what it is. It just never goes away, and when that started taking over *AP*'s audience, it was like either super, super, super whiny screaming stuff like Sleeping with Sirens or Pierce the Veil. Or it was like just the god-awful metalcore like Of Mice & Men. Or it's just bad, just bad bands with bad people in the bands.

REYES: The thing about All Time Low* is I love those guys. And I didn't at first. I remember I was a real dick to Alex at a bar. It really hurt his feelings, apparently. So my friend Brian, who is one of the biggest guitar techs and stage managers on the planet, he was like, "Hey, what you did that night was really mean. You really hurt his feelings." I felt that. So the next time I saw him, I apologized to him and became good friends. Yeah, and again, I'm not crazy about their music, but they're great guys.

HEISEL: People who wanted to be rock stars. Black Veil Brides, the fucking people in that band. A Day to Remember, the fucking people in that band. Avenged Sevenfold, good god. Because they are people who no longer, whether they ever were in the culture of the underground scene, they weren't anymore because they were making money, and they were very quick to talk about how they weren't playing a city, they were playing a market. Everything became dollar signs. Everything became, "How do we make more money? How do we party the hardest? How do we get the most groupies backstage?" It was just this reliving of the '80s: arena rock excess, which is fucking trash. And I was never a fan of that stuff, ever. It's all garbage, right? And so all these bands wanted to be Guns N' Roses, but they were all just fucking Poison or fucking Winger. They were just shitty bands. And we had to cover it, because all the bands we were covering, bands like Fall Out Boy, bands like Panic! at the Disco, those bands had made their difficult albums that their fans abandoned them on. And so we put them on the cover and the covers tanked.

———————————

———————————

* A Maryland pop-punk band that sounded a *lot* like Blink-182, fronted by Alex Gaskarth. They scored a hit with "Dear Maria, Count Me In."

All the attempts to squeeze youth culture credibility out of the emo scene is a testament to how dominant the genre was, as its leading lights were touring arenas and notching hit albums, even if they now often seemed a generation removed from where The Scene was heading. In the summer of 2006, Dashboard Confessional released *Dusk and Summer*, a lush, arena-sized album coproduced by Daniel Lanois, known for his work with U2. The album debuted at number two on the *Billboard* charts, and Dashboard Confessional would headline Madison Square Garden later that year. The album found Carrabba maturing as a songwriter, admitting on the grandiose ballad "Stolen" that sometimes love works out just fine. Carrabba's sensitivity was his selling point, and he was well aware that a cultural tide might be receding. "I remember feeling like the culmination of something," he says. "I felt like I should enjoy this, it won't be like this forever." His old friend and label head Amy Fleisher Madden would also find that times were changing, as she struggled to find her way in the music industry.

Paramore returned in 2007 with *Riot!*, which finally had songs that matched Williams's indomitable voice. Detractors continued to call them mall punk, but the album's highlight, "That's What You Get," proved that Williams was growing as a lyricist, able to ask why she keeps making bad decisions of the heart when she should know better. But "Misery Business," a jealousy-filled missile against a romantic rival that was as misogynist as anything her male counterparts could have come up with, proved that she still had more growing to do.

Paramore hit the Warped Tour in 2008, and after she turned eighteen, Williams would begin a decade-plus relationship with Chad Gilbert, founding guitarist of New Found Glory. He was both married and well into his mid-twenties when the two began dating. "He was already married at twenty-five and divorced his wife and started dating her around the time she turned eighteen," says Heisel. While he says the editorial department of *AP* found this relationship to be disconcerting, the magazine never called it out.

"We weren't writing about relationships. As gossipy as our scene was, we were still focusing our coverage on the music people were making and their personal struggles that created that music. So how do we write that story in 2007 that says it seems pretty sketchy that these people that are happy together have, whatever, an age gap?" he says. "We just didn't have an outlet to really report those things without pissing off managers, labels, all those things. We were still stuck in the old media that we had to protect the relationships."

But while Paramore and Dashboard would continue to ascend, many of their peers were finding themselves butting heads with a music industry that didn't completely understand The Scene but nonetheless wanted to milk it dry before the kids moved onto something else.

Epic Records' new president, Charlie Walk, started heavily dictating Automatic Loveletter's career, forcing Juliet Simms to fire several band members and rejecting a completed rock album, telling her to go make a more pop-focused album. In 2010, the band finally released their debut *Truth or Dare*, only to be dropped by the label shortly afterward. VersaEmerge signed with Fueled by Ramen in 2008 and released a self-titled EP and their full-length debut *Fixed at Zero*, a youthful, optimistic outing that proved there was still some life in the increasingly moribund scene and some of the kids cared more about hooks than their look. They immediately landed on the Warped Tour and the cover of *Alternative Press*. They were also immediately a topic of Scene gossip. In 2014, former bassist Devin Ingelido posted that the band were signed and then placed on the back burner so as to not create competition for Paramore and Williams, a belief that had long been rampant in some corners of The Scene—as were attempts to pit Williams and Kay against each other, a canard neither woman showed much interest in.

"I remember the first time I heard it, being like, 'Absolutely no way. That doesn't make sense. You could have two successful bands. Why would you tank one so one would remain successful?'" Kay says. "But there's definitely times where I'm like, 'Why is this happening to us?' And like, 'Oh shit. Maybe that is true.'"

Motion City Soundtrack was barely able to finish its third album, *Even If It Kills Me*, as Pierre's struggles with substance abuse nearly caused the band to break up. It was a mostly confident, mature work that nonetheless reflected a lack of focus and Pierre's depleted mindset. While *In Defense of the Genre* sold well, Say Anything wasn't selling on the level of Panic! at the Disco or My Chemical Romance, so at the insistence of RCA they teamed with Fall Out Boy producer Neal Avron for their streamlined 2009 self-titled album. But despite having an unapologetic piano-led power ballad with "Eloise," the album didn't break them through to a bigger level, and the band departed the major label system. But Bemis, who had a firsthand look at the absolute heights the genre could achieve when he opened an arena tour for Dashboard Confessional in 2006 and then coheadlined Warped Tour 2008, was starting to get a feeling that the wave was cresting, or at least mutating into something much different.

"Our first big tour ever was with Dashboard, and it was their first big arena tour. It was like, 'They could be the next U2,' but something in me was like, 'He's too good, the world is too shitty, they're not gonna let this happen,'" he says. "I really do think that just like any movement, the commercial stuff affected it. That Dashboard record, *Dusk and Summer*, Daniel Lanois produced it, who did *The Joshua Tree*, and it's awesome," Bemis adds. "Throw a million dollars at the wall and it sounds fucking cool. But I just felt like it wasn't a cultural phenomenon anymore."

Taking Back Sunday had lost two founding members since releasing 2002's *Tell All Your Friends*, but the 2004 follow-up *Where You Want to Be* went gold anyway, as did 2006's *Louder Now*, their debut for Warner Bros., which found the band Coheadlining arenas alongside Jimmy Eat World and scoring MTV2 hits such as "MakeDamnSure." A sturdy if cautious step into the mainstream, the album was just glossy enough for the radio and just shouty enough to appease the base, even if the diehard fans still missed Nolan. Reyes's riffs gave traditional hardcore pummel an arena-sized heft, but the new lineup wouldn't last much longer.

After *War All the Time* didn't turn them into the next Nirvana, Thursday rebounded with 2006's *A City by the Light Divided*. Produced by Dave Fridmann (known for his work with Sleater-Kinney and the Flaming Lips), the album found the band stretching themselves like never before, delving further into their gothic roots for the cinematic ballad "Running from the Rain" and reaching new heights of catharsis with the closer, "Autumn Leaves Revisited."

"That was supposed to be a real left turn for us. We had self-pigeonholed during *War All the Time*. We had started to feel like our idea of what Thursday was, it was becoming very rigid, very claustrophobic: 'It's always gonna be dark, it was always gonna be heavy, it's always gonna be weird,'" says Rickly. "We were overdefining what Thursday did."

Way rarely missed an opportunity to insist that My Chemical Romance was not an emo band, thus cementing that as what people continued to call them. But it's always better to show rather than tell, and one way to set yourself apart from a scene you're not comfortable with is to will yourself into becoming the MySpace Era's answer to Queen. Recruiting producer Rob Cavallo, who'd overseen Green Day's multiplatinum comeback *American Idiot*, the band shrugged off any pretense of punk and channeled the grandiose ambitions of the Beatles and Pink Floyd for *The Black Parade*. The concept was that it was a rock opera about a character's death and journey through the afterlife, but truthfully the whole story line never made much sense.

For one thing, it's doubtful that someone would complain from the great beyond that they found youth culture terrifying, as Way perfectly summarized the feelings of anyone just a bit too old to "get it" with "Teenagers," which hinged on the immortal chorus "Teenagers scare/ the living shit out of me."

But even if the underlying story line was confusing, who cares? The whole album was too fun to get bogged down by self-importance, and when Way hit the "I'm just a man!/I'm not a hero" climax in "Welcome to the Black Parade," it was the cellphone-screens-up moment that era deserved. It also served as the inadvertent curtain call on the whole thing.

CARRABBA: Losing privacy was really fucked up for me. Losing the ability to go to shows anymore and just stand in the audience without having to wear a baseball hat and a sweatshirt to cover my tattoos and stuff like that. I stood out like a sore thumb. And the demands on my time, and the lack of sleep, and the whole year with eleven days off, total. It was just breakneck speed.

AMY FLEISHER MADDEN (FIDDLER RECORDS): By the time *Dusk and Summer* from Dashboard came out, it could have been the peak, but it could have been the beginning of the drop. It's really interesting, because it's also when *The Black Parade* came out, which kind of skewed emo into a more theatrical area than Dashboard would have been comfortable with. Also, *Black Parade* ushered in an entire new generation of younger kids, like twelve-year-olds were buying shirts at Hot Topic. They weren't harping on about the new Dashboard record.

CARRABBA: I was exhausted. I was undernourished. I wasn't eating right. It was my intention to eat right, but the hours we kept were just insane. Waking up early to do radio shows, and then meet and greets, and then record store visits, and then the sound check, and then the show, and then after a show meeting the people that we wanted to meet or had to meet, and then cramming into the van, and then later the bus. We're just falling into bed and trying our best to sleep for maybe four hours, if you got lucky. Usually not a whole four hours. Never getting to shower.

HEISEL: Dashboard was so huge and then vanished. I mean, he worked himself to the bone. He toured super, super hard, and then there was that pivot of The Scene where everything went screaming and he didn't go screaming. And so, you know, he takes time off.

FLEISHER MADDEN: It's still surreal, because it was this small thing that I had helped create. But all of a sudden, it belonged to so many people. And I don't mean in a fan sense, I mean in a behind-the-scenes sense. I'm still not really sure how to think about this.

SIMON: At the time, Chad was seen as someone who was also on the younger side of things, because he started New Found Glory when he was a teenager. So he had a little bit of a Peter Pan air to him, that he was the baby. So to think that a young man is dating a young woman, I don't know if anyone got into the nitty-gritty details of checking IDs and stuff. I mean, there's a whole creep factor, right? And I don't know if you're always able to see the creep factor when you're in it. Only after the fact and with some distance are you able to say, "Huh. That's not quite right."

CAIN: The music video for "Broken Heart," there's a reason we aren't in it, because Justin was in inpatient rehab when we shot that music video. Stuff like that was happening.

PIERRE: It always started with alcohol, and then everything else seemed like a good idea once you get drunk enough. I was directing music videos, and I showed up at this music video just hungover, I was directing a music video completely just brain-dead. I was just waiting to get to the evening so I could drink again. And I would always, even though I'd make them wait two hours or whatever, I'd always get to the van in the morning.

CAIN: We had a third record to do, which is *Even If It Kills Me*, while we were in talks with Sony prior to that, and so we signed a deal with Sony for the records after, and I think the idea was Sony was hoping that they and Epitaph could work together with our next record, but Epitaph was like, "Hell, no." Our goal at that time was we were trying to leverage what was happening, and the label decided that that was backhanded and we shouldn't be doing that.

PIERRE: This one night, there were these really strong drinks at this one place. I was supposed to go to see Minus the Bear play, and I called to see if I could get on the list, like an asshole, last minute. And then I remember getting into the taxi, and then I don't remember anything after that. And I had lost my phone by the time I woke up in the morning, and then Josh was at my house and my dad was there. Brett was on the phone and Josh gave me his phone and I was talking to him, and I'm like, "OK, so I got two choices, I can go to Hazelden, which is like a luxury rehab center. Or I can go to Fairview Riverside, which—I went into outpatient there—scared me, but this time I would go as an inpatient. It was like prison versus the opposite. Brett's like, "Well, I think you know what you have to do." That was like the first time I ever made a decision that went against what I wanted to do, and then from that point on, that's all I did. That turned into doing the thing that I wanted to do. You kinda have to go against your personality until it becomes your new personality.

RICKLY: The label changed hands. Lyor left, most of the staff left Island, and they brought in L. A. Reid.* He came to see us after *War All the Time.* He saw us play, and he was like, "You're a fucking superstar. All we have to do is get somebody who can write you some songs," because he was like, "You don't have songs; you have charisma. You guys are pure charisma: you got style, you got sounds, you don't have a single song."

CAIN: We had seen other bands fail; we've been with bands and watched their careers disintegrate in front of you. It's very obvious. Even when you've seen it happen before, ours was confusing. It was a weird time. People were going to shows and being like "buying music is pshhhh" at the same time. We were on the *Even If It Kills Me* tour playing our biggest venues and biggest shows we've ever played, selling the least amount of records we had ever sold. We were playing shows bigger than a band like Hoobastank played at the time. And they were a radio hit band, so we were like, "There's definitely something, some disconnect somewhere where we could maybe tap into something."

PIERRE: Maybe this is an oversimplification of it all, but I think that people were listening to us, and we were growing in terms of a fan base, but people just weren't spending money on stuff that they didn't have to.

RICKLY: He's like, "So, if we get you somebody to write some fucking songs, you'll be huge, you'll be bigger than Fall Out Boy, you'll be the biggest band on the label." And my response was like, "No, no, we write our own songs." And it was like, right there was the moment when, I didn't realize at the time, but he was like, "Oh yeah, we're not gonna spend any money on this stupid band that thinks they can get big without catchy songs. That's crazy."

---

* A record executive known for his work with Usher and TLC.

CAIN: People weren't as hungry to give you the money and support you in the same way, 'cause there was this misnomer that you make money off the touring and it's fine. Everybody has this idea that [when you buy albums] you're just giving money to the major label. And, yes, they are making the most of the money, but when they make the money, they spend it on us to make more money. If we're not making that money for them, then they stop, and that's a disconnect that whole generation had and the idea of, like, they're sticking it to the man. But they're really sticking it to the musicians, even though we're all in this bad, messed-up relationship with labels already. I think a lot of people got this righteous vibe when they took albums from bands that way, that they were like, "Oh, I still went to a show and bought a T-shirt." Which is great, but you would have gone to the show and bought a T-shirt and the album prior to that, so like . . .

RICKLY: The only thing that was important to me was being in a band and making music. I would never trade that for like, "Well, you'll be famous, but you won't get to make music anymore, you'll have to let somebody else make your music."

MATRANGA: I think often about people like Chris or Geoff, and whatever benefits they've gotten from fame or whatever, it seems like it takes its fucking toll. Once people have invested a lot of money in you, they're going to want their return. If you're a rock singer in a popular band, you are no different than the cog in any other industrial machine. And that was one of the things that I really in my gut knew. I'm not really interested in being a part of this, and I don't think I'm cut out for this.

RICKLY: I had a pretty good grip on how famous I was when I was heading to some award show with somebody pretty high at the label, and I said, "What do you think, next year I can make my way up to the Celebrity C-list?" And she was like, "Why don't you just concentrate on getting [to] the D-list first?" And that was at the height of the band's popularity. That was when we were like on the *Billboard* Top 10. And I was like, "Oh." And she's like, "You're not fucking famous." I was like, "OK." That was all it really took. I was sort of joking, but I also thought maybe I was verging on celebrity. People would run after me on the street to say hi and they loved our music. I would meet somebody that waited online for an hour, and they'd cry because they were meeting me. I don't know, maybe I'm famous? She put it in perspective like, "No. Some people like your music. That's it. You're not fucking famous." And after that, I never really thought about it again.

REYES: When we sold out Madison Square Garden with My Chem and we sold out Nassau Coliseum on Long Island on our own, that's when I was like, "Wow, this shit is different now. All right, we're a big band." Madison Square Garden was a flash. We played and we're off. I thought it was going to peak. But then afterwards Taking Back Sunday kept touring years and years later. Even now, they're still selling out big tours without me.

NEWMAN: Taking Back Sunday were the number one on the MySpace indie bands chart for a long time, like a year. The combination of that and the second record *Where You Want to Be* debuting so high on the *Billboard* chart, it was number three, we got all the gatekeepers' attention. But they had developed their fan base naturally; I think it was a natural progression. I always say, like, I'd be much, much happier having three gold records on my wall than one platinum. There were so many bands that would have a big hit and have their big platinum record and then disappear and couldn't sell ten thousand records after that.

SAPORTA: At the beginning of Cobra Starship, we were voted [by *Alternative Press* readers] the band most likely to be forgotten next year. We did not stop touring for a year straight. We did every fucking tour we could. And then during that tour, we wrote another record. So in the summer, we recorded it and we literally had it out exactly a year after we put out the first record. So we basically had two records in one year. And I think that second record, produced by Patrick Stump, people really love that record. And I think that kind of solidified us into this new scene and really cemented our place. And then the next year in *AP*, we were voted most underrated band, and we got the cover later on that year.

MAX BEMIS (SAY ANYTHING/MAXIM MENTAL): By the third one, it was very much so do-or-die in that world. So basically, the label was like, "You have to make a giant radio record." But I wanted to at that point, just naturally; I was like, "I love the Foo Fighters, I love Blink-182, I haven't gotten to do that." So we hired the guy who made a lot of those records, and we're like, "This is fucking awesome. Listen to how cool the drums sound." It was very sincere, it wasn't trying to sell out or whatever, it was very much so like, "Fuck yeah, we wanna sell out." And so we did that. Didn't work necessarily—but all of this, when I keep saying this and that didn't work, it worked for our fans pretty much unanimously.

SAPORTA: I think the thing about Cobra Starship is if you only hear the singles, you get a certain impression of Cobra Starship. But I think what fans really loved about it is that the albums had a lot of meat to them. There was a lot of commentary and a lot of deeper things on the albums. The second record, *¡Viva la Cobra!*, was a big commentary on celebrity culture. And it's really done from the perspective of someone who is outside of the system, the celebrity institution, but snuck in through the side door. That's literally who we were. We would sneak into parties, but we weren't a part of that world.

FRANK IERO (MY CHEMICAL ROMANCE): It's weird, because coming from where we come from—I think it's a Jersey thing—that term of *rock star* is very derogatory. It even boils down to that feeling of being boastful. People don't ever say that they're good at anything, and if you do, you're kind of a jerkoff. So there's this self-deprecation type thing, but at the same time trying to be the best at what you do. It's a fine line between having confidence and being boastful. So I think that was a constant struggle of wanting to be good at what you do and have that pageantry and be this larger-than-life entity up on stage but also feeling this feeling of inadequacy at all times.

SAPORTA: There was no middle class of artists. The middle class just completely disappeared. I grew up in an era where Mudhoney was huge because they had 200,000 fans that bought their albums. And that's millions of dollars that they could split up and have a nice, comfortable existence as an artist. That was gone. You couldn't sell to your 200,000 core fans. You couldn't sell them an album anymore. So if Cobras would have been big in any other era, I think I probably would have enough money to retire for the rest of my life. I think I'm very lucky that I was able to have any success during that era, because [in] that era there was no monetization.

BEMIS: It was a completely mutual decision [to leave RCA]. Like maybe it was because I knew it would happen as soon as the record came out. I'm like, "This is most likely not gonna be the next Green Day." I think they wanted us to be a band that's artful enough to appeal to indie snobs sometimes and then make power ballads like "Eloise." So if the world wasn't ready for it at that exact time or will never be, whatever the fuck happened, it didn't line up. It hit me hard for a second, and then I just had to adjust to that reality or I would've lost my mind.

SAPORTA: The first song on the first Cobra album, the first line of that album is, "Can you hear me now that I'm dumbing myself down?/And does it make you feel a doubt?" Which is exactly what I knew people were going to say from The Scene, "Oh, that's not really you," or "This invalidates who you are or where you come from." And that's kind of my response to it. "Hey, you know, I don't want to be a martyr, giving ten years of my life to touring and making music and doing The Scene, I'm not going to work at a bar. I've learned some skills, I'm going to be able to make a career from this."

BEMIS: And if you start thinking about life with gratitude, anyone can feel good about their lives. So when that happened, I was like, I'm in a big band. We could headline Warped Tour, I can now maybe sign to Vagrant or Epitaph and do our "reacting to failing" record. I've seen Alkaline Trio do it, I've seen Saves the Day do it. That looks fun.

SAPORTA: The notion of the sellout started to be over. I was over it. If you were still jamming that idea at that time, it felt like it was a little bit of an archaic idea. Like, whatever, dude. No one cares. This came after all these artists who all signed million-dollar major label deals.

JULIET SIMMS (AUTOMATIC LOVELETTER/LILITH CZAR): I fought the "you need to be pop, you need to be pop, you need to be pop" for a very long time.

SAPORTA: I don't think that anyone who liked Midtown was going to a Cobra Starship show, just because they were personally offended by it. Which I get, by the way. I don't hold that against them. I'm the one who's doing something different, and that's OK.

SIMMS: I was the one who signed. It was my record deal, and new people are coming in and saying, "You either get a more professional-sounding, better-looking band, or you're dropped." What do you do?

FLEISHER MADDEN: I went back to college, and the other thing that happened was I met a band called Recover, so I put out a Recover EP, and it became a thing, like every major label that I knew was coming for me for distribution. The meetings that I had were literally like, "You worked with New Found Glory, it did this, you work with Dashboard, it did this, and we hear Recover, and we see it, and we see them." By the time I met with everybody, I think I had six deals to choose from. I just don't want to choose the wrong one. And of course, I chose the wrong one. They might have all been the wrong one, in retrospect. I ended up working with MCA, who—within six months of the deal, the company that had been around for decades imploded. That was supposed to be like the beginning of The Big Next Fiddler. And instead it was the beginning of the end, it kind of sunk my battleship. Not to discredit a band like Fall Out Boy, but I had these bands that could have competed on that level, if they had been given the promised financial support that they needed.

KAY: I didn't even scratch the surface at the level of fame that Paramore had. But there was a bit of success that was definitely overwhelming. And there are little things that I experienced, like, "Jesus, if I was much more successful than this, this would be something I'd probably experience all the time." And that's not fun. I definitely value my privacy. I think when I was younger, I really craved to be in the limelight and be the star of the show. And having that experience has let me sit back and evaluate and ask myself, "What do I want? What is it that I'm after here? Validation of others, because of some deep-seated thing that I can't figure out? Or is it just because I think I have a message to say? Is it really that deep, or is it really not a big deal?"

FLEISHER MADDEN: I was working with Juliette Lewis's band. It didn't occur to me that an entire distribution company would sign a deal just so they could work with a famous person. All of the sudden, these dudes in suits are showing up to be backstage with Juliette Lewis. And it was like, this is so ridiculous. They really didn't want anything to do with me. They wanted to be with her, and she wanted nothing to do with these people, obviously. So it got really confusing. And by 2006, I was like, this is the end.

SIMON: Once record labels start putting together session musicians to form bands, that's the downturn of a scene, and that seemed like the direction that things were going in. It was a very mathematical way to construct a group.

10

INDICTMENT

(Content warning: This chapter contains mentions of abuse and sexual assault.)

IN 2018, WARPED TOUR CAME TO AN END, with Kevin Lyman citing declining ticket sales and a diminishing pool of bands. What might have once been mourned as the end of an era was met with a muted response, if not an outright sigh of relief.

In the wake of the long overdue culture-wide reckoning with patriarchy and misogyny spurred by the #MeToo movement, as well as the fourth-wave feminist movement incubated a decade earlier by social media conversations and websites such as Jezebel, Tiger Beatdown, and Tumblr, writers and fans were now looking at, well, *everything* with a different eye. Or they were finally being heard when they pointed out that things were deeply fucked. Because the hard truth of the matter is the emo and punk scene that the Warped Tour and MySpace supercharged had long been home to abusers.

Jesus David Torres fronted the Orlando, Florida, synth-pop group Blood on the Dance Floor under the name Dahvie Vanity and played the Warped Tour several times. In 2019, the *Huffington Post* reported that at least twenty-one women had accused him of sexual assault, with one of the accusers being Dianna Farrell, who, at age fourteen, met Torres through MySpace. Torres was then twenty-two and known on the site as a proto-influencer named "Dahvie the Elite Hair God." Police let him off with a warning, as long as he promised never to contact her again. But a year later, Torres started Blood on the Dance Floor and clearly became more emboldened. Both Jeffree Star, who collaborated with Torres, and Ash Costello of the group New Year's Day, who toured with him, called him out for taking advantage of underage fans while on Warped Tour and forcing himself on women, with Costello writing in a blog post that "I watched too many fans get abused and I was abused myself by this person."

Jonny Craig was kicked out of two separate bands he fronted, the emo-hardcore group Dance Gavin Dance, which rode a 2006 MySpace demo to multiple Warped Tour appearances, and the band Emorsa. Craig's band Slaves* was kicked off the Warped Tour in 2015 for allegedly assaulting a merchandise worker. He would later be accused by multiple women of sexual assault via social media in 2017, though his behavior had long been whispered about in the industry.

Ronnie Radke, who fronted the metalcore Warped Tour mainstays Escape the Fate and Falling in Reverse, was accused by an ex-girlfriend of domestic assault in 2012 and "landed himself in prison for his involvement with an altercation in the Las Vegas desert that left an eighteen-year-old boy dead," as reported by *Flavorwire*. His band continued to play Warped Tour. He was later accused of rape in 2015, though the charges were dismissed by the police, as happens in far more than half of legitimate rape cases. "He's since sued her for defamation," *Flavorwire* noted, "the ultimate form of silencing a victim."

All of these actions were reported on, either at the time or after the fact, but didn't seem to get much cultural traction, and in some cases clearly didn't affect anyone's career. But the tide turned firmly against the Warped Tour when news broke that Jake McElfresh, the singer-songwriter who performed as Front Porch Step, was allowed to perform a date at the Nashville stop of the 2015 Warped Tour after he had previously been removed from the tour for accusations of, as the *New York Times* reported, "inappropriate text message and social media

---

* In a scene overflowing with terrible band names, this is the worst.

relationships involving at least half a dozen teenage girls, including, in some cases, the exchange of sexually explicit pictures."

Lyman would later defend McElfresh's appearance to the *Nashville Scene* (even as artists such as Hayley Williams and Dan Campbell of The Wonder Years* denounced the action), saying that it was "as part of [an] 8-month therapy program, with his counselors and all his supervisors here." In a postmortem interview with *Billboard*, Lyman downplayed the issue, saying, "Well, that sexual harassment didn't happen on Warped Tour. If you go through every one of those stories, it didn't happen on Warped Tour." Lyman has plenty of defenders, who argue he did what he could, addressed any concerns that arose, and kicked abusers off the tour.

But accounts from the relatively few women who did play Warped Tour† paint a disturbing picture, and confirm that the Warped Tour and The Scene were often not safe or welcoming places for people who weren't straight, white cis men. In a *New York Times* roundup, some women who played Warped Tour over the years praised Lyman for his support and the opportunity, while others lamented the overall lack of female performers, to say nothing of the off-putting atmosphere of bands such as Blink-182 regularly asking the (often largely underage) crowd to flash them during their 1999 performance on the tour.

In an interview with Vulture, Williams (who has apologized for the sexist lyrics of "Misery Business" and promised to stop playing it live) said, "The pop-punk and emo scene in the early 2000s . . . was brutally misogynistic. A lot of internalized sexism, and even when you were lucky enough to meet other bands who were kind and respectful, there was other shit that wasn't." Williams, who was sixteen when Paramore started playing the Warped Tour, recounted how her band was pelted with promotional condoms by male audience members, and that a family member of a Warped Tour band member made a comment about her genitalia that embarrassed her.

---

* When I interviewed Campbell once, he firmly refused to discuss the Warped Tour in any fashion.

† As pointed out by former Jezebel writer Maria Sherman, 53 percent of attendees at the Vans Warped Tour were female, while only 6 percent of its performers were women. "That's ANY woman, in any role, in any group, in the year's lineup of over 120 bands."

Some fans argue that the emo scene once held itself to higher standards than the surrounding mainstream culture and represented an
antidote to the rampant misogyny of the early '00s. The argument goes
that it was the latter-day bands that adopted surface elements of the
culture without understanding that punk and emo saw itself as a safe
haven for the vulnerable.

But that simply wouldn't be true. Abusers and exploiters will always
look for opportunities. Emo's central flaw was that many of the performers (and some, but not all, of their fans) felt they were above the
macho rock music scene but carried a nice-guy entitlement, a belief
that a dollop of self-awareness entitled them to the world, or at least a
girlfriend. It could very often be plain old toxic masculinity, dressed up
in rimmed glasses and vintage sweaters.

To see that there was always a dark side to The Scene, considered
the matter of Jesse Lacey and Brand New. For much of the '00s, Brand
New had the unofficial title of the Emo Band That Non-Emo People
Respected. Due to their complex song structures, experimental tendencies, and Lacey's evocative lyrics, albums such as 2003's *Deja Entendu*
and 2006's *The Devil and God Are Raging Inside Me* were considered
classics of the genre, even earning praise from Pitchfork.

For a while the party line on Brand New was that Lacey was bravely
plumbing the depth of his soul to interrogate the weakest, most petty,
and often hideous parts of himself, putting them on display so we can
all acknowledge that we all have an ugly part of us, hidden away, that
we're not very proud of. Shortly after the release of their 2017 album
Science Fiction, several women came forward to accuse him of inappropriate behavior with teenage fans, with one woman saying that when
she was fifteen and he was in his twenties, he asked for nude photos
and for her to watch him masturbate over Skype.

"[Lacey] solicited nudes from me starting when I was fifteen and
he was twenty-four. Manipulated the hell out of me, demanded specific
poses/settings/clothing, demeaned me, and made it clear that my sexuality was the only thing I had to offer," the woman wrote on a Facebook thread on November 9. "I should've known better by then, but he
had screwed me up so much psychologically that all I wanted was his

approval. It fucked me up to the point that I STILL have nightmares and wake up in a sweat. I still break down and have panic attacks when people play Brand New in a bar."

In response, Lacey, who at that point had avoided publicity for years, wrote a Facebook post in which he offered a blanket apology, noting that he had "a dependent and addictive relationship with sex." Nowhere in the apology did he actually admit that he did what many had accused him of. He hasn't been heard from since and has not faced legal consequences.

In light of these revelations, it became impossible for even the most ardent fans of the genre to just write off Lacey's lyrics—such as those for the 2001 single "Seventy Times 7," in which he hopes a former friend dies in a car wreck—as juvenalia that he later outgrew, or the lyrics of "Me vs. Maradona vs. Elvis," in which he imagines having sex with an intoxicated girl ("I almost feel sorry for what I'm gonna do") as, like he once claimed in interviews, a storytelling exercise in which he imagines the most nightmarish version of who he could have become. Writing about bad deeds does not, obviously, indicate that an artist is a bad person, but it's remarkable the extent to which the lyrics of one of The Scene's heroes exemplified its oft-toxic nature.

But Lacey wasn't the only emo hero held in high regard for his artistic accomplishments who would fall from his station. Chris Conley of Saves the Day, one of the bands that helped to take emo to the wider world, was accused via Instagram in 2021 of abuse, harassment, and allegations of sexual misconduct, including accusations of grooming. In response, Conley denied the grooming accusations but otherwise took ownership of his actions. A planned tour was canceled.

Lacey and Conley's cases were the most extreme examples of the unchecked entitlement that emo could represent, an icky side that's been with the genre since at least the *Pinkerton* centerpiece "Across the Sea," in which Rivers Cuomo writes about becoming obsessed with a teenage fan from Japan, even owning up to masturbating to her letters. It's a genre that can offer a sympathetic outlet to the confused and hurt. It can also plumb the frustration and uglier parts of the human condition in order to facilitate healing catharsis . . . or to unapologetically celebrate being a needy asshole. Artists have the right to explore the gross parts of themselves. But as an adult, I hear *Pinkerton* in a new light. It's a masterpiece I don't like to revisit.

Emo's fans weren't culpable, and many artists of the era handled themselves with dignity. They may have had broken hearts, but they didn't let that pain curdle into something so ugly they'd become something they couldn't recognize. Some artists have some regrets, knowing they could have been better. Others refuse to let the bad actors bring down The Scene they loved, and understandably so.

But these ugly revelations have undeniably cast a pall over the entire era and left both fans and peers wondering what they missed, or didn't want to see—or why people didn't listen when women repeatedly tried to point it out.

The emo scene could feel alienating to anyone who wasn't white, heterosexual, or cisgender. Brannon often felt out of place as a queer man of color who was closeted during the '90s and remembers that when bassist Jason Gnewikow came out in a 1999 *Spin* profile on the Promise Ring, the message board for the band's label became filled with homophobic vitriol, and this was well before the emo scene had any mainstream traction or had developed a reputation for toxic masculinity. This is a scene that's had problems from the beginning.

LESLIE SIMON (*ALTERNATIVE PRESS*): Well, there's a lot to unpack there.

NORMAN BRANNON (TEXAS IS THE REASON): I think being gay in the music world in the '90s was sort of a quick way to sort of ghettoize your band. And at the time I was so protective of the band. And this was all completely, I will say, in my brain. I don't know for sure that coming out during the band's existence would have been something that changed our game, but I will say that my fears were kind of confirmed when Jason from the Promise Ring came out, because the Jade Tree message board completely fucking exploded in homophobia.

EDDIE REYES (TAKING BACK SUNDAY): When bands like Blood on the Dance Floor, those terrible bands, come up to you and they go, "You're the reason why I do this," I'd go, "Not only are you terrible, but you apparently sexually abused underage women. Don't come up to me and try to be my bro."

BRANNON: The entire message board was basically calling Jason a faggot. It was insane. I did not realize that that many people in The Scene were still that vehemently opposed to queer people. And it got to a point where I actually called Tim and Darren* and said, "Look, man, your message board is fucking out of control, saying the worst homophobic shit. Can you shut down your message board and send the URL to an essay about homophobia that I am going to write?" And they were like, "Yeah." That was basically the end of the Jade Tree message board.

SIERRA KAY (VERSA/VERSAEMERGE): I was so young. I was eighteen on my first Warped Tour. There were some bands I loved, but I didn't like all the bands. I wasn't paying attention to their lyrics. I really was just so excited to be there, and I was really in my own little world, and I was just trying to perform well. Also, partying my ass off. I can't really remember a time where I was like, "These lyrics bother me, and that sucks." I was more actually bothered by a lot of the dudes on that tour.

JULIET SIMMS (AUTOMATIC LOVELETTER/LILITH CZAR): I would get music video edits back and I'm like, "How many shots of me bending over do we need?" You know, "We want you in a bikini. We want you in less makeup, to look younger." My A&R is mentioning to my managers, "Is she getting fat? Does she need to be put on a diet?" Men being inappropriate. You know, it's on and on and on and on. But yeah, I think that's something that I don't really want to talk about.

JESS BOWEN (THE SUMMER SET): I didn't come out. I had this stigma in my mind. A lot of it has to do with the fact that I grew up in such a

---

* Darren Walters and Tim Owen, owners of the Delaware independent label Jade Tree, which specialized in emo.

conservative area of Arizona. Being gay wasn't "normal." I didn't have many gay friends around or even anyone that I could look up to, to have the courage to be like, "Oh, OK, if they're gay, like, it's fine." That was never a thing. So, I didn't come out until I guess I was twenty-two. So, that would have been 2012 or 2013 is when I came out.

SIMMS: The pressure as a woman to be a stunning, sexy thing, as if the sands of time have never touched you . . . the pressure I have felt for the years that I've been in the music industry to be very pleasing to look at, I mean, it's left PTSD on my fuckin' soul. I have to practice not giving a fuck what someone thinks about what I look like. Because it's something I dealt with every single day for the last fifteen years.

KAY: I look back on it now, and I'm like, "Holy fucking shit. I was thrown into that really unprotected." I think that my bandmates were young. And honestly, I'm thirty now, I can see that they were young and maybe didn't know how to be protective. Or maybe they didn't care, but I doubt that. I actually got sexually assaulted on Warped Tour.

BOWEN: So, there were a good few years of me being in the band where I was hiding it. And I also felt like . . . I don't know how to say it. I was just scared to be the gay girl in the band. I was like, *I need to be the girl in the band, if there's guy fans that like me.* I felt like I wanted to have that edge. That comes with just being young and thinking like, *Oh, this is quote-unquote "fame." I've got to keep my sexual identity to myself so that like people don't judge me.* I think that probably led to why I drank so much all the time when I was on the road.

KAY: I'm eighteen years old. I'm fresh out of high school. I'm not new—I've been touring for maybe a year or two now—but I'm new to this world. I'm vulnerable, I'm naive, I'm not very sexually experienced, and I was easily preyed upon. And for the most part, I could laugh it off and ignore it. And I also intimidated a lot of men, and I think that helped a lot. A lot of them wouldn't even approach me. But obviously there is some person who felt like they could, and they lured me into a vulnerable position and assaulted me. He was really aggressive, and there was no consent. I had to beg him to stop. I was crying.

BOWEN: This was another thing about being the only girl in the band—I felt like I had to prove myself all the time. So, I always had to be like, "I need to be the girl that can hang with the guys, too." I liked being known as the girl that could out-drink the guys. And that's not healthy.

KAY: I was super ashamed, and I hid it. And they still probably don't know. I never really talked about it, but obviously felt like it was my fault. But now I'm thirty, and I look back, and I'm like, "That was horrific." That absolutely should have been a position I should have never been in, but I just wasn't protected.

BOWEN: I was hiding my identity, and I just was escaping through drinking. And then I think as time went on, I kind of became known as the partier in the band, too, because of it.

KAY: It happened on my own bus, but no one knew what was happening, because it was the back of the bus. It's embarrassing. He stormed off the bus, and when I come out, I'm not going to be like, "Oh, hey, my bandmates and friends, here's this really embarrassing thing that happened. I'm really ashamed. And I'm also fucked up right now. I'm crying and feeling weird." I just knew they weren't going to give me a hug and be protective. I just didn't have that.

BOWEN: As the years went on, you know, I remember in 2016, like Steven [Gomez], my band member, actually brought it up to me and was like, "I think you're drinking too much. Like, we've all thought this." Everyone would want to just come drink with me all the time. And then it felt like this thing I had to always prove then, because I was known as that. So I have to just be able to drink as much as everyone thought I could. The party girl, I guess, is what it felt like.

KAY: They were definitely older than me. I don't know exactly their age, but definitely older than me. They were behind the scenes. I think they were a tour manager. I don't exactly remember their whole thing. When girls started claiming all this shit and the #MeToo movement happened, I'm looking back at that experience, and I was so vulnerable and so naive, and it's absolutely terrifying to think, "I'm going to announce this to the world." I wonder if he thinks about it, during this whole #MeToo movement and all this cancel culture, and is fucking terrified and just waiting for the moment I do it.

BOWEN: Smartpunk was a site that I followed all the time, and then there was one that ended up turning out to be a horrible, horrible website, but I didn't know it until after my band kind of started getting some notoriety, because then I started getting posted on there. It was called StrikeGently. It had been posting about bands and upcoming artists that were in the MySpace scene, and I would always go check it out. But that ended up becoming one of the ones that I pretty much despised because of how misogynistic it was. Whoever was running it ended up putting up fake nude photos of me and stuff, after my band started getting some notoriety. You go to it and in between random posts there would be like some type of pornographic-looking image, using images of girls that were in some of these bands. I happened to be one of them. I obviously freaked out about that, and I was like, "How do I get this taken down?" I honestly don't remember what happened with it. I think I kind of just had to blow it off and just hope that people thought that it was fake. I just know that the site itself ended up getting shut down because, of course, it was illegal what this person was doing. I was like eighteen, nineteen years old at this time.

SIMON: It doesn't stop being disappointing, because you want humanity to be better. You want men to be better. You want elders to be better. And when they're not, it's just such a letdown, because that's how we should treat each other. It should be the rule. It shouldn't be the exception that we're kind and we're caring. These are not the sexiest words, but they're the most important things, especially when you're dealing with under-age artists. Because they need guidance and they need advocates. And if someone like me, who is in their twenties, didn't feel like she had a voice, there's absolutely no way that someone in their teens can possibly feel like they have one.

KAY: It took a long time to get past. But that is something that did happen at Warped Tour, and it's extremely problematic. And when Warped Tour ended, it made sense. We look back at times before ours, and we're like, "How did we let that happen? How was that not a discussion?" It's a different time, and the misogyny was huge. I think back now . . . I could not speak up about anything. I really just had to shut up, grin it, bear it. It was a privilege for me to even be there. So to be there and speak out on things, I feel like I would have been swept under the rug, and this whole dream I had would be taken away. That's the reality of it.

SIMON: As a woman going on tour with these bands and being put in situations that aren't normal—like going to strip clubs, not really normal, sleeping on a bus in mixed company, not really normal for a stranger, but—it was just, "That's what you have to do. That's what it takes." And if you ask too many questions and if you're uncomfortable, you're deemed difficult. You're a bitch. And no one wants to work with the bitch. That definitely played into a fair amount of my opportunities at *AP*. It was, "Does the band want to hang out with you? Are you fun or are you going to be a narc?" My male colleagues didn't go through the same line of questioning that I did. It's not my favorite thing to think about, because it just makes me angry.

AMY FLEISHER MADDEN (FIDDLER RECORDS): I've had a hard time my whole life with being a woman in music. I was nineteen years old, and I got in a van with six dudes I didn't really know and drove around America. And there were just, like, there were so many things that I had to work out for myself with bands that I traveled with. At some point, I had to tell the entire band, "Hey guys, when we stop to go to the bathroom, and we're at a rest stop, and it's 2:00 AM, I need someone to go with me, because I feel like I'm in danger."

BOWEN: I was around men all the time. If there were girls on tour, it was few and far between. I would be the only girl, and I would be hearing horrible jokes and things that they would say about girls or, you know, sexualizing them or whatever it was. And I would just laugh along, and just be like, "Ha, oh yeah." But I will say that that was like more in the beginning of it, because I think, again, I was trying to prove that I could hang. And then after a year, I would be livid. I would just get mad at them. I would say that it kind of ruined my relationship with some of them for a while, because I just saw who they really were. I'm not saying they were bad guys, but they were saying things that were just so inappropriate, and I hated them for it. So I just stopped being nice to them, too. And I feel like it kind of ruined our relationships, because I was like hearing these things come out of their mouths, and I would try to tell them to stop or change, and they would just think that I was, you know, maybe being uptight or something. Like I couldn't take a joke or something.

SIMON: There weren't a lot of women on stage [at Warped Tour]; there weren't a lot of women on staff. Women were treated differently. I think that women in the music industry are unfortunately treated as and seen mostly as maternal window dressing. And if you are not a lovey, dovey, smiley, happy, perky, optimistic cheerleader one hundred percent of the time, you're a bitch. It's either A or B. There's no other option on the Scantron.

KAY: I was specifically told I was fat. They told me I was gaining weight, I didn't look good, and that's hard, because I was a dancer for pretty much a decade before I ever started touring. So I was always in dance class and doing competitions. That was my physical world. So when I stopped and went touring, immediately, my body started changing, because I wasn't doing that. And you're in the limelight, and once again, you have the old bald white guys sitting around saying, "You're fat, you need to change that."

SIMON: I would hope that [Kevin Lyman] and anyone else that was seen as a gatekeeper would take great care of those who participate in [Warped Tour], whether it's on the stage, behind the stage, or in front of the stage. Do I believe that they're omniscient, and they can see everything going on at all times? Absolutely not. Do I hope that they all have good intentions, and the instances that they did hear of where there was questionable behavior, that they acted swiftly and justly? I sure hope so. But how are we to know? There's no expiration date on trauma.

KAY: I wouldn't say I got a full-blown eating disorder, but I was definitely getting obsessive about food and what I was eating and how I put it in my body. And I had to go to a trainer. It definitely was hard. You wanna look pretty. It's something I honed in on. I remember we put out a video or something on YouTube, there'd be one comment or something, like, "She's fat." I was losing my mind. It's sad.

BOWEN: 2010 Warped Tour, there was a guy who was a very notable, well-known sound engineer. Everyone used to go to him to get their albums mixed and mastered and all that. And I remember being cornered by him behind the buses after a barbecue—the barbecues at the end of the shows where everyone would drink and eat and all that stuff, and most everyone just gets really drunk. And he had cornered me behind the back of a trailer or some place and said, "If your band ever wants to get your albums mixed or mastered or whatever by me, you know—basically, you have to hook up with me right now."

SIMMS: It was horrible. My drummer stayed with me from the previous band. The band that we hired, I mean, I guess I kind of got my karma, because I hired this band, and they were fucking assholes. Very, very, very misogynist. They wouldn't listen to me on anything. If I wanted something a certain way I was a diva or a bitch. I constantly overheard them talking shit or rolling their eyes or whatever. And halfway into my first tour with them, a new president comes in and drops me.

BOWEN: He was cornering me, he had me up against the trailer, and thank god one of my friends had noticed that I had gone missing. She somehow found me, and she grabbed me and took me away. I came onto the bus and I told the guys, and I was all flustered and pissed off and like, "Fuck that guy, we're never working with him."

SIMMS: They very much wanted me to pretend like it was a real band. That's oppressive and sexist, if you think about it, it's like, "Oh, you don't think I can stand on my own two feet? I have to have men behind me for it to be believable?" That's something later on down the line I look back at, and I was like, "Fuck you!"

BOWEN: This is the problem when I look back on things. Women weren't as comfortable or open about reporting things. It felt like "Oh, you're being a tattletale." I told the guys in my band, and it just felt like, "Oh, I'm glad they had my back," right? That to me, that was the best-case scenario, that the guys in my band, I was happy that they weren't mad at me. I remember thinking, *Oh my god, they're going to be so mad*, because this was someone we had always wanted to work with. So that kind of shows you a little bit of the mentality that I think we as women—and especially women in this industry—have. It's like, you're scared, but it's still your fault, right? That's how you feel. I'm not even saying this person's name, because I'm still scared.

SCOTT HEISEL (*ALTERNATIVE PRESS* EDITOR): There's a lot of things that bummed me out, and there's a lot of things that I'm upset I didn't know about, that I wasn't aware they were happening. People go, "How do you not know?" Because you just didn't know. I wasn't on tour with these bands. Access is being pulled back as quickly as the bands were getting popular to avoid these stories.

BOWEN: Our band for sure had lyrics, especially on our first album, that were really bad, and anyone could look them up now and be like, "Yeah, what?" We're all in our thirties now. We're like, "Geez, what were we thinking?" We were eighteen years old writing those songs, and you look back on it, and you're just like, "Wow, well, that still exists in the world, but I hope people know that we've really grown up from that." But we just didn't notice till we got older that we were like, "This is really misogynistic."

MAX BEMIS (SAY ANYTHING/MAXIM MENTAL): I knew, everyone knew. But not about illegal stuff, but it was the least surprising thing of all time. Every other guy in The Scene was a cheat. The word *cheater* is a little sus, because a lot of them are legit sex addicts and alcoholics or narcissists or codependents. And they were baby-men. I liked Brand New, and he was a fan of Say Anything, and we became friends for a second. And then as soon as I went from being just a fan of the music to knowing everyone else's business, then you find out this person just has sex with every girl in the world. This person is cheating on their wife.

JONAH MATRANGA (FAR/ONELINEDRAWING): We just didn't have the fucking collective awareness around this. It was never lost on me that The Scene I was singing in was super white and super male. And I was always happy that Far had more women at its shows and up front. And Fugazi was a band that taught me that the mosh pit didn't have to be all angry dudes and to actively push back against that. So I liked the energy, and I was really into that. I don't want to give it too hard a time, but yes, rock 'n' roll, period, is a horrifically patriarchal, misogynistic shit show. There's no way to honestly look at the history and present of rock 'n' roll without acknowledging that fact. I certainly don't think [emo] was worse. I only think maybe it was a little more hypocritical. Because it's like progressive white people not wanting to talk about white supremacy. It's just a lot of them were sensitive, not wanting to talk about that, they were still basically not giving women a chance. I think the only way through these systems is to be honest about it.

BEMIS: I was just relieved that #MeToo happened, and I was just relieved that some of these people were being held accountable, and I was relieved to hold myself accountable for some of the stuff that I did. It was good that I was nervous. I'm very glad that I never did anything illegal or did anything that I wouldn't say publicly or joke about or make fun of, whatever, nothing that makes me unproud to be myself. But if you don't learn something from it, you're a narcissist.

MATT PRYOR (THE GET UP KIDS/THE NEW AMSTERDAMS): So I've wrestled with this in general in my own life in the last couple of years, because as I'm realizing now that . . . punk rock, when I was in high school and throughout my life, has been the closest thing I've ever had to a religion, and it absolutely one hundred percent saved my life, but I think it's failed my kids, to a certain degree, but I think that's changing. I think that the culture is finally becoming more inclusive and intersectional, but it was kinda grappling with the concept that we're all outsiders and we're in this together and then kind of realizing, but we're all straight white cis male outsiders, and so therefore we're excluding other people who are more outside of normal society than we are. This has come up in the last couple of years trying to explain trans issues to people my age.

GEOFF RICKLY (THURSDAY): I have to say, there were fairly popular bands who I would say, like, "Look, hey, I don't like your lyrics. This is why you keep asking us to tour together, and I keep saying no, and the rest of my band really likes your band and thinks that it sucks that I won't tour with you because of your song lyrics. But this is what I'm talking about, and this is what bothers me, and this is what I don't wanna be associated with, and I don't want our fan base to be subjected to X, Y and Z." And the reaction that I got from some of them was like, "Yeah, I was a kid, and you're right, that shit sucks. It's not gonna be like that anymore. We're not gonna write songs like that anymore." And those are the people that we have ended up playing with a lot more later, and I've made friends with. Because as much as I think things should be a certain way, I also think people do stupid shit all the time. They should be allowed to fix those things.

PRYOR: I feel like I was being an ally by not being a bad person, but I realize now that that was not enough, and if anything, that was actually detrimental to the cause. I think the only thing you can do is look at it and go like, "Damn, didn't think about it at the time, but in hindsight, fuck, what a monoculture." But now it's moving forward, it's just like all right, we need to be advocates.

HEISEL: I mean, Jessica Hopper* wrote that big piece years ago, and I think that a lot of it still rings true. I think we were unwitting accomplices

---

* A well-respected music journalist and the author of *The First Collection of Criticism by a Living Female Rock Critic*, her 2003 essay for *Punk Planet*, "Where the Girls Aren't," called the emo scene out for, among other things, its lack of female performers and its monomaniacal focus on men's pain.

for a period of time at *AP* where we didn't necessarily realize it. Our staff was primarily white, primarily men, and we didn't necessarily realize the damage that maybe was being caused by kind of propping all these people up. We eventually kind of caught on to it. I remember at one point we kicked a band out of the magazine. We were going to cover this band, and we read the lyrics and were like, "Nope." I don't remember the name of the band. It was some terrible, terrible, terrible band. They had some song that was all like, "Fuck you, you fucking bitch, I'm going to fuck . . ." That was like the lyrics of a song. I'm like, "We're not covering this band." Like, sorry, no way.

BRANNON: People saw the Internet as the great equalizer, and MySpace was for music, for sure. But if that were true, you would think that there would have been a greater representation of women, of people of color, of queers, of all these people in this scene. There was not. So where was the equalization, why did it fail? And at the same time, what's interesting, too, is that I still equate the rise of a particular type of hip-hop to MySpace. So it's not like people of color were not on the platform.

KAY: Unfortunately I think that there's, first of all, a lot of internalized misogyny that I myself didn't even realize until I was older and had to shed those bits, because I was surrounded by men. I was just always surrounded by boys, constantly, all the time. And wanting to fit in, be a part of it, toughen up, and go with the flow. I wanted to prove that I'm not difficult. I can hang. I can take anything that comes to me, and I had to perform ten times harder than the guys.

BRANNON: I do think that MySpace created more opportunities for people of color and queer people to find each other and to not feel alone. I do know that for a fact. Some of those people reached out to me during that era, through the Texas page or through my own page, to talk about that particular stuff. But in terms of the bands that were actually huge . . . it was the heterosexual white male takeover more so than ever. Obviously, heterosexual white males have always been the primacy of punk in a lot of ways, obviously, but there were things like Bad Brains or like Dead Kennedys or other bands that had people of color in them. But there was something that was distinct about this wave, because of the class factor. I think that a lot of the hardcore stuff and, even in the '90s, I think a lot of the stuff that I was involved in, it was the middle-class people for sure. But this so felt like the experience of upper-middle-class heterosexual white. It was very difficult for me to sort of wrap my head around. But there was definitely a sense to me that that's sort of what you get when the people who are the gatekeepers are all coming from that place. I think coming into rock music, period, I've always felt a bit outside of the lines.

KAY: I was just talking to another female guitarist about this today. I've worked with producers that claim they want to work with me, but really, in the end, they're just trying to sleep with you. And when you say that, it seems like you're narcissistic. They're like, "You think everybody is into you." That's not the truth. I don't think that, but it is a lot of my experience. So when you tell men these things, they're like, "Oh, OK." And you aren't believed right away, and it sucks. That is the female experience, and that, I think, is why so many females are in uproar right now. Like, "Hello, this is what's going on. Please, can we talk about it? Can we address it?" Because I think a lot of men just don't understand.

11

CRASH YEARS

In 2003, MCA's parent company Universal Records absorbed the label into Geffen Records, another label it owned. This sort of dizzying shuffling of the corporate cards had become quite common since 1998, when the alcoholic beverage company Seagrams purchased the entertainment company PolyGram, which owned Universal, which owned major labels ranging from Island to Def Jam to Interscope. What this endlessly complex consolidation meant for the average music fan was that the majority of major labels were ultimately owned by one of three major companies, with the other two being Sony and the Warner Music Group. Consolidation and the lack of competition might be good for a corporation's bottom line, but it's rarely good for fans, artists, or freedom of choice.

For Drive-Thru Records, the end result was Geffen was able to take any bands from the label it wanted, which happened to be New Found Glory and the Starting Line. "They were cursing MCA, all the time," says John T. Frazier. "I guess they got royally screwed, but they did the deal." After a failed attempt at a relaunch, Drive-Thru folded in 2008. Its legacy is a lot of records that made plenty of kids happy and much criticism for the corporatization of pop punk and emo.

Drive-Thru churned out vaguely emo, utterly interchangeable pop-punk bands with machinelike efficiency. But eventually it was swallowed up by the music industry and stripped for spare parts. Eventually, the rest of The Scene would follow.

As the '00s came to an end, MySpace and the Internet were breaking artists quicker than ever before, in all senses of the term. A platform that seemed untouchable just a few years earlier was beginning to feel the bends, and The Scene it fostered was about to go down with it.

In 2007, Fall Out Boy were one of the biggest acts in the world. In December of 2008, they released *Folie à Deux*, in reference to the tense working relationship between Pete Wentz and Patrick Stump. The album garnered some of the band's best reviews yet but didn't even sell half of what *Infinity on High* sold, which itself was considered a commercial letdown compared to *From Under the Cork Tree*.

By the end of 2009, the band unofficially broke up for several years after a show at Madison Square Garden. During this period, Wentz married and had a child with Ashlee Simpson. The relationship was catnip to both the gossip-obsessed scene and the hyperinvasive tabloid culture of the late '00s but was also tumultuous and short-lived. The couple divorced in 2011.

Folie à Deux represented an attempt to move beyond the emo punk they'd made their name on, embracing an artsy classic-pop style that maybe their fans weren't ready for. But the real reason for its muted commercial response was that after the stock market crash of 2008, a lot of people just didn't have money to spend on things like physical media. By the end of 2008, CD sales had sunk to their lowest levels yet, down 14 percent from the year before, and while sales of digital music were on the rise, the *New York Times* notes that "analysts say that despite the growth and promise of digital music—in 2003 just 19 million songs were purchased as downloads—the money made online is still far from enough to make up for losses in physical sales."

Discretionary income was drying up, which meant less money for tickets and merchandise from fans and less patience from the music industry for all but the biggest names. Best Buy cut back on the number of CDs it carried, and MTV shifted its focus even further to reality television programming like *The Hills* and *A Shot at Love with Tila Tequila*, which proved more effective in retaining an audience for more than a few minutes at a time but had the effect of making music feel like a cultural afterthought. No one was having a good time in 2009 and 2010, except perhaps the biggest names in pop. As sales contracted and the economy suffered in the wake of the 2008 economic crash, the recording industry seemingly had no idea what to do. The bubble was bursting, hard.

Wentz formed the group Black Cards with pop star Bebe Rexha and hosted the tattoo competition reality show *Best Ink*, and Stump released the New Wave and Motown–influenced solo debut *Soul Punk*, which was critically acclaimed but ignored both by his fans and a potential listener base that wasn't going to touch a solo project by the Fall Out Boy guy with a ten-foot pole.

SCOTT HEISEL (*ALTERNATIVE PRESS* EDITOR): With *Infinity on High,* I remember seeing them on tour, it was an arena for like eighteen thousand people. Maybe two years later, they're playing a five-thousand-person outdoor amphitheater and there were maybe a thousand people there and that was on tour with All Time Low and, again, Cobra Starship. You could just see it was dead. Things were splintering. That was the end of Fall Out Boy, Mach One. But *Folie à Deux* is the only album of theirs that I like, go figure.

GABE SAPORTA (MIDTOWN/HUMBLE BEGINNINGS/COBRA STARSHIP): At this time, I got into spirituality. I got really into ayahuasca, and I felt like that actually saved my life in a way. And so I wanted to help my friends. So I remember when Pete was going through this whole thing, and he was getting divorced at the same time, too. I just took a flight and went to his house and spent time with him, and he had to go to Japan for something, so I went with him to Japan. I felt like I tried to be there for my friends as much as I could. We had our Fueled By Ramen, Decaydance crew. That's the nice thing, it was a real thing. We were all friends. We hung together, we were all really close. And it felt like everyone was going through shit then. People were starting to pay the price a little bit, and things were getting rough.

HEISEL: The bands were still there and wanted to succeed. But all of a sudden, there wasn't much disposable income. Parents couldn't give their kids a hundred bucks to go buy a hoodie at Warped Tour.

SAPORTA: He was in pain, man. And honestly, seeing Pete get divorced is what made me feel that if I get married, I am going to stop doing music. It's very hard to be married, have kids, and be able to dedicate the time you need to grow a family when you have to go on tour for eight to ten months out of the year.

LESLIE SIMON (*ALTERNATIVE PRESS*): A lot of bands often come to a crossroads where something's got to give. In some cases it is the family. In some cases it's the band. In some cases it's the touring. There's the old adage: you can have it all, just not all at the same time. That's where I think sometimes bands take a break in order to have a life outside of the road. Whether or not they can pick up where they started, that's a different question.

HEISEL: You had bands like Paramore on those 360 deals. The label was seeing the writing on the wall, like, "This is not going to turn around. So we need to get a piece of every bit of your income. So all your sync licensing, all your touring, all your merchandise, all that stuff." So it certainly felt like the pie shrunk a whole lot for our corner of the music industry. Pop artists will always have infinite budgets. Lady Gaga's budget will never get slashed. But you're not going to see Taking Back Sunday have the same budget they had for album number seven as they had for *Louder Now*. They can't. So I think it definitely affected everybody.

Makeoutclub was to MySpace and Facebook what early emo groups like Texas Is the Reason and the Get Up Kids were to My Chemical Romance. They set the groundwork, but they wouldn't be the ones to take it to the masses. Gibby Miller partnered with IndieClick, a media network, and actually saw a boost in traffic in 2008. "We rolled out a bunch of new features that sort of became commonplace on dating apps. So, we had this thing called the Crush List, where you could add somebody on Makeoutclub to your Crush List, totally anonymous. And if they added you, you would both get a note." He retained ownership of Makeoutclub. "That was very important to me," he says, but eventually IndieClick was acquired in 2011 by Demand Media. "The CEO of Demand Media was Richard Rosenblatt," he remembers, "who famously sold MySpace to Rupert Murdoch while wearing shorts and flip-flops. We ended up in the old MySpace, the original offices in Santa Monica, which was a fun time." Eventually, he would form his own small record label and marketing agency. Adulthood had arrived. "I just got to the point where, like, I didn't have time anymore. I couldn't hire staff for Makeoutclub. It cost me money to run it at that point. I'm just over it."

———

Paramore was the most popular young band in America by 2010, with celebrity fans such as Rihanna and Bruce Springsteen, a gold record with the 2009 album *Brand New Eyes*, and a single on the wildly popular *Twilight* soundtrack. You'd think being at the height of your success would be enough to keep a band together, but apparently not. Josh and Zac Farro left Paramore in late 2010, with Josh later writing a blog accusing Williams, her management, and her father of having too much control over the band.* From there, the Paramore lineup would continually shift, as Zac Farro would rejoin in 2016 and Jeremy Davis left in 2015 following disputes over royalties. For a brief period, Williams left the band while seeking treatment for depression, leaving Taylor York, who officially joined for *Riot!* as the only member of the band before she returned.

"When you don't see a lot of women taking center stage, when you do see it, it can mean everything," says Simon. "Hayley is just a powerhouse. She's a one-in-a-million type of person."

Dashboard Confessional returned in late 2009 with *Alter the Ending*, working with producer and songwriter Butch Walker. The album was

---

* In a social media post, Williams would later say the big source of conflict between her and Josh Farro were his retrograde opinions about the LGBTQ community.

met with a muted response from fans and critics. A similar fate awaited Taking Back Sunday, who once again went through a lineup change with the departure of Mascherino, who left after a summer package tour with My Chemical Romance and Linkin Park, a rap-metal band once viewed by emo fans as the enemy. Taking Back Sunday recruited guitarist Matthew Fazzi for 2009's *New Again*, though like Dashboard, they seemed to have gotten lost in the shuffle. Both were too professional to just whiff it, but both albums had the sound of burned-out artists trying hard when they really needed to take a break.

"They just didn't get along," Heisel muses about Taking Back Sunday during this period. "Fred was very much the older brother to Adam, and if you're the good older brother, you can offer your younger brother all sorts of advice and life lessons and try to guide them in the right direction. But the younger brother doesn't want that. They're going to push back and be a brat."

Sherwood would try to shed their Warped Tour ways on *QU*, which found Nate Henry maturing as a singer and the band exploring their love of classic pop. But by the time of its release in 2009, MySpace Records was barely functioning, and the album was barely promoted or even noticed by many critics.

In 2010, Motion City Soundtrack released *My Dinosaur Life* through Columbia Records to stellar reviews, cementing them as The Scene's critical favorites. Hopes were high for the single "Her Words Destroyed My Planet," but first the label had some thoughts on Justin Pierre's appearance, pressuring him to go to a weight loss camp to counter the side-effects of his medication. After the Get Up Kids broke up in 2005, Matt Pryor would focus on family life and his solo career as a singer-songwriter, both under his own name and the project the New Amsterdams. The Get Up Kids would periodically return for albums and tours, such as 2011's *There Are Rules* and 2019's *Problems*, proving that they were all still emo after all these years. Pryor also became a part-time farmer for a while as well. "It was nice 'cause it had nothing to do with the music industry and scenes, politics, jealousy, any of that stuff.

"I didn't have any regrets about our level of success," he adds. "I'm fully aware of the decisions that we made."

Say Anything signed with the indie label Equal Vision. After the straightforward 2012 album *Anarchy, My Dear,* Max Bemis went on a wild run, releasing *Hebrews* in 2014, a string-laden exploration of his Jewish identity, and 2016's *I Don't Think It Is,* an experimental fusion of emo and hip-hop. In 2019, Say Anything released *Oliver Appropriate,* which found Bemis coming out as bisexual and reconciling with the persona he created on earlier albums. He then retired the project to focus on his mental health and spend time with his wife and family. But along the way, Bemis finally found the respect he'd been craving, as he collaborated with young, buzzy bands like Los Campesinos! and Japanese Breakfast's Michelle Zauner, and . . . *Is a Real Boy* started being recognized as a classic of a genre.

"Sometimes I don't appreciate what I have enough or give myself any credit, but then other times I'm just shocked at my luck and the blessing that my life is. It feels good as fuck, because I knew it was good," says Bemis. "I was so jaded. I never thought this would happen."

JONAH MATRANGA (FAR/ONELINEDRAWING): When Napster came around, one of the reasons I was so sad is because really popular, mainstream bands had a fan base that really wasn't interested in all this stuff anyway, they were still buying their stuff. But disproportionately, indie bands and Internet-savvy bands took the brunt of that hit, because all these people thought they were sticking it to the man by downloading music. But they're really just downloading the music of people who actually really needed their support. So they helped gut the insides of their own scene.

NATE HENRY (SHERWOOD): I remember being in the studio making *QU,* and Dan, our guitar player, made a Twitter for Sherwood and he sent out a bulletin and he was like, "Hey, we're on Twitter." And then we immediately got an e-mail from Tom like, "Hey guys, pretty bummed that you put this out on MySpace." And I think he was very self-conscious at that time that other social media networks were winning, and he's a smart guy, so he knew that the writing was on the wall, and then here's one of his bands promoting Twitter. I was using Facebook way more than I was using MySpace, and I remember going, "Shit, if *I'm* using this website, then everyone else is too, so here we go."

MAX BEMIS (SAY ANYTHING/MAXIM MENTAL): Ten years later, you're cool, and then you're not cool, and then you're just pretty much cool for the rest of your career, but you'll never be as popular. I've just seen it play out so many times.

SIMON: I don't know if you know the threshold of bigness until you get that big. How big is too big? You know the feeling when you're blowing up the balloon, you get the tingling in the side of your jaw? No matter how big that balloon is, you're like, "Can I squeeze a little bit more, or should I tie it off now and call it a day? Or am I OK with it popping?" And I think that's what happens to a lot of bands who reach a certain echelon of popularity and notoriety. Can you weather it and still maintain the same height? Or do you have to dip down in order to survive longer? And who knows if they would have weathered, if they stayed together.

HEISEL: [Taking Back Sunday] would have fallen apart if it were not for Fred, because he was older, he had five or six years on [Adam]. But he's like, "I don't want to be in this band anymore, I can't do this." It was just too toxic for him. It's no secret that the band was toxic, right? Look at all the lineup changes, and you know how hard it was. And Adam was not super easy to be around.

HENRY: I think MySpace was kinda diehard, they were like, "Nah, nah, we're still gonna be able to do something," but then the general manager of the record label quit, and we were like, "Uh-oh." The last thing we did was like a radio tour with MySpace. They paid for us to fly all over the West Coast to radio stations and promote a song off that record, but that record was a little bit different than our previous album, and the economy had taken a crash in 2008. It didn't matter what label you were on, everyone was like, "Man, the shows are like less than half of what they were a year ago." The album did come out, but it kinda felt like an afterthought.

JUSTIN COURTNEY PIERRE (MOTION CITY SOUNDTRACK): Oh yeah, the Warped Tour thing, I forget what year it is, I don't even know what they're called, but I remember seeing like a hundred people on stage in a band all wearing bright hot-pink and green outfits and shorts, with tons of tattoos, and somebody was singing these wonderful melodies, and then then they were just like, "*Rrr!*" Like guttural screams and then rapping, and it was so confusing. And people loved it, and I did not understand what was happening with music, and that was when I realized, "Oh, I'm officially old, because I don't get it."

HENRY: I think a lot of the fans of bands in that scene got their money from their parents, and there was just no money. So that took a toll, and then MySpace died to Facebook, and it was a really rough time to be in a band.

JOSHUA CAIN (MOTION CITY SOUNDTRACK): It was a strange experience. We definitely went on Warped Tours that felt less like the Warped Tour we were a part of, right? It felt like "I don't know any of these people; I don't wanna hang out with any of Them. They are like, you know, not my type of people, maybe." They're in that moment where they're starting to blow up and the world's their oyster, and you see these people, and you're like, "Ehh, good luck, and you're also acting like a lunatic, drinking Fireball every night."

PIERRE: I think Tony* reached that breaking point before all of us. He even said, "I'm never doing Warped Tour again."

CAIN: And then when we signed for a Warped Tour, he quit.

HEISEL: Motion City Soundtrack are too fucking smart. They were too goddamn good at it, They could not dumb themselves down if they wanted to, and they tried to dumb themselves down. I want Motion City to be the biggest band in the world, and they can't ever be. But they were like Get Up Kids in that they influenced so many bands. Motion City is like one of the bands where, like, every band is like, "Oh my god, we want to be

---

* Drummer Tony Thaxton.

that band." Whereas, ironically, Motion City wants to be them, because the other bands are bigger.

HENRY: All of a sudden MySpace just wasn't the place to find music anymore, really. We had a hard time connecting with our fans that we connected with on the first record because we could just tell Tom, like, "Hey, send a message to 150,000 people," and then all of a sudden it was like those kids weren't on MySpace. They were on Twitter or they were on Facebook, or they were reading music blogs. All of a sudden it was like there were no rules. There used to be some rules, like, "Oh yeah, if you just do this thing, people will know about your band." And then all of a sudden it's like, "Nope, no one knows about your band anymore."

MySpace was a space for hustling, and Saporta's hustle knew no limits. He began investing in real estate and opened up a restaurant in New York City. Cobra Starship scored a Top 10 *Billboard* hit with "Good Girls Go Bad," which was late '00s mass culture distilled into pop music; it was cowritten and produced by then *American Idol* judge Kara DioGuardi and Black Eyed Peas and Lil Wayne collaborator Kevin Rudolf, with vocals from *Gossip Girl* star Leighton Meester. (She agreed to do the guest appearance in exchange for Saporta giving up studio time he'd already booked.) Naturally, Flo Rida later jumped on the remix, and Saporta cameoed on the show.

While the song had the bottle service thump that the times were increasingly demanding, it was ultimately a goofy, sanitized spin on the sleazed-out dance music overtaking America's clubs at the time, which explains why it did so well. But fame wasn't always fun, as the *New York Times* published Saporta's home address when he purchased a luxury condo, and superfans began stalking him, and the constant cycle of touring, recording, and promoting strained his long-term relationship.

Sherwood was about to hit the limit of what their hustling could achieve without the support of MySpace. To keep the dream alive, they toured as much as possible, including opening dates for '90s teen-pop survivors Hanson.

After leaving Island Records, Thursday signed with Epitaph and released the streamlined and punchy *Common Existence*. It's arguably their heaviest album overall, but one thoughtful enough to have lyrics inspired by the writer David Foster Wallace. Downsizing from a major label and leaving behind other people's expectations was a relief, but the landscape was still rocky, as the band was talked into headlining that year's Taste of Chaos (an indoor version of the Warped Tour for the winter months) with a lineup they were ill-suited for, playing for an uninterested audience that was there for metalcore acts Bring Me the Horizon and Pierce the Veil, who sound exactly like you would expect them to sound. At the time, Geoff Rickly's tendency to self-medicate and abuse his prescription drugs began to lead to a deepening addiction.

The Scene was contracting drastically, and everyone was starting to feel the pinch from the economic crash and the end of the MySpace Era.

For their 2010 album *Streets of Gold*, 3OH!3 were upstreamed to Atlantic Records. Critics came with their knives out, many of them focusing on the lyrics of the single "Touchin' on My." Two more albums followed (*Omens* in 2013 and *Night Sports* in 2016), with neither repeating the success of *Want*. The keg had been tapped, but it's cool. Honestly, they're just happy to be here. The duo kept busy as songwriters and producers, writing for artists ranging from Maroon 5 to Ariana Grande.

After five years of recording and dealing with the collapse of his former label TVT, Lil Jon finally released his official solo debut *Crunk Rock* through Universal Republic. "I sued. I had lawsuits against them, like on the books to see the accounting and all this type of shit," he says of TVT. "And then they went bankrupt, so they didn't have to pay me and probably Pitbull and whoever else." With multiple guests per song, *Crunk Rock* prompted critics to note that it seemed as though his signature Lil Jon-ness had fallen by the wayside. It debuted at number forty-nine on the *Billboard* charts, a surprisingly low number for such a recognizable artist, and Lil Jon has yet to release another solo album. He focused on DJing, producing, and family life for most of the '10s, gaining a comeback single with DJ Snake's multiplatinum EMD single "Turn Down for What" in 2013. He still parties. Less often, but nonetheless, he parties.

NATHANIEL MOTTE (3OH!3): Our metrics of success are a lot different than other bands'. I even avoid the term quote-unquote "*success*," because I think it's more a state of being, man. We're happy people; we're healthy people. The consecutive records didn't sell as much as the other ones, but shit, we're still touring, we're still playing great shows and in a capacity that we love doing, and we're playing a lot of shows for universities where we get to meet a lot of young people who are forward-thinking and interesting. We're delighted with everything that's happened. I think it's natural, in the arc of a band, that people listen to your old shit more. And that's why at our shows, we play probably 85 percent of our shit was released before 2011, and we're fine with that. We're happy to do that.

HEISEL: Thursday might as well have been a classic rock band. They were closing that tour out of respect. But yeah, it was a mass exodus. You had three popular Scene bands in a row. And then it was like, "Oh, it's 9:45. Well, I'm going to go home, because I have school tomorrow." But they were great on that tour.

GEOFF RICKLY (THURSDAY): Thursday did [the] summer of 2008 Warped Tour. Brutal. Like, "Man, what the fuck are we doing here? This doesn't make any sense anymore for us." And then we did Taste of Chaos in 2009, which was really like, "Get me out of here. I hate all this shit."

HEISEL: That tour played Cleveland. By that point, Bring [Me] the Horizon was already super hot. I'd seen them on Warped Tour the previous summer, and even though I didn't like it, I was like, "You guys, we need to be covering this band." The Fall Out Boy issue tanked, and that was like, "OK, now we're officially done, we're going to start doing metalcore." And so we did a Taste of Chaos cover, which was Bring Me the Horizon on one cover and Thursday on the cover. Guess which one sold way more?

RICKLY: We didn't belong there, for one thing. Every other band on the bill belonged together, and we did not. I don't have anything against Pierce the Veil or anything against Four Year Strong. Nothing. Those guys are great. The Bring Me the Horizon guys were not cool to be on tour with at the time—they fucking sucked. I've heard they've grown up a lot since then, but not from the beginning. All the kids who came out to see that tour wanted to see that stuff. That was what was happening there. And Thursday was old news. There'd be shows with like two thousand people at them, and we'd play to a hundred.

HENRY: Hanson, man, it was a blur. Some of us were still single, but imagine doing a tour with a band and like, it was like ninety-eight percent females your age at the shows. It was crazy. It was like all these Hanson fans had grown up, and they were all at that show and they were ready to see some bands play. But Hanson has *the* most hardcore fans of any band I've ever seen. I met my wife on that tour, so it was a good tour in that regard.

RICKLY: I remember very clearly after a discussion that we had in the band, it was like, "Yeah, we're king of the hill, but the hill is shit." And that was mostly because I think we were sort of feeling like a lot of the bands that were influenced by us at the time, or said they were influenced by us at the time, just didn't reflect anything that we cared about. And I think that was very like, "Are we the only ones who don't see . . . that we suck too?"

HENRY: Literally our managers were quitting, our booking agent was kind of moving on, the label was falling apart. Over the course of that tour, we lost everything that we had built over the course of six years. Some guys were making phone calls on the tour, trying to get work.

SIMON: I couldn't understand the Leighton Meester of it all. I don't know if I ever really got an idea of where she comes into all of this. But a lot of things about the music scene were very confusing.

SAPORTA: We did a TRL takeover. Pete and I were announcers on the VMAs. It felt very part of pop culture. And that was one of my goals with doing Cobras. Even though I'm a punk rock kid, I also love pop culture. I genuinely loved *Gossip Girl*. That's why [my cameo] ended up happening, because I was an actual fan at the time. It was also a strange time culturally where you had permission to be into silly stuff. It felt like there wasn't a revolution happening at that time.

LIL JON: I was burnt out by then, because I had been, for ten years or so, producing myself and artists and it just, you know, caught up with me; there's a lot of pressure. The label is always looking at me to make sure I give them hits and singles. So it was a lot of stress on me to get the projects done. So, you know, and that's a lot of work, plus all of the outside tracks and features. So I was, you know, kind of fried.

HENRY: It sucks, because as a band you didn't appreciate the times when your band was as big as it was gonna get, if that makes sense. So we had done a couple headlining tours, and we had sold a couple shows with five hundred, six hundred tickets, and if someone would have pulled me aside and said, "This is as big as your band's gonna get, enjoy this moment, you worked all these years for *this*, it's not gonna get any bigger than this."

SAPORTA: The radio success came on the third Cobra record. I always remember thinking: *Bands only have three good records in them.* So for me personally, on the third record, that felt like the peak, the beginning of the end for me. It definitely felt culturally like it was moving away from band stuff. Electronic music was going crazy. And I think for us, because we had so many electronic elements, we were able to strut the line. And because we went pop a little bit, we were able to really move around, but it felt like The Scene we came from was dying. And I have a fucking song on the third record called "The Scene Is Dead; Long Live the Scene." Even though I was at the height of my success, I was definitely starting to feel the wear of the whole thing.

HENRY: I'm in a place where I can be happy for my friends, like Jack Antonoff* went and blew up after that Hanson tour. It's weird to have

---

* Before he went on to produce for Taylor Swift and start the projects Bleachers and fun., Antonoff fronted the Drive-Thru Records band Steel Train, which also opened that Hanson tour.

been sharing a green room where you're eating Hanson's food to try to save money, and then like a couple years later, they're getting Grammys, and they're writing for Taylor Swift.

SAPORTA: It felt like it was over around 2010. I can't point to any one thing, but it was a bunch of stuff happening at once. *Alternative Press* had no one to write about, nothing was exciting. I think Warped Tour started feeling like, "OK, who are the stars here?" Cobra became very pop, and I didn't know what the next record should be like. Fall Out Boy had broken up. I think even Panic! had taken a break. Ryan Ross left. So a lot of that stuff was like, "Oh, everything's kind of falling apart."

HEISEL: It was becoming a lot more difficult to hit that bullseye with a cover, because you're trying to find a band that people are passionate about, that people want to read more about, but still appeals to our core readership. So we would try bands like the Gaslight Anthem. Great band, the issue tanked. Manchester Orchestra, great band, issue tanked. The bands we think of as being good bands were not resonating, because by that point *AP* was so stigmatized as The Scene magazine that if we went outside of that, people wouldn't buy it. Our fans wouldn't buy it. And our detractors wouldn't buy it, because they hate us already, so we were stuck in this weird middle ground.

SAPORTA: I lost my girlfriend who had been my partner, back before I even started the band, who had been with me the whole time. I was too focused on my sadness. I didn't know how to make a fourth record. My third record was the most successful one. I had a good concept, and I made three records on that concept, and then I just didn't know what the next thing was that I wanted to say or where I wanted to go, and then I had all these personal problems. I also turned thirty, and I was just like, "What am I doing?" It's a young man's game.

HENRY: So I've done a lot of video work. I do a podcast now with a buddy, and I've flipped a couple houses in between. So I've done kinda a bit of everything. Sherwood just did a tour, which was just kind of weird to go back. So we do it now more for fun, and there's still a core group of fans that still care. It was just kind of surreal. I can't believe people still care about these songs when it felt that they were in such a MySpace time.

LIL JON: I started fucking around with *Crunk Rock* when I was still at TVT. So this whole album process was stressful in the sense of getting off TVT, getting a new deal. I signed to Universal. I was on an independent system, and now I'm in a major global system. And we just didn't mesh good. They had an idea of the way they wanted stuff to go. I had an idea where I wanted stuff to go, and I don't think they ever had really dealt with an artist like me, so it just didn't work. But after that, later on, I did "Turn Down for What." So, you know, you have failures, but failures make you stronger, give you more knowledge. In life, you can't just quit, you got to keep working. So, yeah, I was dabbling all along and all of the EDM stuff. So I kept doing records and I stumbled on the record with me and DJ Snake, and we had, you know, that record is a billion fucking YouTube views now. EDM song of the year that year. So yeah, you never quit. No matter what happens, you just keep going.

———

Some people just can't catch a break. Maybe it's timing, maybe it's sexism, maybe it's a music industry that signs artists and then proves they fundamentally don't believe in their talents.

Epic refused to release the Automatic Loveletter rock album *The Ghost We Carry Home*. After the band signed to an indie for *The Kids Will Take Their Monsters On*, Juliet Simms eventually began a solo career, joining the cast of the NBC singing competition *The Voice* for a season. VersaEmerge, which changed its name to just Versa, also struggled with their label, and disbanded after self-releasing the 2014 EP *Neon*. The band had tried to record the more moody, experimental album *Another Atmosphere*. But Sierra Kay felt caught between the album's two producers, Shaun Lopez, formerly of Far and member of the electronic pop group Crosses, and Andrew Dost, who would later form the band fun. This album also never came out.

"We brought in Andrew Dost. Obviously, he's really talented. He's been on a lot of Kanye stuff, he did some stuff for Beyoncé and a lot of big artists," Kay remarks. "I'm not the producer. I'm just writing the songs and singing them. I don't think it really worked. But again, it's one of those things where I can have all the opinions in the world, but I did not really get a say. And that really sucks."

Ultimately, record industry problems paled in comparison to the challenges both Simms and Kay were struggling with. The Summer Set would continue to be Scene mainstays and Warped Tour perennials, even as that world began to deflate in the '10s. Bowen often felt a bit out of place in a very Straight White Male world, a feeling that wouldn't be remediated when she became the touring drummer for 3OH!3.

———————

SIERRA KAY (VERSA/VERSAEMERGE): I don't think they had any intention of fucking us over or anything like that. But things changed at the label. I remember in the middle of our record, our A&R was getting fired, and John Janick's leaving, and all these new people are coming in. They were like, "Write the songs, take care of your voice. We got you a trainer. Stay fit, stay cute, and do your thing. And you don't have to worry about the rest, because we know that it can be a lot and be stressful." But I think being so unattached, not knowing what was exactly going on in the background, did not benefit me. So when things hit a weird wall, I didn't know.

JULIET SIMMS (AUTOMATIC LOVELETTER/LILITH CZAR): So after all that happened, I left RCA. I signed with an indie label, wrote and recorded *The Kids Will Take Their Monsters On*, and then I went on Warped Tour, solo acoustic. And that's when *The Voice* contacted me.

KAY: There was no way for me to protect myself or understand how we even got in that position. So basically, everything was perfectly fine. Great, wonderful. The first record did really well, and when we went in for the second record, there still just wasn't a good budget. So they wanted you to make this great record. It has to do well. We need singles, they want to push to radio. Yet they won't give you a proper budget to go make that record.

SIMMS: The band broke up the moment Epic Records made me hire a professional band. I was still waiting for that big break. My deal with Automatic Loveletter was essentially just me. I was unsigned. So [The Voice] was very attractive. They were like, "You don't have to audition. You're straight to the live portion of the show." They were like, "This is how much you're going to get paid. You're going to get to sing the music that you want to sing." I was like, "All right, well, fuck it. This is what I got to do. Let's do it." I did not want to win the show, though. That's very hard to get rid of, at least from my own point of view at the time. But I look back at that, like, huh? It was fun, and it sucked at the same time; it was awesome, and it was terrible.

JESS BOWEN (THE SUMMER SET): When I did Warped in like 2018 with 3OH!3, like, I was excited about the "nostalgia band," and it was like Simple Plan. You know what I mean? Like, that's the band I was there to get excited about, and they're considered the nostalgia band of that tour. It made me feel old.

KAY: But while we were in this process of making our second record, we had two producers collaborating, and they just weren't seeing eye to eye. Some of our managers were making promises to one person and promises to the other. So it all came to a head. It was this feud between our producers at the time, and then me and Blake were really just stuck in the middle of it, and it was really weird and bad.

BOWEN: When I publicly came out, it actually was through an interview with Alternative Press, and they had initially told me the interview was going to be about our new album, Legendary. Then so I got the call, and like maybe thirty seconds into the interview, it was just "So you came out—you're gay, right? You post pictures on your Instagram with your girlfriend. . ." and blah blah. And so then that's how my story actually like came out, like "out-out"—if that makes sense—into the world, because I obviously was being open, but I never posted like a "Hey, I'm gay." I love all the guys and everyone at *Alternative Press*, and my management was even like, "Do you want us to tell them to not do the story? They can't do that, because they didn't tell us that they were going to be asking those questions." And I was like, "No, let them run it, because at this point, I'm not trying to hide anything."

KAY: And basically, at the end of the day, I've got a bunch of old white guys telling me, "Oh, well, too bad they're not signing off on this. Your whole record's not allowed to come out because they won't sign off on it, and you just have to figure it out." And they basically just left us stranded. So imagine being twenty-three and the rug gets pulled out. Everybody who signed you is now gone. You have different people at the label who don't really know what you're about, don't know what to do with you. And we were just stuck. I'm not bitter or anything, but I've always been like, "Man, if someone listened to me, just once."

SIMMS: Once your season is over, it's done. That's it. And that's shocking to your heart and your soul and your mind. It was like a loss. Everything you thought, everything they were telling you that would happen for you, "You're going to be a huge star. You're going to be the next big thing." You believe it. And then it doesn't happen. And you're just sad. I can laugh about it now. But it was hard. It was really hard.

BOWEN: If I look back to the very beginning of when I started touring, do I think it's gotten better since then? Yes. But do I think it's solved and better? No, not at all. Like, I still deal with the same issues being a female on tour. This still happens to me constantly, where I show up to a venue, and here's other guys that are in the band, and they show up and they don't have their laminates on them, but they walk straight in, don't get asked questions. But the second that I get up and try to walk into the venue, they're like, "Hey, what are you doing? We're not open yet," or "You can't come in." And I'm like, "You just let the rest of my band in. Why am I not allowed in?" Like that still happens just based on my appearance.

KAY: A lot of people wonder why we changed our name. Well, we asked the label to drop us, because they were shelving us and leaving us in a weird position where we just couldn't do anything. So we asked them to drop us, but we couldn't keep our name. We didn't have access to any of our old music. They owned VersaEmerge, so it was an impossible position. So we changed our name to Versa and we tried to move forward with a sound that we really were into.

SIMMS: On *The Voice*, all I did on that show was classic rock. And three of the songs that I sang went to number one on *Billboard*, classic rock, bluesy Motown. And then I get off the show. I get signed by Universal Records, and the first thing they say to me is, "We think you need to do pop." And I was just like, "Oh, here we go again. Why, God?" And so, you know, "Wild Child" was a result of contractually having to do what I was obligated to do. The label said, "This is a hit, it's going to break you." And then they didn't put any muscle or anything behind the song. But I was also a wreck after the show. Heavy, heavy drinking. I was ninety-eight pounds, unhealthy. Not doing well. Very depressed, so much so that I drank myself into rehab.

BOWEN: And then as far as being a queer musician, I just think there's still not enough representation. We are playing a show next month—it's a festival called Change Fest—and it's bands like Jimmy Eat World and Taking Back Sunday. I am literally going to be the only female on stage. The other guy in my band [guitarist John Gomez], he's also gay, but we'll be the only two queer members of that festival as well. Everyone else is pretty much cisgender white male, on that whole festival. So, that's just to put that into perspective.

KAY: It doesn't feel like I'm at a better place. I just had these internal monologues that I had for a long time that were hurtful towards myself and towards other women, whether it was in music or outside of music. So I remember the time I moved to Asheville. When I finally left New York, I moved to Asheville, and I made a great friend who became a mentor for me to get out of these stuck, bitter phases of my failed music career, that I felt I was going through. And she said, "Internalized misogyny." I was like, "Wait, what does that mean?" And she explained it to me, and I was like, "Oh my gosh. Not only do I have it within myself, but also towards my view of other women and how they walk through the world."

When the '00s ended, they ended hard. MySpace was gone in any significant sense, and it seemed like everyone was collectively trying to pretend they never really liked emo anyway. My Chemical Romance returned in 2010 with *Danger Days: The True Lives of the Fabulous Killjoys*, a beguiling electro-pop tinged concept album that represented a hard break from their roots while still keeping their love for theatrical bombast. It was the polar opposite of *The Black Parade*, as colorful and fun as possible, much to the bewilderment of many of their fans. The album went gold, an impressive feat at the time but much lower than the triple-platinum sales for *The Black Parade*. The album's best song was a snide punk anthem called "Vampire Money," which was the band's retort to being pressured to write a song for the *Twilight* franchise.

The band would break up three years later, as they became burned out by the music industry ("Everybody had a f***ing opinion about what MCR should be," said Way in a 2019 interview with the *Guardian*) and sense that with President Obama in office, their role in the world as a lifesaving force in troubled times wasn't as acute. Way would launch a solo career and later turn his acclaimed comic book series *The Umbrella Academy* into a Netflix series.

"They debuted 'Welcome to the Black Parade' live on the VMAs in 2006. What a fucking wild world, right? And when they did *Danger Days*, there's not a chance," says Heisel. "Pop radio had left rock music behind. There was no rock music that was cool anymore. Everything was just pop and hip-hop. So they just got lost in that shuffle."

The major label push Motion City Soundtrack hoped would finally put them on the level of Fall Out Boy and My Chemical Romance did not materialize. They would release two more albums on Epitaph before breaking up in 2016 and reuniting in 2019. During the hiatus, Pierre released the solo album *In the Drink* in 2018.

Taking Back Sunday reunited with their original lineup for 2011's self-titled album and continued to tour and release albums; Reyes would depart the band in 2018. Dashboard Confessional would begin nearly a decade-long hiatus, emerging for the occasional summer package tour or one-off collaboration. Fall Out Boy returned in 2013 with *Save Rock and Roll,* which found them further embracing Top 40 pop and arena rock aesthetics while becoming much more impersonal in the process. After the 2011 Cobra Starship album *Night Shades,* Saporta retired the project to form the talent management firm TΔG // The Artist Group.

Simms found that appearing on *The Voice* did not bring about the mainstream breakthrough she hoped for, and she continued to struggle with a music industry machine that sought to push her into a pop star mold that didn't fit. She began abusing alcohol heavily and was mortified when in 2016 she woke up after blacking out on a plane to find that a video of her assaulting her husband, Black Veil Brides singer Andy Biersack, was on the front page of TMZ. After getting sober, she reinvented herself with the project Lilith Czar, going in a bombastic goth rock direction with a sneering feminist bent. Sierra Kay also reinvented herself after the end of Versa, moving to Brooklyn and completing the emo-to-indie transition, forming the group Neaux with Nick Fit of the buzzed-about punks Trash Talk and releasing the 2016 album *Fell off the Deep End,* a noisy album for which she drew influence from shoegaze music and Sonic Youth.

Hollywood Undead may have been miffed to get unofficially booted from MySpace Records, but they ended up dodging a bullet, at least commercially. Albums such as 2013's *Notes from the Underground* and 2015's *Day of the Dead* topped the *Billboard* Rock charts, but George Ragan's substance abuse, frequently chronicled in his songs (in "Undead" he memorably brags about drunk-driving Cadillacs) led to the band firing him after a disastrous show.

As Rickly's addiction to heroin worsened, Thursday reunited with Dave Fridmann for one last album, the atmospheric, experimental *No Devolución*, before breaking up in 2011. He broke up with his longtime girlfriend and was robbed on two separate occasions, once in New York in 2013 (the thieves bragged on social media about stealing his epilepsy medication) and once in Germany in 2015, after he was poisoned while touring with his new group, No Devotion.

For some artists, like Simms and Kay, the rapid rise to fame and the abuse at the hands of the music industry began to take their toll, and they turned to the coping mechanism they had. Ragan, on the other hand, discovered that fame and success weren't enough to heal the pain he'd carried throughout his life.

———————

GEORGE RAGAN (JOHNNY 3 TEARS/HOLLYWOOD UNDEAD): There was like an absolute downturn. And then also, people stopped buying records. And this is before the advent of streaming as we know it, Spotify and Apple Music, and so on and so forth. So, there was a gap. When records stopped selling, people stopped coming to shows. We would be playing to three thousand people, and all of a sudden we were playing to fifty or a hundred. Which is a lot of bands' dream. Merch wasn't selling anymore, because they didn't have money. Rock has absolutely taken a downturn in that sense, in popularity and stuff like that.

KAY: My whole thing was like, "I can be put in any situation and handle it just fine." But after so many years of that, you feel really empty and you get walked all over. I'm so numb sometimes that I don't know what I'm feeling, because I'm so used to suppressing it. And I also drank a lot to escape my reality. I felt a lot of loneliness on tour, and I would escape that feeling with drinking. And I think that I've accustomed myself to this bit of numbness so I could just push forward and do my job and do what I love to do, so I didn't lose my opportunity, I guess.

RAGAN: Before, I would do coke and shit, meth, whatever. Then all of a sudden you get a bunch of money and I was bananas for like eight years. The only thing that stopped me was I had a kid. Even then, I can't even say I stopped. I kept going. But it kept me to a degree of like, "Oh, I should slow down." But no, I mean, I've had a lot of close calls, but yeah, once you get money and you mix that with addiction, you're in deep fucking shit, deep shit.

KAY: I'm touring around the world with seemingly no authority, which was my dream, because I hated school. I dropped out immediately pretty much into high school. I definitely had a bit of a drinking issue when I was probably eighteen to twenty-three. I would sometimes get way too wasted and would perform badly. There were times I'd hide that I was drinking. I quit a bunch of times and started back up and quit, off and on. I did, in my younger years, my early, early twenties, I definitely attended AA, which was suggested by my managers and stuff like that, because they could just see that I had moments of unhappiness. I was not always thriving. It's a difficult place to be.

SIMMS: I felt like I fucked everything up and fucked my career up by doing the show, and they didn't do what they said they were going to do and what was promised, and they just used me for my fan base and blah blah blah. I felt used. After the show, it became about self-medicating and all of that, and that went on for about a couple of years. I hit rock bottom and I just decided, that's it. I'm going to die, or I can stand back and fucking turn my life around.

RAGAN: My wife left me, with my kid. She finally got to the point where she was like, "I'm fucking done." Even Hollywood Undead, they were sick of me. We were in the Ukraine, and we played a show, and I was so fucking drunk that—we have a song called "Young"—that I did the first verse, twice. The band was like, "Dude, that's it." I knew I was at the end. And it's like "two roads diverged in the wood." Like, Robert Frost. So, I made the right choice, and now I have another daughter with my same wife, and another one on the way.

KAY: It took a long time to not be bitter. There were a lot of years where I was like, "Woe is me. Everybody fucked me over. Why would this happen to me?" I've done that for a long time, and it didn't serve me. I do think that labels really need to be held more accountable. They're just free to scoop things up, throw money where they want, take money away where they want, and hold you hostage—and really compromise the artistic vision of anybody. And I think now, you can be independent and successful a lot easier. I hope that labels are getting scared. I really do.

RAGAN: Let's say you do something and you become successful and you make a bunch of money, and you do all this shit that everybody thinks they want. They *think* they want. If you get to that point where you have all that, it's actually worse in a sense, because then you realize it was not what you wanted. And then you have to ponder, spiritually and mentally, *OK. So if it wasn't the car, or the house, or the girl . . .* You're left wondering, *Oh, I'm still not happy*, then you really have to do some fucking mental gymnastics.

SIMMS: Have you ever toured and drank? It is a nightmare. You feel like you're going to die every single day. In 2019, me and my husband were just like, getting up and exercising, killing it on stage. Healthy sounding, amazing looking. Happy. That was it. I remember, like halfway through that tour, we were both like, "This is so awesome. Why weren't we doing this years ago?"

RAGAN: The reason I wasn't sober was because I couldn't deal, you know? So, you hide. I look back, and you could talk about whether it's [Friedrich] Nietzsche or William Shakespeare, Dostoyevsky, any of these guys. These guys were brilliant beyond anything I'm capable of. And they couldn't figure it out, how the fuck am I going to figure it out? No one figured it out. And that's the thing. There is no answer.

SAPORTA: I put out that fourth record. The fans didn't really like it. I didn't really like it, but we had a huge hit.* We were making good money.

---

* Written by the hitmakers Steve Mac and Ina Wroldsen, "You Make Me Feel . . ." was a worldwide hit, but even the critics who like Cobra Starship thought it was missing an essential *something.*

It was irresponsible to stop. I wanted to stop already, but you also have to be responsible in some way too. We toured the world, did the Justin Bieber tour in 2012. And then I got married, and I took a year off, and then it was 2014. I'm like, "Am I going to do this again?" The label wanted me to do it again. Everyone was like, "Yeah, do it." I put out a song. It did OK. Then I was just like, "Nah, I'm good." I didn't finish the record.

KAY: I went to Sacramento just to crash with a friend for a couple of months, and he messaged me, like, "I've got these really shitty demos, do you want to try to sing on it?" And I was like, "Yes, absolutely." We did a very DIY way of that, and I really enjoyed it. I definitely feared that my credibility wasn't cool enough. I sometimes feel like Versa is not even a ball and chain, but almost like a heavy coat wrapped around me. I sometimes am trying to shake this coat away so people can see that I'm much more than this thing I did when I was, quite frankly, a fucking teenager. I had a great time, and I wouldn't change a thing. But I fear, I think a lot of people feel, that it's hard to get out of that life. Because it was such a phase.

HEISEL: The stock market crash was in 2008, so we took a hit. We lost a lot of advertisers. We had a lot less subscribers at *AP*. We had to go to summer Fridays for a whole summer where we didn't work Fridays. So we all took a 20 percent pay cut, which was never made up. The money coming into The Scene at that point in terms of sponsorships for things and the road became so much harder to get dollars from corporations.

SAPORTA: I had a whole camp the label set up for me, with this producer in Copenhagen, and a bunch of writers came out, and it was a lot of fun. And I was writing, ironically, some of the best stuff that I had written in a while. And while I was out there, I get two calls in one day. The first call that I get was that my wife was pregnant. And then the second call that I get was that the president of my label, Dave Saslow, had had a stroke.

AMY FLEISHER MADDEN (FIDDLER RECORDS): By all means, it could have been the end of MySpace. But I genuinely think that it was generational, because I think the kids that, if they were like fifteen when they got into Jimmy Eat World in 1999, by the time they hit 2006, 2007, 2008, they become grown adults. They wanted to go out, and they wanted to have sex. They didn't want to go to a Dashboard Confessional show and put a pin on their sweater and cry, like, of course, which is very hyperbolic and rude of me to imply either of those things. But I think the fan base aged. One hundred percent you want to go to Misshapes in New York City and get your photo taken by the Cobrasnake.* You now want to be cool. You don't want to be young anymore.

WILL PUGH (CARTEL): Everybody who I remember going to pop-punk and hardcore shows got into the National and Death Cab for Cutie.

CAIN: We had already signed the deal, so [executives from Sony] came out on that tour and they went to the Philadelphia show. The Sony guy mentioned to us, "It's like your genre specifically just doesn't sell albums. We can release an AC/DC album right now, and we'll sell millions of them." Beyoncé's people are gonna buy Beyoncé's album, R&B's gonna sell records, but our specific genre was just people who are not buying records. Not that they weren't coming to the shows, there's plenty of fans, they were just getting it other ways.

KAY: Like I said, I definitely appreciate the journey. I think my experience is really unique, especially starting so young. I think there are definitely some damaging effects, but nothing I can't overcome and learn from. I'm excited to have a band now,† and I refuse to have anybody play or be in my circle that makes me uncomfortable, that I feel like doesn't have my back. I guess I've learned that I deserve better.

HEISEL: The Scene from our perspective was in a super-huge identity crisis. Everyone had outgrown MySpace, but there was no platform that was as artist friendly for musicians to kind of immediately migrate to.

---

* The Misshapes are a DJ duo that were a frequent presence at '00s New York hipster parties; Mark "the Cobrasnake" Hunter is a photographer known for taking candid shots of said hipster parties.
† After Neaux, Kay formed the Americana-leaning project Bad Daughter.

MySpace, for all of its faults, it was very, very humanizing for musicians, for that fan-to-band connection. That's part of the reason why I think The Scene thrived in the first place, was that it was such a direct one-on-one conversational tool. There was such a democratization of fans and bands. The walls broke down, but then the wall started to be rebuilt once that kind of community ended and moved on.

SAPORTA: I'm thirty-three years old now, and I just got married. Am I supposed to keep doing this or not? So I felt when I got those calls, it was a clear sign saying, "OK, it's time to stop." And that was it. I felt happy, because I felt like I had clarity about it. People aren't happy when they don't have clarity. So I felt like I did what was in front of me as best I could until the universe told me that it was done, that it was time to do something else. I told the people at Atlantic, and they were like, "What? You're just going to stop?" "Yeah, I want to work on the business side." I moved to California, had a baby, and started my company.

CAIN: We went to radio with a song, and it didn't take. Then Sony went through a big shift and fired that entire radio department and brought in new people, and they wouldn't take any risks on us, because we had failed once. And then Sony just went through it, and I think they removed every rock act. There's a whole flood of bands that were released at the same time, and I think we are a part of that pool.

RICKLY: I definitely felt like there's no more context. And we made that record in such a different way than we have made any other record. We had a recording session booked and we hadn't written a song, and Dave was just like, "Just come in, you'll write all morning, we'll record the song in the afternoon, and then at nighttime Geoff can come sing it, and we'll just make a record that way, and it'll be painless." And we did, and we just went in there and wrote a record in two weeks. And it was like this completely different existence, where we'd spend a year, seven hours a day, writing our songs. So it just kind of felt like we knew that whatever was going on with Thursday was over and . . . let's do something else. And so we just tried something else and wrote a really different record.

SAPORTA: Most people can't do it, because it's an addiction. Fame is an addiction. But it's actually really easy to do; you just stop feeding the machine. If you stop feeding the fame machine, people stop caring about you. But artists are conflicted about that, because on one hand, they want to do what they love for a living, and that requires being celebrated by people and being known and being famous, even if you're only famous in your scene. It's still a level of fame. Then people are always talking about you, and you have expectations to live up to, and you're being judged, and that can be hard. For me, when I got into it, I made a conscious decision that I was going to play that game and just play it hard, not pussyfoot on it.

CHRIS CARRABBA (DASHBOARD CONFESSIONAL): I'm glad I'm just Internet famous again. It was a bizarre period to be actually famous. I called it mall famous. You can't walk through a Target, you can't walk through a mall, you can't go to a basketball game, you can't do anything without feeling like a spectacle, and that's not what I signed up for. I tried to be gracious during that time. I wasn't always, but I really tried. I eventually would intentionally take a hiatus, a long one, in order to put that part of my life behind me. It's not for everybody.

PIERRE: I soon discovered that a lot of times fans will say that you changed or your music has changed, and they forget to realize that they've changed too.

CARRABBA: I think that fame is ingrained societally now as the ultimate validator. And that is false, but I live in the world, so I understand that railing against that sounds like "Get off my lawn." It's just something I wish was different, so other people could enjoy life without that goal.

CAIN: So when we got dropped and such, we were in this hotel after a tour in Detroit. I was like, "Let's just make an album. I've talked to this guy: a good friend of ours in Arkansas has a studio, he'll give us this crazy rate, we could spend our own money on it—it's only this much money, we can have the studio for three months. Let's just see if we like doing this anymore." It's like, "Should we call it quits?" 'Cause we just got dropped from a major. Is this the moment that we back away and say, "Do we have a career?" Like, what do we feel like doing? 'Cause now it's like the reset, right?

CARRABBA: When Interscope started saying to everyone, including me, that we had to start doing cowrites . . . I tried, I thought maybe I could learn something about songwriting, but no, nothing came of it. It was really about commerce. In my blissful window there was this strange shift in the record-selling industry where it was about artist development, and it was about facilitating the acts to be the best artist that they could be. And then it kind of did a hard shift back to commerce. Once everybody was told they had to do cowrites in order to make their own records, I really felt like the record industry was in peril.

SAPORTA: The publishing thing started happening. All of a sudden you start getting songs written by committee. And I think that's because really smart people that are creative and want to be in the business, they're like, "Dude, there's no way I can make money being an artist, let me just get into a songwriting game." So that was something I dealt with a lot in Cobra Starship. Once you start getting to the point of, "If you want to be on the radio, you've got to work with all these people, because these people know how to make records for the radio." So that was an interesting experience. I don't think a lot of people that came from The Scene had that experience. A few years prior, that wouldn't have happened. One hundred percent.

CARRABBA: They wanted me to make things less personal, more generalized, so they [were] pushing me to change things, which I did do, in the spirit of trying to learn and grow, like changing things from first-person experience to more of a story, even though the story was my story. Instead of saying *me*, I said *they* or *you* or *he* or *she* or whatever, and song structure stuff or tonality stuff. It didn't feel hugely disappointing, except for that I felt disappointed that I listened to so much direction from the label instead of going with my instincts. But it also felt like, "Well, see, this justifies my decision to keep counting on myself."

CAIN: The goal is to be able to do this for the rest of your life, either you're doing it or not doing it, right? You get to a certain size and it kind of snowballs for the rest of your life, and you're taken care of and you can do other ventures, whatever. And you put so much time and effort in to be in a band, it's not like it's a job where you punch in every day and punch out and then go find a new job. When it's over, you're left without a job. As we kind of found around 2016, that's when we're scratching our heads and go—I'm like, "OK, so I only really know how to make up shit out of thin air, and what can you do with that?"

CARRABBA: The thing contracted, and it needed to. It got so fucking bloated. I'm OK with it. The whole thing flatlined. The record tanked; it just came out in a vacuum. I was no longer gainfully employed necessarily, like everybody in the country. Fun money is the first thing to go. And people tightened their purse strings; they had no choice. I had toured so much with Dashboard from 2000 to 2010, just like a machine. And I wasn't burned out, but I could tell that I was right on the cusp, and it felt like I was in danger of phoning it in, and I felt like I had a tacit agreement with my audience that like, "I'll be up here really giving it and really believing in what I'm doing." I felt like if I phoned it in, that'd be the end of the band, and I would rather walk away before that happened than after.

CAIN: I had gone through what they were about to go through and powered through it, and it had devastated my marriage. I was literally at a point where I was like, if the band kept going and we had to do that, I would not be married, I would not have been able to work out the issues that we were having because of my long-term absences and raising a child who was now five. And I'm looking at these guys who are about to have kids, and I'm like, "These guys are not gonna make it through this. It's gonna self-destruct. You do not want this."

CARRABBA: It happened really, really, really slowly. I remember, say, I was in public, and I have people just with their eyes on me. In the early days, there were people that would just come right up to me and talk to me, and I enjoyed that, and then there's the people that look at you and don't talk to you after you get very, very popular, and I didn't like that. And I remember that that kinda switched again. It went back to people now finally just looking at me, recognize me, deciding to come and say hi and talk about music with me for a little bit, and I enjoyed that. I kinda got that back.

CAIN: I did nothing for a while, lived off the money I made from that tour, which wasn't much 'cause I had to pay off a lot of debts with that tour—because the way I lived prior, when you're on labels you get paid in such a weird way, you'd use credit cards, and then I'd get a large lump sum of money, and I just paid it off. At some point that large sum of money never came and I just had massive credit card debt, so when we did that tour, I just kinda righted myself, I was like, "OK, never going on that path again." So the band makes a passive income of some sort, so there's a little bit coming in there. I tried to write music for people and do that kind of thing, and I just wasn't ready to be creative in that way. I felt too much pressure. I ended up just driving Uber for a while. I run into people sometimes and they made it very weird. "Why are you doing this?" Well, everybody needs a fucking job. It's just a fact.

SIMON: I remember being at MTV when *Danger Days* came out, and they played ["Na Na Na (Na Na Na Na Na Na Na Na Na)."] And I thought it was so fucking good. Their label rep came in and played it for a bunch of people with the visuals, and they gave away T-shirts and the whole shilly, cringey major label thing. And I really thought it was going to hit. I thought that it would be something that fans were satisfied with. And I was a little surprised that it didn't seem to take off in the way that I had imagined.

JILL NEWMAN (MANAGER FOR TAKING BACK SUNDAY AND MIDTOWN): So 2009 is the *New Again* era, which was another membership change, which was just not as well received. We had a lot of problems in the recording process, and then the people started leaving at Warner, which made it worse. Our inner guy left the day before that record came out, and he was a big champion. A lot could be said about that era. We just choose not to talk about it too much. And you know, at that point, we could tell the new membership wasn't working. I was basically at the point of telling the band we're not going to survive another membership change. I don't think we should do it. And then Mark was like, "What about John and Shaun coming back?" I'm like, "Well, OK, we would survive that." I think we were lucky we had a pivot like that, because it might have been the end.

EDDIE REYES (TAKING BACK SUNDAY): Honestly, when those guys showed up to Texas, we were like, "Well, this is fucking crazy." It just felt like it never went away. I just felt like two friends disappeared for a little while and came back.

NEWMAN: When we left the major, I was happy. I don't know that all of them were happy about it, you know, and maybe it felt a little bit like not succeeding, but I'm like, "You're in the best position you could ever be in. You only have to please yourselves, nothing else matters at this point. And if you please yourselves, I promise it'll please the fans."

RICKLY: When I found out that it was coming out on the tenth-year anniversary of *Full Collapse*, I was like, "This is gonna be our last record." It's coming out exactly ten years after our breakthrough, and it's this weird, different record that we wrote in two weeks, and it sounds so different, and it's really pretty, and the whole Scene is gone. That was probably just the end of that. We broke up in an afternoon. It went from zero to sixty; we had known that things had gotten weird. But when it ended, it was just like that. I just remember turning to the band and being like, "This is over, right?" And everybody just knew it was.

SIMON: If *Black Parade* was a blockbuster, *Danger Days* was an art house film. And you could tell that it probably represented every single thing that the band wanted, but that might not have been aligned with every single thing that the fans wanted. And that isn't to say that either needs to keep the other in mind, but I don't know if that's what fans expected to be the next thing after they were singing along to the *Parade*.

SAPORTA: Because Cobras were so big, people were finding out about Midtown. So it was cool. I hadn't played an instrument in almost eight years. It took a lot of rehearsal. We rehearsed for six months. We wanted to be really good. And I thought the shows went great. It was special. It was kind of a redemption, because the thing that happened after we broke up and we made that record is everyone fell in love with that record. That happens to a lot of bands that make a weird record. Everyone hates it, and the band gets discouraged. I mean, fucking Weezer broke up after *Pinkerton* for a while. And then everyone fell in love with that record. I actually saw the reunion show in California at the Glass House. It was one of their first shows back, and they were playing *Pinkerton*. They were just so happy. "Oh, this record everyone hated, now people love it." It was kind of the same thing with me. I was like, "Wow, this record that no one liked, now everyone's singing along."

RICKLY: I can't talk about [why they broke up]. But yeah, it was tough, it was a tough ending. And I'm really glad that we've been able to get together and play again, because I would have regretted the way that ended for the rest of my life, I think.

REYES: The band is still doing great. I'm no longer with them. I walked away three years ago. I don't know if I'll ever go back.

RICKLY: It definitely felt like the end of an era. I think to the point where the emo revival is happening, it's a direct result of—it had to crash and burn first. It happened so quick. People still like the music, but it was such a collapse of the whole ecosystem. It was definitely like: "Read the writing on the wall, you guys, this whole thing's done."

REYES: After Warped 2012, I became a full-blown alcoholic, like drinking every day. Bottles of whiskey, vodka. I came home to my bags packed up. I had to move out, get an apartment. My life fell apart. My kids were not seeing their dad.

HEISEL: As a staff at *AP*, or at least editorially, we were very much pushing that underground stuff, the Into It. Over It., the Title Fights, the La

Disputes.* But our readers who cared about that stuff were falling off, because they were seeing the covers every month being your Black Veil Brides or your [Pierce] the Veils, whomever. They were tuning out; it didn't matter how much cool shit we put in the magazine. No one was seeing it anymore. The walls went up. People didn't want to learn about new stuff. They wanted to have their taste reaffirmed to them. That's what *AP* became. It wasn't a way to discover new music, as it was a way to prove what you liked was good.

REYES: I don't think success changed me. I think that I suffer from depression. And there was a lot of things going on in the band that I wasn't happy with and people I wasn't getting along with, and I was just getting sick and tired of it. And I was distancing myself, not realizing it, not being friendly and not hanging out with anyone. Like I just go up on stage, play, and then disappear, and I realized that I did all that, you know, with therapy and counseling and all that, and doing my twelve steps and all that, I realized, "Wow, I was an asshole, you know?" I mean, they were assholes too, but I mean, in my part, I was an asshole. It wasn't like I didn't appreciate the gift I had, the success I had, but I was getting resentment towards it.

RICKLY: I would go to local ear, nose, and throat doctors, and they'd give me bottles of codeine cough syrup and stuff. And then, you know, it just seems sort of harmless in those years. I wouldn't even think of those years as drug-use years. But yeah, sure, I would take a Valium and put myself to sleep in my bunk, get up, have some codeine. Just a little something to take the edge off. Then after the band broke up, it really accelerated a lot more. I didn't have anything to do with my time. A lot of the time, I was kind of at home trying to figure out what came next.

HEISEL: Brokencyde,† Millionaires, Jeffree Star, these purely MySpace creations, which were like, this is complete and utter garbage, right? But

---

* Emo and emo-adjacent acts that began to slowly win acclaim in the '10s but lacked the industry support to do Fall Out Boy numbers.
† A band that made crunkcore, which combined crunk and metalcore. Terrible band, but they deserve credit for calling their debut *I'm Not a Fan, but the Kids Like It!*.

people demanded it. So how do you find a way to meet that demand without totally feeling like you've sold your soul to the devil? And that was the juggling act like the last five years I was there. It got bad.

REYES: They let me go to rehab for two months and they took care of me financially, and I came out when I was sober for a while. And then something happened in my personal life that really fucked me up, and I don't know how to deal with it. So I drank. And then I told them that I did; they were upset with me. And that was just it. That was the end.

HEISEL: You have literally five thousand bands that can't tune their guitar to save their life and are playing to backing tracks every night. Just these awful bands. It became so much about business and back-scratching in a time when we weren't allowed to champion for art, for lack of a better word. We go into these editorial meetings and bash our heads against the wall pitching idea after idea after idea. And none of it would land, so we'd be like, "Well, what's the shittiest band on Rise Records? Well, they're on the cover. Here we go." It was a dark time. I left *AP* in December of 2014. I was fired, but I was already one and a half feet out the door. Like, I didn't want to be there. They didn't want me there. So it kind of resolved itself.

REYES: Hopefully, deep down inside, it sucks for them, and they miss me. If anybody else went through what I went through mentally and becoming an addict and all that, I would have stuck by them, because that's what a brother does. They probably still are, because people hold grudges. I'm also very angry and hurt inside, because things could have been done differently.

RICKLY: I had different day jobs during that time. Kitchen store, I worked some kitchens themselves, some like restaurant kitchens. They always thought that I owned the store. It was just funny to me. I was like: "No, I make thirteen dollars an hour off the books. I don't own this fucking store; I'm just barely getting by."

REYES: I drank myself to the point where I passed out on the floor of my apartment, and my kids came over. Their mom called the ambulance, and they came and revived me. I don't know if I necessarily passed away. I almost did, and they revived me, and I ended up in rehab. I've been in rehab three times. And that was an awakening. You don't know what happens when you drink yourself to a coma. I wasn't trying to kill myself. But at the same time, I didn't care. I was depressed, man.

RICKLY: When Thursday was breaking up, basically, I remember talking to somebody and saying, "Yeah, it kinda freaks me out that somebody might think I'm a has-been at like, thirty-two." And basically, the person said like, "More like a never-were." It was like somebody I worked with too, so I was like, "Damn, that's pretty harsh." But he was also basically trying to say, "Don't break up, man. You'll never establish a name if you break up now, it's a terrible idea." So I remember that and was kinda like, "That's dark, that sucks." And then when the Emo Revival started, and we started getting treated like the grandfathers of The Scene, that was pretty weird too. 'Cause I was like, "No, I'm fucking thirty-four. What do you mean, 'Grandfather of The Scene?' I'm still a young guy."

REYES: Being sober and getting my brain working again and all that, I realized that I had something precious that I took advantage of.

RICKLY: For years I was trying to get off heroin, but . . . to what extent was I willing to go, was the question. At the time, I wasn't really willing to go to any extent, because whenever I felt bad about the fact that I couldn't get off heroin, the thing that would make me feel better was more heroin.

REYES: I saw Mark. I gave him a hug, and I told him I loved him when I was at the airport, and that was the last time I talked to him.

RICKLY: It was hard. Getting off heroin sucks.

NORMAN BRANNON (TEXAS IS THE REASON): I can't even tell you the difference. When he got clean, and when he went to Mexico and did the ibogaine treatment, and came back. I remember he came to my house, and I was just like, I can't even describe it. It had been so long since I'd seen Geoff that clear and alive. I've never seen anything like it. So the transformation was amazing. And I'm amazed that he's been able to hold it together. The alive Geoff is who I see there now.

RICKLY: I still can't believe that I did get off of it. Because I really never thought I would be able to. People would say, "You just gotta take it a day at a time." And I'd think, *A day? Why don't you fucking hold your breath for a day, and tell me that it's just a day?* Yeah, sure. If all it takes is sixty minutes of holding your breath, you think you can do it? Because that's how it feels. I just . . . It's impossible. There's no living without it. It just was such an experience of extreme pain. And that's what I used to think, like, *Oh, that's what withdrawal is. It's turning every single stimulus into a pain response.* And I sort of understood that everything hurts—psychically, physically, everything hurts.

HEISEL: Nothing good lasts forever. Any good scene has about two amazing years, five pretty good years, and then it's just nostalgia for that time period forever. People get old, people grow up, and most music that takes the public by storm, it really just takes the youth by storm. Between the years of middle school, high school, and college, that's eight to ten years max that you as a person have the mental bandwidth to be deeply invested in some schmuck playing a guitar. Right? Because then you get a job and you get a life and you get a spouse and you get a dog and you get kids, you have property taxes, blah blah blah. And it's way harder to still care about what's happening.

12

FALLOUT

A LOT OF THINGS CAN BE SAID about Rupert Murdoch and the corroding effect he had on the world at large. But you don't become one of the richest men in the world if you don't have a pretty firm grasp on ruthless capitalism, and at some point it became clear to him that it was time to stop throwing good money after bad.

After purchasing MySpace, Murdoch had reportedly been distracted by purchasing Dow Jones and the *Wall Street Journal* and figuring out how to integrate them into News Corp. But eventually, he became aware of the scope of MySpace's decline. Murdoch had recently installed the Irish-born Chase Carey, a longtime News Corp executive who'd been away at DirecTV during the MySpace acquisition, as News Corp president and COO. Described by *Reuters* as "a straight-talking, dollars and cents kind of executive whose only obvious extravagance is his remarkable handlebar mustache," Carey had no particular affection for MySpace and told *Reuters* it had "quarters not years" to turn things around.

That attempt to turn things around took the form of a relaunch in October of 2010, when the site's monthly visitors had dropped to around sixty million. (It had been losing a million visitors a month for the past two years.) Rather than fixing problems incrementally, MySpace CEO Mike Jones had decided to save it all for one last push. Instead of competing with Facebook directly, Jones decided to focus on MySpace's reputation as the place where music fans and other pop culture vultures found new artists and traded recommendations.

In retrospect, it seemed like a way to remind people that while Facebook may have been less chaotic, it also had much less personality. The new, cleaned-up feed got rid of the old "a place for friends" logo and operated on a grid system that made it easier to share and organize your favs. It was also easier to sync up with your Twitter and Facebook accounts and for artists to install third-party applications such as the fundraising tool Pledge Music. The relaunch even tried to stay true to the site's discovery ethos with the feature Hunted Real Time Radio, which played the most popular MySpace artists of the last sixty seconds.

It still wasn't enough. Four months later, MySpace's unique visitors had fallen to thirty-eight million, a shocking 30 percent drop. In January of 2011, five hundred employees were laid off, a reduction of 47 percent. Finally, running out of patience, Murdoch began looking for someone to pawn off MySpace on. DeWolfe, backed by the investors Austin Ventures expressed interest, as did Anderson, backed by Criterion Capital Partners LLC, and so did the Chinese Internet holding company Tencent. News Corp also approached Vevo, an online music video site jointly owned, at the time, by Universal Music, Sony Music, and Abu Dhabi Holdings, about a possible venture, and the video game company Activision Blizzard Inc. was also in the running. Eventually, MySpace was purchased by Specific Media, a digital ad network, for $35 million, less than the $100 million that News Corp was hoping for, and much, much, much less than the $580 million News Corp had originally paid for it. Clearly, Murdoch was willing to take a steep loss just to be done.

Specific Media was founded in 1999 by brothers Tim, Chris, and Russell Vanderhook, from Irvine, California. The company originally sold advertising space for websites. It later moved into harvesting users' browsing history, demographic data, and other unique information for targeted advertising. Specific wasn't a well-known company, so the Vanderhook brothers decided to bring in some high-profile help. They also laid off half of the remaining five hundred employees.

In *The Social Network*, David Fincher's 2010 film about the battle over who exactly created Facebook, Justin Timberlake played Napster cofounder Sean Parker. Perhaps that experience unlocked something in Timberlake, because in 2011 Specific Media chief executive Tim Vanderhook said that the pop star turned Serious Actor would help "lead the business strategy" for the relaunch, with a focus on bringing the creative community on board. This seemed to mostly mean the alt-pop artist Kenna, whom Timberlake brought on as a consultant. Vanderhook also said Timberlake had put his own money into the sale for a minority stake but wouldn't specify how much. But people who actually worked at MySpace doubt the official story. "These guys were not afraid to throw money at this purchase that they had," says Kevin Hershey. "So they threw a million dollars to Justin Timberlake and said, "Hey, can we say that you're an investor?"

Vanderhook talked a good game, telling the *Hollywood Reporter* in 2012 that the newly relaunched site would be a "a social network for the creative community to connect to their fans." He said there would be a feature wherein fans would be able to be featured on their favorite artists' page, and that after the initial campaign wore down, the site would "eventually reach out to undiscovered talent and music fans." Along the way, MySpace officially became stylized as Myspace.

SEAN PERCIVAL (VICE PRESIDENT, ONLINE MARKETING): Murdoch was saying we were going to do a billion dollars in revenue. We weren't even close to that. When the bar was that high, the team probably realized, "Oh crap, we'll never get there." But they still sacrificed the product a lot trying to.

BÍCH NGỌC CAO (MYSPACE MUSIC EDITOR): After it was purchased by Specific Media, it wasn't worth anything, because the user base was old and also could not be ported anywhere.

SARAH JOYCE (SENIOR DIRECTOR, CORPORATE COMMUNICATIONS): Everyone who was a MySpace Music person was like, "Can we just become our own thing?" And our only focus was artist tools and connecting artists and fans and just maybe selling merch and tickets and continuing to evolve that product and stay very narrow on that. If they were iterating with that in mind and said, "Let's cut the crap. We've lost the social element of this. We don't need a TV vertical. Let's double down on music," then I would argue MySpace could have kept up and would have been a Spotify competitor. But it didn't. It crashed and burned fast.

KEVIN HERSHEY (DIRECTOR, PARTNER AND LABEL RELATIONS): MySpace being for sale was not a shock. It was expected in my world, because I was sitting here, hearing top-level numbers based on what MySpace music was doing and generating.

PERCIVAL: So the week I started, they actually had laid off, I think, five hundred, six hundred people maybe. So I walked into an office where entire floors were empty. And the first meeting I had with the marketing team, the best way to describe it is depression. They were defeated. You could just see it in their eyes. Half of them had already checked out, and they had just lost half of their department. So I think there was this concern of like, when am I next?

JOYCE: The hardest thing to do is say no. I'd argue they were the first Internet social company to achieve that level. It was phenomenal. I remember being at Comcast before Fox bought it, and I remember telling my boss, "Oh, we should buy MySpace." There was no precedent for that kind of level of explosive growth from both the culture and actual business numbers, driving traffic and being the first of its kind. So they said yes to everything. They lost their way.

PERCIVAL: They felt that we have to eliminate all these silos and get more collaborative. Rupert Murdoch even came to the office. I don't know if he ever came to the office prior to that year. It's a bit like Darth Vader coming on the bridge.

COURTNEY HOLT (MYSPACE MUSIC PRESIDENT): At that time, music was eating MySpace. MySpace as a social network was less valuable to consumers, but the music part of the MySpace business was growing. So MySpace was shrinking, music was growing. And basically the site that we relaunched was almost entirely rooted in music and culture. And it was the right thing to do, but it was probably just too late. And ultimately we were still trying to meet the needs of commercial deals that had been done on the advertising side.

JOYCE: We had two CEOs, and one came from a content entertainment background, the other one came from a tech background. A lot of money, a lot of ego. No one had really had a clear direction. And you got to move before the world moves.

PERCIVAL: We were hemorrhaging so much cash at that point. There were so many liabilities with vendors. I don't know what we were burning per month. I would assume it was at least $10 million. So I wasn't too surprised. I was surprised (it was sold to) such a small company. I was also surprised that it was essentially the same thing as eUniverse and these other things, because that's kind of what they were just doing. They just wanted a lot of ad impressions was the way I looked at it.

HOLT: When Chris, Tom, and Jason were working on this site's relaunch and the rebrand, that was a big pain point, because it was like, "Do you want us to make the company and the site better?" And thereby there's all these things we have to forgo, like ad experience and delivery, in order to make the site more valuable, or "Do you want the thing off the books, because we just need to get rid of it?" And then you could have saved a bunch of time and money in rebranding and relaunching when ultimately the goal was just to get it off the books.

HERSHEY: So for them to sell it for $30 million to a bunch of bros from Orange County who were only known to us as brothers who learned how to traffic ads in their mother's house when they were in their late teens, and somehow by doing that, created this company and it was pretty lucrative for them, we're just kind of sitting there going, "OK, they bought MySpace for $30 million and their forte is trafficking ads. This is not going too well.

Like it's already bad, but they're just going to turn this into a complete and total shit show." As far as the user experience, just being bombarded by eye candy and things that you didn't necessarily sign up for. Now, that eye candy wasn't going to be like gifs and glitter and ponies; it was now going to be ads for FedEx. And that's pretty much what wound up happening.

PERCIVAL: I think they thought, like, *Oh, we'll just gut the entire thing. Even if nobody cares about this thing, it's still going to generate millions of page views every day, and we can make money on that.*

HERSHEY: We're watching all of the other verticals fail, because we're seeing all of the traffic decline when it was supposed to at least maintain, because we were the only legitimate streaming service. But when you have a broken product, you're not the only legitimate streaming service, and that leaves room for other people to come in. We all found out that it sold for $30 million. I can't even do the fractions on that.

JOYCE: I was on maternity leave, and I was let go when they sold it to Justin Timberlake. I mean, we all knew it was coming. People were roaming the halls, eating free ice cream, waiting to be shot in the back of the head. But we all knew we were ghosts of the time past.

ISAC WALTER (MARKETING DIRECTOR AND EDITOR IN CHIEF, MYSPACE MUSIC): And then they're like, "Well, we're selling the company." And I was just like, "All right, I can't." That's when I left. There was not going to be a better situation at that point. I deleted my profile and everything, and I just didn't go back.

HERSHEY: The day we found out we were going to Specific Media, they separated us into two groups. And if you went to one group on the second floor, you were fired. And if you got to stay on the third floor, you were going to stick around and make things work. That was how it all started with Specific Media. And it was just not a great first step forward.

JOYCE: They got all the people that were going to be let go in one room and then a bunch of people went in the other room. The people who were in the room were told, "Hey, you guys all still have jobs." They were so upset, because everyone else got severance, they got paid out of employment. They knew it was over, and all these poor fools would have to quit, get nothing, or try to resurrect this dead fish. So that was the big disappointment, which room you had to go to.

HERSHEY: It was weird to have these guys come in for such a small amount and have all of this traffic. But all they wanted to do was basically just traffic ads. It was just so heartbreaking.

HOLT: In candor, that's why when I left, I didn't want to work in music again. Because I was like, "I can't do this again. It's too hard. It's just too much of getting kicked in the teeth all day long." And then trying to say, "I have this idea, but it's going to require you to suspend disbelief." And then you either have to do it without asking and scale it to a point when then you have the capacity to write the checks to keep them happy, or you've got to go ask permission up front, and then it becomes a painful process. And at Fox, they'd already made the decision; now you have a guy like Chase Carey come in, you basically have a finance guy making the business decisions. They were managing to the bottom line. So a fifty- to one-hundred-million-dollar investment in music, which is probably what it would have taken to build what I would say is a competitive offering, was not something that they wanted to do.

HERSHEY: The disconnect was just so massive. It wasn't about business. It was about them trying to have big swinging dicks and "We own this and we're going to try and leverage our friendships and we're going to turn around something that's never been turned around." And there's a reason that things don't get turned. They have a life span.

ROSLYNN ALBA COBARRUBIAS (HEAD OF ARTIST RELATIONS, MYSPACE): Our MySpace relaunch party was amazing, like Pharrell and Robin Thicke performed. Miley Cyrus was in the audience Justin Timberlake hosted. So it felt like maybe it could come back.

PERCIVAL: I actually requested to be laid off, because I just didn't see it going anywhere.

NGỌC CAO: The thing with Facebook is that they managed to reach a level of prominence that's hard to get rid of. Yeah, whereas MySpace didn't quite reach that point. We were close to it but didn't fully make it there.

HERSHEY: That year of that South by Southwest, it was like, the third relaunch of MySpace Music, but it was the first relaunch for the Specific Media guys. So the labels were really just dogging us 24/7 like, "This fucking sucks. We've been doing this for a couple of years. This is ridiculous. We're not making any money off of this." It was a heavy room, full of execs, and I tried to pull the emotional "Stick with us, you guys know me from my years at other companies and how much I believe in this, blah blah blah blah," and the entire time I was out there, I never will forget this, just the way that I felt in my own head: *Wow. You have become a douche. You are feeding them lines of bullshit to try and just keep the peace. When did you compromise yourself?*

SIR MICHAEL ROCKS (COOL KIDS): I was paying a lot of attention to that, because obviously that's where I got my start. So I wanted to see it win and see it come back. But I don't think that Justin Timberlake was enough. Looking at social media platforms now and how just gargantuan and how much of like powerhouse machines they are, you need a lot more than Justin Timberlake to bring it back.

ALBA COBARRUBIAS: I was a part of the conversations when they were selling. They brought me into a couple of the rooms when they were pitching it out to brands. For a long time, they couldn't explain to people why they would want to buy MySpace, and they had me talk about what MySpace was in its beginning stages. And that's what would get people interested, you know? But what happened is that they brought in too many people that just tried to make it completely different, thinking that's what people wanted. No, they just wanted the same thing, but they wanted the shit to work. They didn't want spam. They didn't want their blogs to be deleted or like it to go sideways instead of like up and down.

HERSHEY: I had a history with Kenna from when I was at MTV and I programmed *120 Minutes*. It was the best job ever. I had run-ins with him early on when Interscope was trying to make him a buzzworthy artist. And I really did believe in him back then. Unfortunately, he was one of the tastemakers that Specific Media hired, because he sold himself as a friend of Justin Timberlake. He wasn't at all. Justin wouldn't even pick up the phone for him. His ego knew no bounds. It was kind of incredible.

ALBA COBARRUBIAS: So Justin Timberlake had a best friend in our office named Kenna. He's actually an artist, too. He was signed to Pharrell's label. And he understood how frustrated I was, and I was sad that I couldn't turn it around. And I was crying, and he asked me, "Do you own this company?" I said, "I don't." He said, "Then get the fuck out. Why are you so sad?" "I helped it grow, and no one's there anymore. And I miss the old days," and he was like, "Just move on," and I made that decision.

HERSHEY: My soul was being crushed every day. These Orange County bros brought in what they thought was the cream of the crop. They hired a bunch of people from *Vice*, that kind of editorial voice. They farmed it out to a bunch of companies to the tune of hundreds of thousands of dollars, what came back was black-and-white side-scroller. OK, so you want to take this website that had Top Eight friends and streaming music and glitter and ponies and now you want to turn it into a high-art concept, black-and-white experience? It was neat on paper, and it looked great. They spent a couple of million dollars on a Super Bowl commercial. It was just the most asinine, marketing-slash-creative approach to a rebrand, besides New Coke or Crystal Pepsi. It was just like, "What? What are you thinking? No!"

WALTER: Watching it get bought and just turn into something stupid was a bummer to me. I took it personally. I took it personally the whole time.

HERSHEY: We had already presented everything to the labels and artists beforehand. We had special tokens to get an invite to the new site so that they could sort of get really ready so that they could give us their feedback.

And the idea behind that feedback is we would effectively make some changes, but those changes never happened. It was just "This sucks, this sucks, this sucks, the side-scroll's kinda cool but everything else sucks." None of those changes were implemented. So whatever the day and date it was that it launched, I'm sure I was sitting in a corner naked, eating a bar of soap, punching myself in the face. You can quote me on that one.

WALTER: It's hard to come back from being the biggest website in the United States. I think if you had broken MySpace Music out of the company and then ditched social networking and all that other stuff, it would have existed, but it definitely wouldn't have been as big. But everybody wants big.

HERSHEY: The guy that they brought in to essentially replace Isac was a former MTV guy, and I couldn't find a single person that I knew and trusted that could tell me anything about this guy that was anything outside of vanilla. So he was calling me saying, "You got to get me into this Coldplay show." So he's calling me left and right, like he's my best friend. It was "You got to get me into the VIP balcony seat," which I did. And then on Monday, I got the random meeting request, and I immediately was like, "OK, I'm going to open the door, and HR is going to be in there, and this is it for me." Which is exactly what happened. I was elated, because I finally got to sort of unload a little bit and say, "How was that show on Friday night? Did you and your girlfriend enjoy that? Did you know the strings I had to pull to do that? And you knew you were going to fire me?"

The new MySpace announced itself with a $20 million advertising campaign that featured a video in which Pharrell Williams and then breaking stars such as Mac Miller, Chance the Rapper, and Sky Ferreira cavorted, hula-hooped, and skateboarded around in a white room with a bunch of young influencer types, with a closing message of "Check us out on Myspace." If the clear white rooms were supposed to be a metaphor for a cleaner design, it was an artistic choice that was too subtle for the intended audience.

"I didn't go to the shoot on principle," says Hershey. "To spend that amount of money on such a silly commercial. People didn't even understand it! It didn't say: 'MySpace is creating something new.' I don't even think there was text or a graphic. Like, what the actual fuck? Seriously, like if you are going to spend this amount of money, explain to people what your product is."

After a soft launch in late 2012, the new MySpace went public in January 2013; it had dropped to 27.4 million monthly visitors the month before. The redesign was heavy on entertainment news and featured a unique (and counterintuitive) horizontal scroll, as opposed to the industry standard of scrolling down to read. Users were given the option to sign in with their old MySpace password, if they still had it, or their Facebook or Twitter accounts, and once in they could post songs and playlists to their profiles.

As *Wired* noted at the time of the relaunch, "The new MySpace is everything the old one wasn't towards the end: Simple, non-confusing, modern, clean, and focused." But *Wired* also asked "Will anyone care?"

It was a fair question. By 2013, the free version of the streaming service Spotify had started to catch on, and Facebook and Twitter reached new heights of popularity, especially once the explosive popularity of smartphones made it easier than ever for people to get online and update their statuses from anywhere. (In 2014, the Nielsen group found that two-thirds of Americans had smartphones and that 60 percent of Internet usage came from mobile devices instead of desktops.)

Anybody who's taken even one business class knows that one of the founding principles of sales is that it's more important, and cost-effective, to keep an existing customer than chase after a new one. But once you lose the trust of a customer, it's very difficult to get it back. In MySpace's case, it didn't help that users who could remember their old log-in information began to realize their old profiles and friends had not carried over to the new redesign. Everyone had to start over, including the stars. As blogger Brenden Mulligan pointed out for TechCrunch, "Britney Spears has about 1.5 million friends on the old MySpace. She has fewer than 7,000 connections on the new MySpace."

Despite Timberlake's efforts to cosplay as a social media mogul, MySpace never gained a second wind. But while MySpace didn't recapture its cultural clout, it held onto about fifty million monthly visitors. Specific Media's parent company renamed itself Viant in 2015 (and also went by Interactive Media Holdings for a bit), and the company's ability to wring money out of targeted online advertising was enough to get it scooped up by Time Inc. in 2016 for a reported $87 million. The century-old brand had been struggling, as Facebook and Google continued to hoover up all the advertising money. Time Inc. wanted Viant to help make its brand's advertising more targeted and efficient. Acquiring control of MySpace was an afterthought, like a basket of dinner rolls that comes free with your meal. Two years later, Time Inc. was purchased by the Meredith Corporation, publisher of *Better Homes and Gardens*, *Shape*, and, once upon a time, *Family Circle*.

As MySpace continued to change hands, it moved ever further from God's light and became akin to a still-touring classic rock institution that features no original members, such as Blood, Sweat & Tears or Canned Heat. A website aggregating entertainment news and streams of years-old pop songs still exists at MySpace.com, though it's unclear why anyone would visit. It gives the impression that maybe, if you and your friends pooled your pocket change, you might be able to buy the site and give it another try. Maybe you'd finally get it right this time. There's certainly been enough lessons on what *not* to do.

In a final sign of what a complete afterthought MySpace had become, in 2019 the company released a statement admitting that a year prior, it had lost any song or profile made before 2015 in a server migration, wiping out an estimated fifty million songs from about fourteen million artists, which is in essence an act of cultural vandalism against an entire generation. But the fact that MySpace essentially deleted itself and no one even noticed typified the ignoble end of a former cultural behemoth.

But it also could have been much worse. While MySpace lost everything that made it MySpace and died a quiet death, at least it didn't stick around long enough to become something akin to Facebook—that is, a cultural plague that actively makes the world worse by breeding conspiracy theories and misinformation and that finally found its final form as the platform where you can learn which of your high school classmates tried to overthrow the American government on January 6, 2021.

Perhaps time and market forces would have led to MySpace becoming just as bad as Facebook, especially without Anderson at the helm. (It's arguably naive to believe that something owned by Murdoch wouldn't eventually be used as a weapon in the culture wars of the twenty-first century.) Or perhaps Facebook was a uniquely soulless platform made by a uniquely soulless man. But the fact that MySpace died young as a victim of corporate shortsightedness rather than becoming a malevolent force gives the site a nostalgic sheen that nothing Zuckerberg creates will ever approach.

"It ended at a good time. There are a lot of bad things that could have happened," says Alba Cobarrubias. "I can't imagine Tom going to Congress or if Donald Trump was on MySpace."

———

HERSHEY: I did know that they deleted all the servers, which just sounds idiotic to me, because why would you buy something and then delete it? You're buying the history.

ANDREW NOSNITSKY (COCAINE BLUNTS): It's crazy that I did some writing for them when they tried to rebrand. I did an annotated Lil Wayne Discography that was like fifty thousand words or something. It was insane. And they took it down after four days and didn't tell me anything. I think there were some legal issues, because they posted audio from everything. I was like, "If you're asking me to do this, I guess you have the legal information sorted out." But apparently they didn't. But so that was the extent of my experience with the Myspace relaunch. One of the reasons I was psyched to work on that: they were like, "We have the best archive of music." And then two years later they're like, "Actually, we deleted all of it."

CHRIS CARRABBA (DASHBOARD CONFESSIONAL): Social media's become a real passive thing. You scroll, you have music playing, the TV's on, you're flipping through your phone, your iPad, your computer has something different on them, and it's all this nonsense. And I love new technology, but the majority of the time you're on there, you're just passively checking it out, probably not with your whole attention. That's not how it was then. Then it was a really active thing where you were fully engaged.

NOSNITSKY: I don't think tech people understand the value of history. I think so much of their MO is disruption and moving things forward. It's like, "No, actually what you need to be doing is you need to find the MySpace account that Tyler, the Creator* had when he was fourteen, and get somebody to write about that. You have all this shit that's truly priceless, and you're just gonna delete it?"

GABE SAPORTA (MIDTOWN/HUMBLE BEGINNINGS/COBRA STAR-SHIP): The thing about MySpace that was special at the beginning is it was the place for The Scene, because Scene bands and artists didn't have anywhere to go. They weren't let into mainstream things or anything like that. So everyone just piled in at once, which is awesome. I think the problem we have now is that there are a lot of OK options and not one great one.

GARETH DAVID (LOS CAMPESINOS!): There was a period where I kept trying to log in to my old MySpace and the band's old MySpace, and it just made it impossible to do so. There doesn't seem to be anything left over. If you go onto MySpace and click onto the music tab, it'll try to have you listen to "24K Magic" by Bruno Mars. I just couldn't imagine what anybody would use it for.

JONAH MATRANGA (FAR/ONELINEDRAWING): It's just especially sad when it happens with art and idealism, because they're supposed to be neat and creative and free. And so when you start trying to commodify neat and creative and free, you end up with these like shitty facsimiles of neat, creative, and free, and that's good for no one.

---

* Leader of Odd Future, the most influential rap group of the '10s. Though he's more associated with Tumblr, he had a MySpace page as a teenager.

In 2016, pop megastar Taylor Swift appeared in an advertisement for Apple Music in which she sang Jimmy Eat World's hit "The Middle," referring to it as a song she loved in middle school. For a while, that seemed like what the general public thought of as emo: something that belonged in the past, a slightly embarrassing reminder of youth. The popularity of MySpace had supercharged the popularity of The Scene, but it seemed that the copycat artists and silly signifiers had obscured what drew in people in the first place: empathic, honest, vibrant music. For a while, it seemed like emo was just another thing that Murdoch's News Corp had ruined.

But to paraphrase Jimmy Eat World's other crossover hit, people were still listening. Starting in the middle of the '10s, a group of artists began the process of discarding the tacky and toxic and focusing on the yearning for connection that had always powered the genre. Dubbed Fourth Wave Emo as well as the Emo Revival, artists such as Modern Baseball, Touché Amoré, Joyce Manor, Foxing, the Hotelier, and The World Is a Beautiful Place & I Am No Longer Afraid to Die began winning over skeptical critics and brought a much-needed energy to an indie rock scene that had become a bit too enamored with music that prioritized vibes above all else. They didn't become as huge as the previous wave, but they rebuilt a community for the people who needed it, and later women-led bands such as Pool Kids and Home Is Where made it clear this was fully *their* scene as well.

Eventually, the leading lights of the old guard would also discover that people still cared. Thursday reunited in 2016 for a series of shows, prompting Rickly to seek help for his addiction. He got sober in 2017. Dashboard Confessional returned in 2018 with *Crooked Shadows,* and a My Chemical Romance tour set for 2020 sold out quickly but was pushed back due to the COVID-19 pandemic. A younger cohort of writers and critics and artists used this resurgence as an opportunity to reappraise the '00s movement, pointing out that while much of it deserved scorn, actually, some of it held up quite nicely. There was clearly a lot that was toxic, but there was also an honest empathy and compassion at the heart of the best stuff, and that needed to be held onto, remembered, and built upon.

———————

CARRABBA: It really means something to me, and it means something, again, within The Scene and outside of The Scene, it's starting to mean this again. It was too bloated. It was a catchall that really began to mean nothing to me and probably to most fans. And it seemed to be more about how people dressed, which was not something that was relevant in my graduating class of emo, with the Get Up Kids and Saves the Day and Jimmy Eat World and such. There was a brief period where I just really, truly felt that it didn't apply to me anymore. It's necessary that the slate gets wiped clean pretty often.

SAPORTA: Ultimately, what is a kid from The Scene? The kid from The Scene is someone who music saved their life, in a way. Everyone listens to music. Not everyone is obsessed by music, not everyone wants to be a part of a scene. The people that do want that are the people that have troubles at home, right? They have a hard life growing up. And music is salvation for them, and that's a beautiful thing. And that's amazing. And I think in a way it always feels difficult, even when you're in The Scene, because you're still tortured about it. Sometimes you have a hard time enjoying and really appreciating the amazing thing you're a part of, because you're around a lot of people that are also tortured.

GEOFF RICKLY (THURSDAY): Those [reunion shows] were tough for me. I was off drugs, but not to the extent that I needed to be. I was trying to replace it; I was trying to drink my way out of it. I knew that I couldn't be on heroin anymore, but sobriety wasn't working for me yet, so I wish I had gotten sober before that. Because we just did two nights in every city, we were just fucking destroying it.

SCOTT HEISEL (*ALTERNATIVE PRESS* EDITOR): I think that those fans will always be around and those records will live on for a long, long time. I was DJing a wedding over the weekend and I played "Sugar, We're Goin Down," and the dance floor went crazy. A bunch of twenty-seven-year-olds losing their minds.

NORMAN BRANNON (TEXAS IS THE REASON): Well, I think any time a genre persists through age, you start to see a history that's more difficult to erase. And once you have legacy artists, you've cemented something. So I think that at this point, there's probably no putting the genie back in the bottle. It's almost like, why are we even counting waves anymore, this is gonna be endless, and I really believe that it is gonna be endless. And I think part of that is also because now you have some of the values that made emo blow up in the first place: the vulnerability and the authenticity, the sincere expression of who you are. Now, those ideals are sort of baked into the culture, and they're certainly baked into the very being of at least the last two generations, Gen Z and the millennials. These are all things that now are being used to market everything from razor blades to manscaping gear. They're appealing to emotion, and I think people are . . . As long as people continue to respond to that, that's not gonna change.

LESLIE SIMON (*ALTERNATIVE PRESS*): I love that new fans are rediscovering some of these albums for the first time. I also love that people are taking some of these records off the shelf or, I guess, off the Spotify, more appropriately, and relistening. And you do get to hear what stands up and what doesn't. And a lot of the great bands of that era are still great. They haven't lost their luster. They just capture a moment in time, and I happen to have a lot of really great memories from that moment in time.

JOSHUA CAIN (MOTION CITY SOUNDTRACK): There was a period of time where I was like, "Yeah, I was in a band. We did well." People would say, "I loved you in high school." And we're like, "Thanks." No, shit. I'm sorry that we didn't stay with you. But we started playing some shows, and I was like, "Oh god, people like our band a lot, this is a big deal to them."

BRANNON: When Texas Is the Reason came out, I wouldn't say that that was the nature of the culture that we were going into. Mainstream pop at this point is just dark emo, and I love it. The Internet has created it so that we have new languages and new signifiers for these things. So everyone speaks therapy talk now, everybody's talking about their trauma and their PTSD and whatever it is, and that's now part of pop music. And people wanna hear about your trauma in pop music, where back then people would be like, "These emo bands, stop complaining—what do you have to complain about?" Now it's like complaining is where it's at. And let's face it. All this therapy talk and all that stuff, this is a direct line to like . . . "I'm Not Okay," right? That's exactly what this is. It's not just angst, we're understanding things on a deeper level now.

EPILOGUE:
SPACE WAS THE PLACE

IF YOU'RE A NORMAL PERSON with a normal (which is to say, fairly casual) relationship with music, it's very likely you remember MySpace as the site that got beat by Facebook. But if music is your lifeblood and fuel source, then the MySpace Era was a special, exciting, and strange time, and perhaps it gives you cold comfort that, unlike Mark Zuckerberg or Twitter's Jack Dorsey, Tom Anderson has never been called before Congress to answer for undermining America's national security or playing a part in incubating a new generation of white supremacists.

It's not wise to get *too* nostalgic for a website that was, at one point, part of the portfolio of one of the world's most conservative men. But when we miss MySpace, we don't just miss a fun, silly, and often chaotic website. We miss an era that now stands as the bridge between the twentieth century, when traditional media largely decided which artists would get access to the spotlight, and what we have now, where there are more options and avenues for music lovers than ever, but less ability for all but a few superstars to cut through the noise and make a cultural impact.

"Music sucks now" is, to put it eloquently, a rather dumb thing to say. There's garbage, magnificence, and magnificent garbage in every era, and if you can't find something to like, that's on you for not trying hard enough. Tuning out of music is the surest sign that you've gotten old at heart, and you will have to drag me to the nursing home as my fingernails scrape the floor bloody to get me to stop finding the next song that will once again explain the human condition to me for three minutes at a time. But the music culture that has flourished in the wake of MySpace's Era's slow dissolve? That sucked, and that's not the fault of the artists or their fans.

A terrified and cash-starved music industry lost interest in even trying to develop artists and desperately flailed around for the safest bets. The decline of print journalism and the slow dissolve of the blogosphere meant there were fewer outlets for voices with something to say, and many that did survive often found themselves covering the same music as everyone else, losing something about their distinctive character in the process. Good work was still being done, though, and the rampant misogyny and willful ignorance that had long undergirded music and fan culture was finally being addressed, while important questions about mental health and racial and gender inequality were being asked.

But sometimes you wondered if anyone was having fun anymore. The spirit of finding the next new band that would change the lives of you and your friends, and that being *everything*, was giving way to a culture that, much like the MySpace Music in the later years, preferred one already huge superstar to ten smaller acts that needed the push more and usually had more to offer.

Streaming services became the dominant means of music discovery in the '10s. On one level, after the smorgasbord days of Napster and the flatlining of CD sales, artists were happy to get any money for their music at all. But services like Spotify are often pilloried for not paying artists nearly enough for their music. As pointed out by the Ringer (which is now owned by Spotify) in a piece titled "Is Spotify's Model Wiping Out Music's Middle Class?," the cellist Zoë Keating "generated 2 million streams from 241,000 fans in 65 countries who listened to her music for a combined 190,000 hours." Her payout was "$12,231, or about half a penny per stream."

The result is that fewer smaller and mid-tier artists are able to support themselves, which eventually leads to fewer smaller and mid-tier artists, period—thus robbing fans of potential favorite albums they'll never hear, because making music for a living became something akin to managing a Blockbuster or working at a coal mine. Many artists found that music was no longer sustainable, now something they had to abandon or just do on their time off from work.

We lose out when artists from all walks of life and genres don't get the support they need to potentially become something great or to sustain themselves enough to continue the artist-fan dialogue over the years.

Maybe what made MySpace special was that it was made by an emo kid. It was often frustrating, but it was also alive and messy in the best way. It was made by a fan, for other fans. And what's taken its place treats fandom like a loss leader, a means to an end.

MySpace had all the elements needed to find fans and bands in one place. It offered just enough structure that anyone could navigate it and enough freedom that you could always stumble upon something new and exciting. It was just enough, before it all became too much. That exact balance, that contained chaos, has proven nearly impossible to replicate, even by people who ended up owning the MySpace name.

As unlikely as it is to link Far East Movement to Thursday to Lil Jon to Hollywood Undead to Kate Voegele, they all shared quite a bit in common. They went through the MySpace Era, and they went through it together. We all did, in our way.

GARETH DAVID (LOS CAMPESINOS!): Everything you did on MySpace seemed monumental and important. And everything you do on Twitter is just stream-of-consciousness and relentless, I guess because of the traffic that Twitter gets now. Unless you're using it consistently and relentlessly, it's hard to get noticed. I do think that it's a shame bands don't have anywhere, the go-to place to showcase their music anymore. You could get your music easily on Spotify and Apple Music, but there is nothing as good as recording your demo, uploading it to a MySpace player, and people being able to clunkily download that for free.

SIR MICHAEL ROCKS (COOL KIDS): Nowadays with Instagram and Twitter and stuff, like, I work for this. Always, I have to post. If I don't post, the algorithm will punish me.

LESLIE SIMON (*ALTERNATIVE PRESS*): MySpace comes in and you're able to do these rabbit-hole scavenger hunts for your next favorite obsession, whether it's music, movies, books, graphic novels, whatever. It's like traveling. You have a passport and you never have to go on a plane. You can just stay in your seat at home and be comfortable and see the world and discover all the things that you thought maybe existed but wouldn't have been open to you otherwise. And that's something that MySpace, more than any social platform of the time, offered its users.

BÍCH NGỌC CAO (MYSPACE MUSIC EDITOR): There really was no algorithm for MySpace, so it was like me stumbling around and finding things. Now there's a lot of stuff that does get referred to me that I do like, but the bands I really love are when friends are telling me about what they're listening to. But it's a little harder as we get older. Most people, I believe there's a study that shows that at age thirty-three is when you stop listening to new music for most people, and I was about thirty-three when I read that, so I was very alarmed. But I still listen to new music.

SCOTT HEISEL (*ALTERNATIVE PRESS* EDITOR): Everyone wants to have that discovery moment, even though that's been robbed of them now with the algorithm. The algorithm discovers things for you. Nothing will beat your friend saying, "Hey, check out this band."

JIM MERLIS (PUBLICIST, BIG HASSLE): Today is so much more of a streaming world and more about individual songs. And I feel like with MySpace it was the last years of artists and albums.

GEOFF RICKLY (THURSDAY): Facebook beating MySpace sucked. I hated that. I always thought Facebook was painfully fucking corny. My friends were like, "That's where the cool kids are." I was like, "These people are fucking lame." I was like, they don't even like music. There's not even a design element, it's so boring. This is like the Ivy League bullshit version of what it's like to be a boring normie. I was super not into Facebook, and I feel very vindicated by how evil that company has been over the years.

DAVID: This is gonna make me sound like an old-timer, but I think the music industry is worse off with it not existing anymore. It seems to be the turning point from when bands could control things themselves. That was really the pinnacle, and everything since then, the bands have lost that power.

CHUCK INGLISH (COOL KIDS): I've been in this long enough to know how the money changes hands. And there is no underground, there is no independence, there is no way for an artist that makes music that isn't pop right now to say, "Oh, this bought me a house." There is no middle class of nothing. There's literally just struggle. You can feed yourself or you're rich as fuck. There's no in-between. That's not by accident. I think that without an artist union or some way that a legal action is brought where they can audit it or there's some sort of discovery into how money changes hands . . . we're fucked for a little bit. It's just what it is. I'm not sad about it, 'cause everything changes over. The streaming era will be extremely forgotten, I promise you that.

NGỌC CAO: The middle is what I always loved.

ROCKS: They're Skynet now, like social media platforms are more of these overarching parts of our lives. When they used to just be a small corner of our life, they used to just be like, "Hey, I'm out of school, I'm off work. Let's go surf the web, let's go get on MySpace for a little bit." But now you're never not on Instagram. You wake up and you're on Instagram. Basically right now, like I am an Instagram employee. I wasn't a MySpace employee. I never felt like I had to work for MySpace.

KATE VOEGELE: There was an aspect of MySpace that like somehow mirrored going to the record store and like browsing through CDs or records to sort of find your next favorite album. There was something about that analog experience of finding your next favorite artist that they captured digitally. I don't know exactly what the ingredients were, but you could feel it. The fact that it was a platform created by somebody who was such a music fan, Tom, that contributed.

GRAHAM WRIGHT (TOKYO POLICE CLUB): The Internet in 2002 was just a beautiful, weird, esoteric space for a nerdy kid to surf. And maybe it's still like that if you're sixteen, and I'm just being a curmudgeon. I hope that's the case. I don't mind if it's just me, but it certainly doesn't feel fun. So nothing has ever been as much fun as MySpace. But then again, I've never been as twenty years old as I was when I was twenty years old, so it's hard to separate the two. The Internet fucking sucks. It's shitty now. It's ugly and self-devouring and capitalized and just full of bad vibes.

NORMAN BRANNON (TEXAS IS THE REASON): I miss having one centralized place to find everything I wanna know about a band or about an artist. And also that directness of it, I feel like you don't get that on Facebook. What do I look at now? If I wanna know about an artist, I go to Wikipedia. I don't know. Where do people go?

JONAH MATRANGA (FAR/ONELINEDRAWING): Because the MySpace days, for whatever it's worth, was the last gasp of small-scale interpersonal communication on the Internet. After that, it was off to the social network races.

VOEGELE: I'm hopeful that there will be some sort of streamlining of all of it for the artists' sake, but also for the fans' sake. At the end of the day, I just wanna connect to the people who are excited about my music or the people who maybe don't know my music yet but would love it and share what I'm making with the world. That's really all any of us want to do.

ISAC WALTER (MARKETING DIRECTOR AND EDITOR IN CHIEF, MYSPACE MUSIC): There's no place where I can go to find music. I don't have that anymore. There's no magazines. Where do you discover music now?

MATRANGA: If I pay the right people, I can get a bunch of streams on Spotify. The technology isn't lost on me. It's just gotten more and more payola driven. You know, unless you're really committing yourself to huge amounts of time spent on these platforms and/or spending huge amounts of money investing in advertising on these platforms and promotion via these platforms, it's tough sledding out there.

BRANNON: Spotify is a passive experience. MySpace was really about user engagement. Spotify is my music library, and MySpace was more than that.

GIBBY MILLER (MAKEOUTCLUB): The Internet's just become something horrendous. For everything that Friendster and MySpace did and had going on, they never felt fucking evil like Facebook. They never felt as corporate and as gross as the Internet does now.

BRANNON: Spotify is in an untenable position, because there's a lot of scrutiny about their payment right now. And artists aren't necessarily going out of their way to partner with Spotify for promotional reasons, 'cause they're just sort of like, "Why? You're making all the money." And so right away, you've got a flawed platform when your entire platform is based on a group of people who don't trust you. I don't think MySpace had that problem. Artists loved MySpace. Artists personally logged in and did the shit. When an artist was controlling their own MySpace, you knew it, and people fucking followed it. That's special and cool, and that was what they wanted. It was just having that one place that was meaningful and useful and potent.

MATRANGA: It's been a long, slow slide of watching what I thought was potentially interesting about the Internet be subsumed by a, just, kind of a strip-mall buffet Vegas mentality.

FRANK IERO (MY CHEMICAL ROMANCE): I have a Facebook for my solo project. I actually wish it was set up like MySpace. Maybe it's because I'm an old person, and I don't really know how to fuckin' work anything, but it doesn't seem as user friendly as previous platforms. Just like, what the fuck, this isn't fun at all; this is really stressful.

MEIKO: I feel so lucky. Lots of artists who are starting out now, they didn't have the platform or the stepping stones that MySpace gave me. They're putting their songs on SoundCloud, or they're trying to have an artist page on Facebook. It's not as easy. So I feel like I did catch a wave, and I'm grateful for that.

SIERRA KAY (VERSA/VERSAEMERGE): But I feel like it's really hard to authentically grow an audience without promoting yourself on social media to all ends. You don't need to go to a record shop. Today, you can buy promotions on Instagram just to get people to see it and hopefully click it. Or you make a TikTok that goes viral, and then people are listening to the one song that has blown up. But I don't think all causes are lost. I think there's really cool niche scenes and subcultures that are still very, very much alive, with an authentically growing audience. I don't think that goes anywhere.

MEIKO: All of these new platforms, they just kind of do one thing. But MySpace kind of had it all, which makes it tragic that it had to end, because it was really helpful.

LIL JON: People try to say music is terrible now, but it's actually a lot of good artists that you have to dig to find—you got to be turned on to them. So it's a good and a bad thing.

JOSH BROOKS (MARKETING AND PROGRAMMING CHIEF FOR MYSPACE): I think everybody bemoans the world where there were only big funnels of information. TV dominated because it was the only thing people could get in their home, or radio, right, it was the one pipe you could get in your home or in your car, and when those giant pipes were at their height, they could really make or break bands, because there were no options. MySpace was the only tech equivalent of that, where it was the giant pipe that a bunch of stuff was going through, but the features were really a meaningful part of the band's campaign, and once that changed, there's so many other places to go get information now. It turned out to be a bunch of other things to fill that void.

LIL JON: Everybody and their mom is trying to fucking break their music and whatever. It is fucking hard, hard, hard, hard to try to cut through.

CHRIS CARRABBA (DASHBOARD CONFESSIONAL): I think what we have today uses the building blocks of MySpace, but I do miss the music-centric nature of MySpace, and I don't think anything's kinda come close to that. That's just solely as a music fan. It comes down to being a music fan. Not as a professional musician, just as a music fan.

NATE HENRY (SHERWOOD): People will still write us now like, "I can't believe you guys have a new record—I didn't even know. You're like one of my favorite bands." And *that* to me is always just like, wow, you can be somebody's *favorite* band, and they have *no* idea you have an album coming out. That *never* used to be the case. I got a wife and kids now, I can't keep up with music like I used to. That just, that used to be my life, but now it's like, "Jimmy Eat World put out a new record *last year*, what??' I think what MySpace meant for a lot of people . . . it was one place where you knew what was going on, even if you didn't like any of the genres of the music that was getting promoted. At least it felt like there was this hub, this train station that everything had to go through.

SIMON: I just wish I could recover my password to see what photos still exist on my profile. But I think that I would have to talk to tech support about that.

WALTER: Had they just bought fucking Facebook at the time, I feel like none of this would have happened.

HENRY: I still think it's worth it. If it's in your blood, you gotta go out and do it. I mean, looking back on it, I wish we spent more time writing better songs than promoting what we had on MySpace.

———————

MySpace would later prove to be the canary in the coal mine of the Internet. Rich men with more money than taste began scooping up every website that earnest, snarky, excitable, and kinda dorky fans and writers spent too much time on and stripping them for parts, with seemingly no idea what made them special, why people liked them, or anything else that a data analyst can't tell you. Many websites either folded or became so desperate for the remaining advertising not scooped up by Google and Facebook that they lost their character in the rush for clicks, ruined by overseers.

Some days it feels like *everything* became the Internet—and not the good, fun Internet, but the often-flavorless Internet we have today. Venture capital firms continue to scoop up everything in their path, jettisoning the flavor and soul out of the world.

But it doesn't necessarily always have to be this way. The MySpace Era ended, as surely as what we have now will as well. But we need to remember that while it was built by Anderson and his collaborators, MySpace was truly made by the fans, artists and weird kids who gave it the spark of life and fueled it with the magic of fandom. He built MySpace, but we did too.

Even amidst a sea of digital noise, the bond between fans and artists, fans and other fans, and weirdos and other weirdos is an endlessly renewable source of energy, and it will continue to endure as long as people want to express themselves and someone else wants to feel something. That connection might get exploited and drained dry, but the feeling will never be sucked out fully. And whether that connection can serve as the basis to something even better than the MySpace Era is a question we all get to answer together.

ACKNOWLEDGMENTS

FIRST OFF, THANK YOU TO my wife Holly. Without her support and encouragement, this book would not exist, nor would anything else worthwhile about my life. She also told me it was time to stop working before I went mad, as she is much wiser than I am. She had a rad MySpace page, back in the day.

Thank you to all of my friends who read drafts, helped with transcription, reminded me that everything was going to be fine, and listened patiently as I described the finer points of the 2005 Warped Tour. There's too many to name here, but special acknowledgement to Dan, Minerva, Ken, Andrew, Erik, Susanne, Jamie, Hanuman, Lynn, Sadie, Kate, Anna, Emma, Maria, and Adam. I promise I'll shut up about emo for a while now.

Thank you, and sorry again, to anyone who knew me in the MySpace days who still talks to me.

Thank you to my parents, Warren and Susan. Your kindness and humanity have been the lighthouse I have tried to follow my entire life.

Thank you to my agent Tim, for believing in me.

Thank you to Scott Lapatine and my Stereogum family. They gave me a chance to become the writer I always wanted to be, and I will forever be grateful.

Thank you to Rob Sheffield, both for being a genius and for his truly astounding generosity and notes. He is the standard by which everyone in the game judges themselves.

Thank you to everyone who talked to me for this book. I truly appreciate it.

And finally, thank you to my editor Kara. See, I told you we'd get there.

THE WHO'S WHO
OF MYSPACE

The following artists, executives, and writers participated in this oral history. Their time and candor are all greatly appreciated.

A-Trak, aka **Alain Macklovitch**, is a DJ, producer, and cofounder of the record label Fool's Gold. His group **Duck Sauce** was nominated for a Grammy for the 2010 single "Barbra Streisand."

Nate Auerbach was a tour manager before joining MySpace as a marketing manager and later was key in building the MySpace Music brand. He also chartered MySpace Canada as the director of marketing and content. Later he served as head of music strategy and outreach for Tumblr. Nate is currently the co-owner of the music culture and marketing firm Versus Creative and the label OFFAIR Records.

Max Bemis is a songwriter and author who lives in Tyler, Texas. His band **Say Anything** released their acclaimed debut album . . . *Is a Real Boy* in 2006. He has also made music with the projects **Two Tongues, Perma**, and **Maxim Mental**. He has also written comic books for Boom! Studios and Marvel Comics, including a turn on the series *Moon Knight*.

Jess Bowen is the drummer for the Scottsdale, Arizona, pop-punk group the Summer Set, which released its debut album *Love Like This* in 2009. She has also played drums in 3OH!3.

Norman Brannon is a musician and author, best known for playing in Texas Is the Reason, whose 1996 debut *Do You Know Who You Are?* is considered an early classic of the emo genre. He has also played in New End Original, 108, Shelter, Resurrection, and Thursday. He has also worked as a cable TV presenter, music journalist, and university lecturer, and founded the zine *Anti-matter*.

Josh Brooks was a marketing and programming chief for MySpace, with a focus on music, film, and comedy. He managed Queens of the Stone Age and was a founding member of Fanscape, a leading digital marketing agency. He also partnered with Selena Gomez to launch the app Postcard on the Run. He currently oversees brand marketing and strategy for Jam City, a mobile-games company created by MySpace cofounder Chris DeWolfe.

Colbie Caillat is a California-based singer-songwriter. Her song "Bubbly" was a viral hit, making her, for a time, the most popular unsigned artist on MySpace. Shortly afterward, her debut *Coco* was released via Universal Republic Records in 2007. Her album *The Malibu Sessions* was self-released in 2016.

Joshua Cain is the cofounder and lead guitarist of the Minneapolis alternative rock band Motion City Soundtrack, which released its debut album *I Am the Movie* in 2003 and scored a hit single in 2005 with "Everything Is Alright." He also produced the pop-punk band Metro Station's 2007 self-titled debut.

Chris Carrabba is a singer-songwriter from South Florida who performed in Dashboard Confessional and fronted the groups the Vacant Andys and Further Seems Forever. Dashboard Confessional released its debut album *The Swiss Army Romance* in 2000, and the band became one of the first to find a following through Napster and LiveJournal, with the break-out single "Screaming Infidelities" winning the MTV2 award at the MTV Video Music Awards. In 2022, Dashboard Confessional released the album *All the Truth That I Can Tell.*

Roslynn Alba Cobarrubias was the former head of artist relations at MySpace.com, helping to launch MySpace Music, MySpace UK, MySpace Mexico, and MySpace Latino. She was there since its early stages in 2004 and left the company in 2013. Most recently, she created ROS. Marketing, an agency producing television shows, events, and content for international brands like ABS-CBN International and MYX, as well as NBA teams like the L.A. Clippers.

Gareth David is the front man for the Welsh indie rock group **Los Campesinos!**, which generated buzz among bloggers and record labels after posting singles such as "Death to Los Campesinos!," "It Started With a Mixx," "Sweet Dreams, Sweet Cheeks," and "You! Me! Dancing!" to their MySpace page. Their debut album *Hold on Now, Youngster . . .* was released via Wichita/Arts & Crafts in 2008. *Sick Scenes* was released via Witchita in 2017.

Sean Foreman is one half of the Boulder, Colorado, party-rap group **3OH!3**. Their MySpace following earned them a deal with Atlantic Records, and they scored a Top 10 *Billboard*-charting hit with "Don't Trust Me." He has produced for artists such as Lil Jon and Ke$ha.

John T. Frazier is the owner and founder of the independent record label Spartan Records. He has also served as the marketing director for Tooth & Nail Records and Drive-Thru Records and was the marketing manager of Crank! A Record Company.

Scott Heisel served as managing editor of the Cleveland-based national music magazine *Alternative Press*, the primary document of the MySpace-fueled emo boom of the 2000s, for which he wrote cover stories on Weezer, Blink-182, Paramore, and others. He has also written for UPROXX, the A.V. Club, *Paste Magazine*, Consequence of Sound, and more. He currently teaches music at Cleveland's School of Rock.

Nate Henry is the singer and bassist for the California-based rock group **Sherwood**, who, after amassing a fan base with their online presence, earned a deal with MySpace Records, which released their second album *A Different Light* in 2007. For a while, Sherwood had an online television program, created by Henry, on MySpace. Sherwood's most recent album, *Some Things Never Leave You*, was self-released in 2016 following an Indiegogo crowdfunding campaign. Henry currently lives in Tennessee, where he does freelance video work and cohosts the podcast *Don't Feed the Trolls*.

Kevin Hershey was the director for partner and label relations for MySpace Music from 2008 through 2013, for which he worked with record labels and artists' teams to create promotions and live events. Before he took this job he worked at MTV, where he programmed the alternative showcase *120 Minutes*, as well as EMI Music Publishing. Since leaving MySpace, he has worked at Disney and NBC.

Courtney Holt is a longtime music industry veteran who worked as the global head of podcasts and new initiatives for Spotify and was the president of MySpace and MySpace Music from 2008 to 2011. He has also worked at MTV, Interscope Geffen A&M Records, and Atlantic Records.

Frank Iero played rhythm guitar in **My Chemical Romance**, one of the most commercially successful rock groups of the 2000s. Their 2004 album *Three Cheers for Sweet Revenge* and 2006's *The Black Parade* both went multiplatinum. Following My Chemical Romance's dissolution in 2013, he released his debut solo album *Stomachaches* in 2014. My Chemical Romance reunited for a world tour in 2022.

Chuck Inglish, aka **Evan Ingersoll**, is one half of the Chicago hip-hop duo **Cool Kids**, who developed a fan base via MySpace and scored a viral hit with the song "Black Mags." The Cool Kids debut EP *The Bake Sale* was released in 2008.

Sarah Joyce was a senior director of corporate communications for MySpace from 2009 to 2011. After leaving MySpace, she worked at Apple doing corporate communications and then at Beats by Dre as global head of corporate communications.

Sierra Kay, aka Sierra Kay Kusterbeck, was the singer for the Port St. Lucie, Florida, emo group VersaEmerge, which released its debut album *Fixed at Zero* on Fueled by Ramen in 2010. In 2016, she formed the post-punk group Neaux, and she has also released music under the project name Bad Daughter.

Lil Jon, aka Jonathan Smith, is a producer, rapper, DJ, and an unofficial ambassador for his hometown Atlanta and the musical genre crunk. He was also an A&R for the label So So Def. As a solo artist, leader of the rap group Lil Jon & the East Side Boyz, and producer for artists such as Usher, Ludacris, Pitbull, Ying Yang Twins, Ciara, Steve Aoki, and LMFAO, to name just a few, he has scored numerous Top 10 *Billboard* hit singles, including "Get Low," "Turn Down for What," and "Freek-a-Leek." He won a Grammy Award for Best Rap/Sung Performance for his Usher and Ludacris collaboration "Yeah!" His last solo album was 2010's *Crunk Rock*.

Amy Fleisher Madden started the label Fiddler Records, an offshoot of her zine *Fiddler Jones*, when she was sixteen years old. She released the first Dashboard Confessional album, *The Swiss Army Romance*, in 2000 and the EP *It's All About the Girls* by New Found Glory in 1997, and later worked at Vagrant Records. Her first novel, *A Million Miles*, was released in 2014.

Jonah Matranga has sung for the emo and alternative rock bands Far, Gratitude, and New End Original and has collaborated with artists ranging from Thursday to Lupe Fiasco. His 2002 album *Visitor*, released under the project name onelinedrawing, is often considered a sleeper emo classic. He continues to self-release music and self-book tours.

Melissa McAllister Sheppard, aka Meiko, is a singer-songwriter from Roberta, Georgia, who moved to Los Angeles and made her name playing at The Hotel Café. Her popularity on MySpace led to her song "Reasons to Love You" being used on *Grey's Anatomy* and to her self-titled debut album being rereleased by MySpace Records in 2008. She self-released her album *In Your Dreams*, lives in Germany, and will gladly play at your wedding.

Jim Merlis is the founder and owner of the music publicity firm Big Hassle, which has worked with clients ranging from MySpace to Dashboard Confessional to the Strokes. He previously worked at Columbia Records and Geffen Records.

Gibby Miller is the founder of the early music-centric social networking site Makeoutclub. He is also a DJ and the founder of Dais Records. He is the cofounder of the online marketing company FieldTest and was the vice president of the online advertising agency IndieClick.

Nathaniel Motte is the cofounder of the rap group **3OH!3**, which he formed while a student at the University of Colorado at Boulder, and which earned a record deal from Atlantic Records because of their MySpace popularity. 3OH!3's album *Need* was released in 2021.

Jillian Newman is an artist manager and founder of Jillian Works Here Inc. She has overseen the careers of Midtown and Taking Back Sunday. She has also worked at Vagrant Records, A&M Records, and the online marketing company Fanscape.

Bích Ngọc Cao was the music editor of MySpace, as well as a producer, from shortly after the website's founding until 2006. She was also the cofounder and community outreach manager for the charity (RED), and she has worked at Warner Bros. Records and Harvest Records. She was a director for media projects at the *Los Angeles Times* and is a senior advisor for the Los Angeles Unified School District. She remains good friends with MySpace cofounder Tom Anderson.

Kev Nish, aka **Kevin Nishimura**, is a rapper, producer, and cofounder of the electro-pop group **Far East Movement**, which self-released its debut album

Folk Music in 2006 and had a worldwide hit with the song "Like a G6." He is the cofounder and co-CEO of the entertainment company Transparent Arts.

Andrew Nosnitsky, aka **Noz**, is the founder of the music blog Cocaine Blunts and is often considered one of the best hip-hop writers of the blog era. He has also written for MySpace, NPR, *Complex*, and the Fader.

Sean Percival was the vice president of online marketing for MySpace from 2009 to 2011. He has been a content manager for online marketing companies such as Tsavo Media, and was the growth marketing advisor for Innovation Norway.

Justin Courtney Pierre is a filmmaker and the front man for the Minneapolis alternative rock band **Motion City Soundtrack**, which had a commercial breakthrough with the 2005 album *Commit This to Memory*. The band's 2007 follow-up *Even If It Kills Me* debuted at the top of *Billboard*'s Independent Albums chart. In 2018, he released the solo album *In the Drink*.

Jon Pikus played drums in the Los Angeles band **Campfire Girls** and recorded the demos that helped earn Weezer a major label deal with Geffen Records before transitioning into a career as an artists and repertoire scout for major labels such as Interscope Records and Columbia Records. He was senior director of A&R at MySpace Records and is currently the music director at Mixer, a private social network for creatives.

Prohgress, aka **James Roh**, is a rapper, producer, and cofounder of the electro-pop group **Far East Movement**, which used MySpace to build an online following, eventually releasing the hit album *Free Wired* on Interscope in 2010. The group self-released their 2016 album *Identity*. Roh is the cofounder and co-CEO of the entertainment company Transparent Arts, which focuses on supporting Asian talent in the music industry.

Matt Pryor is the front man of the Kansas City, Missouri, emo group the **Get Up Kids**, which released its debut album *Four Minute Mile* in 1997.

Released by Vagrant Records in 1999, their album *Something to Write Home About* is considered a classic of late 1990s emo. In 2019, Get Up Kids released the album *Problems*. Pryor also has a more singer-songwriter style project the New Amsterdams and has made children's music with the project the Terrible Twos.

Will Pugh was the front person of the Conyers, Georgia, pop-punk group **Cartel**, which had a hit with the song "Honestly" from its 2005 debut *Chroma*, released by Epic Records. In 2007, the band starred in the MTV reality show *Band in a Bubble*, for which they worked on their self-titled second album. In 2013, Cartel self-released the album *Collider*.

George Ragan, aka **Johnny 3 Tears**, sings in the Los Angeles rap-rock group **Hollywood Undead**, whose intense MySpace popularity earned them a deal with MySpace Records. They scored a rock radio hit with the single "Undead" from their 2008 album *Swan Songs*. Hollywood Undead's albums *New Empire, Vol 1* and *Vol 2*, were released in 2020, the same year they launched their signature cannabis strain Dove and Grenade.

Cassie Ramone, aka **Cassie Grzymkowski,** formed the Brooklyn indie rock trio **Vivian Girls** in 2007, taking the name from a book by the artist Henry Darger; their self-titled debut album was released a year later. The Vivian Girls broke up in 2014 but reunited and released the album *Memory* in 2019. A guitarist, singer, and songwriter, Ramone also formed the band the **Babies** with songwriter Kevin Morby and released a solo album titled *The Time Has Come* in 2014.

Eddie Reyes was the founding guitarist of the Long Island emo group **Taking Back Sunday**, which released the sleeper hit *Tell All Your Friends* in 2002 and scored a hit single with "MakeDamnSure" from the 2006 album *Louder Now*, which was released via Warner Bros. Records. He left the band in 2018. He has also played in the post-hardcore bands **Mind Over Matter, Clockwise**, the **Movielife**, and **Fate's Got a Driver**.

Mark Richardson was the editor in chief and executive editor of Pitchfork and the rock and pop music critic for the *Wall Street Journal*. He is the author of the book *Zaireeka* about the Flaming Lips and has written for *Billboard, Village Voice,* and *L.A. Weekly.*

Geoff Rickly is the front man of the emo/post-hardcore group **Thursday** and the founder of Collect Records. The song "Understanding in a Car Crash," from the 2001 album *Full Collapse,* was one of the first emo crossover songs, and the band released the album *War All the Time* in 2003 via Island Records. After their breakup in 2011, Thursday reunited in 2016. Rickly also produced the first My Chemical Romance album, *I Brought You My Bullets, You Brought Me Your Love,* and performs in the bands **No Devotion** and **United Nations.**

Sir Michael Rocks, aka **Antoine Reed,** is one half of the Chicago hip-hop duo **Cool Kids,** one of the first rap groups to break through MySpace and blog coverage. After a series of delays, the Cool Kids' debut album *When Fish Ride Bicycles* was released in 2011. In 2014, he released the solo album *Banco.* In 2022, the Cool Kids returned with the album *Before Shit Got Weird.*

Gabe Saporta is the former front man of the New Jersey pop-punk band **Midtown,** which released their debut album *Save the World, Lose the Girl* in 2000 through Drive-Thru Records, and the electro-pop group **Cobra Starship,** which scored a record deal when their song "Hollaback Boy," a parody of Gwen Stefani's "Hollaback Girl," went viral on MySpace. Cobra Starship's "Good Girls Go Bad," from the 2009 album *Hot Mess,* hit the *Billboard* Top 10. Saporta also hosted television programs for Fuse and MTV and is a restaurateur. After the release of 2011's *Night Shades,* Saporta retired the project and formed the talent management firm TΔG // The Artist Group.

J Scavo is the former executive director of Hollywood Records and the general manager of MySpace Records. In 2016, he founded the digital marketing and strategy company Daemon.

Juliet Simms was the front woman of the Florida pop-punk band **Automatic Loveletter.** After a demo she made as a teenager earned her a feature on MySpace, she was signed to Sony BMG, which developed a rock band around her. Their debut album *Truth or Dare* was released in 2010. After dissolving that band, she was a contestant on the NBC singing competition *The Voice*, coming in second place. She released several singles, and in 2021 she debuted **Lilith Czar**, a goth-rock alter ego, with the album *Created from Filth and Dust*.

Leslie Simon was the managing editor of *Alternative Press* and wrote cover stories on Fall Out Boy, My Chemical Romance, Panic! at the Disco, and more. She has also worked for MTV and Warner Bros. Records and is currently an editorial director for Paramount+. She is the coauthor of the book *Everybody Hurts: An Essential Guide to Emo Culture* in addition to being the author of books like *Geek Girls Unite: How Fangirls, Bookworms, Indie Chicks, and Other Misfits Are Taking Over the World* and *Wish You Were Here: An Essential Guide to Your Favorite Music Scenes*.

Kate Voegele is an Ohio-born singer-songwriter who gained an online fan base as a teenager after posting MP3s such as "Only Fooling Myself" and "It's Only Life" to MySpace. After being invited to open for John Mayer and Counting Crows, she signed to MySpace Records, which released her debut album *Don't Look Away* in 2007. She also had a recurring role on the television drama *One Tree Hill* from 2008 through 2011. Her most recent album, *Canyonlands*, was self-released in 2016.

Isac Walter was the marketing director and editor in chief of MySpace Music from 2005 to 2011. He directed editorial coverage of which bands would be highlighted on MySpace Music and spearheaded the MySpace Secret Shows project. Before this job, he was a music editor for *Heckler Magazine* and worked at Capitol Records. He is the owner and founder of Project Mersh, a music and entertainment merchandising company.

Ron Wasserman was a member of the rock band **Fisher**, which was the first band to ever achieve mainstream success through the Internet. Their song "I Will Love You" was the number-one song on the website MP3 .com, leading to a deal with Interscope Records, an appearance on the Internet-music showcase Farmclub, and Fisher's songs being placed in television shows such as *Dawson's Creek* and *Ally McBeal.* Fisher's last album was 2014's *3.* Wasserman also wrote the theme songs for the 1990's *X-Men* cartoon and *Mighty Morphin Power Rangers.*

Graham Wright plays keyboards and guitar in the Ontario indie rock band **Tokyo Police Club**, which released their debut EP *A Lesson in Crime* in 2006 on Paper Bag Records and their first full-length album, *Elephant Shell,* on Saddle Creek in 2008. Tokyo Police Club remains active, releasing *TPC* in 2018.

BIBLIOGRAPHY

Introduction: Why We Miss MySpace

Gallucci, Nicole. "'The Office' Fansite That the Cast Actually Obsessed Over." *Mashable*, accessed December 1, 2022, https://in.mashable.com/culture/17707/the-office-fansite-that-the-cast-actually-obsessed-over.

1. Back in the Day

Dewey, Caitlin. "Whatever Happened to LiveJournal, Anyway?" *Washington Post*, June 10, 2014.

Greenwald, Andy. "Geek Love." *Spin*, November 2001.

MTV News. "Pioneering Webzine Addicted to Noise Folds." June 30, 2000.

Nussbaum, Emily. "My So-Called Blog." *New York Times Magazine*, January 11, 2004.

Press, Gil. "Why Facebook Triumphed over All Other Social Networks." *Forbes*, April 8, 2018.

Sawa, Dale Berning. "An Oral History of the AIM Away Message (by the People Who Were There)." inVision, August 12, 2019.

Schwedel, Heather. "Why Did Fans Flee LiveJournal, and Where Will They Go After Tumblr?" *Slate*, March 29, 2018.

Wingfield, Nick. "The Well, a Pioneering Online Community, Is for Sale Again." *New York Times*, June 29, 2012.

2. The My Generation

Arrington, Michael. "Myspace Cofounder Tom Anderson Was a Real Life "WarGames" Hacker in 1980s." TechCrunch, August 30, 2008.

Associated Press. "Clear Channel Completes Deal." *New York Times*, August 31, 2000.

Berendt, Abby. "The Effect of Clear Channel Radio." *Talking Back* 2, no. 1 (2002).

Boehlert, Eric. "Why the Record Industry Is Killing the Single." Salon, December 19, 2001.

DiCola, Peter, and Kristin Thomson. "Radio Deregulation: Has It Served Citizens and Musicians? A Report on the Effects of Radio Ownership Consolidation Following the 1996 Telecommunications Act." The Future of Music Coalition, November 18, 2002.

Fiegerman, Seth. "Friendster Founder Tells His Side of the Story, 10 Years After Facebook." Mashable, February 3, 2014.

Jagernauth, Kevin. "Steven Soderbergh's No Brainer Idea for Remakes: Take on Movies That Didn't Work the First Time, Not Famous Films." IndieWire, May 1, 2013.

Jones, Tim. "Clear Channel to Sell 72 Stations for AMFM Merger." *Chicago Tribune*, March 7, 2000.

Moerer, Keith. "Who Killed Rock Radio?" *Spin*, February 1998.

Rivlin, Gary. "Friendster, Love and Money." *New York Times*, January 24, 2005.

———. "Wallflower at the Web Party." *New York Times*, October 15, 2006.

Sellers, Patricia. "MySpace Cowboys." *Fortune*, August 29, 2006.

Sherman, Maria. "The Future According to NSYNC: 20 Years of 'No Strings Attached.'" NPR, March 20, 2020.

3. The Lonely Hearts Club

Beaujon, Andrew. "That Other Rock." *Spin*, January 2002.

———. "The Spin Top 40." *Spin*, April 2001.

Cohen, Ian. "How Jimmy Eat World Survived Emo Rock and Stopped Writing Themselves Off." The Ringer, November 5, 2019.

Dark, John. "Dashboard Confessional, *The Places You Have Come to Fear the Most*." Pitchfork, 2002.

Kane, Dan. "How Mike Shea Turned a 1,000-Copy Fanzine into the National Alternative Press." *Repository*, July 16, 2015.

Kuge, Mara Schwartz. "Am I Emo?" *Seventeen*, August 2002.

Kurland, Jordan. "The Scene Is Now: Emo-Core," *CMJ*, May 1998.

Payne, Chris. "Former New Found Glory Guitarist Accused of Lewd Acts with a Minor." *Billboard*, March 12, 2014.

Pettigrew, Jason. "Geoff Rickly on Understanding in a Car Crash." *Alternative Press*, May 6, 2013.

Salamon, Jeff. "Emotional Rescue." *Spin*, November 1999.

4. Top Eight

Greenwald, Andy. "The Crying Game." *Spin*, March 2003.

Jackson, Nicholas, and Alexis Madrigal. "The Rise and Fall of MySpace." *Atlantic*, January 12, 2011.

Rivlin, Gary. "Friendster, Love and Money." *New York Times*, January 24, 2005.

Williams, Alex. "Do You MySpace?" *New York Times*, August 28, 2005.

5. Enough Space for Everyone

Billboard Staff. "Kevin Lyman, Warped Tour 'Family' Members on How the Tour Keeps Rolling." *Billboard*, April 6, 2012.

Bream, Jon. "Success Bubbles Over for MySpace Fave Caillat." *Baltimore Sun*, November 15, 2007.

Ellis, Josh. "Party in the USA." *Spin*, July 2010.

Greenwald, Andy. "They Came from Outer Jersey." *Spin*, June 2005.

Hansell, Saul. "For MySpace, Making Friends Was Easy. Big Profit Is Tougher." *New York Times*, April 23, 2006.

Hiatt, Brian. "How Fall Out Boy Went from Heartbreak to Stardom." *Rolling Stone*, March 9, 2006.

Keiper, Nicole. "Paramore Is a Band." *Spin*, March 2008.

Krol, Charlotte. "My Chemical Romance Mark 20 Years Since 9/11, the Reason They Formed." *NME*, September 13, 2021.

Lynskey, Dorian. "We're Here to Fight Evil." *Blender*, April 2005.

Marco, Meg. "Hot Topic Likes Your Art So Much . . . They're Selling It!" *Consumerist*, September 30, 2008.

Pearlman, Mischa. "An Oral History of Taking Back Sunday." *Kerrang*, 2019.

Robinson, Syd. "17 Secrets and Stories from People Who Worked at Hot Topic in the Early 2000s." *BuzzFeed*, November 29, 2020.

Snapes, Laura. "Paramore's Hayley Williams: 'A Lot of My Depression Was Misplaced Anger.'" *Guardian*, March 12, 2020.

Williams, Alex. "Do You MySpace?" *New York Times*, August 28, 2005.

6. Top of the World

Angwin, Julia, and Emily Steel. "Founders Step Aside at MySpace." *Wall Street Journal*, April 23, 2009.

Artyhur, Kate. "Tila Tequila's Descent into Nazism Is a Long Time Coming." BuzzFeed, November 22, 2016.

Byrom, D. Cory. "Panic! at the Disco *A Fever You Can't Sweat Out*." *Pitchfork*, November 28, 2005.

Kelly, Trevor. "Crazy Days." *Alternative Press*, September 2004.

Lieberman, David. "MySpace Debacle Vindication for Fired Viacom CEO Tom Freston." *Deadline*, June 30, 2011.

Massony, Theresa. "Jeffree Star Responded to a Resurfaced Offensive Pic After Fans Rightfully Called Him Out." *Elite Daily*, June 24, 2020.

Montgomery, James. "Cobra Starship Owe Success to Talking Snake from the Future." MTV News, July 27, 2006.

———. "Panic! at the Disco Fight for Cred, Swear They Have No Beef with the Killers." MTV News, February 2, 2006.

Sawyer, Miranda. "Pictures of Lily." *Guardian*, May 21, 2006.

Snapes, Laura. "How Arctic Monkeys' Debut Single Changed the Music Industry and 'Killed the NME.'" *Guardian*, October 22, 2015.

Swash, Rosie. "Lily Allen: Social Networker of the Decade." *Guardian*, November 28, 2009.

Tedder, Michael. "Anthony Green on Getting Sober and Staying Healthy." Spotify for Artists, September 7, 2018.

Tenbarge, Ken. "Jeffree Star Accusers Say the Makeup Mogul Has a History of Sexual Assault, Physical Violence, and Hush-Money Offers." *Insider*, October 1, 2020.

7. Warning Signs

ABC News. "Victim's Parents Want Action Against Online Predators." February 11, 2009.

Adegoke, Yinka. "Special Report: How News Corp Got Lost in MySpace." *Reuters*, April 7, 2011.

Gaither, Chris. "For Musicians, MySpace Is Site to Be Seen and Heard." *Los Angeles Times*, July 5, 2005.

———. "MySpace Making Room for Advertisers." *Los Angeles Times*, July 18, 2006.

Hansell, Saul. "For MySpace, Making Friends Was Easy. Big Profit Is Tougher." *New York Times*, April 23, 2006.

Kaye, Randi. "How a Cell Phone Picture Led to Girl's Suicide." CNN, October 7, 2010.

Mulligan, Brenden. "MySpace Squandered the Only Thing It Had Left." TechCrunch, February 2, 2013.

Poulsen, Kevin. "MySpace Sued over 2006 Teen Suicide." *Wired*, February 25, 2008.

Saillant, Catherine. "Testing the Bounds of MySpace." *Los Angeles Times*, April 8, 2006.

Sellers, Patricia. "MySpace Cowboys." *Fortune*, August 29, 2006.

Smith, Andrea. "A Parent Learns About MySpace." ABCNews, March 7, 2006.

Waters, Richard, and Aline van Duyn. "Google in $900M Ad Deal with MySpace." *Financial Times*, August 8, 2006.

Zetter, Kim. "Prosecutors Drop Plans to Appeal Lori Drew Case." *Wired*, November 20, 2009.

8. Face Off

Adegoke, Yinka. "Special Report: How News Corp Got Lost in MySpace." *Reuters*, April 7, 2011.

Angwin, Julia, and Emily Steel. "Founders Step Aside at MySpace." *Wall Street Journal*, April 23, 2009.

Ante, Spencer E., and Catherine Holahan. "Generation MySpace Is Getting Fed Up." *Bloomberg Businessweek*, February 6, 2008.

Arango, Tim. "MySpace Set to Lay Off 400 Workers." *New York Times*, June 16, 2009.

Arrington, Michael. "Facebook No Longer the Second Largest Social Network." TechCrunch, June 13, 2008.

———. "MySpace Ditches New Playa Vista Offices." TechCrunch, June 5, 2009.

———. "The Perks of Being the MySpace CEO Include, Apparently, Paris Hilton." TechCrunch, August 8, 2008.

Consumer Affairs. "Connecticut Opens MySpace.Com Probe." February 2, 2006.

Frerking, Beth. "Military Families Hit by Ban on Social Sites." *Politico*, May 16, 2007.

Garrahan, Matthew. "Candidates Put Faith in MySpace." *Financial Times*, May 28, 2007.

Gaston, Peter. "Operation MySpace Blows Through Kuwaiti Desert." *Spin*, March 11, 2008.

Johnson, Bobbie. "MySpace Spammers Fined $230m." *Guardian*, May 14, 2008.

Kincaid, Jason. "MySpace Reshuffles Its Music Label." TechCrunch, January 15, 2010.

Leeds, Jeff. "Universal Music Sues MySpace for Copyright Infringement." *New York Times*, November 18, 2006.

McGirl, Ellen. "MySpace, the Sequel." *Fast Company*, September 1, 2008.

Reuters. "MySpace Overtakes Yahoo in Display Ad Views." August 29, 2008.

Rosmarin, Rachel. "Open Facebook." *Forbes*, September 11, 2006.

Stelter, Brian. "MySpace Might Have Friends, but It Wants Ad Money." *New York Times*, June 16, 2008.

Stone, Brad. "Facebook Expands into MySpace's Territory." *New York Times*, May 25, 2007.

Terdiman, Daniel. "At Home with Mark Zuckerberg and Jarvis, the AI Assistant He Built for His Family." FastCompany, December 19, 2016.

Walsh, Mark. "Facebook Tests More Than Three Ads Per Page." Online Media Daily, April 3, 2009.

9. Bad Scene, Everyone's Fault

Alipour, Sam. "Runner's High." *ESPN The Magazine*, February 1, 2013.

Castillo, Arielle. "Denny's Adopts Rock Bands." *Houston Press*, June 4, 2008.

Jones, Evan C. "Cartel Mounts Comeback After 'Bubble' Bust." *Billboard*, October 5, 2009.

"My Chemical Romance's Gerard Way Taps Another Nail into 'Emo' Coffin." *Rolling Stone*, September 20, 2007.

Notopoulos, Katie. "The Weird Denny's Pop-Punk Experiment of 2009." BuzzFeed, December 27, 2012.

Pompilio, Natalie. "Denny's After Dark: Rockin'." *Inquirer*, July 16, 2009.

Sherman, Maria. "MTV's Pop-Punk Reality Show Experiment, 'Band in a Bubble,' Was All Too Real." Thrillist, June 6, 2017.

Thill, Scott. "Is Denny's Rockstar Menu a Sign of the Apocalypse?" *Wired*, August 26, 2008.

10. Indictment

Barlow, Eve. "In Conversation: Hayley Williams. The Front Woman on What Went Wrong with Paramore, Warped Tour War Stories, and Her New Solo Life." *Vulture*, May 6, 2020.

Cook, Jesselyn, and Sebastian Murdock. "Dahvie Vanity Raped a Child. Police Gave Him a Warning. Now 21 Women Accuse Him of Sexual Assault." *Huffington Post*, April 5, 2019.

Coscarelli, Joe. "A Pop-Punk Singer and the Blurred Line Between Digital Fan Mail and Trouble." *New York Times*, January 9, 2015.

Dangelo, Joe. "Brand New Singer Goes Long, Fears Turning into Soccer Star Maradona." MTV News, August 5, 2003.

Deville, Chris. "Slaves Voted Off Warped Tour for Allegedly Assaulting Merch Girl, Dumping Sewage." *Stereogum*, July 2015.

DiVita, Joe. "Saves the Day's Chris Conley Responds to Abuse + Sexual Misconduct Accusations." LoudWire, May 15, 2021.

Knopper, Steve. "'It Was 11 Guys on a Bus, and Then Me': Women on the Warped Tour." *New York Times*, June 21, 2018.

Kreps, Daniel. "Brand New's Jesse Lacey Apologizes After Sexual Misconduct Allegations Surface." *Rolling Stone*, November 12, 2017.

Mapes, Jillian. "Pop-Punk Keeps Forgiving Sexual Harassers, to the Detriment of Its Teen Girl Fanbase." FlavorWire, July 16, 2015.

MetalSucks. "Blood on the Dance Floor's Dahvie Vanity Accused of Sexually Assaulting Multiple Women, Many While They Were Underage." August 1, 2018.

Rotter, Jeffrey. "Naughty by Nature." *Spin*, November 1999.

Salamon, Jeff. "Emotional Rescue." *Spin*, November 1999.

Seling, Megan. "Kevin Lyman Explains Why Front Porch Step Played Today's Warped Tour: 'This Was a One-Time Supervised Part of a Rehabilitation Process.'" *Nashville Scene*, July 1, 2015.

Sherman, Maria. "The Miserable Business of Emo Masculinity." Jezebel, October 12, 2020.

11. Crash Years

Barbanel, Josh. "No Battle Scars Here." *New York Times*, October 28, 2007.

CNNMoney. "Seagram Buys PolyGram." May 21, 1998.

Cooper, Leonie. "Gerard Way on the End of My Chemical Romance: 'It Wasn't Fun Any More.'" *Guardian*, February 9, 2019.

"Drive-Thru Ponders Its Future." *Billboard*, April 5, 2007.

"Fall Out Boy to 'Save Rock and Roll' in May." *Billboard*, February 4, 2013.

Ganz, Caryn. "How Hayley Williams Saved Herself (and, BTW, Paramore)." *New York Times*, March 4, 2020.

Gonzalez, John. "How Did MTV Become the 'Ridiculousness' Network?" The Ringer, September 15, 2020.

Sisario, Ben. "Music Sales Fell in 2008, but Climbed on the Web." *New York Times*, December 31, 2008.

12. Fallout

Adams, Russell, and Emily Steel. "Lead Bid Emerges in Sale of MySpace." *Wall Street Journal*, June 29, 2011.

Adegoke, Yinka. "How MySpace Blew It." Reuters, April 7, 2011.

Baltin, Steve. "Justin Timberlake's MySpace Gears Up for Relaunch." *Hollywood Reporter*, September 24, 2012.

Barr, Jeremy. "SEC Filing Gives Clues to Price Time Inc. Paid for MySpace Parent Viant." *AdAge*, May 9, 2016.

Bhattacharya, Ananya. "Time Inc. Now Owns MySpace, More or Less by Accident." The Verge, February 11, 2016.

Dredge, Stuart. "MySpace—What Went Wrong: 'The Site was a Massive Spaghetti-Ball Mess.'" *Guardian*, March 6, 2015.

Fiegerman, Seth. "MySpace Promotes Relaunch with $20 Million Ad Campaign." Mashable, June 12, 2013.

Halliday, Josh. "Justin Timberlake Buys His Own Social Network with MySpace Investment." *Guardian*, June 30, 2011.

Kiss, Jemima. "The MySpace Redesign: Voice of a Generation—or Dressed up to Sell?" *Guardian*, October 2010.

Lee, Amy. "MySpace Collapse: How the Social Network Fell Apart." Huffington Post, June 30, 2011.

Mulligan, Brenden. "MySpace Squandered the Only Thing It Had Left." TechCrunch, February 2, 2013.

O'Reilly, Lara. "MySpace Has Undergone a 'Surprising Renaissance' and Now It's Going After Teens." *Business Insider*, September 15, 2015.

Phillips, Casey. "How Smartphones Revolutionized Society in Less than a Decade." *Chattanooga Times*, November 20, 2014.

Pineda, Dorany. "MySpace Loses 12 Years of Music Uploads, an Estimated 50 Million Songs." *Los Angeles Times*, March 18, 2019.

Smith, Catharine. "MySpace Sold to Specific Media for $35 Million." Huffington Post, June 29, 2011.

Spranger, Todd. "Time Inc. Buys MySpace Parent Company Viant," Variety, February 11, 2016

Tedder, Michael. "Anarchy in Worcester, Mass." Stereogum, May 19, 2016.

Van Buskirk, Eliot. "MySpace Relaunches with New Justin Timberlake Single 'Suit & Tie.'" *Wired*, January 15, 2013.

Epilogue: Space Was the Place

Hermann, Andy. "Independent Music Publicists Grapple with a Shrinking Media Landscape." *Billboard*, January 14, 2019.

Lipman, Joanne. "Tech Overlords Google and Facebook Have Used Monopoly to Rob Journalism of Its Revenue." *USA Today*, June 11, 2019.

Luckerson, Victor. "Is Spotify's Model Wiping Out Music's Middle Class?" The Ringer, January 16, 2019.

Mathis-Lilley, Ben. "Facebook and Google Need to Start Paying Journalists What They Owe Us." *Slate*, January 24, 2019.